# Paul, Women & Wives

*Marriage* AND *Women's Ministry* IN THE *Letters* OF *Paul*

CRAIG S. KEENER

This book is dedicated to all our sisters in ministry, especially those who have had to endure opposition to follow God's call. May God fulfill all the work of your calling.

**Paul, Women & Wives: Marriage and Women's Ministry in the Letters of Paul**

P. O. Box 3473
Peabody, Massachusetts, 01961-3473

Printed in the United States of America

Eighth Printing — August 2009

ISBN 978-0-943575-96-4



**Library of Congress Cataloging-in-Publication Data**

Keener, Craig S., 1960–
Paul, women & wives: marriage and women's ministry in the letters of Paul / Craig S. Keener.
p. cm.
Includes bibliographical references and index.
ISBN 0-943575-96-6
1. Women in the Bible. 2. Women in Christianity—Biblical teaching. 3. Marriage—Biblical teaching. 4. Bible. N.T. Epistles of Paul—Theology. 5. Women in Christianity—History—Early church, ca. 30–600. I. Title. II. Title: Paul, women, and wives.
BS2655.W5K44 1992
261.83′442—dc20 92–26515
CIP

# Table of Contents

# Preface (2004)

As *Paul, Women, and Wives* enters a new printing, I am grateful for the opportunity to revisit some of the issues this work raised and to bring it more up to date. My primary academic interests are exegetical and historical, and I hope to have time in years to come to develop those questions in future commentaries on some of the New Testament letters addressed in this book. (Questions about particular Pauline letters' authorship raised by some critical reviewers would also need to be addressed more fully in those works.)

Nevertheless, I also have a pastoral interest in the subject (how we apply Paul's teaching in the twenty-first century), which will not be addressed so easily by purely academic works. Further, most of the response to this book has been theological, and since I am less convinced that I will have opportunity to revisit this book's theological questions in future works, I am especially grateful to be able to offer the present preface.

In some circles, debates over the pastoral application of Paul's teachings on gender are settled, but in others they are just warming up. Among those Christians who regard Paul's teaching as authoritative, the debate over gender roles is probably more polarized now than it was when this book was first written. Political and rhetorical battle lines have been drawn, and many Christians have suffered wounds at the hands of fellow Christians. Having no desire to add to the rhetorical bloodshed, I urge readers to take this book's insights as an exegetical study with pastoral implications. At the same time, I want to remain clear where I think the pastoral implications point. Since writing *Paul, Women, and Wives* I have served in ministry under women pastors and alongside women colleagues and am certain that the body of Christ would have been far poorer without the spiritual fruit of their ministry.

In addressing introductory issues where I need to supplement the book, I begin this preface with some comments on gender roles in antiquity (directed more toward advanced students). Then, on a less academic level, I summarize aspects of the shape of the current debate among readers seeking to apply Paul's teaching, especially among evangelicals. Finally I conclude with comments on the hermeneutical principles that necessarily underlie my (and most other egalitarians') approach.

## GENDER ROLES IN ANTIQUITY

This section may appeal primarily to specialists, yet it is important for me to include. Scholars have published numerous works on women in both early Judaism and the Greco-Roman world since I completed my original manuscript for *Paul, Women, and Wives.*[1] A number of these works significantly advance our views of the diverse positions held by women in antiquity. Although they do not alter the central thrust of this book, they would influence how I would write the book if I were starting it today.

*Paul, Women, and Wives* did note the diverse roles of women, both Jewish and Gentile, in different parts of the Empire,[2] but I have long wished that I had emphasized this point more fully. It is more helpful to compare Paul with a range of his contemporaries, and then rank him among the more progressive of them (as I think the evidence warrants), than to enter into fruitless debates over who was the "most progressive." Among the options articulated in his day, he (like most other "progressive" voices) sometimes sided with dominant practices in his culture, just as he supported obedience to the state under normal circumstances (Rom. 13:1–7) and other writers supported allegiance to the king (1 Pet. 2:13). Sometimes the reasons for maintaining such popular arrangements were explicitly apologetic, both addressing the behavior of slaves (1 Tim. 6:1–2), wives (Titus 2:5; cf. 1 Tim. 5:15), and others (Titus 2:8).[3] This was an important concern to a minority religious movement in an environment where such movements were sometimes charged with social subversion. On other occasions, however, Paul's statements fit among the most progressive of his contemporaries (as this book emphasizes).

The same may be even more the case for his comments on slavery. Although the wilderness Essenes and some other radical communities rejected slavery in principle (generally because they rejected all private property), the most progressive views expressed among those in mainstream society generally promoted only slaves' equality in nature and their fair treatment. By arguing not only for their human equality but for something like mutual submission between slaves and slaveholders (Eph. 6:9), Paul was easily among the more progressive voices of his day.

Where I do *not* think the evidence points is that everyone, or even most people, would have been as progressive as Paul. Scholars have rightly collected many examples of highly educated upper class women, but those who depend on such collections without reading the entire range of ancient sources will fail to distinguish the exceptions from the general practice. (A person actually surveying the ancient sources directly will recognize that the preponderance of sources do not suggest anything close to gender equality.) Likewise, Jewish women attended synagogue and learned the law, but, with possibly rare exceptions, were not raised to recite it the way most boys were. While we should take note of the exceptions (which provide a context for the many "exceptions" also in the New Testament), we should not lose sight of the fact that these were (in most of the Empire) exceptions.

Although we know of women in positions of prominence, they constituted a far smaller percentage than men. Of course, the same is true in Paul: the women in visible ministry were a small percentage compared to the men in such ministry, and their percentage tended to be higher in locations (and perhaps classes or occupations) where women had more social freedom. But the point must be that Paul *approved* of these women's activities, in contrast to the tendencies of a good number of his contemporaries. Likewise, while there is plenty of evidence for diverse positions in different parts of the Mediterranean world, none of these suggest a society that would allow women to vote or to engage in activities alongside men in the way that almost all of us (at least in western society and some other cultures) take for granted today. Again, it may be objected that Paul does not, so far as we have record, press beyond his society by advocating women's (or anyone's) suffrage; he addressed the issues of his culture. But again, I stand by my argument in this book that Paul does make statements about gender (such as Rom. 16:1–3, 6–7, 12; 1 Cor. 11:5, 11–12; Gal. 3:28;

Phil. 4:3; cf. Col. 4:15) that rank him among the more progressive voices of his day. That he also has more conservative statements (the focus of the body of this book) does not negate the more progressive ones, especially if, as I argue in this book, he articulates these for culturally strategic reasons.[4]

We may compare Paul, for instance, with the much earlier writer Xenophon, who was also very "progressive." Various ancient writers spoke of forms of mutuality while preserving (in various degrees) a measure of hierarchy (an observation important, for example, in the exhortation to children in Eph. 6:1–3).[5] Xenophon, who offers a remarkably progressive view in classical Athens, argues for partnership *(koinōnia)* between spouses (*Oec.* 7.18, 30), yet argues that nature has suited wives' bodies better for indoor work and husbands' for work outdoors (*Oec.* 7.22–23, 30). The husband has more courage (*Oec.* 7.25), but both are equals in memory and self-control (*Oec.* 7.26–27).[6] Xenophon's position restricts women more than most complementarians (gender hierarchicalists) would today; but he has moved significantly beyond the typical views of his Athenian contemporaries, and it is in this context that we must judge him historically.

Paul does move beyond such statements in emphasizing mutual *submission* (Eph. 5:21),[7] and this contrast is instructive, but should not be overstated. On the one hand, the statement of mutual submission in Ephesians 5 is so directly connected with the wife's submission as to challenge his society's usual understanding of that relationship. On the other, Paul presumably did expect wives to honor the accepted roles of their society for the sake of the gospel (as he also expected submission to other authorities in the society). As I suggest in the last three chapters of this book, that is presumably the reason for his household codes.

But pastoral interest takes us beyond the historical question to the hermeneutical one. Granted that Paul probably expected wives to follow accepted roles in first-century society, would he have expected wives in *our* society to directly follow the accepted roles of wives in first-century society? The way that he adapts the traditional codes in the direction of mutuality suggests that he was not personally committed to all his contemporaries' usual values on the matter. (Most modern readers who wish to apply pastorally Paul's words on slavery take this difference of cultural settings into account; consistency suggests that we do the same for the hierarchical character of ancient marriage. Note my discussion of hermeneutics below.)

As another example, the Stoic thinker Musonius Rufus viewed women as equal to men in nature, though their roles were different, and he often disagreed with the restrictive roles to which his society had limited women.[8] He was hardly a modern feminist, but given his setting, he was certainly articulating a more egalitarian ideal than most of his contemporaries, and in another setting his understanding might have supported a more fully egalitarian direction. Paul's thinking at points parallels this particularly progressive stream among his contemporaries (e.g., 1 Cor. 11:11). Would Paul have gone farther in a setting where a progressive vision was more culturally workable? Because he grounds his version of the household codes (Eph. 5:22–6:9) in the universal Christian model of serving others, it is reasonable to suppose that he would have allowed that gender-specific expressions of service could vary from one culture to another. (Even among hierarchicalists, specific expressions of submission do in fact vary from one culture to another.)

Although further study in ancient sources has required more attention to nuance, most of my work subsequent to *Paul, Women, and Wives* has reinforced my general picture of a world whose range of gender options was quite different from ours. I have provided considerable documentation in several essays focused specifically on those historical questions.[9] I have today much more information than even when I authored those essays; further publication, however, will need to wait several years, due to my current work on other projects. Interested scholars need not wait for my (or other scholars') work, however; most of the ancient sources are already available, and enough has been collected for students who are not specialists to pursue these questions on their own.

## RECENT DEBATE AMONG EVANGELICALS

I have updated my response to the current debate (at somewhat greater length, hence with more documentation than here) in my essay in *Two Views on Women's Ministry*.[10] Here, however, I offer some basic observations most relevant to the current book.

Although evangelicals were not the sole audience for *Paul, Women, and Wives*, they have been a central part of that audience. While some circles are concerned only with historical questions or, by contrast, with evaluating Paul's acceptability for modern readers, some evangelical circles are disputing (either internally or externally) the practical question of women's ordination. I was aware when I wrote this book that the issue of women's ordination was controversial among evangelicals, but it was not until after this book was published that I became aware of just how volatile the subject was. I now have written twelve books, the best known being commentaries, and expected my works on Revelation, the gifts of the Spirit, and divorce to be my most controversial.[11] Unquestionably, however, my work on gender issues in Paul (my second book) has proved my most controversial, and the firestorm took me mostly by surprise.

Most of the evangelical circles I knew best (the Pentecostal and charismatic circles that first nurtured my faith; the local African-American Baptist association in which I was ordained and ministered; and InterVarsity Christian Fellowship) supported women's ministry, as do many mainline evangelicals. I did have evangelical friends and colleagues who disagreed, but our disagreement on the matter was charitable and we continued to work together in ministry. I was thus shocked to learn, after the book's release, that some fellow evangelicals questioned the genuineness of my evangelical commitment because I supported women's ordination! While I had often labored on the evangelical side of other debates in academic circles, had led many people to Christ in other settings and had sometimes even been beaten for my witness, I now discovered that some people who did not know me (and had not read the book) had heard my name and considered me "liberal." While in some circles that title means "generous" or "charitable," it had less friendly connotations in the circles that applied it to me!

Such criticism inducted me into the current evangelical conflict, and I soon found that most scholars who have written on either side of the issue have suffered the effects of their opponents' strong feelings. Both sides believe that the message of Scripture supports their case, and the temptation in the face of harsh criticism (for either side in the debate) is to return it in kind. Polarizing the debate, however, only makes dialogue and genuine persuasion more difficult; truth emerges better in open discussion than from ecclesiastical or academic politics. Political polarization works by categorization and sound bites; scholarly dialogue (and even Christian correction; cf. 2 Tim. 2:24–25) ought to think through arguments more carefully. In discussion with several scholars who oppose women's ordination (most of whom I interacted with at least in footnotes of this book), I discovered that they had also been treated less than charitably by some people on my side of the debate. Happily a number of us, some of us friends outside the debate, have been able to dialogue across the divide of our positions in friendly ways.[12]

Accepted terminology has changed in the few years since the book was written. For many, the label "feminism," which has carried a variety of connotations to different people in different decades of the past century, has become too loaded a term for continued use in the evangelical debate. The preferred title for most evangelical scholars who accept women's ministry today is "egalitarian." The preferred title for what was previously called the traditionalist or hierarchical position is "complementarian." Each title risks misrepresenting the other side of the debate: most "complementarians," for example, insist on the equality of persons (while maintaining gender-assigned differences in role). "Egalitarians" reject hierarchy yet accept the reality of (nonhierarchical) gender differences, hence speak of man and woman as complementary.

While the debate is polarized into two sides, there is in reality a range of views. Craig Blomberg, for example, a friend whose scholarship I respect, accepts a range of women's ministries and believes that women are excluded only from the office of senior pastor. Although the politics of the debate has defined this position as "complementarian," I see it as closer to the egalitarian position than to complementarians who completely prohibit women from teaching the Bible to men. In more conservative evangelical circles (as opposed to most mainline evangelical circles), Blomberg's mediating position functions as quite progressive, allowing women far more freedom than is usual. What appears conservative or progressive to us often depends on the circles in which we move. (No less than in the first century, social context still matters.)

*Paul, Women, and Wives* focuses on the general question of women's ministry, not on the specific office of senior pastor (or of "offices" in general, a term that does not appear in Scripture). Yet it has implications, I believe, for the pastoral question as well. If women could be prophets (the most common ministry of God's message in the Bible as a whole); occasionally apostles (at least alongside a husband, Rom. 16:7);[13] or even a judge over all Israel (Judg. 4:4), why could not a woman be a pastor in a house church (the form of churches dominant in the first century)?[14] Probably most such churches could hold twenty to fifty people (i.e., families and some individuals) and probably had a plurality of leaders; there are women who teach and organize much larger Sunday School classes than this today. No one argues that women teaching the Bible or exercising authority were the majority among biblical prophets or early Christian leaders, but if we grant the divinely sanctioned existence of any of them, then we dare not rule out candidates today based purely on gender.

One complementarian friend conceded my objection that it seems inconsistent for women to be prophets, judges, or apostles, but not pastors; yet he responded that he nevertheless felt constrained by 1 Tim. 2:11–12 to forbid them to be senior pastors. Yet (as I argued in response) the passage does not mention "senior pastors," "offices," or standing behind a "pulpit," all of which are ideas and practices from after the first century. It commands women to keep silent, and not to teach authoritatively (or, as some have argued persuasively, neither to teach nor to exercise authority). To make the silence absolute would prohibit women from singing in church; by contrast, to attribute this strictness to a particular situation invites the consideration of what other elements of the text may be situation-specific. This invites evangelical interpreters to explore carefully, not whether there is a transcultural point, but certainly what that point might be.

Paul does not name specific persons (whether men or women) as "pastors" (though he speaks of those who certainly do work elsewhere attributed to "pastors"). Yet his most common ministry titles for men ("fellow worker"; "minister/servant" *[diakonos]*) he applies at least on occasion to women (Rom. 16:1, 3). Following prior biblical tradition (Exod. 15:20; Judg. 4:4; 2 Kgs. 22:14; 2 Chron. 34:22; Isa. 8:3; cf. Luke 2:36) and contemporary Christian practice (Acts 2:17–18; 21:9), he allows women to pray and prophesy (1 Cor. 11:4–5), so long as their heads are covered (on which see chapter 1 of this book). For another passage, then, to entirely silence women from speaking for God appears remarkable.

Do we see the stricter passages as contradicting the more affirming ones (as many argue)? Do these passages envision two levels of ministry, i.e., senior pastor (which is not specifically mentioned) being a higher "office" than apostles or prophets (a position which, I have argued, is difficult to maintain)? Are the prohibitions universal principles and the conflicting examples merely exceptions (in which case we might accept some exceptions today)? For reasons offered below (and more fully later in the book), I prefer a fourth solution: the so-called "exceptions" indicate a pattern acceptable to God (though not common for cultural reasons), and the prohibitions (consisting on this point of two passages) merely address exceptional circumstances. Why would I favor this fourth alternative?

The first passage, 1 Corinthians 14:34–35, seems to address a particular kind of speech ("asking questions"); it certainly cannot restrict public prayer or speaking God's message (1 Cor. 11:4–5; see chapter 2 of this book).[16] More importantly, it can hardly be coincidence that the one passage that is most restrictive (1 Tim. 2:11–12) also appears in the one set of letters in the Bible that we specifically know addressed a congregation where false teachers were targeting women. This claim is explicit in 2 Timothy 3:6–7, and is probable in 1 Timothy 5:13, where some widows are spreading a form of "nonsense."[17] Since false teachers needed homes for house churches, it made most sense to target the most theologically vulnerable homeowners: widows who owned homes on account of widowhood and had less access to training because of their gender.[18]

What complicates matters is that the 1 Timothy passage goes on to cite Scripture, including, complementarians point out, an argument from the creation order (1 Tim. 2:13). What many interpreters overlook is that Paul applies precisely the same argument for head coverings in 1 Corinthians 11:8. Yet some who vilify those who disregard "creation order" as transcultural in 1 Timothy do precisely the same themselves in 1 Corinthians! Paul usually applies Scripture in a straightforward way, but he also makes *ad hoc* applications frequently enough, as a survey of his citations and their original contexts makes clear (e.g., 1 Cor. 14:21; Gal. 3:16; Eph. 4:8).[19] The two most relevant comparisons in Pauline literature are the comparisons with Eve's creation sequence (1 Cor. 11:8) and, more explicitly, her deception (2 Cor. 11:3); the former involves head coverings and the latter Paul applies specifically to the Corinthian church.[20] In view of abundant biblical evidence for women's ministry, this text should not be pressed against the others in a way that consistent exegesis does not require.

## HERMENEUTICAL ISSUES

Much of the debate finally comes down to hermeneutical approaches, although that is not always where scholarship has focused its energy in the debate. Since the first publication of *Paul, Women, and Wives,* the lexical debate has gone much further—and without much further resolution. Complementarians have argued that *authentein* (1 Tim. 2:12) means simply "have authority," based on all the pre-Christian uses of the verb—though there are two to four of them (plus only a handful of others after 1 Timothy not potentially influenced by the interpretation of the passage).[21] Some egalitarians have countered that those few examples actually mean "dominate" rather than "exercise authority."[22] The lexical debate continues, but if Paul was addressing a specific situation, the debate over such a small range of evidence becomes less pressing.

Most egalitarians have continued to argue that *kephalē* means "source," and complementarians that it means "authority over" or "ruler." Although I am an egalitarian (and recognize that there are *some* cases where the meaning "source" is more likely), as an exegete I am more inclined to think that the complementarians' usual lexical preference is more relevant (especially in Eph. 5). I base my preference on the few uses in the Septuagint that preserve the Hebrew idiom, and the use of the image in Latin (which would also be relevant in Corinth).

Given how Paul transforms Aristotle's household codes and some other ideas common in his culture, however, we must look at particular texts to see how Paul applies the term: a dictionary provides a term's potential range of meaning, but only specific contexts show what elements in that range are relevant and how they are used. A context of mutual submission (Eph. 5:21), or mutual dependence (1 Cor. 11:11), raises questions as to whether Paul's focus is (as pure focus on lexical questions could be used to argue) male authority. He calls the wife (like slaves or others subject to others' authority) to submit, but the husband's only specified obligation is to love self-sacrificially (Eph. 5:25). If Paul's particular adaptation of language leads us to question whether he thinks he is mandating a transcultural hierarchy, his cultural setting should make us even more cautious.

Important as lexical questions are, the fixation on them in the debate can lead us to overlook the larger cultural questions. Here I believe that egalitarians have the edge, but we also have a problem. While virtually all scholars (from complementarians to egalitarians to traditional critical scholars) acknowledge the importance of taking cultural context into account, on a popular level most Christians do not.[23] Further, even some scholars, while using culture to explain a text, are not willing to limit a text's application to the sorts of situations a text addresses. Thus, for example, some point to a number of apparently transcultural commands in the Pastoral Epistles to argue that everything in these epistles was intended transculturally.[24]

Yet such reticence to read Scripture (and especially letters) as addressing particular situations cannot be followed consistently. A brief survey of New Testament letters will indicate that, like letters today, they usually address people in particular historical settings (for example, "the saints at Rome," "the church in Corinth," or "Timothy"). Neither Paul nor other early Christian authors wrote in English, Chinese, Korean, or Spanish for modern readers, or otherwise showed an interest in readers outside their first-century Mediterranean audience. While Paul undoubtedly would be happy to welcome later readers to "listen in" on his message and reapply the principles to other settings, he no more wrote with such readers in mind than he wrote in a language other than Greek.[25] Granted, Paul drew on transcultural principles, but he applied them to specific situations. We learn by analogy: if Paul addressed a situation in, say, Thessalonica in a particular way, what would he have said to us in our somewhat different setting? On some issues, Paul's corpus (and Scripture as a whole) speaks with a unified voice (for example, on sexual morality); on others, it varies, at least often because it addresses different cultures or situations (for example, on women's work outside the home, Prov. 31:16, 24).

Many Christians today who restrict women's speech in church do not require them to cover all their hair (as Paul apparently wanted them to do in Corinth). Other Christians (like some of my friends and coworkers in northern Nigeria) do expect head coverings, but not holy kisses (which are commanded in Scripture five times as often). (By contrast, in Central Africa, where my wife is from, kisses are used in greeting, hence in church, but the use of head coverings varies.) Many churches in the western world once prohibited jewelry (1 Tim. 2:9; 1 Pet. 3:3) or required head coverings (1 Cor. 11:2–16); many today that prohibit women in the pulpit nevertheless relegate biblical remarks on such external matters to "ancient culture." What is the standard for consistency?

Paul commands the church in Corinth to lay up offerings for the Jerusalem church every Sunday (1 Cor. 16:1–3). Should all churches today obey this command? Certainly, the passage provides transcultural principles, but whether the transcultural principle it models is caring for the poor, the unity of Jewish and Gentile

Christians, or something else cannot simply be assumed without argument. In the Pastorals, Paul tells Timothy to bring his cloak from Troas (2 Tim. 4:13). How many of us have sought to obey that command? Have we gone to Troas, tried to find the cloak, and (most difficult of all, now that he is dead) tried to get it to Paul?[26]

We recognize such a direct application of a limited statement as absurd, but we should be consistent. We learn by analogy from such commands, but we recognize that the biblical writers addressed specific situations (and even specific audiences, like Timothy). Before we can apply a text appropriately, we must take into account the situation being addressed to apply its point to analogous situations. (My dictum for my hermeneutics students is: All Scripture is for all time, but not every Scripture is for all circumstances. When you preach from a text, make sure you get the analogy right.) Some interpreters apply this hermeneutic selectively: when a command seems absurd, it is not for today, but otherwise it is for today. Often, individuals simply allow their respective church traditions to unconsciously determine what they consider acceptable or absurd: for example, no women in the pulpit, but neither mandatory head coverings (despite the same creation order argument in the passages behind both teachings). In the end, consistency is a demanding rule, and we cannot ignore the cultural question altogether without committing hermeneutical suicide.

Today, some complementarians accuse egalitarians of a similar inconsistency, claiming that they simply follow the lead of modern secular culture. This is an *ad hominem* argument, and also historically inaccurate. Egalitarian interpreters (including Catherine Booth, cofounder of the Salvation Army, and some other nineteenth-century evangelicals) actually preceded the culture in many respects.[27] Some evangelical movements ordained women before the practice was accepted in mainline denominations (before the mainline denominations included their current range of theological options).

Some complementarians object that the majority of Christendom historically rejected women's ordination. We should keep in mind that the church's historic *reason* for this rejection was women's ontological inferiority in understanding.[28] While we do well to take seriously the common tradition of the church on major issues, the dominant historic voice of the church on some issues clearly contradicts the church's Scripture: much of its history is stained with anti-Semitism, cultural insensitivity, and neglect of central doctrines like justification by faith. Like anti-Semitism, restrictions on women may have flowed from the broader culture into the church. Various minority, back-to-the-Bible movements often challenged this view and, as noted above, the challengers included many nineteenth-century evangelicals. The church's history is full of reformers who challenged traditional interpretations on various issues when they believed the biblical burden of proof strong enough to do so. If some aspects of their environment added persuasiveness to their arguments (as in the case of the Reformation), we need not for that reason dismiss their arguments as capitulation to secular culture.

Following the traditions of a particular church, like following the lead of one's culture, can introduce biases. If we press beyond *ad hominem* charges of bias, how can we use cultural background *consistently* in our interpretation of Scripture? As F. F. Bruce argued in advocating the full ministry of women, the principles of the gospel take precedence over first-century forms.[29] Though egalitarians often reconstruct the setting differently (for example, Catherine Clark Kroeger on one hand and Gordon Fee on the other), we share a common, culturally sensitive hermeneutic. William Webb has recently produced a detailed and careful study demanding hermeneutical consistency in the use of backgrounds for the gender (and other) debates; despite detractors, it is the most rigorous attempt to develop a consistent method so far.[30]

In my effort to be rigorously consistent and learn from the Bible with sensitivity to its original cultures, I have tried to make available, on a fairly popular level, background for all New Testament texts (especially in *The IVP Bible Background Commentary: New Testament*).[31] It was also an attempt to be hermeneutically consistent that led me to the conclusions I hold on women's ministry. While not everyone will agree with my conclusions in this particular case, I reiterate a plea offered in the original work: that those whose interpretation of the text differs from my own would not misrepresent my different interpretation as stemming from lack of commitment to Scripture's authority. If I did not genuinely believe Scripture supported the position I herein articulate, I would not have willingly endured for it the scorn I have encountered in some circles. No matter how strongly different groups of Christians may feel about and defend our respective views, we are not free to misrepresent each other. The gospel obligates us to keep loving each other.

## NOTES

1. E.g. (among many others), Tal Ilan, *Jewish Women in Greco-Roman Palestine* (Peabody: Hendrickson, 1996; Tübingen: J. C. B. Mohr, 1995); Bruce W. Winter, *Roman Wives, Roman Widows* (Grand Rapids: Eerdmans, 2003).

2. E.g., *Paul, Women, and Wives,* pp. 160, 163, 243, 254.

3. See esp. Alan Padgett, "The Pauline Rationale for Submission: Biblical Feminism and the *hina* Clauses of Titus 2:1–10," *EQ* 59 (1987): 39–52. For relevance to our culture today on a practical level, see also Rich Nathan, *Who Is My Enemy?* (Grand Rapids: Zondervan, 2002), pp. 141–59.

4. I treated briefly this tension between his strategic social conservatism and his more progressive interests in "Paul: Subversive Conservative," *Christian History* 14 (3, 1995): 35–37.

5. As I already noted from Plut. *Bride* 11, *Mor.* 139CD. Cf. Greek views of Egyptians in Diod. Sic. 1.27.2.

6. For Xenophon the wife rules (like a queen bee) over matters inside and the husband things outside (*Oec.* 7.33, 39), but if she works harder at her role she merits greater honor, making him a voluntary servant (*Oec.* 7.42). Cf. Mus. Ruf. 14, p. 92.38–94.1.

7. If the claim of *mutual* submission was unusual, it would invite attention all the more graphically; cf. the discussion of tropes on pp. 124–25 in Galen O. Rowe, "Style," in *Handbook of Classical Rhetoric in the Hellenistic Period 330 B.C.–A.D. 400,* ed. Stanley E. Porter (Leiden: Brill, 1997), pp. 121–57.

8. On virtues being the same for both, see, e.g., Mus. Ruf. 4, p. 44.10–35 (Lutz); for role distinctions in expressing virtue, see, e.g., Mus. Ruf. 3, p. 40.25–28.

9. Craig Keener, "Marriage," pp. 680–93; "Family and Household," pp. 353–68; "Headcoverings," pp. 442–46; and related articles in *Dictionary of New Testament Background,* ed. Craig A. Evans and Stanley E. Porter (Downers Grove: InterVarsity, 2000).

10. Edited by James R. Beck and Craig L. Blomberg (Grand Rapids: Zondervan, 2001); a newer edition in a different format is being published. Linda Belleville, the other egalitarian contributor to that volume, engages the complementarian objections more vigorously, and should be consulted for many current arguments I cannot detail here ("Women in Ministry," pp. 77–154 in *Two Views;* see also Linda L. Belleville, *Women Leaders and the Church* [Grand Rapids: Baker, 2000]). Two (among many) other recent egalitarian works of note in the evangelical debate include Rebecca Merrill Groothuis, *Good News for Women* (Grand Rapids: Baker, 1997); Stanley J. Grenz with Denise Muir Kjesbo, *Women in the Church* (Downers Grove: InterVarsity, 1995); from the complementarian side, one of the most compelling is Andreas J. Köstenberger, Thomas R. Schreiner, and H. Scott Baldwin, eds., *Women in the Church: A Fresh Analysis of 1 Timothy 2:9–15* (Grand Rapids: Baker, 1995). Another egalitarian work, Richard Clark Kroeger and Catherine Clark Kroeger, *I*

*Suffer Not a Woman* (Grand Rapids: Baker, 1992), was released at the same time as *Paul, Women, and Wives,* hence my book interacts with only their articles.

11. *And Marries Another* (Peabody: Hendrickson, 1991), somewhat controversial; *Gift & Giver: The Holy Spirit for Today* (Grand Rapids: Baker, 2001), mostly ignored; *Revelation,* NIV Application Commentary (Grand Rapids: Zondervan, 2000). The major commentaries include *The Gospel of John: A Commentary,* 2 vols. (Peabody: Hendrickson, 2003); *A Commentary on the Gospel of Matthew* (Grand Rapids: Eerdmans, 1999).

12. Wayne Grudem, Robert Yarbrough, and Tom Schreiner, among others, dialogued with me on this and other issues. Some egalitarians who recoil at the citation of one or two of these names should be aware that complementarians recoil no less at the names of well-known egalitarians engaged in the debate. (For the most part, those on either side of the debate who have not written on the subject have happily escaped the acrimony.) In a friendly public dialogue at Dallas Theological Seminary several years ago, Darrell Bock modeled charity in a particularly noteworthy way.

13. "Junia" is clearly a woman's name; the method used to contract Greek names into similar forms is irrelevant in the case of Junia, which is not Greek but Latin. See Richard S. Cervin, "A Note Regarding the Name 'Junia(s)' in Romans 16.7," *NTS* 40 (1994): 464–70 (brought to my attention by Prof. Michael Holmes).

14. I am not comfortable with the question of "rank" in texts describing first-century ministry, but to the extent that one does discuss it, pastors do not rank above apostles and prophets (1 Cor. 12:28).

15. See my objections above and in "Women in Ministry," pp. 31–32.

16. I offer another argument for the same basic position in my essay for the forthcoming book, Ronald W. Pierce, Rebecca Merrill Groothuis, and Gordon D. Fee, eds., *Discovering Biblical Equality: Complementarity without Hierarchy* (Downers Grove: InterVarsity, 2004).

17. Gordon Fee sent me a list of every use of the term in extant Greek literature, along with relevant contexts; the sense is generally "nonsense," with an emphasis on false or improper teaching in didactic contexts.

18. For the relative lack of training, see, e.g., *Paul, Women, and Wives,* pp. 83–84. Because I documented this in chapter 2 rather than later, one reviewer of the book who read only chapter 3 thought that I did not document the claim.

19. See much more extended discussion in my "Women in Ministry," pp. 27–73 (in the 2001 ed.).

20. On interpretations of the fall narrative in its own context, see briefly ibid., pp. 62–63.

21. See the careful study by Scott Baldwin, "A Difficult Word: *authenteō* in 1 Timothy 2:12," in *Women in the Church,* pp. 65–80.

22. Belleville, "Women in Ministry," pp. 134–35. Others also appeal to the cognate noun (cognates sometimes point toward similar meanings, though one cannot always depend on them to do so).

23. It is understandable that it is difficult even for many scholars, regardless of their views on gender, to read biblical texts consistently in their ancient settings. Basic familiarity with those settings typically takes years of rigorous study.

24. Cf. the somewhat more nuanced argument in David Gordon, "A Certain Kind of Letter: The Genre of 1 Timothy," in *Women in the Church*, pp. 53–63. See my review of this book in *JETS* 41 (Sept. 1998): 513–16.

25. He might have also been surprised to discover that history outlasted the first century (1 Thess. 4:17).

26. See my "Women in Ministry," pp. 46–49, 55–58 (in the 2001 edition); in the Pastorals, for culture-specific statements note, e.g., 1 Tim. 4:7; 5:9–13, 23.

27. See, e.g., Catherine Booth, *Female Ministry: Woman's Right to Preach the Gospel* (New York: Salvation Army, 1975; first published 1859); esp. Ruth A. Tucker and Walter Liefeld, *Daughters of the Church: Women and Ministry from New Testament Times to the Present* (Grand Rapids: Zondervan, 1987); Grenz and Kjesbo, *Women in Church*, pp. 36–62; and Nancy Hardesty, *Women Called to Witness: Evangelical Feminism in the 19th Century* (Nashville: Abingdon, 1984).

28. See Daniel Doriani, "History of the Interpretation of 1 Timothy 2," in *Women in the Church*, pp. 213–67.

29. F. F. Bruce, *A Mind for What Matters* (Grand Rapids: Eerdmans, 1990), chap. 17, "Women in the Church: A Biblical Survey," pp. 259–325. Of course, because application of biblical ethics involves cultural recontextualization (for a variety of cultures, as missiologists point out), we need to take account of the forms of receiving cultures into which the message is translated; for a useful sociological study, see Mary Stewart Van Leeuwen, *Gender & Grace* (Downers Grove: InterVarsity, 1990).

30. William Webb, *Slaves, Women & Homosexuals: Exploring the Hermeneutics of Cultural Analysis*, foreword by Darrell L. Bock (Downers Grove: InterVarsity, 2001). See earlier Willard M. Swartley, *Slavery, Sabbath, War, and Women* (Scottsdale, Pa.: Herald, 1983).

31. Downers Grove: InterVarsity, 1993. If *Paul, Women, and Wives* has been my most controversial book, the background commentary (with over 200,000 copies in print to date, including translations) has been the most widely accepted. This is perhaps because background itself, apart from a consistent hermeneutic for its use, does not lead to many self-evident conclusions (though some may quote this admission of mine out of context).

# Acknowledgments

Some of the ground I cover in this book will be familiar to those who have read other books on the subject. It will also become obvious to the person who peruses the endnotes that my field of scholarly study is the New Testament and its ancient historical context. . I am far less adept in modern Christian writers' debates about women's roles in the Bible, a weakness I frankly admit. The strength of this work is its documentation of primary sources from my own research. Many of this book's proposals appear to be new, although others turn out to parallel previous work that has been done, which I have cited when I have come across it in my reading. I am thus content to hope that this book will be useful, more than that it will be entirely original.

My lack of familiarity with most other modern Christian literature on the subject has been somewhat met by the help of Gretchen Gaebelein Hull, who provided me with a short reading list before I finally sat down to write the final draft of this book. The one book I read on the subject before starting to write this book is one that I read some years ago, which has no doubt influenced my thinking more than my endnotes would reveal. That is Don Williams' helpful book, *The Apostle Paul and Women in the Church*. But the argumentation reflected here is my own, except where my notes indicate dependence, and my citations from the primary sources come directly from my own reading of those sources, except where I have noted otherwise.

I was introduced to the growing body of scholarly literature on women's studies in Greco-Roman antiquity particularly by Duke University Professor Mary T. Boatwright. Professor Boatwright guided me to many of the secondary sources in preparation for one of my preliminary doctoral exams on this subject.

I also wish to express my gratitude to Hendrickson production editor Phil Frank and to Linda Withrow Purnell of Duke's Perkins Library (who went beyond the call of duty in securing for me volumes not in Duke's holdings). Such technical assistance has contributed to making this the useful work I trust it will be.

I am, of course, indebted also to my undergraduate and seminary instructors for their advocacy of women's ministries. I am likewise indebted to my students for their helpful interaction with my arguments, especially to Cecilia Barnes, who single-handedly kept urging me to take a public stand on my views until she finally persuaded me. I am indebted to my women colleagues in evangelical ministry who trusted me enough to share their concerns with me. I am certain that these colleagues could close this book with greater passion and eloquence than I, because the issues in this book are issues they must confront every day. But I nevertheless hope that this book will strengthen the case in the body of Christ for justice on their behalf.

# Abbreviations

## MODERN JOURNALS, TEXTS, AND COLLECTIONS

| | |
|---|---|
| AARAS | American Academy of Religion Academy Series |
| AB | Anchor Bible |
| *AJA* | *American Journal of Archaeology* |
| *AmAnth* | *American Anthropologist* |
| *AncSoc* | *Ancient Society* |
| ANET | *Ancient Near Eastern Texts Relating to the Old Testament*, ed. Pritchard |
| *ANRW* | *Aufstieg und Niedergang der Römischen Welt* |
| APAACS | The American Philological Association, American Classical Studies |
| ASNU | Acta Seminarii Neotestamentici Upsaliensis |
| *ASSR* | *Archives de sciences sociales des religions* |
| AZLGHJ | Arbeiten zur Literatur und Geschichte des Hellenistischen Judentums |
| *BA* | *Biblical Archaeologist* |
| *BAR* | *Biblical Archaeology Review* |
| *BASOR* | *Bulletin of the American Schools of Oriental Research* |
| *BibSac* | *Bibliotheca Sacra* |
| *BiTod* | *Bible Today* |
| *BJRL* | *Bulletin of the John Rylands Library* |
| *BTB* | *Biblical Theology Bulletin* |
| *BZ* | *Biblische Zeitschrift* |
| *CB* | *Classical Bulletin* |
| CBNTS | Coniectanea Biblica New Testament Series |

| | |
|---|---|
| *CBQ* | *Catholic Biblical Quarterly* |
| CCWJCW | Cambridge Commentaries on Writings of the Jewish and Christian World 200 BC to AD 200 |
| *CH* | *Church History* |
| *CHL* | *Commentationes Humanarum Litterarum* |
| CHSHMC | The Center for Hermeneutical Studies in Hellenistic and Modern Culture |
| *CJ* | *Classical Journal* |
| *ConJud* | *Conservative Judaism* |
| *CQ* | *Classical Quarterly* |
| *Cruc* | *The Crucible* |
| *CT* | *Christianity Today* |
| *CTM* | *Concordia Theological Monthly* |
| CynEp | *The Cynic Epistles,* ed. Malherbe |
| *DA* | *Dissertation Abstracts* |
| *DR* | *Downside Review* |
| *DSar* | *Daughters of Sarah* |
| DSS | Dead Sea Scrolls |
| *EgTh* | *Eglise et Théologie* |
| EHR | Etudes d'Histoire des Religions |
| *EPROER* | *Etudes Préliminaires aux Religions Orientales dans l'Empire Romain* |
| *EQ* | *Evangelical Quarterly* |
| *ExpT* | *Expository Times* |
| *FV* | *Foi et Vie* |
| GNS | Good News Studies |
| GP | *Gospel Perspectives,* ed. France, Wenham, and Blomberg |
| *GR* | *Greece and Rome* |
| *GRBS* | *Greek, Roman and Byzantine Studies* |
| *GTJ* | *Grace Theological Journal* |
| *HeyJ* | *Heythrop Journal* |
| HeyM | Heythrop Monographs |
| HNTC | Harper New Testament Commentary |
| *HR* | *History of Religions* |
| HSS | Harvard Semitic Series |
| *HT* | *History Today* |
| *HTR* | *Harvard Theological Review* |
| ICC | International Critical Commentary |
| *Interp* | *Interpretation* |
| *JAAR* | *Journal of the American Academy of Religion* |

| | |
|---|---|
| *JAC* | *Jahrbuch für Antike und Christentum* |
| *JAF* | *Journal of American Folklore* |
| *JBL* | *Journal of Biblical Literature* |
| *JETS* | *Journal of the Evangelical Theological Society* |
| *JFSR* | *Journal of Feminist Studies in Religion* |
| *JHS* | *Journal of Hellenic Studies* |
| *JJS* | *Journal of Jewish Studies* |
| *JNES* | *Journal of Near Eastern Studies* |
| JPFC | *The Jewish People in the First Century*, ed. Safrai and Stern |
| *JRS* | *Journal of Roman Studies* |
| *JSNT* | *Journal for the Study of the New Testament* |
| *JSOT* | *Journal for the Study of the Old Testament* |
| *JTS* | *Journal of Theological Studies* |
| LEC | Library of Early Christianity |
| LLA | The Library of Liberal Arts |
| MBCB | Mnemosyne: Bibliotheca Classica Batava, Supplementum |
| MFC | Message of the Fathers of the Church |
| MNTC | Moffatt New Testament Commentary |
| NCB | New Century Bible |
| *NedTT* | *Nederlands Theologisch Tijdschrift* |
| *Neot* | *Neotestamentica* |
| NIBC | New International Biblical Commentary |
| NICNT | New International Commentary on the New Testament |
| *NovT* | *Novum Testamentum* |
| NovTSup | Novum Testamentum Supplement |
| *NTA* | *New Testament Abstracts* |
| *NTS* | *New Testament Studies* |
| *NTT* | *Norsk Teologisk Tidsskrift* |
| OBT | Overtures to Biblical Theology |
| OCPHS | Oxford Centre for Postgraduate Hebrew Studies |
| OTP | *Old Testament Pseudepigrapha*, ed. Charlesworth |
| *PBSR* | *Papers of the British School at Rome* |
| POTTS | Pittsburgh Original Texts and Translations Series |
| PTMS | Pittsburgh Theological Monograph Series |
| *RAfT* | *Revue Africaine de Théologie* |
| *RefJ* | *Reformed Journal* |
| *RestQ* | *Restoration Quarterly* |
| *RHR* | *Revue de l'Histoire des Religions* |

| | |
|---|---|
| *RSB* | *Religious Studies Bulletin* |
| SB | Stuttgarter Bibelstudien |
| SBL | Society of Biblical Literature |
| SBLBMI | Society of Biblical Literature Bible and Its Modern Interpreters Series |
| SBLDS | Society of Biblical Literature Dissertation Series |
| SBLGRRS | Society of Biblical Literature Greco-Roman Religion Series |
| SBLMS | Society of Biblical Literature Monograph Series |
| SBLTT | Society of Biblical Literature Texts and Translations |
| SBS | Sources for Biblical Study |
| SBT | Studies in Biblical Theology |
| *ScSoc* | *Science and Society* |
| *SEAJT* | *South East Asia Journal of Theology* |
| SHRSN | Studies in the History of Religions, Supplements to Numen |
| SJLA | Studies in Judaism in Late Antiquity |
| SNTSMS | Society for New Testament Studies Monograph Series |
| SPB | Studia Post Biblica |
| SSCS | Suny Series in Classical Studies |
| SUASIA | Skrifter Utgivna Av Svenska Institutet I Athen, 8° |
| *SvExÅrs* | *Svensk Exegetisk Årsbok* |
| TDGR | Translated Documents of Greece and Rome |
| *ThZ* | *Theologische Zeitschrift* |
| *TJ* | *Trinity Journal* |
| UBS | United Bible Societies |
| UCP | University of Canterbury Publications |
| UNDCSJCA | University of Notre Dame Center for the Study of Judaism and Christianity in Antiquity |
| *USQR* | *Union Seminary Quarterly Review* |
| *VerbDom* | *Verbum Domini* |
| WBC | Word Biblical Commentary |
| *WD* | *Wort und Dienst* |
| *WTJ* | *Westminster Theological Journal* |
| *ZNW* | *Zeitschrift für die Neutestamentliche Wissenschaft* |

## ANCIENT WORKS CITED

### Old Testament

| | |
|---|---|
| Gen. | Genesis |
| Exod. | Exodus |
| Lev. | Leviticus |
| Num. | Numbers |
| Deut. | Deuteronomy |
| Judg. | Judges |
| 1 Sam. | 1 Samuel |
| 2 Sam. | 2 Samuel |
| 1 Kgs. | 1 Kings |
| 2 Kgs. | 2 Kings |
| Ps. | Psalms |
| Prov. | Proverbs |
| Isa. | Isaiah |
| Jer. | Jeremiah |
| Lam. | Lamentations |
| Ezek. | Ezekiel |
| Dan. | Daniel |
| Hos. | Hosea |
| Mic. | Micah |
| Nah. | Nahum |
| Mal. | Malachi |

### Apocrypha

| | |
|---|---|
| 1 Esd. | 1 Esdras |
| Tob. | Tobit |
| Jdt. | Judith |
| Wisd. | Wisdom |
| Sir. | Sirach |
| Bar. | Baruch |
| Sus. | Susanna |
| 1 Macc. | 1 Maccabees |
| 2 Macc. | 2 Maccabees |

### New Testament

| | |
|---|---|
| Matt. | Matthew |
| Rom. | Romans |
| 1 Cor. | 1 Corinthians |
| 2 Cor. | 2 Corinthians |

| | |
|---|---|
| Gal. | Galatians |
| Eph. | Ephesians |
| Phil. | Philippians |
| Col. | Colossians |
| 1 Thess. | 1 Thessalonians |
| 1 Tim. | 1 Timothy |
| 2 Tim. | 2 Timothy |
| Tit. | Titus |
| 1 Pet. | 1 Peter |
| 2 Pet. | 2 Peter |
| Rev. | Revelation |

## Qumran Texts

| | |
|---|---|
| CD | Damascus Document |
| 1QH | Qumran Hymns |
| 1QM | War Scroll |
| 1QpHab | Pesher commentary on Habakkuk |
| 1QS | Manual of Discipline |
| 1QSa | Commentary on 1 Samuel |
| 4QNah | Pesher commentary on Nahum |
| Gen. Apoc. | Genesis Apocryphon |

## Rabbinic Works: Mishnaic Literature

| | |
|---|---|
| m. | before tractate title = Mishnah |
| t. | before tractate title = Tosefta |
| b. | before tractate title = Babylonian Talmud |
| p. | before tractate title = Palestinian Talmud |
| 'Ab. | 'Aboth |
| 'A. Z. | 'Abodah Zarah |
| B. B. | Baba Batra |
| Bez. | Beza |
| B. M. | Baba Metzia |
| Git. | Gittin |
| Hag. | Hagigah |
| Hor. | Horayoth |
| Hul. | Hullin |
| Kel. | Kelaim |
| Ker. | Keratoth |
| Ket. | Ketuboth |
| Kid. | Kiddushin |
| Meg. | Megilla |

| | |
|---|---|
| Men. | Menahoth |
| Mid. | Middoth |
| M. K. | Mo'ed Katan |
| Naz. | Nazir |
| Ned. | Nedarim |
| Pes. | Pesahim |
| R. H. | Rosh Hashanah |
| Sanh. | Sanhedrin |
| Shab. | Shabbath |
| Sot. | Sotah |
| Suk. | Sukkoth |
| Taan. | Ta'anith |
| Ter. | Terumoth |
| Yeb. | Yebamoth |

**Rabbinic Works: Midrashim**

| | |
|---|---|
| Mek. | Mekilta de-Rabbi Ishmael |
| Shir. | Shirata |
| Sifra | Sifra |
| VDDeho. | Vayyiqra Dibura Dehobah |
| A. M. | Aharé Mot |
| Qed. | Qedoshim |
| Sifre Num. | Sifre Numbers |
| Sifre Deut. | Sifre Deuteronomy |
| Gen. Rab. | Genesis Rabbah |
| Exod. Rab. | Exodus Rabbah |
| Lev. Rab. | Leviticus Rabbah |
| Num. Rab. | Numbers Rabbah |
| Deut. Rab. | Deuteronomy Rabbah |
| Koh. Rab. | Ecclesiastes Rabbah |
| Song Rab. | Song of Songs Rabbah |
| Lam. Rab. | Lamentations Rabbah |

**Other Rabbinic Collections**

| | |
|---|---|
| Ab. R. Nathan | Aboth de-Rabbi Nathan |
| Pes. Rab. | Pesikta Rabbati |
| Pes. Rab Kah. | Pesikta de-Rab Kahana |

**Other Jewish and Christian Works**

| | |
|---|---|
| Apoc. Abr. | Apocalypse of Abraham |
| Apoc. Adam | Apocalypse of Adam |

| | |
|---|---|
| Apoc. Moses | Apocalypse of Moses |
| Apoc. Sedrach | Apocalypse of Sedrach |
| Apost. Const. | Apostolic Constitutions |
| Asc. Isa. | Ascension of Isaiah |
| Athenag. | Athenagoras |
| *CIJ* | *Corpus Inscriptionum Iudaicarum* |
| *CPJ* | *Corpus Papyrorum Judaicarum* |
| Did. | Didache |
| Ep. Arist. | Epistle of Aristeas |
| Euseb. | Eusebius |
| *Eccl Hist* | *History of the Church* |
| *Pr. Ev.* | *Preparation for the Gospel* |
| 1 Clem. | 1 Clement |
| 1 En. | 1 Enoch |
| 4 Macc | 4 Maccabees |
| Gr. Ezra | Greek Apocalypse of Ezra |
| Hippol. | Hippolytus |
| *Ref.* | *Refutations* |
| Ign. | (Pseudo-)Ignatius |
| *Antioch.* | *To the Antiochenes* |
| Jos. | Josephus |
| *Ag. Ap.* | *Against Apion* |
| *Ant.* | *Antiquities* |
| *War* | *The Jewish War* |
| Jos. & As. | Joseph and Asenath |
| Jub. | Jubilees |
| Justin | Justin Martyr |
| *1 Apol.* | *First Apology* |
| *Dial.* | *Dialogue with Trypho* |
| Mart. Poly. | Martyrdom of Polycarp |
| Min. Fel. | Minucius Felix |
| *Oct.* | *Octavius* |
| Ode Sol. | Odes of Solomon |
| Ps-Philo | Pseudo-Philo's *Biblical Antiquities* |
| Ps-Phocyl. | Pseudo-Phocylides |
| 2 Bar. | 2 Baruch |
| 2 Clem. | 2 Clement |
| 2 En. | 2 Enoch |
| Sent. Sextus | Sentences of Sextus |
| Sib. Or. | Sibylline Oracles |
| Syr. Men. | Syriac Menander |

| | |
|---|---|
| *Epit.* | *Epitome* |
| *Sent.* | *Sentences* |
| Tert. | Tertullian |
| *Apol.* | *Apology* |
| Test. Abr. | Testament of Abraham |
| Test. Job | Testament of Job |
| Test. Mos. | Testament of Moses |
| Test. Sol. | Testament of Solomon |
| Testaments of the Twelve Patriarchs | |
| Test Asher | Testament of Asher |
| Test. Benj. | Testament of Benjamin |
| Test. Iss. | Testament of Issachar |
| Test. Jos. | Testament of Joseph |
| Test. Jud. | Testament of Judah |
| Test. Levi | Testament of Levi |
| Test. Naph. | Testament of Naphtali |
| Test. Reub. | Testament of Reuben |
| Test. Sim. | Testament of Simeon |
| Test. Zeb. | Testament of Zebulon |
| Theoph. | Theophilus |
| 3 Bar. | 3 Baruch |
| 3 Enoch | 3 Enoch |
| 3 Macc. | 3 Maccabees |
| V. Adam | Vita Adam et Evae |

**Greco-Roman Works**

| | |
|---|---|
| Ach. Tat. | Achilles Tatius |
| *Clit.* | *Clitophon and Leucippe* |
| Apul. | Apuleius |
| *Metam.* | *Metamorphosis (The Golden Ass)* |
| Aristoph. | Aristophanes |
| Arist. | Aristotle |
| *E. E.* | *The Eudemian Ethics* |
| *N. E.* | *The Nicomachean Ethics* |
| *Pol.* | *Politics* |
| *Rhet.* | *The Art of Rhetoric* |
| Artem. | Artemidorus |
| *Oneir.* | *Oneirocriticon* |
| Athen. | Athenaeus |
| *Deipn.* | *Deipnosophists* |

| | |
|---|---|
| Char. | Chariton |
| *Chaer.* | *Chaereas and Callirhoe* |
| Cic. | Cicero |
| *Acad.* | *Academica* |
| *Invent.* | *De Inventione* |
| *Leg.* | *De Legibus* |
| *Offic.* | *De Officiis* |
| *Oratore* | *De Oratore* |
| *Par. Stoic.* | *Paradoxa Stoicorum* |
| *Re Publ.* | *De Re Publica* |
| *Senect.* | *De Senectute* |
| *Tusc. Disp.* | *Tusculan Disputations* |
| Diod. Sic. | Diodorus Siculus |
| Dio Chrys. | Dio Chrysostom |
| *Or.* | *Orations* |
| Diog. Laert. | Diogenes Laertius |
| *Lives* | *Lives of Eminent Philosophers* |
| Epict. | Epictetus |
| *Disc.* | *Discourses* |
| *Encheir.* | *Encheiridion* |
| Eurip. | Euripides |
| Bacch. | The Bacchants |
| Gaius | Gaius |
| *Inst.* | *Institutes* |
| Greek Anth. | The Greek Anthology |
| Herod. | Herodotus |
| *Hist.* | *Histories* |
| Hor. | Horace |
| *Ep.* | *Epistles* |
| *Poet.* | *Ars Poetica* |
| *Sat.* | *Satires* |
| Isoc. | Isocrates |
| *Demon.* | *To Demonicus* |
| *Nic./Cypr.* | *Nicocles* or *The Cyprians* |
| *Panath.* | *Panathenaicus* |
| Juv. | Juvenal |
| *Sat.* | *Satires* |
| Lucian | Lucian |
| *Alex.* | *Alexander the False Prophet* |
| *Dem.* | *Demonax* |
| *Dream* | *The Dream*, or *Lucian's Career* |
| *IgnBC* | *Ignorant Book-Collector* |

| | | |
|---|---|---|
| | *Lucius/Ass* | *Lucius*, or *The Ass* |
| | *Peregr.* | *Peregrinus* |
| | *Swans* | *Amber*, or *The Swans* |
| | *SyrG* | *The Syrian Goddess* |
| Lucr. | Lucretius | |
| | *Nat.* | *De Rerum Natura* |
| Macrob. | Macrobius | |
| | *Satur.* | *Saturnalia* |
| Marc. Aur. | Marcus Aurelius | |
| | *Med.* | *Meditations* |
| Mart. | Martial | |
| | *Epig.* | *Epigrams* |
| Mus. Ruf. | Musonius Rufus | |
| Paus. | Pausanias | |
| | *Desc. Greece* | *Description of Greece* |
| Persius | Persius | |
| | *Sat.* | *Satires* |
| Petr. | Petronius | |
| | *Sat.* | *Satyricon* |
| Philostr. | Philostratus | |
| | *V. A.* | *Life of Apollonius of Tyana* |
| Plato | Plato | |
| | *Alcib.* | *Alcibiades (books 1 and 2)* |
| | *Charm.* | *Charmides* |
| | *Crat.* | *Cratylus* |
| | *Rep.* | *Republic* |
| | *Symp.* | *Symposium* |
| Pliny | Pliny | |
| | *Ep.* | *Epistles* |
| Plut. | Plutarch | |
| | *Ages.* | *Agesilaus* |
| | *Alex.* | *Alexander* |
| | *Bride* | *Advice to Bride and Groom* |
| | *Def. Orac.* | *De defectu oraculorum (Decline of Oracles)* |
| | *Dial. on Love* | *The Dialogue on Love (Amatorius)* |
| | *Div. Veng.* | *On the Delays of Divine Vengeance* |
| | *Educ.* | *On the Education of Children* |
| | *Eum.* | *Eumenes* |
| | *Fort. Rom.* | *Fortune of Romans* |
| | *G. Q.* | *Greek Questions* |
| | *Isis* | *Isis and Osiris* |
| | *Lyc.* | *Lycurgus* |

| | |
|---|---|
| *Mor.* | *Moralia* |
| *Or. at Delphi* | *The Oracle at Delphi* |
| *Par. Stories* | *Parallel Stories* |
| *Plat. Q.* | *Platonic Questions* |
| *R. Q.* | *Roman Questions* |
| *SRom.* | *Sayings of Romans* |
| *SSpart.* | *Sayings of Spartans* |
| *SSpartW.* | *Sayings of Spartan Women* |
| *Superst.* | *On Superstition* |
| *Tim.* | *Timoleon* |
| *T.-T.* | *Table-Talk* |
| *Uneduc. Ruler* | *To an Uneducated Ruler* |
| Pythag. Sent. | Pythagorean Sentences |
| Quint. | Quintilian |
| Rhet. ad Herenn | Rhetorica ad Herennium |
| Sen. | Seneca |
| *Ben.* | *On Benefits* |
| *Clem.* | *De Clementia* |
| *Dial.* | *Dialogues* |
| *Ep. Lucil.* | *Epistles to Lucilius* |
| Sext. Emp. | Sextus Empiricus |
| *Out. Pyrr.* | *Outlines of Pyrrhonism* |
| Strabo | Strabo |
| *Geog.* | *Geography* |
| Suet. | Suetonius |
| *Calig.* | *Caligula* |
| *Claud.* | *Claudius* |
| *Tib.* | *Tiberius* |
| Tac. | Tacitus |
| *Agric.* | *Agricola* |
| *Ann.* | *Annals* |
| *Germ.* | *Germany and Its Tribes* |
| *Hist.* | *History* |
| Theon | Theon |
| *Progymn.* | *Progymnasmata* |
| Val. Max. | Valerius Maximus |
| *Mem. Deeds* | *Memorable Deeds and Sayings* |
| Varro | |
| *Lat. Lang.* | *On the Latin Language* |
| Xenophon | |
| *Oec.* | *Oeconomicus* |

# Introduction

Because the question of Paul's teachings on women's roles has been debated on several levels of discourse, this book is likewise written on several levels. Whereas the following chapters are devoted primarily to a serious investigation of Paul's teaching using the relevant historical and cultural tools, the introduction, conclusion, and some of the arguments address or presuppose some of the more popular concerns raised by this issue today. The extensive documentation is for those who wish to consult it, but the text itself is written to be useful to the general reader as well as to the biblical scholar.

Besides its academic contribution, I hope that this book will help Christian spouses to serve one another better, and that it will benefit the body of Christ as a whole by encouraging it to raise up more laborers for the harvest. This nontechnical introduction is directed especially toward those who share my convictions about the Bible's authority but who are still struggling with whether the Bible really advocates the full equality of men and women.

## MY INTEREST IN PAUL'S VIEW OF WOMEN'S ROLES

It could be suggested that since I am a man I have nothing to gain or lose by taking a position on the issue of women's roles in the church. But while such a suggestion could be offered either to challenge my commitment to the subject or to praise my objectivity, it would actually only underline the wrong thinking that has dominated discussion of the issue in recent years. As members of the body of Christ, we are all called to look out for one another's interests, and if certain ministries are denied to half (or over half) of God's people, then that should concern all of us, for the ministry of the entire body of Christ will surely suffer from this denial.

Since my conversion, much of my Christian life has been spent in fellowship with charismatic and Pentecostal circles which do not oppose women in ministry. Indeed, many of the pioneers in the Pentecostal and Holiness movements were women, and denominations such as the Assemblies of God have repeatedly affirmed the right of women to ordination.[1]

I am ordained by the National Baptist Convention, a traditional black denomination in which women have played an active role since its earliest days.[2] Although the issue of women's ordination does not command a consensus,[3] the local association in which I was ordained supports it and hosts many effective women ministers who command our utmost respect. AME Zion, another black denomination, was the first Methodist communion to ordain women, and it began to do so twenty-six years before women received the right to vote in the United States.[4] The black church has been traditionally ahead of American culture in this regard in part because free black women in the antebellum North nearly always had to work outside the home so their families could survive.[5] Another factor, however, may be the black church's sensitivity to the injustice of discrimination; interestingly, many of the black abolitionists also spoke up for the emancipation of women.[6]

I have thus never been a part of a movement that excludes women from ministry, and consequently I do not feel as though I am engaging in polemic in writing this book; for much of contemporary Christianity, including my own evangelical Christianity, this book will only confirm what its readers have already believed or suspected.

At the same time, it is common knowledge that a significant stream of Christianity severely limits the roles of women in the home and the church. Indeed, even in the less restrictive circles, some ordained women have complained about the unofficial restrictions many of their brothers in Christ place on them. These sisters have begun to sensitize many of the rest of us to the importance of the issue and to the need to address the proof-texts that are often marshalled to support women's subordination or to restrict them from teaching Scripture.

I did not always hold the views I hold now. When I began my undergraduate theological education about fifteen years ago, I was listening to some very traditional friends. They had warned me that some women teachers would argue for their right to teach the Bible, that my Greek teachers might think that other Bible translations besides the KJV could be accurate, and that I might meet people who liked contemporary Christian music. Like many others who hold to wholesale theological positions without having time to investigate their points, I thought it safer to stand on the more conservative side—which at the time I thought meant the more "traditional" side—until I could know for certain. I was, of course, mistaken; it would simply have been better for me not to have taken a stand at all until I could know for certain.

Not everyone who opposes women teachers is equally restrictive or traditional in all areas; indeed, my own feelings on some issues would still be considered at least "conservative" and perhaps even "restrictive." Yet some people hold many views simply because these views are part of a "conservative" package. It is precarious, however, to interpret the Bible by simply assuming the more "conservative" or traditional interpretation to be correct—given the variety of traditions in the body of Christ, interpreting the Bible on the basis of traditions would surely lead to the impossibility of dialogue between different Christian groups! (Unfortunately, it sometimes has.) Thus, to be conservative in some evangelical circles is to oppose women's ordination; in some other equally evangelical circles (such as my own), it is conservative to defend it.

What is ultimately at issue for those who regard the apostolic tradition as normative is not what subsequent traditions teach, but what the writers of the Bible teach. Yet understanding what the Bible means is not always a simple matter; certain passages in the Bible might appear as though women are excluded from teaching the Bible (if interpreted consistently, from teaching Sunday School as well as from explaining Scripture from the pulpit).[7] Those with the more restrictive view must then read the passages in the Bible about women who taught or prophesied as exceptions that prove the rule, if exceptions actually do that.

Inclined as I once was toward the more traditional restrictive view, I encountered two main problems: (1) I kept meeting committed women who were sure that God had called them, and I did not have sufficient conviction to tell them that they had to be mistaken. I would have to be pretty sure of my position before I used it to judge another person's call, because if I made her stumble, it was none other than God to whom I would have to answer. And if I as a male minister could question the sincerity of her call, how could any of us men argue that we were certain that *we* had been called to ministry?[8]

(2) An initially less pressing problem was the response most students gave to my view, the same response they gave to Paul's admonition that women cover their heads in church: "That's just cultural." "But it's part of the Bible!" I protested. "If you throw this part out, you have to throw everything else out, too." I cannot recall anyone having a good response to my objection, but even as a freshman I knew very well that if I were consistent in my stance against using culture to interpret the Bible, I would have to advocate women's head coverings in church, the practice of holy kisses, and parentally arranged marriages. (I admittedly did not inform my parents of my questions concerning the last-mentioned view.)

Sooner or later I had to come to terms with the claims of the biblical texts themselves. If Paul says in 1 Corinthians that he is writing a letter to the Corinthians, am I not disrespecting his words if I ignore Paul's own claim that this is what he is doing? I had to come to grips with how the Bible itself invites us to interpret it. It became clear as I continued to immerse myself in Scripture that most of the books of the Bible were originally written to different audiences, and that the Bible's original readers would have to have read each book by itself. The Corinthians, for example, would read Paul's letter to them as a letter addressing their own situation, and they could not cross-reference to Romans or Revelation to figure out what Paul meant. In other words, at the very least, there has to be enough in 1 Corinthians, in the situation it addresses, and in the Old Testament, to tell me what it means without my taking recourse to other texts unavailable to the Corinthian Christians.

Few biblically informed readers would try to take all the symbols in Revelation "literally," without accounting for the historical context Revelation addresses. We recognize that the book of Revelation belongs to a certain literary genre called prophetic or apocalyptic literature. But Paul's letters belong to a distinct literary genre no less: they are *letters.* And letters also nearly always address specific situations. To apply what Paul said to his churches to our own circumstances today requires more than simply reading the words on a translated page of the Bible; it requires understanding the principles those words were meant to evoke for the first readers. This is the only proper way to respect the author's inspired message, as opposed to constructing an entirely new meaning based on a naïve modern reading of an ancient text.

In time, I came to the costly conclusion which I had long resisted, namely, that I was going to have to start learning the culture and history of the biblical world if I were to be faithful to my call. I decided that I would thus need to spend time reading a book besides the Bible that would give me all the necessary background. Unfortunately, no one book seemed adequate or trustworthy, so I had to start reading several. Then I discovered that these books sometimes contradicted one another. Only at this point did I begin to realize that accepting the validity of cultural-historical context for biblical interpretation had started me on a very long road. If I were to expound the Scriptures adequately, I would have to know the culture. I hoped one day to be able to produce books that would keep others in my situation from having to do all the same work. Those undergraduate questions eventually led me through a Ph.D. and a detailed study of the milieu in which the New Testament was written.

I had not been at such research long before I came to realize that a lot of what Paul wrote about women (not just concerning their head coverings) had to address a specific congregational or cultural situation. While I insisted that whatever principles Paul applied to that situation were transcultural, I had to acknowledge that those principles would have to be reapplied in different ways in different cultural settings: all biblical passages may be for all time, but all biblical passages are not for all *circumstances*. I later learned, particularly in my missions courses in seminary, that this approach—called "contextualization"—is standard practice for missionaries and Bible translators. What I learned the hard way, many people already knew; but I am all too aware that many Christians have not yet discovered this approach to reading the Bible.[9]

## BIBLICAL INTERPRETATION OR FEMINIST AGENDA?

On the one hand, many people today claim to follow the Bible, yet prejudice their interpretation of the Bible by merely using it to legitimize their own prior agendas. On the other hand, many other people claim to follow the Bible, and yet fail to apply its principles to our own situations today. While Christians should not read their agendas into the Bible, we should ask how the Bible relates to the culture in which we live.

Since this book deals only with Paul's teachings on women's roles in ministry and in the home, it is not meant to address modern feminism or most of the issues associated with that movement. Because it advocates full equality in the church and home for women and men, however, many will place this book in an ideological category called biblical feminism. The complication with placing this book in such a category, of course, is that not everyone defines either "biblical" or "feminism" in the same way, so it would not contribute anything to the discussion to embrace the title without defining what sort of issues this book addresses and what sorts of issues it does not address.

Whether readers consider themselves "feminists" or not, most will agree with at least some concerns often characterized as feminist, while questioning other such concerns. Many ideas that have been advocated in the name of the women's movement are not only in harmony with Christian principles, but demand the support of all Christians: for instance, opposition to rape, other forms of sexual and physical abuse, sexual harassment, and pornographic exploitation. Some other ideas that have often been associated with the modern women's movement, such as "abortion rights," or much less often associated with it, such as worship of a "mother goddess," are far less agreeable to most evangelicals, including myself.

If our allegiance is to biblical teaching, we do not need to accept or reject uncritically *everything* associated with any particular movement. For instance, the women's movement in the 1800s, originally initiated and dominated by evangelical Christians,[10] largely opposed abortion.[11] There are also prolife feminists today (such as a group known as "Feminists for Life"). A polarization between defending women and defending the unborn, or between equality of the genders and peace in the home, may be a polarization the world around us accepts, but Christians need not buy into such forced-choice logic. Why can we not support both?

There are issues where most biblically conservative Christians, including myself, disagree with prominent elements in the feminist movement (as do some elements of the feminist movement itself). But there are other concerns which nearly all Christians, including myself, and nearly the whole women's movement plainly share. All of us would call for justice against the oppression of women that takes place in the world today. All of us oppose the exploitation of tens of thousands of female (as well as male) children who run away from home each year in our country, many of whom end up selling their bodies to survive on the street. All of us oppose young men getting their girlfriends pregnant then leaving them to raise the children alone.

Of course, agendas of justice on behalf of women cannot be narrowly limited to the questions traditionally entertained among many North American feminists, as African-American writers and writers from the Two-Thirds World often remind us.[12] But here again Christians would find much common ground with other women's movements, objecting to the oppression many women face around the world. Although "bride-burning" is now illegal in India, it still happens frequently; a bride whose dowry is insufficient may be burned to death so that her husband can find a new partner. There is no investigation, of course, because it is said that she simply poured cooking oil over herself and set herself on fire accidentally.[13] Whereas in my church my sisters complain that there are not enough men to go around, in India the situation for marital prospects is reversed: discrimination against women extends even to the womb, and at one hospital there, 7,999 of the 8,000 abortions reported were of female fetuses.[14]

In lands like Afghanistan and Bangladesh, women are denied educational opportunities on the basis of their gender; in the former, they must leave school at ten or eleven to begin weaving carpets. Although it is reported that two thirds of the world's food is produced by women, they have little control over the products of their labors. In rural Uganda, for instance, women do the hardest physical work in the fields, besides caring for the children, and also grow up expecting beatings from their future husbands.[15] As in most parts of rural Africa, a woman labors from 5 A.M. till 9:30 P.M.[16] It is reported that women own less than 1% of the world's property, and though they work over 60% of all hours worked, they only receive 10% of the world's income.[17]

Lest we think that discrimination against women is limited to Islamic and other non-Western societies, however, we should note that the first nation to grant women the right to vote was New Zealand—in 1893. Women did not receive the right to vote in the United States or Canada until 1920, in Great Britain and Germany until 1928, and in France until 1945. As late as 1970, women still could not vote in the European nations of Switzerland, Portugal, or Liechtenstein.[18]

It should be remembered that long after the slaves had been freed and black American men were allowed to vote, black women, like their white counterparts, were still denied this right. As Sojourner Truth, a black abolitionist woman, warned in 1867, "if colored men get their rights, and not colored women theirs, the colored men will be masters over the women, and it will be just as bad as it was before."[19] It was the young women's movement, backed by many Christians with their roots solidly planted in evangelical revivalism, that pushed for women to have the right to vote.

A Rhode Island Rape Crisis Center Study of 1700 teenagers, cited in a 1990 InterVarsity magazine, reported that 65% of the boys and 47% of the girls in seventh through ninth grades say that a man may force a woman to have sex with him if they've been dating for more than six months. Eighty-seven per cent of the boys and 79% of the girls responded that rape was acceptable if the couple was married. This thinking warns us where our culture is headed, incited by commercials that exploit human sexuality and movies that glamorize violent death, especially of women as sex objects. It is not hard to understand why "date rape" has become common and why rape concerns all of us, men as well as women; it threatens men's sisters, girlfriends, wives, or daughters. In a survey conducted at Duke University, 13% of the women students said that someone had tried to rape them, and 80% said that they knew their assailants.[20]

Wife-beating seems to have been a well-established practice in many patriarchal families of the 1800s.[21] This should not surprise us, given how common it remains today; sometimes it even occurs in professedly Christian homes.[22] (Indeed, it has sometimes been practiced under the supposed sanction of biblical passages about wives' submission,[23] although not even the most traditional interpreters of those passages believe that this is what they mean.) Court officials, neighbors, and pastors have sometimes suggested that the wife must have done something to provoke the abuse, which only adds to the cruel oppression these women face.[24] This is a far cry from the New Testament teaching about loving one's wife as Christ loved his church and gave himself for her. Those of us who stand aloof from their pain are also a far cry from the biblical teaching about loving one's neighbor as oneself.

But while some Christians may have once been content to cite proof-texts about women's subordination to justify their ignoring this sort of oppression, virtually all of us would today recognize that oppression and exploitation of any sort are sinful violations of Jesus' commandment to love our neighbor as ourselves and to love fellow-Christians as Christ loved us. Nor is protest against women's oppression a new phenomenon in Christian circles; biblical Christians led much of the fight for women's rights in this country:

> The feminist movement is not new—nor is its connection with biblical principles. The first U.S. women's rights convention, held in 1848 in Seneca Falls, New York, was an outgrowth of both the religious revivalist and abolitionist movements. Many of these women had a renewed desire to study Scripture and were quick to see the parallels between slavery and female subordination.[25]

Wherever Christians come down on the issue of women in the pastorate or women's place in the home, *no* Christians would advocate beatings, ridicule, or sexual exploitation. *All* Christians must affirm the equal humanity of men and women, that they are both made in God's image (Gen. 1:26–27), and that women should be treated with respect and honor by their husbands. Since I do not know any Christians (or non-Christians, for that matter), who would today oppose women attending college or voting, I suppose that all Christians would acknowledge the intellectual as well as spiritual equality of women and men. Even the people I know who believe that a mother's role is mainly to care for the children at home (contrast Prov. 31:10–31) would not for that reason deny women a place in the work force.

While we may disagree on the flexibility of roles mentioned in the Bible, the secular generalization that Christians (both men and women) who respect the Bible oppose women's rights is an inaccurate caricature of these Christians—a caricature into which a few traditional Christians themselves have unfortunately bought. And the view that some conservative Christians hold of the women's movement as concerned only with advocating abortion or destroying the home[26] is likewise a caricature that ignores the common ground that exists between biblical Christianity and the women's movement on a number of issues.

In the broadest sense of the term "feminism" (regarding women and men as equal and actively opposing women's oppression), then, perhaps all Christians should consider themselves biblical feminists. But the phrase "biblical feminist" usually applies to a much more specific set of questions than those listed above.

The issue is not just whether women should be respected and treated with dignity; the issue is also whether they should properly fill the same roles as men. This then is the question with which this book will deal. The biblical argument of this book is that, in fact, women are as capable of filling those roles as men are. This is indeed a question of women's rights, too, but in addressing the differences of opinion among Christians on this issue,[27] it is important not to overlook the large area where all Christians agree and can work together for women's (and others') rights in the world. Given that large area of agreement, it is the area on which we disagree—smaller but large enough to dramatically affect every phase of our church and home life—which this book addresses.

Equal treatment for women (or, indeed, for any people made in God's image) is not, as some would argue, an agenda borrowed from the secular world. The *subordination* of women, on the contrary, is an idea practiced (often in brutal ways) by most non-Christian cultures in history.[28] It could thus be easily argued that the subordination of women in Christian history was borrowed from the "secular world," and that it tells us more about the societies in which those Christian rules were formulated than about God's eternal purposes. As I hope this book will help to demonstrate, treating women as men's equals was far closer to the spirit of Paul than making them subordinate. This is significant, since it is to Paul that the alleged repression of women in the New Testament is most often attributed.

## THE NATURE OF THIS BOOK

Those who advocate the subordination of women traditionally appeal to a limited number of passages to support their position;[29] those of us who advocate women's equality do the same, except, of course, with different passages. This book does not devote much space to arguments for women's equality in the Bible, except where those arguments touch briefly on the subject of our study.

The sole purpose of this book is to examine four passages in Pauline literature which have traditionally been used to argue for the subordination of women. Two of these texts address women's roles in family relationships, and two address women's speaking in the church. One of each is in a letter universally accepted as written by Paul; the other two are from letters whose authorship is questioned in varying degrees by different scholars, but which I accept as Pauline.

This book, like my last one, *And Marries Another*,[30] attempts to combine the scholarly and popular genres in a manner that will be most useful to pastors and others familiar with the biblical texts we are addressing. For this reason, I do not discuss extensively the proposed date of sources I cite, or evaluate in detail the references in the notes. But the notes should be helpful to those who wish to pursue these issues further.[31]

Not all this book's conclusions will appear to be of equal exegetical weight to those who do not accept the importance of cultural context for understanding the Bible. On the one hand, for instance, that the God of the Bible calls women to teach the Scriptures is, in my opinion, beyond dispute, supported by clear biblical evidence and challenged only by the interpretation of several comparatively ambiguous texts. On the other hand, this book's arguments concerning the submission of wives to their husbands involve the question of application. There, if my models of going from interpretation of the text to modern application were to prove flawed, my application would suffer correspondingly, as some of my students (women as well as men) have delighted to point out to me. This requires me to demonstrate that those who disagree with my method of interpretation on this issue in practice accept the same method elsewhere. The sixth chapter of this book thus calls for a method of application on which most Christians today would agree with regard to Paul's teaching about slavery.

I trust that this book is exegetically sound, and I hope that it is persuasive. But even if some readers are only partly persuaded, I hope that my suggestions will in *practice* be equally useful for the nonoppressive traditionalist and the loving egalitarian: mutual submission means that we should look out for one another's interests, and that is a difficult enough call in itself to demand our dependence on the Holy Spirit. Mutual submission does not reduce the wife's responsibility articulated in the traditional position; it merely reminds the husband that he, too, must submit to his wife as a fellow-heir of the grace of life.

While I do not expect everyone to agree with my conclusions, I do hope that those who disagree will honestly address the issues raised in this book and not repeat the sort of accusations a few writers have leveled against equally evangelical colleagues. I hope that those who disagree will challenge my interpretations, rather than question my commitment to the authority of Scripture because my interpretation is different from theirs. My relationship with Jesus Christ is the most important thing in my life; my call is to expound his message faithfully. I have been beaten and had my life threatened for sharing Christ on the streets, and I do not doubt that it will happen again. I try to live simply according to what I believe the Bible says about possessions, and take a lot of other Scriptures more literally than do many of those who might wish to attack those who disagree with their interpretation which subordinates women.

That I should need to defend myself in advance on these points reflects the unfortunate level of discourse on which discussions of this issue have sometimes been conducted in recent years. But what I offer in this book I offer in love, believing that this is an important issue that affects how over half the body of Christ is being treated.

## NOTES

1. Cf., e.g., the entire February 1991 issue of *Mountain Movers*, an Assemblies of God (AG) missions periodical, and the statement adopted by the General Presbytery of the AG, August 1990.

2. On women's prominent roles in the black Baptist church, see especially Evelyn Brooks, "The Women's Movement in the Black Baptist Church, 1880–1920," Ph.D. dissertation, University of Rochester, 1984. This is not to say that women always had access to the pulpit, but to argue that the black church was ahead of much of U.S. culture. The prominent black Baptist educator Nannie Helen Burroughs started the National Training School for Women and Girls; this school is said to have sent out more women missionaries than any other school in the country.

3. A large percentage still disapprove of women as pastors (in contrast to some other black denominations like AME, AME Zion, and CME); see C. E. Lincoln and L. H. Mamiya, *The Black Church in the African American Experience* (Durham, N.C.: Duke, 1990), pp. 292–93). But most of the younger clergy in black churches support women as pastors (ibid., p. 290), which probably reflects the trend of the future.

4. Lincoln and Mamiya, *Black Church*, p. 58. Far earlier than this, Bishop Richard Allen, founder of AME, let Jarena Lee (b. 1783) preach in his pulpit; for her ministry, see M. C. Sernett, *Afro-American Religious History* (Durham, N.C.: Duke, 1985), pp. 160–79.

5. See Dorothy Sterling, ed., *We Are Your Sisters: Black Women in the Nineteenth Century* (New York: W. W. Norton & Co., 1984), pp.

87–104, 215–16. This was the case in spite of the popular societal ideal to the contrary (ibid., pp. 220, 255).

6. Such as Frederick Douglass, an AME Zion deacon, and prominent female religious figures such as Sojourner Truth and Harriet Tubman (J. H. Cone, *For My People: Black Theology and the Black Church* [Maryknoll, N.Y.: Orbis, 1984], pp. 123–25; in general, see pp. 122–39). For the position of white evangelical abolitionists such as Finney and Oberlin College, see N. A. Hardesty, *Women Called to Witness: Evangelical Feminism in the 19th Century* (Nashville: Abingdon, 1984), pp. 15, 37, 44. The recognition of past oppression against the black community was a major reason for our local Baptist association's explicit support of women's ordination (Lincoln and Mamiya, *Black Church*, p. 41, on the East Cedar Grove Association).

7. This is stricter than the usual traditionalist position, which allows women to teach (as long as it is in Sunday School, and not in the pulpit) and to be missionaries (of which there have been very many; see e.g., Ruth Tucker and Walter Liefeld, "Women in Foreign Missions," pp. 56–76 in *World Christian Summer Reader 1990* [Pasadena, Calif.: World Christian, 1990]).

8. Harriet Tubman testified eloquently to her call (see in Sterling, *Sisters*, p. 397). Not only did she successfully smuggle hundreds of slaves northward on the Underground Railroad, but she led black Union soldiers through the South in slave-freeing raids without losing a single soldier, just like the Israelites in many OT "holy wars" (see in ibid., p. 259).

9. What we argue here has long been advocated by pastorally minded Bible scholars concerned with applying the text in the church today; e.g., B. H. Streeter and Edith Picton-Turbervill, *Women and the Church* (London: F. Fisher Unwin, 1917), p. 54: "We see again and again how our Lord, while enunciating eternal principles, conformed to the customs of the day. Customs, however, pass away while eternal principles remain." The writers use this interpretive principle to explain why there were no women among the twelve apostles, given the "customs of the East."

10. See especially Hardesty, *Women*.

11. E.g., Tim Stafford, "The Abortion Wars: What Most Christians Don't Know," *CT* (Oct. 6, 1989): 18.

12. Jacquelyn Grant, *White Women's Christ and Black Women's Jesus: Feminist Christology and Womanist Response*, AARAS 64 (Atlanta: Scholars Press, 1989), pp. 195–201, rightly criticizes much of the feminist movement in the U.S. for starting from a purely white American perspective. Unlike many liberationist approaches, the present book begins from the evangelical premise that the original meaning of Scripture is the starting point and can provide an authoritative critique of church tradition. But Scripture must be *applied* to concrete situations now just as when it was written, and Dr. Grant's perspective on contextualization is very useful (cf. especially pp. 209–22).

13. Gretchen G. Hull, "Under the Yoke: Facing the Challenge of Global Oppression," pp. 16–19 in *World Christian Summer Reader 1990* (Pasadena, Calif.: World Christian, 1990): 18.

14. "India's Lost Women," *World Press Review* (April 1991): 49.

15. Hull, "Yoke," p. 18. Several of my Ugandan friends also confirmed this report.

16. Steven Myers, "Crown of Beauty Instead of Ashes," pp. 20–25 in *World Christian Summer Reader 1990* (Pasadena, Calif.: World Christian, 1990): 23.

17. Ibid., p. 22. New reports surface continually about the abuse of women around the world (e.g., "Against Their Will: Rape and Sexual Abuse in Custody," *Amnesty Action* [Jan./Feb. 1992], p. 6).

18. Myers, "Crown," p. 22.

19. Sterling, *Sisters*, p. 411.

20. *The Chronicle*, Nov. 15, 1988, p. 8.

21. The footnote in Sterling, *Sisters*, p. xii, referring to traditional white families, reads: "An 1868 editorial in the *Nation* noted that working class families remained intact because husbands enforced obedience 'by blows and abuse.' " She points out that slave wives experienced relative equality with their husbands since both were equally subject to the master's authority (ibid., pp. 37–38).

22. For short treatments, see e.g., James and Phyllis Alsdurf, "Battered into Submission," *CT* (June 16, 1989): 24–27; H. W. Green, "Wife Abuse: When Submission Goes Too Far," *Charisma* (July 1985): 44–54; more extensively, James and Phyllis Alsdurf, *Battered Into Submission* (Downers Grove, Ill.: InterVarsity, 1989).

23. The Matthew's Bible, in a note to 1 Pet. 3, endorsed beating the fear of God into a disobedient wife (R. W. Fogel and S. L. Engerman, *Time on the Cross* [Boston: Little, Brown & Company, 1974], p. 146).

24. E.g., Hull, "Yoke," p. 18.

25. G. G. Hull, "Biblical Feminism: A Christian Response to Sexism," *ESA Advocate* (Oct. 1990): 14.

26. David Ayers, "The Inevitability of Failure: The Assumptions and Implementations of Modern Feminism," pp. 312–31 in *Recovering Biblical Manhood and Womanhood: A Response to Evangelical Feminism*, ed. John Piper and Wayne Grudem (Wheaton, Ill.: Crossway, 1991), pp. 322–23. It appears to me that many conservative Christians were polarized against feminism because NOW embraced a prochoice stance, but this was not an official stance of the women's movement before 1967, and groups such as Feminists for Life today evidence that prolife feminism remains a continuing option.

27. R. K. Johnston, "Biblical Authority and Interpretation: The Test Case of Women's Role in the Church & Home Updated," pp. 30–41 in *Women, Authority & the Bible*, ed. Alvera Mickelsen (Downers Grove, Ill.: InterVarsity Press, 1986), emphasizes that it is not just a question of one's commitment to the Bible that determines how one reads the biblical evidence on the subject; he notes that there are committed conservative evangelicals on both sides of the issue. This is not to say, of course, that both sides *correctly* represent the biblical position.

28. Cf. e.g., Don Richardson, *Peace Child* (Ventura, Calif.: Regal, 1974), p. 272, for Christianity's raising women's standard of living in a culture. It could easily be argued that this widespread subordination (and usually oppression) of women reflects the effects of the curse on Eve. The

question then arises: Should we as Christians work for or against the curse? (Camus similarly questioned whether Christians are consistent to work against a plague if they believe God sent it as a judgment.) We ought to be consistent in our response; if the existence of the curse means that we should help the effects of the curse along, then we also ought to advocate sin and death as much as possible, since these are also effects of the curse. God judged the Babylonians for crushing Judah, though they were unwittingly fulfilling God's purposes; and God may similarly send judgments but call us to work for healing.

29. E. A. Clark, *Women in the Early Church*, MFC 13 (Wilmington, Del.: Michael Glazier, 1983), pp. 15–16, notices this practice as early as the church fathers. Patricia Gundry, *Women Be Free* (Grand Rapids: Zondervan, 1977), pp. 43–54, provides numerous examples of the abuse of Scripture in history (e.g., to support slavery, to oppose inoculations, to advocate burning suspected witches, etc.).

30. *And Marries Another: Divorce and Remarriage in the Teaching of the New Testament* (Peabody, Mass.: Hendrickson, 1991).

31. Those most familiar with current scholarship in early Judaism will recognize that I have drawn from a wide variety of Jewish sources, including later Palestinian and Babylonian sources. This is because our sources particular to Asian or Achaian Judaism in the first century are severely limited, and I feel that it is best to provide the broadest possible context based on the convergence of the largest amount of data. Minimal commonalities are more crucial to our study of these NT texts than are detailed analyses of particular regional developments, as much as the latter are to be appreciated. Thus, for example, A. T. Kraabel, "Judaism in Western Asia Minor Under the Roman Empire" (Th. D. dissertation, Harvard, 1968), p. 6, points out that Asian and Palestinian Judaism are different (though cf. the connections on pp. 30–32); but he admits that the Asian evidence on religious life is sometimes "meager indeed" (p. 13). We have attempted to construct the picture based on the evidence we do have, rather than hypothesize on the basis of silence in cases where evidence is lacking. Local and early evidence should, however, be weighted more heavily than other evidence, particularly where differences are evident.

# PART 1

## THE ROLES OF WOMEN IN THE CHURCH

The first part of this book examines those passages in Paul that have been advanced to support women's subordination in the church. The second part addresses the main passage used to argue for women's subordination in the home.

The first passage we will examine is 1 Corinthians 11:1–16. This passage allows women to minister in the congregation, but calls them to cover their heads lest they detract from God's glory by distracting men from the worship of God. Paul covers all his bases by marshalling several arguments that will appeal to various groups of readers; one of his arguments for women covering their heads is based on the creation order. The cultural issue addressed in this passage is probably that women of higher wealth and status were decking themselves out and distracting men by their artificial beauty. Paul sides with the lower-status, more conservative elements in the congregation for the sake of propriety and church unity.

The second passage we will examine is 1 Corinthians 14:34–35. This passage could be read as enjoining absolute silence on all women in all churches, but this interpretation would contradict the context and the earlier passage in 1 Corinthians 11, where women are praying and prophesying. More likely, this second passage addresses women who are asking misguided questions during the teaching period of the church service, thereby slowing everyone down, and Paul's admonition refers only to this situation. The cultural situation is the inferior training of women, which Paul seeks to correct by urging husbands to take a more active interest in their wives' spiritual and intellectual maturation.

The third passage we will examine is 1 Timothy 2:8–15. This is the *only* passage in the entire Bible explicitly forbidding or limiting women's teaching role. This passage is therefore problematic, since Paul elsewhere commends fellow ministers who were women. Again, the cultural situation is in view; women were in general less trained than men, and Paul does not want people susceptible to false teaching to be in leadership positions when heresy is so rampant in the church. But here again he proposes a long-range solution for the Christian women in that congregation: they *should* be educated as the men had been.

He bases his argument against allowing these particular women to teach first of all on the creation order, the same basis for the requirement that women in Corinth wear head coverings. The second basis for his argument is the parallel between the deceivable women of Timothy's congregation and deceivable Eve, similar to his earlier parallel between the deceivable Corinthian Christians of both genders and Eve. But, as in 1 Corinthians 11, he ends up qualifying his argument so that no one takes him too far; Eve's curse is removed for those who persevere in Christ.

There is in the entirety of the New Testament no evidence for the subordination of women that is practiced in many of our churches today, and certainly not sufficient evidence for men to rule out the validity of women's calls to minister the word of God. When men claim that God has called them, we do not question their call if their lives and ministry bear witness to that claim; when women claim that God has called them, we ought to evaluate their calls on the same terms. If we judge other people's calls on the basis of a narrow and ill-considered interpretation of several texts, ignoring the clear examples of other texts, we may succeed only in silencing some of God's servants needed for our generation. And if we do that, we invite God to pass judgment on our own call as interpreters of God's word.

# 1

# Head Coverings in 1 Corinthians 11:2–16

One passage generally acknowledged to address a specific cultural situation is 1 Corinthians 11:2–16. Paul presents four basic arguments for why married women should wear head coverings in church worship services: the order of the home, the order of creation, the order of nature itself, and church custom. Although many churches would use arguments like these to demand the subordination of women in all cultures, very few accept Paul's arguments here as valid for covering women's heads in all cultures. "Men preaching and teaching is something for all cultures," they say, "whereas women wearing head coverings was only an issue back then."

This seems to me a curious form of reasoning, however: the same argument Paul uses in one passage for forbidding women to teach he uses in another passage to argue that married women (i.e., nearly all adult women in his day) must cover their heads in church. In the one passage, Paul does not want the women of a certain congregation to teach; in the other passage, he wants the women of a certain congregation to cover their heads. We take the argument as transculturally applicable in one case, but not so in the other. This seems very strange indeed.

Someone who advocates women's subordination may object that Paul would understand that styles of apparel are different in our day than they were in his, so that a modern woman could attend church without a hat, and a man might even venture to wear one. But to this we would reply that Paul would understand that styles of ministry, the educational level of women, and the moral and social significance of women teaching is different from what it was in Paul's day, and that he would therefore approve of women teaching in church.

In this chapter I will address only 1 Corinthians 11, examining the nature of head coverings and each of Paul's arguments for why the Corinthian women ought to wear them. Because some of Paul's arguments in this passage are difficult for modern readers to follow, the discussion will necessarily be involved at times. But the basic points of his argument are not difficult to grasp.

## INTERPRETATIONS OF 1 CORINTHIANS 11:2–16

The following survey of views is not exhaustive, but it is representative of the different sorts of positions that other writers have taken concerning this passage.[1]

Some deal with this troublesome passage by excising it entirely, claiming that a later writer inserted it into Paul's letter.[2] In one major academic journal, a scholar argued that this passage was an interpolation (an insertion);[3] another scholar responded, "No, it's not";[4] and still another scholar responded, "Oh yes, it is."[5] Those who feel that the passage is an insertion argue that it is not consistent with the way Paul thinks elsewhere, a thesis that is more than a little questionable. But even if the text stood in tension with what Paul writes elsewhere, we must remember that it was not uncommon for ancient writers to write things that sometimes stood in tension with each other; modern writers do the same thing, especially when they address different issues.[6] And the textual basis for removing this passage is impossibly weak.[7]

Other scholars accept the passage as authentic but ask whether its instruction is specific to that culture or universal in its import. At least one scholar does suggest that Christian women should still cover their heads in church today,[8] and I admire his consistency on the matter, even though I disagree with him. Less consistent, though surely more popular, is the view that a head covering was simply the ancient cultural manifestation of a wife's subjection to her husband; the head coverings are no longer necessary, but the subjection is.[9] My objection to this approach is: how do we know that the subjection was not also cultural?

Those who view Paul as reflecting the standards of his culture vary in the extent to which they accept his teaching here as valid for all cultures. Ramsay suggests that Paul was merely a child of his age on the matter of head coverings, but that his eternally valid view is presented in Galatians 3:28, "in Christ there is . . . neither male nor female."[10] Perhaps more sympathetic to the Paul of 1 Corinthians 11 is the related view of Morna Hooker:

> Because it seemed to Paul (conditioned as he was by his Jewish upbringing) that the only way of avoiding scandal in the particular social conditions of first-century Corinth was for women to wear something on their heads in public, women continued to be expected to wear hats in church for almost 1900 years thereafter. Could there have been a greater distortion of the spirit of Paul, who insisted that religion was not a matter of law, than to turn him into a great lawgiver?[11]

One increasingly common view is that Paul is refuting a *Corinthian* view that women in the congregation should cover their heads, and is arguing that the women should resist this requirement.[12] But this view strains our sense that Paul could write clearly; although Paul sometimes cites Corinthian views before qualifying and correcting them, the whole tenor of this passage is that he does indeed want the Corinthian women to cover their heads.

A related and more likely position is that while Paul acknowledges these women's authority over their own heads (11:10), he calls on them to submit to the head coverings so as not to cause offense.[13] This position has in its favor the entire preceding context of surrendering one's own "rights" (the same term Paul uses in 11:10 for "authority") to avoid causing others to lose faith in Christ.[14] Since 1 Corinthians 8 and 10 address various issues raised by the practice of food offered to idols, with Paul using himself as an example of sacrificing one's own rights in chapter 9, this makes the most sense of the passage in the context. In the rest of the chapter Paul returns to a discussion of eating, although there he states his case far more forcefully than he does regarding head coverings, because the next issue is less morally ambiguous (contrast 11:2, 17).[15]

What then do we make of Paul's arguments in 11:2–16? I will argue later in this chapter that Paul's arguments here (as often elsewhere) are meant to persuade his readers in terms of the logic of their own culture. Paul was a masterful missionary, and he was skilled enough in debate to understand the Corinthians' own views, and to probe the Corinthians for consistency until he could persuade them to change their positions. This does not mean that his logic is the same sort of logic a Christian philosopher would use today. Had any one of his arguments here been an absolute, unambiguous, universal proof, Paul could have settled for one argument instead of four.[16] As Gordon Fee notes, Paul here appeals to "shame, propriety, and custom" rather than to outright declarations or commands; this is a cultural issue, not a "life-and-death matter" like the abuse of the Lord's Supper.[17]

## WOMEN'S HEAD COVERINGS IN ANTIQUITY

When we speak of head coverings, we are normally speaking of a shawl that covered a woman's hair instead of a face-veil. Although some of our evidence, especially from the eastern Mediterranean, may suggest the use of face-veils such as now are in vogue in traditional Middle Eastern societies, most of our evidence points to a covering that concealed only the hair from view.[18] Since veils were one *kind* of head covering, we subsume evidence for them under our discussion below on head coverings in general.

Some scholars have argued that neither a veil nor a shawl was in view in this passage, but rather hair put up high on one's head instead of being let down. For example, James Hurley suggests that the accepted custom of wearing one's hair up in church was being violated by controversial women who were letting their hair down.[19] He cites 1 Timothy 2:9 (which addresses wealthier women who are showing off their faddish hairstyles in church) to show that women in Pauline congregations did not wear veils.[20] But we might cite the same passage to show why Paul *wanted* them to cover their heads—to avoid showing off their fashionable hairstyles in church! Hurley's position is problematic, as Fee points out; if an "uncovered" head simply means "having her hair down," how is "the man's not covering his head in v. 7 . . . the opposite of this?"[21] It is thus clear that head coverings, not merely long hair, are in view.

In this first section of our discussion of the custom of head coverings in antiquity, we start with the possibly related question of the seclusion of women in some aspects of Greek culture.

### Seclusion of Women in Classical Antiquity

The practice of women covering their heads in public may be related to the old Greek tradition that restricted women in many ways to the domestic sphere.[22] In theory, at least,[23] women in fourth century BCE Athens could not go to the market and were not to be seen by men who were not their relatives.[24] The orators especially attest the separation of male and female spheres of life in classical Athens,[25] and "one speaker in court seeks to impress the jury with the respectability of his family by saying that his sister and nieces are 'so well brought up that they are embarrassed in the presence even of a man who is a member of the family.' "[26] Under classical Athenian law, a wife who needlessly entered the public sphere placed her honor as a faithful wife in grave danger.[27]

This ideal seems to have continued to some degree in conservative parts of the Greek-speaking Mediterranean world, through the period directly before the spread of Christianity. Thus marriage contracts from first or second century BCE Egypt could include the demand that the wife not leave the home without her husband's permission.[28] Even in a later period, it could be thought scandalous to force a man to bring his wife before the public contrary to his wishes, especially if he wished to keep others from gazing on her beauty.[29]

Thus in ancient romances, a beautiful virgin might never have appeared in public before meeting her lover, so that her lover was the first to behold her.[30] A wisdom work, probably Jewish, advises its readers: "Guard a virgin in firmly locked rooms, and do not let her be seen before the house until her wedding day."[31]

Roman women were, however, much less secluded, although some moralists ideally wished them to be more secluded than they were. It was reported that in an earlier period a husband might have divorced his wife for going into public unveiled, or disciplined his wife or daughter for conversing publicly with another man.[32] Writing in Greek in the Roman period, Plutarch extols the modesty of the virtuous woman who, when a man praised the beauty of her suddenly exposed arm, retorted that its beauty was not meant for the public. Plutarch goes on to explain that a woman's talk should also be kept private within the home.[33] For him, "keeping at home and keeping silence" are joint aspects of a wife's virtue; she "ought to do her talking either to her husband or through her husband."[34] He further recommends that "a virtuous woman ought to be most visible in her husband's company, and to stay in the house and hide herself when he is away."[35]

But while writers upheld this traditional seclusion of wives as an ideal,[36] it had never been more than an ideal.[37] We cannot suppose that all levels of society hearkened to the moralists (the moralists themselves were well aware that this was the case), and other writers like the satirists (who instead exaggerate public immorality) certainly suggest that reality was far from the moralists' ideal in their own time.

Jewish women in Palestine were expected to go to the marketplace,[38] but in towns of the Greek east they followed the Greek customs of relative seclusion.[39] Philo, a prominent Jewish thinker in first-century Egypt, declares that it is best for women to stay indoors, to avoid matters apart from their household concerns, and to remain secluded.[40] In 4 Maccabees, a document written outside Palestine, the righteous mother of martyrs reminds her children that she had been a pure virgin who had not gone outside her father's house.[41] Even in Jewish Palestine, however, great modesty was expected in public; according to laws later set down by Jewish legal scholars, "a husband was compelled to divorce his wife if she appeared in public in torn clothing or bathed together with men, as was the Roman custom."[42]

Throughout most of the first-century empire, women generally were not required to remain at home, but it does appear that they were more restricted in their public activities than their husbands were, and that this was often due to the fear that they would prove too attractive to other men. Some ancient writers, especially Jewish teachers, used the same rationale to get women to cover their heads, as we shall see shortly. First, however, we must investigate several other suggestions about ancient practices that might have led Paul to suggest that women in Corinth cover their heads.

### *Prostitutes or Pagan Prophetesses?*

Why would the Corinthian Christian women's uncovered heads have caused offense? One recurrent suggestion is that an uncovered head was the traditional garb of prostitutes.[43]

Dress could indeed sometimes indicate that a woman was a prostitute, and some morally disreputable members of high society purportedly liked this kind of apparel: "typically, bright colours, a tunic showing part of their legs, diaphonous fabrics and a toga instead of the customary cloak. Elaborate hairdressing and make-up were part of the self-presentation for the better-class whores."[44]

But the evidence for *head coverings* distinguishing wives from prostitutes is slender; very few traditions from the Near East attest it. Ancient Assyrian women were not to go out with their heads uncovered, but if a prostitute were caught with a veil on she would be flogged with staves fifty times and have pitch poured over her head. Female slaves, who, as in other cultures, often served as prostitutes for their masters, were likewise forbidden to veil themselves.[45] If a man veiled a woman, he thereby made her his wife.[46] But these rules are from far to the east of Paul's cultural world, and from well over a thousand years before him (i.e., the twelfth century BCE).

The idea of prostitutes going unveiled may have continued in the eastern Mediterranean, since the practice is assumed by an anonymous third-century rabbi,[47] who argues that Judah had trouble believing that Tamar was a harlot because her face was covered.[48] But, as we shall note below, head coverings typified married women in general in Jewish Palestine, so that an uncovered head could indicate a virgin seeking a husband as easily as it could connote a prostitute. The rabbi no doubt thought Tamar's head covering problematic only because it would have normally identified her as a married woman in his culture.[49]

Others, noting that the issue in the context is how women pray and prophesy, have suggested instead that Paul may have been thinking of the "uncovered and dishevelled heads" of pagan prophetesses.[50] As we shall see below, in most Greek religious activities women uncovered their heads, and this may be significant. But it is doubtful that Paul or the Corinthians would have thought specifically about pagan prophetesses' hairstyles; such prophetesses, like the Pythoness, mantic priestess of Apollo, were generally secluded from public view.[51] Even if one were to compare the Christian prophetesses to their pagan counterparts (Paul was not necessarily above this; cf. 1 Cor. 12:3), it is unlikely that hairstyle would have been one of the first comparisons to have come to mind.

Disheveled hair may have also characterized female demons in popular Jewish conceptions,[52] but again our evidence is too slight and too late to draw any conclusions about what might have been the standard view among Corinthian Christians on this matter.

### *Mourning or Shame?*

Covering one's head was sometimes associated with mourning;[53] the practice was a standard sign of grief, for both men and women.[54] Plutarch says that it is a Roman custom for mourning women to dress in white robes and white head coverings.[55] Elsewhere, a woman weeping at her plight is said to cover her head.[56] Palestinian Jewish texts also speak of covering one's head for mourning[57] and compare a woman's head covering to that of a mourner.[58] The evidence for this mourning custom is not altogether unambiguous, however; during the funeral procession itself, Roman sons would cover their heads, while daughters would "go with uncovered heads and hair unbound."[59]

The ambiguity of the practice is not the strongest argument against seeing it as background for our passage. Since this custom normally applied to both genders, it must not be in view in 1 Corinthians 11, where Paul gives different instructions to the men and the women. He cannot be implying that he wishes men to pray and prophesy without mourning, but wishes women to mourn when they do it!

Then again, the related senses of shame and dishonor could be in view. Walking about bareheaded seems to be a sign of social respectability for a man,[60] and he might "cover himself"—hide his face—if moved to shame.[61] It seems that either covering[62] or uncovering[63] one's head could be used as a sign of reverence or humbled awe. In 2 Maccabees 4:12 head coverings may symbolize humiliation; when the king subjugated the Jews, he made them cover their heads. But this passage may simply mean that he forced them to adopt certain Greek manners of dress.

Some Jewish teachers explained Palestinian Jewish women's head coverings in this manner:

> Why does woman cover her head and man not cover his head? A parable. To what may this be compared? To a woman who disgraced herself and because she disgraced herself, she is ashamed in the presence of people. In the same way Eve disgraced herself and caused her daughters to cover their heads.[64]

It is unlikely that most Palestinian Jews viewed the head covering as a symbol of women's *humiliation*, but at the least a head covering was a necessary sign of public *modesty* for all Palestinian Jewish women who could afford it. One story tells of a woman so destitute that she could not afford a head covering, so she had to cover her head with her hair before going to speak with Rabbi Johanan ben Zakkai.[65] A Jewish teacher in the late first century heavily fined a man for uncovering a woman's head in the marketplace. When she later uncovered her own head, Rabbi Akiba said that she had compromised her own self-respect, but noted that this was her choice; the man's penalty nevertheless stood.[66]

We need not suppose that all Palestinian Jewish women cared to be modest by these Pharisaic standards, but it is unlikely that the Pharisees invented the custom themselves. Modesty was no doubt a major purpose of the head covering in Palestinian Judaism and in all the cultures we shall consider below. Those who wished to save their beauty for their husbands probably viewed this modesty as a form of chastity.

### *Veiling Customs and Geography*

Veiling customs varied geographically.[67] Veiling seems to have prevailed in parts of the eastern Mediterranean, in places like Syria, Arabia, and southern Asia Minor (modern Turkey), including Paul's home city of Tarsus.[68] There is much more evidence for the veiling of women in these regions than many scholars have traditionally recognized.[69]

Evidence for this custom in Greek life, however, is sparse; the standard citation from Aristophanes is half a millennium earlier, with little later evidence to support it.[70] The issue of head coverings, especially veils, could thus have divided Corinthian Christians between native Greeks and eastern immigrants to Corinth; the problem with this solution is that it assumes a much larger eastern immigrant population in the church than we would expect from the demography of Corinth. (The solution becomes less problematic if many of the immigrants to Corinth were Palestinian Jews, or, as is also possible, a substantial number of the Corinthian Christians were drawn from the ranks of the non-Greeks from the east who had settled there.)

The Palestinian Jewish custom is much easier to document than the Greek custom. Male head covering customs like the yarmulke are far too late to be of relevance here,[71] but the covering of women seems to have been standard, long before Jewish teachers had to find biblical proof to make it a requirement.[72]

It is possible that this Jewish custom of veiling married women was also followed in some Jewish communities outside Palestine: one Jewish text from Egypt mourns women who were "carried away unveiled."[73] But the meaning of this text is not entirely clear, and though it is likely that Egyptian Jews were familiar with the custom of veils or other kinds of head coverings (see p. 29 below on Philo, and Joseph and Asenath), we cannot assume it certain that most Jewish women would have necessarily worn head coverings as far away as Corinth.

We therefore have a variety of evidence for women wearing head coverings in antiquity, but so far little that sheds light on the nature of the conflict about head coverings in the Corinthian church. Since Paul addresses the issue only in the context of church worship (nothing in 1 Cor. 11 suggests a practice that requires women's heads to be covered all day long), it may be helpful to examine the use of head coverings in ancient religious contexts.[74]

### *Head Coverings in Religious Contexts*

In general, Greek women were expected to participate in worship with their heads uncovered. Their relative seclusion to the domestic sphere did not include their seclusion from public religious life. Of course, Greek men were also to worship bareheaded. An early inscription provides rules for those about to be initiated into a Greek mystery cult: "Women are not to have their hair bound up, and men must enter with bared heads."[75]

In contrast, Roman women had to cover their heads when offering sacrifices.[76] The custom was old enough by Plutarch's time to have elicited a variety of contradictory explanations,[77] and the several exceptions[78] merely serve to prove the rule that Roman women worshiped with heads covered. This does not apply to all Roman religious functions,[79] but it does contrast significantly with the usual Greek practice. But again, Roman men would also pull the toga over their head at sacrifices.

Corinth was a Roman "colony" in Greece during this period. Its citizens conducted business in both Greek and Latin. Social differences between traditional Roman and traditional Greek elements may have caused tensions in the worship in the house churches. It is unlikely, however, that this is the main reason for conflict over women wearing head coverings in worship, because the same conflict should have arisen over the *men* wearing head coverings. This explanation would provide no reason for why Paul would give certain instructions to the men but entirely different instructions to the women.

### *Hair, Beauty, and Lust*

Jesus did not accept the traditional male excuse that a man's lust was a woman's fault (Matt. 5:28), but many other people in his day did; that excuse was used even more commonly in antiquity than it is today. Indeed, in our culture, saturated with the commercializing of the human body, we might have little sympathy for our ancient counterparts, who could be moved to lust at the sight of bare arms.[80]

What was true of uncovered parts of the body in general was especially true of the hair. Thus cutting off a woman's hair would spoil all her beauty, even if she were Venus herself,[81] and a young man given to lust might go down the street staring at women's head and hair, rehearsing the images in his mind when he got home.[82] It was, one such man thought, the beauty of the head that mattered most, and after noting this he went on to praise a woman's hair.[83]

Loosening a woman's hair could reveal her beauty and subject her to male lust in both Greek[84] and Jewish tradition.[85] Early Roman women were divorced for not wearing veils precisely because their action laid them open to the suspicion that they were looking for another man.

A Jewish woman who ventured into public with her hair down and exposed to view, or who otherwise could be accused of flirtatious behavior, could be divorced with no financial support from her marriage contract.[86] A woman uncovering her head could be described as nearing the final stage in seducing a man.[87] Jewish teachers permitted loosing a woman's hair only in the case of an adulterous woman, who was publicly shamed by exposure to the sight of men;[88] but even in this case they warned that it should not be done with women whose hair was extremely beautiful, lest the young priests be moved to lust.[89]

The most noble and desirable woman to an Egyptian Jewish man seems to have been one whose very appearance was virgin and unstained by the eyes of other men; in an Egyptian Jewish romance novel, the ideal virgin Asenath seems to have worn a veil as a virgin to keep men from gazing on her.[90] She even wore a bride's veil when she went before Joseph, perhaps as a sign of newfound modesty.[91] Probably a more reliable index of Egyptian Jewish sentiment is the writing of Philo, the well-to-do Jewish philosopher from Alexandria, who "says that if a woman keeps even her hair uncovered, it is a sign that she is not modest."[92]

It is not hard to understand how the practice of veiling and not veiling related to expectations concerning certain male reactions. In older Greek society, the Spartans were said to have veiled only their married women, for an important reason: "When someone inquired why they took their girls into public places unveiled, but their married women veiled, he said, 'Because the girls have to find husbands, and the married women have to keep those who have them!' "[93] Although this example is from long before our period, it seems to provide the simplest rationale for why married women would have covered their heads, whereas single women did not need to do so. Men were interested in protecting their solitary rights to the beauty of their wives, and married women who went into public with their heads uncovered could be considered immodest or seductive.

It is probable that some well-to-do women thought such restrictions on their public apparel ridiculous, especially if they were from parts of the Mediterranean world where head coverings were not considered necessary. But to other observers, these women's uncovered heads connoted an invitation to lust. The issue in the Corinthian church may thus have been a clash of cultural values concerning modesty, and Paul wants the more liberated elements within the church to care enough about their more conservative colleagues not to offend them in this dramatic way.

### *Class Conflict in Corinth?*

Today many churches avoid social conflicts by keeping people from different backgrounds in different churches. Whatever we may think of that practice today, churches in Paul's day did not have that option. Believers had to meet in homes large enough to accommodate them, and that meant meeting in the homes of well-to-do members. Since most members in the Corinthian church were not well-to-do,[94] people from very different social classes would be brought together. Many of the other issues in 1 Corinthians revolve around this clash between the socially powerful ("the strong") and the socially weak members of the church,[95] and the issue of head coverings may be one further example of this problem.

Most women in Greco-Roman statues and other artwork from this period have uncovered heads, because most of the families who could afford to commission such works were well-to-do[96] and presumably more concerned with current fashion than with lower-class women's interpretation of modesty. As historian Ramsay MacMullen points out,

> women who imitated the changes in style that went on at the imperial court, changes depicted in the provinces by portraits of the ladies of the imperial house, were the richer ones, the more open to the new ways, and the more likely to belong to families on the rise. Women of humbler class went veiled.[97]

When we discuss 1 Timothy 2:9–10 in chapter 3, we shall examine the desire of upper-class women to show off their fashionable hairstyles as well as other impressive array. Moralists saw such ostentation as a problem in high society, and Paul viewed its cheaper imitation as a problem in the church. For Paul, church was not meant to be a fashion show for women or for men, especially when some of those styles could strike "less fashionable" members of the congregation as willfully seductive.[98] But Paul does not regulate anyone's garb outside the church, leaving that to the discretion of the person and the meaning their clothing styles will bear among the company they keep.[99]

This background for 1 Corinthians 11:2–16 makes good sense, but it still remains for us to examine how Paul develops his argument to persuade women members of the congregation to cover up. In ancient debate, one might give arguments for a position that were different from the reasons one held to the position oneself. Paul has to address the issue of women's head coverings in Corinth with the arguments that would most readily persuade his ancient readers.

## PAUL'S ARGUMENTS: FAMILY, CREATION, NATURE, AND CUSTOM

In 11:3–16 Paul sets forth four main arguments. In this context, he could have simply said, "Do not cause your brother or sister to stumble," but as in the case of food offered to idols, he instead presents a variety of supporting arguments to make a convincing case for all his readers.

Not all of Paul's arguments make sense to us today on a first reading, but that is because Paul is trying to persuade the Corinthian women to wear head coverings, not women today. Had he been writing a letter to *us* he would have dealt with entirely different issues and reasoned a different way. It is easy for modern Western readers to assume that cultures elsewhere think as we do; we are impatient with other cultures' logic. Paul, a pastor and a missionary, is concerned about getting his point across to his people, not with impressing modern Western readers with arguments that would work transculturally. Paul employs a transcultural argument only when he is making a transcultural point, and the wearing of head coverings, as we have suggested above, is not one of those points.

### *The Husband as the Head: 1 Corinthians 11:3–6*

Paul's argument here involves two analogies: an analogy between a wife's literal head (part of her body) and her figurative head (her husband), and an analogy between her artificial head covering (a veil) and her natural head covering (her hair).

Before we can grasp Paul's first argument about head coverings, we must understand his play on the word "head."[100] Although an argument based on a play on words may sound irrational to us today, to many ancient readers it would have made sense.[101] Paul knew his audience, and he knew the most effective ways to convince them to change their behavior. So Paul initiates a play on the word "head": it is both the part of the woman's body whose covering is in dispute, and the woman's husband.

But right at the outset, we are faced with a problem. When Paul calls the husband the "head" of the wife (as Christ is the "head" of the man, and God of Christ),[102] what does he mean? To be the "head" of something today normally means to be in charge, but was this the way the phrase would have normally been taken in Paul's day?

This modern sense of "head" is rare, though not unknown, in ancient Greek. The oldest Greek lexicons do not attest this meaning,[103] but it is attested in the one document Greek Christians knew best: the Septuagint, the Greek translation of the Old Testament. The Hebrew word for "head" (*rôš*) usually referred to a part of the body, but when it was used figuratively, it could mean "leader" or "boss." Yet the Septuagint rarely translates *rôš* (in the sense of leader) literally as "head"; most often it uses other Greek words that mean "leader." It retains "head" for leader less than one tenth of the time, despite the Hebrew usage.[104] In other words, "leader" is not a very common meaning for the Greek word for "head."[105]

This is not to say that "head" never means "leader" in Greek: the few uses of the term that did come through the Greek translation naturally influenced Jewish and Christian writers like Philo[106] or the church fathers.[107] The question is whether this figurative use of the term "head" is common enough that we should *automatically* read it into the present passage, and the answer is that it is not. Indeed, as Fee points out, the only "authority" mentioned in the entire passage is the woman's own (11:10), and 11:11–12 "explicitly qualify vv. 8–9 so that they will *not* be understood" hierarchically.[108] The woman is not the man's subordinate in this passage; she is his "glory" (or "reputation," "honor," "splendor"), the one who brings him shame or honor.[109]

Other possible nuances of the term "head" exist, such as "the honored part." "Head" is sometimes contrasted with "tail" in the Old Testament because the head, as the most prominent part of the body (and the part that on men was normally uncovered) was the most honored part.[110] Paul seems to imply in the next chapter that those parts of the body which need to be covered are more honored, the covering representing the special attention and honor given to them (12:22–24), but there is no indication that he has the discussion of 11:2–16 in view as he writes this. More likely, in 11:2–16 he is speaking of the natural honor accruing to the head, and suggesting that the wife by virtue of the creation order owes her husband reverence. Husbands receive glory or shame from their wives, just as Christ receives glory or shame from the behavior of men.[111]

But if Paul means this argument in this way (which he may), he seems to be making an argument that he would not wish to enforce universally. Cannot *women* in the church also bring reproach or honor on the cause of Christ (cf. 1 Tim. 5:13–15)? If Paul is referring to the husband's honor—which in some sense, we shall argue, he is—the nature of his argument cannot extend very far beyond the particular application he wishes to draw from it.

Other scholars have argued that "head" means "source."[112] A number of scholars have compiled references to this sense of the term "head" in antiquity,[113] a sense which occurs in Paul's own usage elsewhere.[114] This meaning of "head" certainly makes sense in this context, where Paul states that woman was derived from man (11:8).[115] The only objection to interpreting head as "source" here seems to be the statement that God is the source of Christ, but this objection fails if the text refers to Jesus' source as the Father from whom he proceeded at his incarnation as a human being.[116] If the incarnation is in view, then 11:3 is in chronological sequence, as Bilezikian points out: Christ is the source of Adam, Adam of Eve, and God of Christ.[117]

The meaning "source" has been hotly disputed. Evangelical scholar Wayne Grudem argues that this meaning for "head" is not attested, whereas the metaphorical use of "head" usually implies authority.[118] His argument has, however, been seriously challenged by other evangelical scholars.[119] Gordon Fee observes that only forty-nine uses of "head" in ancient Greek literature are metaphorical, and of these:

(1) Twelve appear in the New Testament, which is the subject under consideration and thus must not be included in the count (especially since some of them *do* mean "source").

(2) Eighteen are from the Greek translations of the Old Testament, where they represent a very small percentage of exceptions to the rule that the translators usually bent over backward to *avoid* translating "head" in this way.

(3) In most of the remaining nineteen instances the sense "authority over" that Grudem finds is disputable.

(4) Finally, Philo clearly does use "head" to mean "source" sometimes.

Fee concludes that Grudem has shown that "head" can sometimes mean "leader," although even in these cases it need not mean "authority over." But in Fee's view, Grudem has failed to bring into question the meaning "source" or to show that "head" is normally a term of authority.[120]

That "head" sometimes means "authority," sometimes means "prominence, honor, or respect" in other ways, and probably sometimes means "source" does not tell us which possible meaning is in view in our text. Context is the key to determining how a particular term is being used in a given passage, and the context here indicates nothing about the husband's "authority." But for the sake of argument, let us assume that "head" here means "authority," which I believe Grudem has shown is a possible nuance of the term. If Paul is using "head" here in the sense of "authority," he could simply mean that the husband was the one in the position of authority over the wife in that culture, without demonstrating that all husbands are to rule over their wives in all cultures (cf. Rom. 13:1; 1 Pet. 2:13); he might have expressed himself very differently to an audience in whose culture husbands were not in a position of authority over wives. Thus the debate about the meaning of the term cannot ultimately settle the issue unless Paul plainly argues for the husband's transcultural rule over his wife.

Whatever particular nuances Paul may have wished to call to his readers' minds, he uses a wordplay to facilitate his point: the woman who brings dishonor on her head is bringing dishonor upon her husband, and thus upon the Christian family. That is Paul's point in this context, not that her display of independence in removing the culturally significant head covering would bring reproach on any husband in any culture.

In 11:5 Paul indicates how seriously a woman dishonors her "head" by worshiping with it uncovered. He makes an analogy between her praying without a head covering and her praying with her head shaved; whether she is without her specific cultural covering or her natural, God-given covering, humiliation is involved. Paul is using here the ancient debating principle of reductio ad absurdum: reducing the position of his opponents to the absurd. If they want to bare their heads so badly, why don't they bare them altogether by removing their hair, thus exposing themselves to public shame?

Unlike the act of *uncovering* his head, a Greek man's *shaving* his head could represent mourning,[121] a response to great catastrophe like shipwreck, or it could be associated with illness or recovery from it.[122] Priests of Isis were said to shave off all their hair, so this act could imply the shame that certain pagan cultic associations bore in Greco-Roman antiquity.[123]

Shaving the head could also imply the disgrace of the loss of womanly attractiveness; by ancient standards, it would deprive women of beauty and make them look like boys.[124] A Roman satirist complains that a Roman matron overly concerned with her hair ought to have it shaved off with a razor.[125] The ultimate example of the shame involved in shaving one's head is that it is the final stage of desperation to which Satan reduces Job's wife in a Jewish story about Job's trials.[126]

Some have suggested that Paul's argument at this point appeals to something more than the general shame of a shaven head. Perhaps, as some scholars have argued, Paul opposes the removal of symbolic gender distinctions;[127] an uncovered head and short hair have precisely this point in common: both reflect a disregard for customary marks of gender identification.[128] As Wayne Meeks puts it, Paul stresses equivalent rights and duties for both parties in marriage (1 Cor. 7:2–4), but "objects to *symbolic* disregard for sexual differences in the dress of male and female prophets."[129] This may have been in intentional opposition to certain pagan cults that encouraged sex role reversal,[130] but it would make enough sense simply on its own terms here: gender interchange was regarded by Paul as "against nature" (Rom. 1:26–27; cf. Deut. 22:5).[131]

Whether or not Paul is addressing gender reversal here, another more central issue seems to be at work. The woman's uncovering or shaving her head brought disgrace not only on her own physical head, but also on her husband. The idea that a wife could shame her husband by her behavior[132] or by revealing his secrets[133] was common in the ancient world. Even though Plutarch advises that the husband has to set the example if he expects his wife to live honorably,[134] he was no doubt conscious of the idea that one person's dishonorable behavior could bring reproach on the whole family.[135] The common view is reflected by an accuser of Stilpo, who noted that Stilpo's married daughter was profligate and charged "that she was a disgrace to him."[136] Thus some marriage contracts include the stipulation that the wife avoid shaming her husband.[137] Moralists could insist that wives please only their own husbands;[138] if wives were not "socially retiring . . . and submissive to their husbands," they would "bring dishonor to the household."[139]

The point of Paul's opening arguments about the head therefore calls us as believers to give up personal rights for the sake of honoring our families. Although his specific addressees in Corinth were women, the principle he articulates could be applied to any of us. If our dressing a certain way in public will cause discomfort to our spouse, we ought not to do it. Paul is clearly less concerned with the particular apparel worn in a given culture than he is with its effects.

### *Creation Order: 1 Corinthians 11:7–12*

Paul's second argument is based on the creation of Eve from Adam in Genesis 2. This argument is really part of his first one, for it carries on the idea of headship and the wife's relationship to her husband.

> For a man is obligated not to cover his head, since he is the image and glory of God [his ultimate head and source, 11:3]; but the woman is the glory of man [her direct head and source, 11:3].

> For the man did not come from the woman, but the woman from the man; for the man was not created through the woman, but rather the woman through the man. Therefore the woman is obligated to have authority over her head on account of the angels. Nevertheless, in the Lord, neither is the woman apart from the man, or the man apart from the woman; for just as the woman was taken out of the man, man comes into the world through woman; but all things are [really ultimately] from God (11:7–12).

In short, Paul says, because woman was taken from man, she reflects man's image, and therefore she ought to cover that image in worship lest it distract observers from attention to God's image.[140] It is not that Paul is unaware that woman and man together make up God's image. It is impossible that he had not read the explicit statement to that effect in Genesis 1:27,[141] and he speaks elsewhere of all believers being conformed to that image in Christ (1 Cor. 15:49; Rom. 8:29; 2 Cor. 3:18). It seems rather to be another reminder that the way the wife dresses will in that culture affect whether honor or shame comes to her husband. It is far more gracious to say that than to state, "Women are too beautiful and will distract the eyes of undisciplined men during the worship services," although that may have been part of the problem in Corinth.

How could women as "men's glory" (or "honor," "splendor") distract men from the worship of God during church services? Although the following analogy is probably a little more extreme than the Corinthian problem, it may convey the general point. We might imagine a laid-back church today where the women entered wearing bathing suits, prepared for the baptismal service in the ocean after morning worship. If the men lusted, the women would be right to say that the men should take responsibility for their own actions; but out of concern for their brothers in Christ, the women could avoid the problem by simply wearing something less revealing than bathing suits to church. The same principle would apply, of course, for men who wished to assert their proper right to wear bathing suits to church; a bathing suit may not be intrinsically sinful, but one should do everything possible to avoid causing one's fellow Christian to stumble from the way of Christ. Many ancient men had a lower tolerance level for exposed skin than we do today because they saw much less of it. Apparently just seeing a woman's hair was enough to disturb them.

Despite the potential seriousness of this problem, however, Paul is not ordering these well-to-do women to change their church wardrobe; he is trying to persuade them to choose to do so. Paul emphasizes that it is the woman's right to choose what she will wear (v. 10); yet he is asking her to use her right to dress how she wills to honor rather than shame her husband, just as he called on others, including himself, to give up their own rights for the sake of others (chs. 8–10).[142]

Not everyone sees Paul as affirming a woman's authority to choose what to wear on her head in 11:10. Some translations and commentators interpret the text as if it spoke of the woman's being *under* someone's authority,[143] or as if the head covering merely symbolized her dignity;[144] but these are not natural ways to read the Greek text here.[145] Others think that an Aramaic term for head covering is here mistranslated "authority,"[146] but not only would the Corinthians not have known Aramaic,[147] the supposed play on words does not actually *work* in Aramaic.[148] The only normal way to read the Greek phrase is to read it that the woman has "authority over her own head."[149] It is not even optional for her to recognize this authority; she "ought" to demonstrate it.[150]

Paul not only affirms that the woman has authority over her own head, but he even qualifies his argument concerning man being woman's source. Paul explicitly says that woman being derived from man is not the whole story; even though it was the only part of the story he needed to state to make his point, he did not want the Corinthian Christians to misunderstand him.[151] Paul affirms that woman and man are mutually dependent in the Lord,[152] using the same language that other early Jewish writers had used to make the same point.[153] Women and men are each derived from the other in some sense, and the ultimate source or head of both is God.

Paul's clarification of his point about man being woman's source (taken from Gen. 2) may reflect the creation story in Genesis 1. Woman and man are together said to represent God's image (1:27). There is some evidence that the Corinthian Christians may have separated the two accounts of human creation in Genesis 1 and 2,[154] as did some other Jewish thinkers of the period.[155] Paul apparently appeals to their understanding of Genesis 2, but then qualifies their view of that passage by reading it in the light of Genesis 1.

The idea of women as men's glory would not have been too difficult for Paul's readers to have grasped; in some Jewish traditions, a wife's domestic expertise brought public "glory" to her husband.[156] His readers would have especially followed his case if they knew the Scriptures well enough to recognize how he was applying them. He uses "glory" here to mean virtually the same thing as "image" (1 Cor. 15:43, 49), adapting the phrase "image and likeness" of Genesis 1:26 to read "image and glory" (1 Cor. 11:7).[157]

Here again, Paul relates to some of the ideas of his culture. Although some ancient Jewish traditions repeat the biblical view that both men and women are created in God's image,[158] others could declare that while man was made in God's likeness, woman was made in man's image.[159] The Greek writer Plutarch similarly compares a wife to a mirror: a good wife will reflect her husband's likeness well, but a bad wife will reflect it poorly.[160]

When Paul later notes (11:15) that a woman's long hair is a "glory" to her, his point would also make sense to his readers; a woman in antiquity could prize her long and beautiful hair.[161] In contrast, an adulteress, who had ignored God's honor or glory by her unfaithfulness to her husband, herself received dishonor when the priests disheveled her hair.[162] Much of Paul's argument here revolves around wordplays about "glory" and "image."

This much is not hard to grasp; what is more problematic is Paul's statement that the woman has authority on her head "on account of the angels." What could this obscure phrase mean?

### *Because of the Angels: 1 Corinthians 11:10*

Several explanations have been proposed for the obscure phrase "because of the angels." We shall examine the most commonly proposed explanations of the phrase.[163] One is that the angels of holiness are present for the worship of the community, as in some other early Jewish texts;[164] on this interpretation, the problem is that the worshiping angels will be offended by the breach of propriety involved in a woman's uncovering her head.[165] Since it was only a breach of propriety in that culture, Paul need not be implying that these angels are culture-bound or squeamish; this view could mean that they are simply offended by the symbolic disrespect shown to the women's husbands.

Then again, if the issue in the congregation is that some men would be tempted to lust after these women who were showing off their fancy hairstyles, another traditional interpretation may be more likely. It had become a very common belief that many angels had fallen into sin long ago by lusting after beautiful women. On this view, Paul would be saying: "By leaving your hair open to public view, you are inciting not only men, but also angels, to lust."[166]

Before some readers dismiss this view as ludicrous from our modern perspective, we ought to examine how such an argument would have appeared to Paul's original readers in Corinth.[167] Ancient mythology in many cultures is replete with stories of gods and goddesses chasing mortal consorts of the other (or sometimes the same) gender.[168] The "sons of God" having intercourse with the daughters of men in Genesis 6 is likewise interpreted as fallen angels copulating with human women in most[169] early Jewish traditions.[170] This is probably reflected in 2 Peter 2:4,[171] Jude 6,[172] and 1 Peter 3:19–20[173] as well, so it may be a valid Christian interpretation of Genesis 6.

Thus it is said that these angels, the "Watchers" (as they are called in 1 Enoch) who observed the earth, lost their heavenly abode due to illicit sex.[174] One tradition of uncertain date puts it this way: Women seduced the Watchers by the beauty of their adorned heads and faces, and the Watchers,

> filled with desire for them, perpetrated the act in their minds. Then they were transformed into human males, and while the women were cohabiting with their husbands they appeared to them. Since the women's minds were filled with lust for these apparitions, they gave birth to giants. For the Watchers were disclosed to them as being as high as the heavens.[175]

Jewish people believed that evil spirits still occasionally lusted after women,[176] in the most extreme stories even killing women's suitors to keep the women for themselves.[177] Such ideas may also be reflected in the common view that demons could reproduce.[178]

The main problem with the "lusting angels" view is what it would seem to imply on a wider scale. If angels lusted after women's hair in Corinth, Paul would have had to have supposed that they could lust after women's hair anywhere in the world where it was not covered. Perhaps he thought this was just a stumbling block for angels gathered for worship, but the view that Paul thought angels were always in danger of falling because of uncovered body parts on women would make his argument a little broader than he intends. Paul would surely have made much more of these angels in his writings than a mere phrase, because this would have been a transcultural, enduring argument for all women in all cultures to wear head coverings. This does not seem to fit the way the rest of his argument goes.

Another major possibility remains: Paul speaks of the angels who run the structures of the world system. Although some have objected that Paul nowhere speaks of hostile angels,[179] this objection ignores some of the evidence. Some scholars have pointed out that these may be the angels of the created order we see in 1 Corinthians 6:3,[180] and Romans 8:38 connects hostile angels with the "rulers" in the heavens.

Terms like "rulers and authorities" normally meant simply political powers in the world (e.g., Rom. 13:1).[181] But many groups in the ancient world believed that there were also spiritual powers, such as the gods of various nations, influencing the course of those nations.[182] In Jewish thought, those spiritual powers[183] were angelic authorities appointed by God;[184] in some Jewish sources, they had become malevolent powers and would be judged at the end of the age.[185] While this way of looking at the world became common only in postbiblical Jewish sources,[186] it was already established as early as the book of Daniel chapter 10,[187] and we may be certain that both Paul and his readers were familiar with the idea.

How would this meaning fit 1 Corinthians 11:10? It would function in a manner quite similar to the statement in 6:3 that Christians will judge angels; if they will judge angels, they should be able to arbitrate disputes among themselves. The argument of 11:10, in the context of the preceding verses, would be that Christ is head of the husbands; husbands are heads of their wives; Christ and his church together are destined to be above the principalities and powers, or angels of the nations, which are over the rest of the world. Paul's rhetorical question, "Do you not know?" (6:3), probably implies that they should indeed have known that the "saints," those set apart for God by faith in Christ, would judge angels; hence they could have grasped his brief clause "because of the angels." If, as we believe, Paul also wrote Colossians, the dual picture of Christ as head, both of the church (Col. 1:18) and of the created order of spiritual powers (2:10; cf. 1:15–17), would indicate that such images are not foreign to his thought.

On this reading of 1 Corinthians 11:10, Paul mentions the angels to show where these women stand. Although they should choose to wear a head covering, submitting to their husbands' honor for the sake of the gospel, yet they have authority over their own heads; so much authority, in fact, that they will judge the angels. Thus Paul is saying, "You will judge angels someday. Surely you can make responsible choices about your head apparel now."

The main weakness of this proposal is that it reads "because of the angels" as "because of what you know about your future relation to those angels." But such a concise and therefore difficult allusion on Paul's part would not be uncharacteristic of him or of ancient Jewish teachers in general, and it may make more sense than supplying "because of the angels present at worship," or "because of lusting angels." While I would not propose that this view is beyond dispute, it seems to fit Paul's usage elsewhere better than either of the other views proposed above.

Whatever conclusion one ultimately reaches about the angels, Paul does not spell out in detail the meaning of the phrase, and it is not his main argument. It is therefore proper for us to move to his next arguments. Paul's arguments to this point have presupposed an interpretation of the Genesis narrative, but his final arguments express ways of thinking that were standard in Greek culture.

## An Appeal to the Natural Order: 1 Corinthians 11:14

> Judge this matter for yourselves: it is fitting for a woman to pray to God with her head uncovered? Doesn't even nature itself teach you that if a man has long hair, it brings him dishonor,[188] whereas if a woman has long hair, it brings her glory?[189] For her long hair is given to her[190] as a natural covering.[191]

Paul's appeal to nature was a standard Greco-Roman argument, used especially by Stoics,[192] but also by Epicureans,[193] other philosophers,[194] and, for that matter, just about everyone else.[195] This sort of reasoning has become more or less discredited today; no one says any longer, "If people were meant to fly, they would have wings." But it was a very common sort of argument in Paul's day. Our question is, What did Paul and other ancient writers mean by their appeal to nature?

Sometimes writers meant by "nature" pretty much what we mean by the term today: the created order.[196] They could speak of nature as the force or order controlling and arranging natural existence in the cosmos.[197] Nature is said to teach us the way things really are,[198] often through our natural endowments[199] or through the nature of the world around us.

Usually writers used these examples from nature to advocate a specific kind of moral behavior,[200] or simply exhorted living in general in accordance with nature.[201] For instance, the Stoic thinker Epictetus points out that if one has a cold, nature supplied us with hands to wipe our nose rather than just to sniff in the mucous all day.[202] In the same way, Plutarch reasons that nature teaches mothers to nurse their own babies by providing them the ability to produce milk.[203]

Many gender distinctions were also considered part of nature, rather than a matter of mere social convention.[204] Thus, one of Cicero's examples of a natural way to categorize types of humans is male and female.[205] More significantly, Epictetus can speak of hair as a mark of gender distinction: "Can anything be more useless than the hairs on a chin? Well, what then? Has not nature used even these in the most suitable way possible? Has she not by these means distinguished between the male and the female?"[206]

Beards were quite out of fashion in the Roman world of Paul's day, and he was therefore not likely to impose them on his readers as a mark of gender distinction; but perhaps he would have agreed with Epictetus' basic point: "we ought to preserve the signs which God has given; we ought not to throw them away; we ought not, so far as in us lies, to confuse the sexes which have been distinguished in this fashion."[207] In the same way, some in antiquity saw gender reversal[208] and homosexual behavior[209] as being "against nature" (Rom. 1:26–27).

It was not sexist or sexually exploitive to wish to preserve gender distinctions; they were already matters of natural endowment, and to keep them explicit was entirely in accordance with nature. Thus F. F. Bruce may well be right when he suggests that Paul's appeal to nature here is an appeal to the fact that women's hair *naturally* grows longer than men's.[210]

Other scholars suggest that by "nature" Paul refers to cultural custom.[211] Although "nature" might occasionally mean custom,[212] the term is normally used to mean exactly the opposite of custom: that which is innate in the order of things, which cannot be acquired.[213] But it cannot be denied that the Greco-Roman *custom* at this time was for men to have shorter hair than women.[214] The fact that Paul must have been aware of the exceptions to this custom would indicate that he speaks in a general sense of what was acceptable for usual societal norms in his day.[215] The exceptions were various: Artemidorus lists "a wise man, a priest, a prophet, a king, a ruler and for stage performances."[216]

In a few cases men may have worn long hair as a sign of gender reversal, or to show their disdain for the traditions of gender distinctions.[217] Ancient Spartan men, like the heroes of an earlier period in Greek history and like statues of some Greek gods,[218] wore their hair long;[219] in earlier Sparta, perhaps as an expression of Sparta's duty-centered warrior character, Spartan brides often cropped their hair short and dressed like men.[220] In Paul's day, the ecstatic priests of Cybele were said to have long hair;[221] since they were also emasculated, their long hair may have been a sign of gender reversal.[222] Long hair may also have been associated with luxury or wantonness.[223] Conversely, a woman might cut her hair if she wished to disguise herself as a man.[224] Not everyone took well to unnecessary gender reversals. Thus Epictetus charges,

> Are you a man or a woman?—A man.—Very well then, adorn as a man, not a woman. Woman is born smooth and dainty by nature [*physei*], and if she is very hairy she is a prodigy, and is exhibited at Rome among the prodigies. But for a man *not* to be hairy is the same thing, and if by nature he has no hair he is a prodigy, but if he cuts it out and plucks it out of himself, what shall we make of him? Where shall we exhibit him and what notice shall we post? "I will show you," we say to the audience, "a man who wishes to be a woman rather than a man."[225]

Epictetus' remarks verge on the crude when he suggests that the one who wishes to look like a woman by plucking his hairs ought to "make a clean sweep of the whole matter," chopping off the source of his masculine hairiness, so he may be a full woman and not half and half.[226] That the context of his remarks may suggest that the object of Epictetus' ridicule is from Corinth may be of more than passing interest.[227]

Some philosophers apparently advocated obliterating marks of gender distinctions,[228] but most philosophers who wore their hair long probably did so only as a sign of their simple, extrasocietal lifestyle.[229] Epictetus was not the only philosopher to ridicule an "effeminately attired" man.[230]

The general custom accords also with Diaspora Jewish antipathy toward transvestism in hairstyles: "If a child is a boy do not let locks grow on (his) head. Do not braid (his) crown nor the cross knots at the top of his head. Long hair is not fit for boys, but for voluptuous women."[231] Although certain exceptions were permitted in the Bible for long hair, such as the Nazirites,[232] a later rabbi could argue that the long hair was to set the Nazirite apart from normal society, making him repulsive and uncomfortable.[233]

Whether Paul's argument is that women by virtue of creation have longer hair than men, or that the social norms of his day demand women's hair to be longer under normal circumstances, does not in the end need to be decided. In either case, Paul would seem to be making an argument that addresses symbolic gender distinctions, and requiring men and women to recognize those differences between them.

From natural gender differences, he can easily argue that clothing styles ought to reflect those differences.[234] Women in Corinth should thus cover their heads, and men should not, to identify their differences. This is a case of distinguishing the two, however, not of ranking one over the other.

### *Paul's Appeal to Custom: 1 Corinthians 11:16*

Although Paul's appeal to "nature" in 11:14 may not be an appeal to custom, 11:16 certainly is. It is not an appeal to universal practice, but only an appeal to the practice of those who "count" on the matter of church attire, the churches of God.[235] They are the ones who count, of course, because they are the ones whose behavior best supports Paul's argument to get the well-to-do Corinthian wives to cover their heads in church and avoid division among the Christians in Corinth.

This was a standard way for an ancient lawyer or speech writer to argue a case;[236] for instance, Isocrates appeals to common knowledge when he writes what "the myths relate and all men believe" about Zeus,[237] even though clearly there were exceptions to "all men" of which even Isocrates must have known in his day. Theon, the writer of an important rhetorical handbook, notes that one can refute an argument if it is contrary to the common account or view; the burden of proof was strongly on anyone opposing established custom or view.[238] This practice is no less common in rabbinic texts, although the standard there was determined specifically by rabbinic tradition.[239]

Some philosophers in the ancient world actually accepted no other argument except one drawn from custom.[240] Although it is unlikely that there were disciples of any of these thinkers, called the Skeptics, in the Corinthian church, their position illustrates the importance attributed to custom in ancient thought. Paul, who often must challenge accepted custom in proclaiming the truth of the gospel, here finds it on his side and is able to appeal to it.

## CONCLUSION

The arguments one uses to persuade readers in a given setting may not be the same as one's own reasons for articulating a position. Paul's arguments in 11:2–16 are different from his reasons for writing this passage. Probably he was dealing with social division in the church, as he was in most of the rest of 1 Corinthians. But as elsewhere, he must come up with supporting arguments that would work for his readers. Although we do not believe that he was making a transcultural argument in favor of women wearing head coverings in church, we can notice some transcultural points in his argument: one should not bring reproach upon one's family or upon the Christian gospel; one should not seek to destroy symbolic gender distinctions by pioneering unisex clothing styles; one should respect custom and do one's best to avoid causing someone to stumble.[241]

Why did Paul try to persuade the uncovered women to cover up, rather than trying to persuade the covered women to uncover? One reason may have been that he agreed with some of the moral objections to showing off one's fashions in church. Another reason may be that, in that society, these women's adorned hair would distract men from the worship of God, perhaps in the way that bathing suits would distract many of us in church today. Paul never questioned the well-to-do women's right to dress as they pleased—indeed, he affirmed it—but he asked them to sacrifice that right for the sake of those in the church who would have a very hard time understanding it.

I hope that this chapter will not be used by anyone to enforce rigid dress codes in churches today. If we really understand the chapter and what it communicates about the right of the women to dress as they please, it seems that it would be better to ask only for modesty. None of us should dress extravagantly and embarrass those who have little, or in a manner that might be interpreted as sexually enticing in our culture. Beyond this, we must keep in mind that Paul's purpose was to make Christianity available to more people, to increase its cultural appeal to the majority of those who would be interested in it. If our churches' dress codes turn people away from the church rather than bring them in, we have failed to catch Paul's motives or his message.

Finally, and most significantly for this book, we should note that *nothing* in this passage suggests wives' subordination. The only indicator that *could* be taken to mean that is the statement that man is woman's "head," but "head" in those days was capable of a variety of meanings, and nothing in this text indicates that it means subordination. As many scholars have been pointing out in the past few years, if we want this passage to teach subordination, we have to read subordination into the passage. The only clear affirmations here, besides that men and women are different and should not conceal that fact, is the equality and mutual dependence of men and women.

## NOTES

1. For a listing of major divergent views on 22 different points of interpretation in this passage, see S. D. Hull, "Exegetical Difficulties in the 'Hard Passages,' " in Gretchen G. Hull, *Equal to Serve: Women and Men in the Church and Home* (Old Tappan, N.J.: Revell, 1987), pp. 252–57.

2. G. W. Trompf, "On Attitudes Toward Women in Paul and Paulinist Literature: 1 Corinthians 11:3–16 and Its Context," *CBQ* 42 (2, April 1980): 196–215 (regarding 1 Cor. 14:33–35 in the same way).

3. W. O. Walker, Jr., "1 Corinthians 11:2–16 and Paul's Views Regarding Women," *JBL* 94 (1, March 1975): 94–110. He sees three separate non-Pauline fragments here.

4. Jerome Murphy-O'Connor, "The Non-Pauline Character of 1 Corinthians 11:2–16?" *JBL* 95 (4, Dec. 1976): 615–21. He points out that denying that the text is Pauline may save face for Paul, but it does not do justice to the textual evidence (p. 621).

5. Lamar Cope, "1 Cor 11:2–16: One Step Further," *JBL* 97 (3, Sept. 1978): 435–36.

6. "Tensions" need not be contradictions; they can be semantic differences rather than contradictions on the level of meaning.

7. Neither the Nestle–Aland nor the UBS text notes any texts omitting it, and B. M. Metzger's textual commentary (*A Textual Commentary on the Greek New Testament*, 2d ed. [New York: United Bible Societies, 1975], pp. 561–62) has no discussion of the "problem." It is not, indeed, a textual problem, but a question of removing a difficult passage. This is the more so if E. Schüssler Fiorenza, *In Memory of Her*

(New York: Crossroad, 1983), p. 226 (following H. Wendland), is correct that 11:1–16 and 14:34–35 form an inclusio around Paul's comments on the pneumatic worship service; this may well be correct, although 11:17–34 seem to me to continue the preceding section on foods.

8. B. K. Waltke, "1 Corinthians 11:2–16: An Interpretation," *BibSac* 135 (537, Jan. 1978): 46–57.

9. G. R. Osborne, "Hermeneutics and Women in the Church," *JETS* 20 (4, Dec. 1977): 337–52.

10. W. M. Ramsay, *The Teaching of Paul in Terms of the Present Day* (London: Hodder & Stoughton, 1913), pp. 214–15; so also A. M. Hunter, *The Gospel According to St. Paul* (Philadelphia: Westminster, 1966), p. 48. Cf. Jean Héring, *The First Epistle of Saint Paul to the Corinthians,* trans. A. W. Heathcote and P. J. Allcock (London: Epworth, 1962), p. 103.

11. M. D. Hooker, *A Preface to Paul* (New York: Oxford University, 1980), p. 17.

12. T. P. Shoemaker, "Unveiling of Equality: 1 Corinthians 11:2–16," *BTB* 17 (2, April 1987): 60–63 (11:2–9 vs. 11:10–16); Alan Padgett, "Paul on Women in the Church: The Contradictions of Coiffure in 1 Corinthians 11.2–16," *JSNT* 20 (1984): 69–86; idem, " 'Authority Over Her Head.' Toward a Feminist Reading of St. Paul," *DSar* 12 (1, 1986): 5–9 (11:4–7 vs. 11:7–16).

13. C. L. Thompson, "Hairstyles, Head-coverings, and St. Paul: Portraits from Roman Corinth," *BA* 51 (2, June 1988): 112.

14. Gundry, *Women,* pp. 67–68, rightly cites 10:23, 31; 11:1.

15. It deals with status differentiation in the church, allowing those who are socially or economically inferior in the world to bear the same inferior status in the church.

16. For the view that they were ad hominem arguments, see also F. F. Bruce, " 'All Things to All Men': Diversity in Unity and Other Pauline Tensions," in *Unity and Diversity in New Testament Theology: Essays in Honor of G. E. Ladd,* ed. R. A. Guelich (Grand Rapids: Eerdmans, 1978), p. 95; R. N. Longenecker, *New Testament Social Ethics for Today* (Grand Rapids: Eerdmans, 1984), p. 81; idem, "Authority, Hierarchy & Leadership Patterns in the Bible," in *Women, Authority & the Bible,* ed. Alvera Mickelsen (Downers Grove, Ill.: InterVarsity, 1986), p. 74. Such arguments were common in Aristotle (see W. A. Meeks, *The Moral World of the First Christians,* LEC 6 [Philadelphia: Westminster, 1986], p. 19, cited below). Explanations based on (ancient) logic were also common in rabbinic exegetical material; they appear in the Talmud at nearly three times the number of explanations from Scripture, ten times those from the Tosefta, and eighteen times those from the Mishnah (A. J. Avery-Peck, in *Talmud of Israel,* vol. 6: *Terumot,* ed. Jacob Neusner, et al. [Chicago: University of Chicago, 1988], p. 37).

17. Gordon Fee, *The First Epistle to the Corinthians,* NICNT (Grand Rapids: Eerdmans, 1987), p. 530. This may also be reflected in the fact that Paul can praise them for keeping traditions in v. 2 (though these may well not include their behavior with head coverings; see ibid., p. 500), whereas in v. 17, introducing the Lord's Supper issue, he

protests, "I praise you not" (cf. Diogenes 17, to Antalcides [*CynEp,* pp. 110–11]), possibly reflecting an ancient epistolary emphasis on praise and blame that could even define certain types of letters (S. K. Stowers, *Letter Writing in Greco-Roman Antiquity,* LEC 5 [Philadelphia: Westminster, 1986], pp. 77–90).

18. Ramsay MacMullen, "Women in Public in the Roman Empire," *Historia* 29 (1980): 210, n. 4.

19. J. B. Hurley, "Did Paul Require Veils or the Silence of Women? A Consideration of I Cor. 11:2–16 and I Cor. 14:33b–36," *WTJ* 35 (2, Winter 1973): 200, citing no sources. (Cf. Fiorenza, *Memory,* p. 239, n. 67, following Hurley, who does cite J. P. V. D. Balsdon, "Women in Imperial Rome," *HT* 10 [1, Jan. 1960]: 24–31; but Balsdon clearly shows that the piled-up hairstyle dates to the end of the first and early second century, not before [pp. 24–25, and only the pictures on pp. 24 and 27]). On p. 197, Hurley argues that the only verse mentioning a shawl is v. 15, which actually says that long hair is given *instead* of a shawl. But Fee, *1 Corinthians,* p. 496, points out that v. 15 speaks of long hair, not piled-up hair, which would not support Hurley's thesis, either.

20. Hurley, "Veils," p. 200.

21. Fee, *1 Corinthians,* p. 496. He offers a more thorough refutation on pp. 528–29, especially to the view that long hair is given "instead" of a shawl; he addresses the parallels cited by others in sufficient detail on pp. 506–7.

22. Men also might not appear in public for certain reasons, e.g., grief (Chariton *Chaer.* 2.1.1), but these were temporary and not directly related to the pervasive restrictions on women.

23. The matter was probably not as universal as some have thought; see W. Den Boer, *Private Morality in Greece and Rome: Some Historical Aspects,* MBCBS (Leiden: Brill, 1979), p. 251.

24. S. B. Pomeroy, *Goddesses, Whores, Wives, and Slaves: Women in Classical Antiquity* (New York: Schocken, 1975), p. 72; cf. p. 170; Boer, *Morality,* pp. 243–44.

25. John Gould, "Law, Custom and Myth: Aspects of the Social Position of Women in Classical Athens," *JHS* 100 (1980): 47. There were, of course, significant exceptions, e.g., in the theater; see H. P. Foley, "The Conception of Women in Athenian Drama," in *Reflections of Women in Antiquity,* ed. H. P. Foley (New York: Gordon & Breach Science Pub., 1981), p. 161. The exception in the theater may be related to the status attained by certain mythic women; cf. Dorothy Willner, "The Oedipus Complex, Antigone, and Electra: The Woman as Hero and Victim," *AmAnth* 84 (1, March 1982): 58–78.

26. K. J. Dover, "Classical Greek Attitudes to Sexual Behavior," in *Women in the Ancient World: The Arethusa Papers,* ed. John Peradotto and J. P. Sullivan, SSCS (Albany, N.Y.: State University of New York, 1984), p. 145.

27. D. C. Verner, *The Household of God: The Social World of the Pastoral Epistles,* SBLDS 71 (Chico, Calif.: Scholars, 1983), p. 31.

28. Verner, *Household,* p. 38.

29. Chariton *Chaer.* 5.4.10.

30. Chariton *Chaer.* 1.1.4–6; cf. similarly Jos. & As. 2:1–6 (in some editions, 2:1–11).

31. Ps-Phocyl. 215–16 (*OTP* 2:581; Greek version, p. 111).

32. MacMullen, "Women in Public," p. 209; cf. also P. E. Harrell, *Divorce and Remarriage in the Early Church* (Austin, Tex.: R. B. Sweet, 1967), p. 31 (Val. Max. 2.9.2; 5.3.10–12).

33. Plut. *Bride* 31, *Mor.* 142CD.

34. Plut. *Bride* 32, *Mor.* 142D (LCL).

35. Plut. *Bride* 9, *Mor.* 139 (LCL). In *Bride* 30, *Mor.* 142C (LCL), he suggests that "most women, if you take from them gold-embroidered shoes, bracelets, anklets, purple, and pearls, stay indoors." Cf. Artem. *Oneir.* 1.8.

36. Perhaps under Greek influence.

37. See e.g., J. P. Hallett, "The Role of Women in Roman Elegy: Counter-Cultural Feminism," in *Women in the Ancient World,* p. 245.

38. Even here, they probably remained indoors most of the day since all their "duties" were domestic; see Martin Goodman, *State and Society in Roman Galilee, A.D. 132–212,* OCPHS (Totowa, N.J.: Rowman & Allanheld, 1983), p. 37.

39. Verner, *Household,* pp. 46–47, citing especially Philo *Special Laws* 3.169–171; *Flaccus* 89.

40. See Philo *Special Laws* 3.169–175 (conveniently available in R. S. Kraemer, *Maenads, Martyrs, Matrons, Monastics* [Philadelphia: Fortress, 1988], p. 29).

41. 4 Macc. 18:6–7.

42. S. Safrai, "Home and Family," in *JPFC,* p. 762, citing t. Ket. 7:6; m. Ket. 7:6; cf. b. Git. 90ab; p. Git. 9, 50d. See J. R. Wegner, *Chattel or Person? The Status of Women in the Mishnah* (New York: Oxford University, 1988), pp. 18, 40, 145–67.

43. Longenecker, *Ethics,* p. 80; Richard and Joyce Boldrey, *Chauvinist or Feminist? Paul's View of Women* (Grand Rapids: Baker, 1976), p. 59. The Boldreys cite E. A. Leonard, "St. Paul on the Status of Women," *CBQ* 12 (1950): 319, but Leonard cites L. Delaporte on a *Mesopotamian* custom—quite far removed in place and time from Paul's Corinth! Gundry, *Women,* p. 65, cites "Many pictures on vases and wine jars from early Greece" showing prostitutes "with short hair and without headdress of any kind"; but it is not clear that the evidence she cites would still hold true in Paul's day.

44. J. F. Gardner, *Women in Roman Law & Society* (Bloomington, Ind.: Indiana University, 1986), p. 251, citing Mart. *Epig.* 10.52; Juv. *Sat.* 2.68, but noting (p. 252) that prostitutes were not forced to dress this way.

45. Middle Assyrian Laws, trans. T. J. Meek, in *ANET,* p. 183 (Tablet A, §40).

46. Ibid. (Tablet A, §41).

47. I am supposing that the rabbi was no later than the third century, because R. Johanan, a third-century rabbi, seems to build on this tradition.

48. Gen. Rab. 85:8.

49. I am thus in agreement with Fee, *1 Corinthians,* p. 511, n. 80, who notes that "there is no contemporary evidence" to support the view that short or shaved hair (or lack of head coverings) would indicate prostitutes. Indeed, m. Kel. 24:16 could suggest that prostitutes wore head coverings, too (the meaning of 28:9 is less clear).

50. E.g., F. F. Bruce, *1 and 2 Corinthians,* NCBC (Grand Rapids: Eerdmans, 1980), p. 105; idem, "All Things," pp. 94–95; Fiorenza, *Memory,* p. 227. Fee, *1 Corinthians,* pp. 507–8, provides nearly the opposite suggestion, as just one possibility among others: the prophet in the Isis cult wore a head covering (according to one fresco from Pompeii), so Christian male prophets were to avoid this practice. But I think this is as unlikely here as Bruce's proposal.

51. It is true that ecstatic dance in the more frenzied cults (cited in Fiorenza alongside the prophetic elements) was more naturally and easily conducted with heads uncovered, but we have no evidence of such activity in the Corinthian church.

52. Test. Sol. 13:1. *OTP* 1:974, n. a, compares the Greek Medusa and the artwork of demons on Aramaic incantation bowls.

53. In Athen. *Deipn.* 12.523b, closely cropped hair is associated with mourning. It is possible that this custom was extended to those who were sick (Petr. *Sat.* 101).

54. The woman Callirhoe in Chariton *Chaer.* 8.1.7; perhaps also 1.3.6. Her husband Chaereas also covers his head for mourning (3.3.14). This work is a novel, but the customs it assumes must have been authentic for the narrative to have been intelligible to the original readers.

55. Plut. *R. Q.* 26, *Mor.* 270D (*kekryphalous*).

56. Chariton *Chaer.* 1.11.2.

57. See p. M. K. 3:5, §20.

58. See Ab. R. Nathan 1 A.

59. Plut. *R. Q.* 14, *Mor.* 267A. Petr. *Sat.* 111 reports this as a standard custom in the Greek east, in Ephesus, as well.

60. Petr. *Sat.* 57.

61. Epict. *Disc.* 1.11.27; see also m. Sot. 9:15.

62. See 1 En. 14:24, where Enoch covers his face and trembles as he approaches God. (I have at this point followed Knibb's translation as against Isaacs'.)

63. For uncovering the head, in awe before a king, see R. Berechiah's parable in Pes. Rab Kah. 9:5. This evidence is late.

64. Ab. R. Nathan 9, §25 B (trans. Saldarini, p. 83). See similarly Gen. Rab. 17:8.

65. Ab. R. Nathan 17 A. Johanan ben Zakkai lived in the first century, but this tradition could, of course, be later.

66. Ab. R. Nathan 3 A.

67. Cf. e.g., the Chalcedonians, whose men customarily covered one side of their face when meeting outsiders, in Plut. *G. Q.* 49, *Mor.* 302E.

68. Thompson, "Hairstyles," p. 113, citing Dio Chrys. *33d (1st Tarsic) Discourse* for Tarsus, and paintings elsewhere.

69. See especially MacMullen, "Women in Public," pp. 209–10, with notes.

70. Archibald Robertson and Alfred Plummer, *A Critical and Exegetical Commentary on the First Epistle of St Paul to the Corinthians*, ICC, 2d ed. (Edinburgh: T. & T. Clark, 1914), p. 230, citing Aristoph. *Thesm.* 838. The woman with the covered head in Petr. *Sat.* 14, 16, is a devotee of Priapus, which could make her exceptional, or from the east.

71. Thompson, "Hairstyles," p. 104; cf. Fee, *1 Corinthians*, p. 507, on the *tallith*.

72. Sifre Num. 11.2.2. Num. Rab. 9:16, a later text, also affirms that covering their heads was the custom of Israelite women, without offering any polemic against unreligious women who failed to do so; it was thus no doubt standard practice. Fiorenza, *Memory*, p. 116, properly points to Jdt. 10:7; 11:21; 15:9, to prove that Judith's beauty was publicly admired, and that she therefore must have been unveiled. But Judith was not married, the provenance of this text in Greek may be non-Palestinian, and it may reflect a Jewish understanding that in earlier times women were not always veiled; and contrast Susanna's veil (Sus. 32). At the same time, Fiorenza's observation may point in a helpful direction: at least upper-class, hellenized women probably ignored the custom (see below).

73. 3 Macc. 4:6. In 3 Macc. 1:4, Arsinoë, sister of Ptolemy IV Philopator, went about the ranks with "her braided hair hanging loose," perhaps because she was taking on a traditionally masculine role; Ptolemy opposed the Jewish community till the end of the book, when he changed his mind, so Arsinoë's example may not be relevant.

74. This observation was made by James Moffatt, *The First Epistle of Paul to the Corinthians*, MNTC (London: Hodder & Stoughton, 1938), pp. 149–50.

75. In F. C. Grant, ed., *Hellenistic Religions: The Age of Syncretism*, LLA (Indianapolis: Bobbs-Merrill, 1953), pp. 26–27. The inscription is early, but these rules continued in force through the second century CE. Hans Conzelmann, *1 Corinthians: A Commentary on the First Epistle to the Corinthians*, trans. James W. Leitch, Hermeneia (Philadelphia: Fortress, 1975), pp. 184–85, cites evidence that this was a normal practice in the mysteries, while observing that the custom at the Isis festival in Corinth seems to have been the opposite. His evidence on the Isis festival is from Apuleius, who writes in Latin for Roman readers, but we may suppose that Apuleius nevertheless knew and correctly represented the custom. Roman culture was quite prominent in Corinth.

76. Varro *Lat. Lang.* 5.29.130. The contrast between the Greek and Roman custom is also pointed out by Moffatt, *Corinthians*, pp. 149–50; and in much greater detail by R. E. Oster, "When Men Wore Veils to Worship: The Historical Context of 1 Corinthians 11.4," *NTS* 34 (4 Oct. 1988): 494–96.

77. Plut. *R. Q.* 10, *Mor.* 266C. They are, however, to uncover to show respect to honorable men (ibid.).

78. For Saturn (*R. Q.* 11, *Mor.* 266E) and the god Honor (*R. Q.* 13, *Mor.* 266F–267A). The concept of honor may again be significant.

79. Cf. Thompson, "Hairstyles," p. 112.

80. Test. Jos. 9:5; Chariton *Chaer.* 6.4.5, imagining Callirhöe dressed as a huntress, like Artemis.

81. Apul. *Metam.* 2.8. Cf. similarly Deut. 21:12–14, to determine whether one's attraction is related more to lust or love.

82. Apul. *Metam.* 2.8.

83. Apul. *Metam.* 2.8–9.

84. Chariton *Chaer.* 1.14.1; she had covered it back in 13.11.

85. See the warnings on the adulteress, note 89 below.

86. M. Ket. 7:6 (referring to the ketubah, which is both the marriage contract and the dowry she brought with her into the marriage). R. Meir (second century) is said to have reaffirmed that the law required a man to divorce such a wife, because she was clearly pursuing other men (Num. Rab. 9:12).

87. Ab. R. Nathan 14, §35 B.

88. See b. Sot. 9a; p. Sot. 1:5, §5; Num. Rab. 9:16. Cf. Sifre Num. 11.2.1 (R. Ishmael, early second century); Pes. Rab. 26:1/2 (suggesting a face-veil).

89. Sifre Num. 11.2.3; p. Sanh. 6:4, §1 (both late second to early third century). Cf. Num. Rab. 18:20.

90. Jos. & As. 15:1–2.

91. Jos. & As. 18:6.

92. Samuel Belkin, *Philo and the Oral Law: The Philonic Interpretation of Biblical Law in Relation to the Palestinian Halakah,* HSS 11 (Cambridge: Harvard University, 1940), p. 230.

93. Charillus 2, in Plut. *SSpart., Mor.* 232C (LCL).

94. See especially Paul's rhetorical insult in 1 Cor. 1:26. They were, however, better off financially than many of Paul's other church communities (2 Cor. 8:1–3); Corinth as a whole was a relatively prosperous urban center by ancient standards.

95. See e.g., D. B. Martin, *Slavery as Salvation: The Metaphor of Slavery in Pauline Christianity* (New Haven: Yale University, 1990) (especially on 1 Cor. 9); Gerd Theissen, *The Social Setting of Pauline Christianity,* ed. and trans. John H. Schütz (Philadelphia: Fortress, 1982).

96. Thompson, "Hairstyles," p. 112.

97. See MacMullen, "Women in Public," pp. 217–18; cf. also Catherine Kroeger, "The Apostle Paul and the Greco-Roman Cults of Women," *JETS* 30 (1, March 1987): 37.

98. For instance, the adulteress whose head is uncovered in b. Sot. 9a is said to have plaited her hair for the sake of the adulterer. Although this is a later text, it is consistent with other evidence cited above, under notes 81–93.

99. One may take as an example the African tribe where missionaries forced tribal women to cover their breasts; only later did they learn that covered breasts in that society marked adulteresses, and that they had damaged the witness of these women by forcing them to conform to the style of Western culture, where bare breasts would be seductive and immodest. None of the men in Paul's day wore ties to church; our dress must accommodate the particular culture we address. It should also be noted that Paul is talking here about causing severe spiritual offense, of

the order that could hinder the ministry of the body of Christ and turn people away from Christ; he is not referring to others' personal tastes. Paul requires his readers to consider other people's interpretations of how they dress ("seductive!" "disrespectful!"), but he is most certainly *not* requiring them to keep up with fashions, even church fashions.

100. That he is using a wordplay is also noted by others, e.g., Boldrey, *Chauvinist*, p. 33; Bruce, "All Things," p. 95.

101. In Greco-Roman tradition, e.g., Diogenes in Diog. Laert. *Lives* 6.2.55, 68; Suet. *Calig.* 27 (a farce writer's double entendre); Martin Dibelius, *From Tradition to Gospel*, trans. Bertram Lee Woolf (reprint, Cambridge: James Clarke, 1971), p. 157. In Jewish texts, where a common method of midrashic interpretation is to interpret one word as another (by revocalizing the vowels or sometimes even by modifying the consonants, in Dead Sea texts as well as in the rabbis), see e.g., CD 8.10–11; Ps-Philo 2:1; Sifre Deut. 306.22.1; 318.4.7; 321.8.6; 345.2.2, 3.1; b. Tamid 32a; p. R. H. 3:9, §§1–3; T. H. Gaster, *The Dead Sea Scriptures* (Garden City, N.Y.: Doubleday, 1976), pp. 481–85; W. H. Brownlee, "Light on the Manual of Discipline (DSD) from the Book of Jubilees," *BASOR* 123 (Oct. 1951): 32; cf. b. Ber. 55b; Pes. Rab. 14:6; 21:6. W. G. Braude lists over 200 examples in Pesikta de-Rab Kahana (*Pesikta de-Rab Kahana*, trans. Braude and I. J. Kapstein [Philadelphia: Jewish Publication Society, 1975], pp. 585–93). Fallacious etymologies were also standard: Hierocles *Duties. Fatherland* 3.39.34 (in A. J. Malherbe, *Moral Exhortation: A Greco-Roman Sourcebook*, LEC 4 [Philadelphia: Westminster, 1986], p. 89); Plut. *Isis* 2, *Mor.* 351F; Marc. Aur. *Med.* 8.57; Anthony Hanson, "Philo's Etymologies," *JTS* 18 (1, April 1967): 128–39; cf. John 9:7 (R. E. Brown, *The Gospel According to John*, 2 vols., AB 29 [Garden City, N.Y.: Doubleday, 1966–70], 1:373).

102. W. J. Martin, "1 Corinthians 11:2–16: An Interpretation," in *Apostolic History and the Gospel: Biblical and Historical Essays presented to F. F. Bruce on his 60th Birthday*, ed. W. W. Gasque and R. P. Martin (Grand Rapids: Eerdmans, 1970), pp. 231–42, makes much of comparing the woman to the church, and the man to Christ. This may be implied in the passage, though it is not explicit in the way we find it in Eph. 5.

103. Berkeley and Alvera Mickelsen, "What Does *Kephalē* Mean in the New Testament?" in *Women, Authority & the Bible*, p. 99.

104. Mickelsen, "*Kephalē?*" pp. 101–3; cf. Fee, *1 Corinthians*, pp. 502–3. Rabbinic texts such as the baraita in b. Shab. 61a naturally reflect the Semitic idiom and do not affect our picture of the Greek sources.

105. P. B. Payne, "Response," in *Women, Authority & the Bible*, pp. 118–19, thinks that "leader" is never a valid meaning for the term in pre-Byzantine Greek.

106. Note the figurative application of the literal use of "head" in Philo *Special Laws* 3.33, §184; Test. Zeb. 9:4; cf. Artem. *Oneir.* 1.35 (where a head can stand for a master, but a head is also said to be the cause, i.e., source, of life; cf. 1.2). The head is the ruling part of the body and seat of life (ruler or source?) in the medical texts of Galen and Hippocrates (C. E. Arnold, *Ephesians: Power and Magic*, SNTSMS 63 [Cambridge: Cambridge University, 1989], pp. 81–82; Markus Barth,

*Ephesians,* 2 vols., AB 34 [Garden City, N.Y.: Doubleday, 1974], 1:187, but noting [p. 191] that Paul speaks of the head, not the brain). It is where reason is established as a pilot in Plut. *Plat. Q.* 9.1, *Mor.* 1008A; "the chief member of the body" (because on top?) in Quint. 11.3.68 (cf. the head-tail contrast even in the OT and in 1 En. 103:11, etc.).

107. See R. A. Tucker, "Response," in *Women, Authority & the Bible,* pp. 111–17.

108. Fee, *1 Corinthians,* p. 502.

109. Ibid., pp. 503–4.

110. Deut. 28:13, 44; Isa. 9:14–15; also Jub. 1:16.

111. See especially W. L. Liefeld, "Women, Submission & Ministry in 1 Corinthians," in *Women, Authority & the Bible,* pp. 139–40, and the data he cites. Herman Ridderbos, *Paul: An Outline of His Theology,* trans. J. R. de Witt (Grand Rapids: Eerdmans, 1975), p. 385, sees the idea of "representation" as most appropriate here.

112. E.g., Bruce, *The Message of the New Testament* (Grand Rapids: Eerdmans, 1981), p. 37; idem, "All Things," p. 95; Letha Scanzoni and Nancy Hardesty, *All We're Meant to Be* (Waco, Tex.: Word, 1974), p. 30; Robin Scroggs, "Paul and the Eschatological Woman," *JAAR* 40 (3, Sept. 1972): 284, following Stephen Bedale, "The Meaning of *kephalē* in the Pauline Epistles," *JTS,* n.s. 5 (1954): 211–15, who is cited by most subsequent sources. Cf. also S. F. B. Bedale, "The Theology of the Church," in *Studies in Ephesians,* ed. F. L. Cross (London: Mowbray, 1956), pp. 69–70, 72.

113. E.g., C. C. Kroeger, "The Classical Concept of *Head* as 'Source'," Appendix 3, in Hull, *Equal to Serve,* pp. 267–76 (not all the examples are equally compelling, but some are quite convincing, especially her examples from the church fathers; the problem is that these do not predate the NT). R. W. Crabb, "The *KEPHALĒ* Concept in the Pauline Tradition with Special Emphasis on Colossians" (Th.D. diss., San Francisco Theological Seminary, 1966), traces metaphorical meanings, including those of authority and priority of being, and Philo's use of that which structures the forces of the universe (DA 29.04A, pp. 1280–81).

114. Gilbert Bilezikian, *Beyond Sex Roles: What the Bible Says About a Woman's Place in Church and Family* (Grand Rapids: Baker, 1986), pp. 157–62, traces the evidence well; cf. also Mickelsen, "*Kephalē?*" pp. 105–8 (Eph. 4:15; Col. 2:19). We should mention in passing that alleged differences between the usage of body imagery in 1 Cor. 12 and Rom. 12 on the one hand and that in Ephesians and Colossians on the other has been used to argue against the Pauline authorship of the latter; but other writers of Paul's day used head/body and body cosmological images interchangeably. See A. Van Roon, *The Authenticity of Ephesians,* NovTSup 39 (Leiden: Brill, 1974), pp. 275–93 (favoring authenticity). One could propose that Paul uses head/body imagery for husband and wife because of his use of this for Christ and his church (or the reverse, since husband and wife in Gen. 2:24 were said to become "one flesh").

115. E.g., Fee, *1 Corinthians,* pp. 503–4.

116. Ibid., p. 505.

117. Bilezikian, *Roles,* p. 138.

118. Grudem, "Does *kephalē* Mean 'Source' or 'Authority Over' in Greek Literature? A Survey of 2,336 Examples," *TJ,* n.s. 6 (1, Spring 1985): 38–59. He argues that the current lexicons do not cite "source" as a meaning (p. 40), and that it does not occur in ancient literature (pp. 43–46). The different count is due to the different ways scholars interpret the ancient texts, not due to any attempt to misrepresent the data.

119. I followed Grudem in my own article, "Is Paul's Teaching 'Sexist'?" *Cruc* 1 (1, Fall 1980): 9, n. 34; but while much work went into Grudem's research, I find Fee's objections persuasive. J. A. Fitzmyer, "Another look at *KEPHALĒ* in 1 Corinthians 11.3," *NTS* 35 (4, Oct. 1989): 506–11, also argues that "head" means "authority," apparently independent of Grudem. Grudem, "Appendix 1: The Meaning of *Kephalē* ('Head'): A Response to Recent Studies," in *Recovering Biblical Manhood and Womanhood: A Response to Evangelical Feminism,* ed. J. Piper and W. Grudem (Wheaton, Ill.: Crossway, 1991), pp. 425–68, provides a detailed and reasoned response to his critics, especially when he points out that "head" nowhere means "source" in the LXX (pp. 451–53) or when applied to a person (p. 433). His response to Liefeld's suggestion of "honored part" (p. 458) seems less persuasive, but scholarship has undoubtedly not heard the last of this dispute.

120. Fee, *1 Corinthians,* pp. 502–3, n. 42.

121. Cf. Plut. *Isis* 4, *Mor.* 352D.

122. Artem. *Oneir.* 1.22. Cf. Paus. *Desc. Greece* 2.3.7 in Jerome Murphy-O'Connor, *St. Paul's Corinth: Texts and Archaeology* (Wilmington, Del.: Michael Glazier, 1983), p. 33. Contrast the Jewish custom of letting one's hair grow long in mourning (Deut. 21:12 [cited by Conzelmann, *1 Corinthians,* p. 186, n. 46]; Gen. Rab. 98:15).

123. Plut. *Isis* 4, *Mor.* 352C; cf. Artem. *Oneir.* 1.22.

124. Ach. Tat. *Clit.* 5.19.2. In the case of a boy who was appealing to older homosexual men, shaving the head also repulsed potential suitors (Diog. Laert. *Lives* 7.3.166).

125. Mart. *Epig.* 2.67.

126. Test. Job 23:7–10 (*OTP* 1:849)/23:8–11 (ed. Kraft, pp. 44–47); 24:9–10; ch. 25.

127. Jerome Murphy-O'Connor, "1 Corinthians 11:2–16 Once Again," *CBQ* 50 (2, April 1988): 265–74 (though basing it on hair rather than head covering); idem, "Sex and Logic in 1 Corinthians 11:2–16," *CBQ* 42 (4, 1980): 482–500; Kroeger, "Cults of Women," pp. 37–38.

128. Fee, *1 Corinthians,* pp. 510–11.

129. W. A. Meeks, *The First Urban Christians: The Social World of the Apostle Paul* (New Haven: Yale University, 1983), p. 161; cf. pp. 71, 220, n. 107.

130. Kroeger, "Greco-Roman Cults," pp. 37–38. Scholars provide evidence that such reversal was practiced, e.g., in the cult of Dionysus (Albert Henrichs, "Changing Dionysiac Identities," in *Jewish and Christian Self-Definition,* ed. E. P. Sanders et al., 3 vols. [Philadelphia: Fortress, 1982], 3:138–39, 158); for Cybele, see below.

131. Epict. *Disc.* 1.16.10 and our discussion of Paul's argument on "nature" (11:14) below may bolster the argument that Paul has this in mind here. The belief of some contemporary American churches that Deut. 22:5 precludes women from wearing pants is not very sound: that text refers either to transvestism in general or to ancient Near Eastern magical transvestism. For examples of the latter, see "Tale of Aqhat," trans. H. L. Ginsberg, in *ANET,* p. 155 (though cf. the interpretation of P. C. Craigie, *Ugarit and the Old Testament* [Grand Rapids: Eerdmans, 1983], p. 60); Hittite "Ritual Against Impotence," trans. A. Goetze, in *ANET,* pp. 349–50; cf. H. A. Hoffner, Jr., "Symbols for Masculinity and Femininity: Their Use in Ancient Near Eastern Sympathetic Magic Rituals," *JBL* 85 (3, Sept. 1966): 326–34; C. H. Gordon, *The Common Background of Greek and Hebrew Civilizations* (New York: Norton, 1965), p. 168; J. C. Moyer, "Hittite and Israelite Cultic Practices: A Selected Comparison," in *Scripture in Context II: More Essays on the Comparative Method,* ed. W. W. Hallo et al. (Winona Lake, Ind.: Eisenbrauns, 1983), pp. 27–29. (Ritual transvestism is sometimes associated with the possession trance in traditional religions today; cf. Raymond Prince, "Indigenous Yoruba Psychiatry," in *Magic, Faith, & Healing: Studies in Primitive Psychiatry Today,* ed. Ari Kiev [New York: Free, 1964], p. 109.) Further, ancient men wore what modern observers might consider dresses, and most men who complain today about women's wearing pants would not wear women's pants (implying a recognition that women's pants are really women's clothing, not men's).

132. So a daughter's shameless (promiscuous) behavior in Sir. 42:11.

133. Ab. R. Nathan 14, §35 B; Ab. R. Nathan 7 A.

134. Plut. *Bride* 17, *Mor.* 140C.

135. Mart. *Epig.* 2.56 attributes wrongdoing to someone's wife in order to reproach the husband. In 4 Macc. 9:2 one should avoid shaming one's ancestors by departing from their customs. One's honor or disgrace affects the honor or disgrace of one's family or tribe; cf. Sifra Emor par. 14.242.1.11.

136. Diog. Laert. *Lives* 2.114. Stilpo is said to have replied, "No more than I am an honor to her," flouting conventional wisdom.

137. Verner, *Household,* p. 38, citing second/first century BCE Egyptian contracts.

138. Ps-Melissa to Kleareta (in Malherbe, *Exhortation,* p. 83).

139. Verner, *Household,* p. 65.

140. W. H. Leslie, "The Concept of Woman in the Pauline Corpus in Light of the Social and Religious Environment of the First Century" (Ph.D. diss., Northwestern University, 1976), pp. 107–8: "Since the goal of worship is to glorify God, woman needs to be covered during worship in order to hide man's (humanity's) glory." Bilezikian, *Roles,* p. 141: "humanity twice recognized." Boldrey, *Chauvinist,* p. 37, appropriately compares Moses' veil in 2 Cor. 3. Cf. G. W. Knight III, "The New Testament Teaching on the Role Relationship of Male and Female with Special Reference to the Teaching/Ruling Functions in the Church," *JETS* 18 (2, Spring 1975): 86. One of the first writers to point this out

is M. D. Hooker, "Authority on her head: An Examination of I Cor. XI.10," *NTS* 10 (3, April 1964): 415–16.

141. Against Moffatt, *1 Corinthians,* p. 152, who thinks that Paul, like most rabbis, stressed Gen. 2 to the exclusion of Gen. 1:27 here. A third-century rabbi in Gen. Rab. 18:2 argues that God created Eve from a covered part of Adam's body so that she would be modest. Sometimes the rabbis did read the accounts together; Ab. R. Nathan 9, §25 B, speaks of man always seeking his missing part, because woman comes from man, but this presupposes the rabbinic hermaphrodite interpretation of Gen. 1, as well as presupposing Gen. 2. But cf. especially the tradition attributed to R. Ishmael and R. Akiba's discussion, probably early second century: man and woman together were created in God's image and likeness, so "neither man without woman nor woman without man, nor both of them without the *Shechinah*" (Gen. Rab. 22:2, trans. 1:181; the same tradition is attributed to third-century R. Simlai in Gen. Rab. 8:9). The context seems to be procreation (E. E. Urbach, *The Sages: Their Concepts and Beliefs,* 2d ed., 2 vols. [Jerusalem: Magnes, 1979], 1:227–28; Moffatt, *1 Corinthians,* p. 153).

142. As noted also by others, e.g., Liefeld, "Women," pp. 145–46; cf. Scanzoni and Hardesty, *Meant to Be,* p. 66. Fee, *1 Corinthians,* p. 521, suggests that "authority" is their own term, and that they have been seeking their "rights."

143. E.g., Moffatt, *1 Corinthians,* p. 153.

144. Williams, *Paul and Women,* p. 64. Cf. the headdress in W. M. Ramsay, *Luke the Physician and Other Studies in the History of Religion* (London: Hodder & Stoughton, 1908), pp. 175–76.

145. See especially W. M. Ramsay, *The Cities of St. Paul: Their Influence on his Life and Thought* (London: Hodder & Stoughton, 1907), p. 203, who notes that the former idea is such unnatural Greek that no one would have thought of it but for their presupposition on how to read this passage.

146. E.g., Boldrey, *Chauvinist,* pp. 38–39, following Gerhard Kittel, who first proposed it.

147. The preservation of Aramaic in 1 Cor. 16:22 is often attributed to liturgical use (e.g., J. A. T. Robinson, *Twelve New Testament Studies,* SBT 1/34 [London: SCM, 1962], pp. 154–57; idem, *Jesus and His Coming,* 2d ed. [Philadelphia: Westminster, 1979], pp. 26–27; Oscar Cullmann, *Early Christian Worship,* trans. A. S. Todd and J. B. Torrance [Philadelphia: Westminster, 1953], p. 13; idem, *The Christology of the New Testament,* trans. S. C. Guthrie and C. Hall [Philadelphia: Westminster, 1959], pp. 201–2; R. N. Longenecker, *The Christology of Early Jewish Christianity,* SBT 2/17 [London: SCM, 1970], pp. 121–22; G. E. Ladd, *A Theology of the New Testament* [Grand Rapids: Eerdmans, 1974], p. 341; Adolf Deissmann, *Paul: A Study in Social and Religious History* [New York: Harper & Brothers, 1927, p. 127), although it need not be associated with the Eucharist as some (e.g., Robinson, Cullmann) have supposed; at any rate it need not imply that most Jewish Christians in Greek-speaking parts of the Diaspora would have known Aramaic.

148. E.g., Conzelmann, *1 Corinthians,* p. 188; Fee, *1 Corinthians,* p. 520. Cf. Günther Schwarz, "*Exousian echein epi tēs kephalēs* (1 Korinther 11:10)," *ZNW* 70 (3–4, 1979): 249, who provides a better suggestion on the Aramaic, although we reject the idea that Aramaic is used here.

149. Cf. e.g., Test. Reub. 5:1: women do not have authority "over a man," employing the same construction. This view is now accepted by many commentators, e.g., Bruce, *1 and 2 Corinthians,* p. 106; Longenecker, *Ethics,* p. 82; Hurley, "Veils," p. 208; Liefeld, "Women," p. 145. This insight was noticed as early as the 1600s (John Lightfoot, *A Commentary on the New Testament from the Talmud and Hebraica,* 4 vols. [Oxford: Oxford University, 1859], 4:236–37) and is noted by Ramsay (above), but has been increasingly accepted since Morna Hooker's article ("Authority," pp. 410–16). Commentators differ on whether the authority is over her head (as I and some others have taken it), authority to pray publicly (e.g., Hooker, "Authority," p. 415, arguing that women in Judaism could not pray or prophesy; Liefeld, "Women," pp. 145–46), or authority over the angels mentioned in the text (Hurley, "Veils," p. 208).

150. T. R. Schreiner, "Head Coverings, Prophecies, and the Trinity: 1 Corinthians 11:2–16," in *Manhood and Womanhood,* p. 135, rightly points to the language of obligation here, but wrongly supposes that this justifies translating "authority over" as "authority on."

151. He could have easily been misunderstood by Greek-speaking Jews, had he not qualified his statement. Philo, for instance, uses the temporal priority of man's creation to argue that men take precedence in other ways (*Special Laws* 2.25, §124).

152. Roger Nicole, "Biblical Authority & Feminist Aspirations," in *Women, Authority & the Bible,* p. 45; Fee, *1 Corinthians,* p. 523; cf. Gundry, *Women,* p. 69.

153. 1 Esd. 4:14–17, 22, especially 4:17, upon which Paul's language here is probably dependent. Cf. Gen. Rab. 22:2, cited above, and 8:9. Josef Kürzinger, "Frau und Mann nach 1 Kor 11,11f.," *BZ* 22 (2, 1978): 270–75 (followed by Fiorenza, *Memory,* p. 229), reads the Greek of 1 Cor. 11:11 as "different from" rather than "apart from," seeing this as an affirmation of equality; but the point may be the same either way.

154. This would be a natural way for Greeks to read the text. The idea that women and men have different kinds of glory goes back to Aristotle, who cites Sophocles to prove that a woman's glory, but not a man's, is silence (quoted in M. R. Lefkowitz and M. B. Fant, *Women's Life in Greece & Rome* [Baltimore, Md.: Johns Hopkins University, 1982], p. 64, §86).

155. See the extensive discussion of Philo in B. A. Pearson, *The Pneumatikos-Psychikos Terminology in 1 Corinthians,* SBLDS 12 (Missoula, Mont.: Scholars, 1973).

156. 1 Esd. 4:17. Cf. Sent. Sextus 237, an early Christian work: "A self-controlled wife is her husband's glory" (*eukleia*); cf. also a related idea in the Latin Jewish epitaph in Adolf Deissmann, *Light from the*

*Ancient East* (reprint, Grand Rapids: Baker, 1978), p. 448. The familial sharing in glory or dishonor also extended to other relationships: Sir. 3:11.

157. R. A. Batey, *New Testament Nuptial Imagery* (Leiden: Brill, 1971), p. 22; cf. Conzelmann, *1 Corinthians,* p. 183. This usage of "glory" for "reflection" began in the LXX and continued in Greek-speaking Judaism, especially Philo (Conzelmann, *1 Corinthians,* p. 187).

158. Apoc. Moses 29:10; Gen. Rab. 22:2. Eve is more apt to appear in a positive light in earlier than later sources; cf. Tob. 8:6.

159. Sib. Or. 1:23, 33. This may be because she was *from* Adam. Children, of course, bear the images of their parents (Gen. 5:3; 4 Macc. 15:4; Ps-Philo 50:7), which protects against adultery (Ps-Phocyl. 178; t. Sanh. 8:6; Pes. Rab Kah. 11:6; perhaps Wisd. 4:6; cf. the Greco-Roman idea in Chariton *Chaer.* 2.11.2; 3.8.7; Pythagorean treatise, third–second century BCE, in Lefkowitz and Fant, *Women's Life,* p. 104, §107; in Platonic group marriages, Arist. *Pol.* 2.1.13, 1262a). A fourth-century rabbi, purportedly conveying second-century tradition, said that Eve's image was "transmitted to the reigning beauties of each generation," such as Sarah (Gen. Rab. 40:5, trans. 1:329).

160. Plut. *Bride* 14, *Mor.* 139F.

161. Artem. *Oneir.* 1.18.

162. Sifre Num. 11.2.3; Num. Rab. 9:33; cf. also Joseph Bonsirven, *Palestinian Judaism in the Time of Jesus Christ* (New York: Holt, Rinehart & Winston, 1964), p. 61; David Daube, *The New Testament and Rabbinic Judaism* (New York: Arno, 1973), p. 301. The greatest "glory" is to bring honor to God (Ep. Arist. 234; cf. 224).

163. Other possibilities, such as a link with proposed angelic spirits of prophecy in 14:32 (on the idea in 14:32, cf. E. E. Ellis, "Christ and Spirit in 1 Corinthians," in *Christ and Spirit in the New Testament: Studies in Honour of C. F. D. Moule,* ed. Barnabas Lindars and S. S. Smalley [Cambridge: Cambridge University, 1973], pp. 275–76; I take 14:32 as referring to human spirits, which seems to me the only sound way to read it in context, would take us too far afield).

164. 1QSa 2.8–9 (A. Dupont-Sommer, *The Essene Writings from Qumran,* trans. G. Vermes [Gloucester, Mass.: Peter Smith, 1973], p. 108); so also the armies in holy war (1QM 7.4–6; 12.7–9). Cf. 4QCryptic, on astrological physiognomy, cited by P. Alexander on 3 Enoch, *OTP* 1:250. The prohibition of physical abnormalities in OT tradition is paralleled by other sacerdotal customs in antiquity as well (Plut. *R. Q.* 73, *Mor.* 281C; the Doric inscription in Grant, *Religions,* p. 7). Participation in angelic liturgy was a common concept, too, in Jewish sources, as documented by A. T. Lincoln, *Paradise Now and Not Yet,* SNTSMS 43 (Cambridge: Cambridge University, 1981), p. 112.

165. J. A. Fitzmyer, "A Feature of Qumrân Angelology and the Angels of I Cor. XI.10," *NTS* 4 (1, Oct. 1957): 48–58; repr. in idem, *Essays on the Semitic Background of the New Testament,* 2d ed., SBLSBS 5 (Missoula, Mont.: Scholars, 1974), pp. 187–204 (with a 1966 postscript on p. 203); H. J. Cadbury, "A Qumran Parallel to Paul," *HTR* 51 (1, 1958): 1–2. This view is followed by Edwin Yamauchi, "Magic or Miracle? Diseases, Demons & Exorcisms," in *The Miracles of Jesus,* ed.

David Wenham and Craig Blomberg, GP 6 (Sheffield: JSOT, 1986), p. 126; Bruce, *1 and 2 Corinthians,* p. 106; R. P. Spittler, *The Corinthian Correspondence* (Springfield, Mo.: Gospel Publishing, 1976), p. 56, against the view that these are lusting angels. This view actually predates the Qumran discoveries (cf. Robertson and Plummer, *1 Corinthians,* p. 233; perhaps Moffatt, *1 Corinthians,* p. 153).

166. Cf. Wilhelm Bousset, *Kyrios Christos* (Nashville: Abingdon, 1970), p. 257; Héring, *1 Corinthians,* pp. 106–7 (with the qualification that the Corinthians might not have known these ideas; but given their pervasiveness in early Judaism and Christianity, I would guess that they did know of them).

167. The argument of Fee, *1 Corinthians,* p. 521, that lusting angels would require face and not merely head coverings, would falter if, as we have argued above, hair was itself a standard object of lust, and uncovered hair could be interpreted as signifying immodesty or a promiscuous invitation to look lustingly.

168. E.g., Sib. Or. 3:390–91; W. F. Otto, *Dionysus: Myth and Cult* (Bloomington, Ind.: Indiana University, 1965), p. 65; W. K. C. Guthrie, *Orpheus and Greek Religion: A Study of the Orphic Movement,* 2d ed. (New York: Norton, 1966), p. 27. Justin *1 Apol.* 5 interprets these as demons; cf. 1 En. 19:1. The fallen angels of Gen. 6 sounded enough like the fall of the Titans in Greek mythology for Diaspora Judaism to exploit the connection (Sib. Or. 1:307–23; 2:231); on the use of the term "Tartarus" (see below) in 2 Pet. 2:4 in this connection, see R. J. Bauckham, *Jude, 2 Peter,* WBC 50 (Waco, Tex.: Word, 1983), p. 249; cf. J. N. D. Kelly, *A Commentary on the Epistles of Peter and Jude* (reprint, Grand Rapids: Baker, 1981), p. 331 (by now "fully acclimatized in Hellenistic Judaism").

169. In early Jewish and Christian texts, only the rabbis seem to have played down this interpretation, although some seem to have known the tradition (bar. in b. Yoma 67b; Pes. Rab. 34:2); in Justin *Dial.* 79, Trypho, advocating a rabbinic position, holds Justin's view of fallen angels to be "blasphemous" (perhaps Justin's exaggeration). See P. S. Alexander, "The Targumim and Early Exegesis of 'Sons of God' in Genesis 6," *JJS* 23 (1, 1972): 60–71 (starting with R. Simeon ben Yohai, mid-second century CE); cf. M. Delcor, "Le mythe de la chute des anges et de l'origine des géants comme explication du mal dans le monde, dans l'apocalyptique juive. Histoire des traditions," *RHR* 190 (1, 1976): 3–53 (OT, LXX, and rabbinic texts demythologize, in contrast to other literature); R. C. Newman, "The Ancient Exegesis of Genesis 6:2, 4," *GTJ* 5 (1, Spring 1984): 13–36. In some rabbinic traditions male and female demons were descended from sexual acts as early as Adam (Pes. Rab Kah. 5:3; 2 Bar. 56:10–11 suggests that Adam's sin affected the angels willing to fall); the view that Satan rebelled in Adam's time (e.g., V. Adam 12:1; 13:1—16:4), treated below under Eve's deception, is preserved as late as the Qur'an (Sura 2:34); one rabbi suggested that evil spirits accompanied Noah on the ark (Gen. Rab. 31:13). The fall of the sons of God is treated by many of the rabbis (as by many today) euhemeristically—as a tale of ancient heroes (e.g., Gen. Rab. 26:5); for brief treatments of Euhemerism

in antiquity in general, see R. M. Grant, *Gods and the One God,* LEC 1 (Philadelphia: Westminster, 1986), p. 61; J. F. Gardner, *Leadership and the Cult of the Personality* (London: Dent, 1974), p. xxiv; and the excerpt from Euhemerus' *Sacred History* in Grant, *Religions,* pp. 74–76.

170. Philo *On the Giants* 4, §16 (with a significantly unorthodox view on angels!); *On the Unchangeableness of God* 1, §1; 1 En. 6:2; 19:1; 69:5; 106:13–15; Jub. 4:22 (on "polluted"; cf. Jude 6); 5:1; 7:21; 2 Bar. 56:13–15; Test. Sol. 6:3; 2 En. 18:5–6; probably CD 2.18; Gen. Apoc. 2.1; cf. J. A. Fitzmyer, "The Aramaic 'Elect of God' Text from Qumran Cave IV," *CBQ* 27 [4, Oct. 1965]: 369–70; Gaster, *Scriptures,* pp. 522–23 ("The Epochs of Time"); texts in Geza Vermes, *The Dead Sea Scrolls in English,* 2d ed. (New York: Penguin, 1981), pp. 259, 267; H. A. Wolfson, *Philo: Foundations of Religious Philosophy in Judaism, Christianity, and Islam,* 2 vols., 4th rev. ed. (Cambridge: Harvard University, 1968), 1:384–85; D. S. Russell, *The Method and Message of Jewish Apocalyptic,* OTL (Philadelphia: Westminster, 1964), pp. 249ff.; Joseph Klausner, *From Jesus to Paul* (New York: Menorah, 1979), p. 567; Margaret Barker, "Some Reflections upon the Enoch Myth," *JSOT* 15 (1980): 7–29.

171. The language of 2 Pet. 2:4–7 probably reflects Sir. 16:7–8: God did not spare the giants or Lot's city (cf. also Test. Naph. 3:4–5 for the connection); possibly also 1 En. 10:4–6; cf. 10:12–13; 16:1; 22:4; 45:2–3; 84:4; Jub. 5:6, 10 (cf. CD 2.19; using 2 Kgs. 25:7); 10:7–9; Sib. Or. 1:102, 180. If 2 Peter's opponents claimed mystic revelations as support for their views, promethean motifs of fallen angels as secret-revealers in 1 Enoch may be significant; cf. P. D. Hanson, "Rebellion in Heaven, Azazel, and Euhemeristic Heroes in 1 Enoch 6–11," *JBL* 96 (2, June 1977): 226; G. W. E. Nickelsburg, "Apocalyptic Myth in 1 Enoch 6–11," *JBL* 96 (3, Sept. 1977): 405.

172. E.g., Kelly, *Peter,* p. 257; E. M. Sidebottom, *James, Jude, 2 Peter,* NCBC (Grand Rapids: Eerdmans, 1982), p. 86; James Moffatt, *The General Epistles: James, Peter, and Judas,* MNTC (Garden City, N.Y.: Doubleday, Doran, 1928), p. 232; Bo Reicke, *The Epistles of James, Peter, & Jude,* AB 37 (Garden City, N.Y.: Doubleday, 1964), p. 199; Martin McNamara, *Palestinian Judaism and the New Testament,* GNS 4 (Wilmington, Del.: Michael Glazier, 1983), p. 68; Wesley Carr, *Angels and Principalities* (Cambridge: Cambridge University, 1981), p. 132. The background is essentially the same as in 2 Peter, which may apply Jude's language to a more specific problem.

173. The preaching of 3:19 as a proclamation of triumph over the fallen spirits (cf. 3:22); "spirits" is never used to refer to the deceased in the NT without explicit clarification (usually not in other texts either [e.g., Jub. 10:8; Test. Job 27:2], though there are exceptions, e.g., 1 En. 22:3, 5). See R. T. France, "Exegesis in Practice: Two Examples," in *New Testament Interpretation: Essays on Principles and Methods,* ed. I. H. Marshall (Grand Rapids: Eerdmans, 1977), pp. 264–78; Ladd, *Theology,* p. 601; idem, *The Last Things* (Grand Rapids: Eerdmans, 1978), p. 38; Kelly, *Peter,* p. 154; E. G. Selwyn, *The First Epistle of St. Peter,* 2d ed. (London: Macmillan, 1947), pp. 353–54; Ernest Best, *1 Peter,* NCBC

(Grand Rapids: Eerdmans, 1982), pp. 142–43; most thoroughly, W. J. Dalton, *Christ's Proclamation to the Spirits: A Study of 1 Peter 3:18–4:6,* AnBib 23 (Rome: Pontifical Biblical Institute, 1965); idem, "The Interpretation of 1 Peter 3,19 and 4,6: Light from 2 Peter," *Bib* 60 (4, 1979): 547–55; idem, "Christ's Victory over the Devil and the Evil Spirits," *BiTod* 1 (18, 1965): 1195–1200; idem, "Proclamatio Christi spiritibus facta: inquisitio in textum ex Prima Epistola S. Petri 3,18–4,6," *VerbDom* 42 (5, 1964): 225–40 (NTA 9:372) (with too much emphasis on an Enoch "typology"—though Rendel Harris went so far as to emend the text, followed in Moffatt, *Epistles,* p. 141). The connection between the fallen angels and the flood (due to their proximity in Gen. 6) appears often in the texts we have cited above, e.g., Jub. 7:21; Test. Naph. 3:5. Others hold that this refers to Christ's preaching through Noah in Noah's day (J. S. Feinberg, "1 Peter 3:18–20, Ancient Mythology, and the Intermediate State," *WTJ* 48 [2, Fall 1986]: 303–36; Wayne Grudem, "Christ Preaching Through Noah: 1 Peter 3:19–20 in the Light of Dominant Themes in Jewish Literature," *TJ* 7 (2, Fall 1986): 3–31), or Christ's preaching to the dead before his resurrection (C. E. B. Cranfield, "The Interpretation of I Peter iii.19 and iv.6," *ExpT* 69 [12, 1958]: 369–72; Reicke, *Epistles,* p. 109, sees these *and* the fallen angels of Gen. 6!), but this seems to ignore the clear chiasmus in 3:16—4:4, paralleling the spirits of 3:19 and the heavenly rulers of 3:22 (4:6 functions as a conclusion recalling 3:18, not 3:19). Descents to the underworld are frequent in ancient Near Eastern and Greek texts, and some later Jewish and Christian apocalypses (e.g., Vision of Ezra).

174. 1 En. 16:2; 2 Bar. 56:14 (the reason for and time of expulsion is quite different in Rev. 12:4); cf. 1 En. 69:28. Ps-Philo 60:3 (most MSS) can use the Greek language of Tartarus as the rightful abode of demons; cf. Test. Sol. 6:3; for people, Sib. Or. 1:101 (= Gehenna, 1:103); 2:291, 302 (if not a Christian interpolation).

175. Test. Reub. 5:6 (*OTP* 1:784). This may be modeled on the basically magical fertility practice of Gen. 30:37–43, which God seems to have blessed only because it was Jacob (31:8–13). I am not as persuaded as some that the bulk of the Testaments of the Twelve Patriarchs is pre-Christian with only Christian interpolations, but I cite this passage because it is representative of data appearing in other texts.

176. Test. Sol. ch. 4, perhaps 5:3. Text 1:12–13 in C. D. Isbell, *Corpus of the Aramaic Incantation Bowls,* SBLDS 17 (Missoula, Mont.: Scholars, 1975), p. 18, speaks of demons "who appear . . . to men in the likeness of women and to women in the likeness of men." According to 1 En. 106:5–6 and Gen. Apoc. 2.15–16 (first thought a "Lamech Apocalypse"), Lamech initially thought that Noah was descended from angels because he was so extraordinary (rabbinic tradition transfers most extraordinary birth material to Moses). Apocryphal rabbinic stories, such as Satan disguised as a woman tempting R. Akiba, may be related to such traditions.

177. Tob. 6:14.

178. Test. Sol. 2:4; Ab. R. Nathan 37 A; Gen. Rab. 8:11; 14:3; cf. Jub. 10:5; Apoc. Abr. 14:6 (first–second century CE or later); also

b. Hag. 16a, cited in W. M. Alexander, *Demonic Possession in the New Testament: Its Historical, Medical, and Theological Aspects* (Edinburgh: T. & T. Clark, 1902), p. 28. Heavenly angels did not procreate (1 En. 15:6–7; contrast possibly 69:5, from the later Similitudes). In some traditions, humans would become like angels in the world to come (Matt. 22:30; cf. 2 Bar. 51:10, not specifically referring to marriage) and have no passion (b. B. B. 58a; Sib. Or. 2:328 is probably a Christian interpolation based on Matt. 22:30) or perhaps even no gender (Brian McNeil, "Asexuality and the Apocalypse of Zosimus," *HeyJ* 22 [2, 1981]: 172–73, though I am not at all persuaded this is non-Christian or non-Gnostic Judaism). The view that the heavenly angels do not eat is also attested in Jewish tradition (Test. Abr. 4, 6 A; Ab. R. Nathan 1 A; Gen. Rab. 48:11, 14; Exod. Rab. 32:4; Lev. Rab. 34:8; cf. D. Goodman, "Do Angels Eat?" *JJS* 37 [2, 1986]: 160–75).

179. E.g., Boldrey, *Chauvinist,* p. 41.

180. G. B. Caird, *Principalities and Powers* (Oxford: Oxford University, 1956), pp. 17–18, noted by D. E. H. Whitely, *The Theology of St. Paul* (Oxford: Basil Blackwell, 1964), p. 26; Bruce, *1 and 2 Corinthians,* p. 106 (though still reading these in the light of the Qumran evidence for angels gathered for worship). It is commonly argued that Paul demythologized these powers, although retaining their demonic force; e.g., F. F. Bruce, *Paul: Apostle of the Heart Set Free* (Grand Rapids: Eerdmans, 1977), p. 422; idem, *Message,* p. 39; idem, "Myth and History," in *History, Criticism and Faith,* ed. Colin Brown (Downers Grove, Ill.: InterVarsity, 1976), p. 89.

181. With F. F. Bruce, "Paul and 'The Powers That Be,' " *BJRL* 66 (2, Spring 1984): 78–96; J. L. C. Abineno, "The State, According to Romans Thirteen," *SEAJT* 14 (1, 1972): 23–27; and others, against Oscar Cullmann, *The State in the New Testament* (New York: Scribner's, 1956), pp. 100, 108; idem, *Christ and Time,* trans. Floyd V. Filson (Philadelphia: Westminster, 1950), p. 194.

182. E.g., Plut. *Fort. Rom.* 11, *Mor.* 324B, speaks of the *daimōn,* or guardian spirit, of Rome. Cf. Harold Mattingly, *Christianity in the Roman Empire* (New York: Norton, 1967), p. 19. The concept appears frequently as a pagan one (occasionally adapted by Israel) in the OT, and the picture of God's heavenly court (possibly demythologizing the 70 gods in El's Canaanite pantheon) may suggest that the idea of guardian angels of the nations predates Daniel and LXX Deuteronomy.

183. Philo speaks of "powers" as mediatorial manifestations of God, similar to Stoic (Diog. Laert. *Lives* 7.1.147) or *later* Platonic thought (C. G. Rutenber, "The Doctrine of the Imitation of God in Plato" [Ph.D. diss., University of Pennsylvania, 1946], p. 17; cf. Wolfson, *Philo,* 1:217–26; John Dillon, *The Middle Platonists: 80 B.C. to A.D. 220* [Ithaca, N.Y.: Cornell University, 1977], p. 161); e.g., *On the Unchangeableness of God* 109–10; *On the Confusion of Tongues* 136ff.; 171, 174–75; *Who is the Heir?* 170; *On Flight and Finding* 69; *Special Laws* 1.47, 209; 4.187; *Questions and Answers on Genesis* 20; *Questions and Answers on Exodus* 18, 45, 65, 68. They seem to vacillate between being attributes and being personal beings. In Jewish mysticism, see G. G. Scholem, *Jewish*

*Gnosticism, Merkabah Mysticism, and Talmudic Tradition* (New York: Jewish Theological Seminary, 1965), p. 33.

184. Mek. Shir. 2:112ff.; b. Ber. 16b–17a; Yoma 77a; Exod. Rab. 32:3; Pes. Rab. 17:4; 3 En. 29:1; 30:1–2.

185. Jub. 15:21–32; 35:17; 49:2–4; 1QM 17.7–8 (Michael's rulership elevated "among the gods" and Israel among all flesh; the verb governs both clauses); 17.5–6; 14.15–16 (gods overthrown in context of evil spirits being smitten); 15.13–14 (wicked spirits = hero/warrior gods); Test. Sol. 6:4; 8:10; see P. J. Kobelski, "Melchizedek and Melchiresa: The Heavenly Prince of Light and the Prince of Darkness in the Qumran Literature" (Ph.D. diss., Fordham University, 1978), p. 123. The later rabbis often described their specific hostility toward Israel (3 En. 26:12; Sifre Deut. 315.2.1; Gen. Rab. 77:3, 78:3 [keeping in mind that Edom often stood for Rome]; Exod. Rab. 21:5; Lev. Rab. 21:4; Deut. Rab. 1:22–23; Song Rab. 2:1, §3; 8:8, §1) and judgment (e.g., Pes. Rab Kah. 4:9; 27:2; Song Rab. 8:14, §1).

186. 1 En. 40:9 (reading with Knibb against Isaacs); 61:10 (both references from the later Similitudes); 2 En. 20:1 (longer version); Test. Levi 3:8; Test. Job 49:2; Asc. Isa. 1:3; 2:2 (but 1:4 sounds suspiciously Christianized); 3 Bar. 12:3; in early Gnostic texts, e.g., Apoc. Adam 1:4; Hypostasis of the Archons. Angels could also be designated with terms of military rank, especially Michael as Archistrategos (e.g., Test. Abr. 14 A). J. Y. Lee, "Interpreting the Demonic Powers in Pauline Thought," *NovT* 12 (1, 1970): 54–69, thinks Paul derives these terms from Jewish apocalyptic tradition, but others from gnosticizing traditions; Pierre Benoit, "Pauline Angelology and Demonology. Reflexions on the Designations of the Heavenly Powers and on the Origin of Angelic Evil According to Paul," *RSB* 3 (1, 1983): 1–18, thinks he borrowed the language but did not deal with how evil angels became evil. Carr, *Angels,* p. 40, questions whether any of the language is clearly pre-Pauline, the best possibility being in 1 En. 61:10—from the Similitudes of Enoch, the date of which is uncertain.

187. Cf. C. C. Caragounis, *The Ephesian Mysterion: Meaning and Content,* CBNTS 8 (Lund: Gleerup, 1977), pp. 157–61; Cullmann, *State,* p. 68. For the LXX of Deuteronomy, see Russell, *Apocalyptic,* pp. 244–49; A. S. Peake, "Colossians," in *The Expositor's Greek Testament,* ed. W. R. Nicoll (Grand Rapids: Eerdmans, 1979), 3:479; C. H. Dodd, *The Bible and the Greeks* (London: Hodder & Stoughton, 1935), pp. 18–19.

188. Lit., "it is a dishonor to him . . . glory to her"; I have sought a more idiomatic rendering. It might be even more idiomatic English to translate "it would embarrass him," but it is unlikely that most long-haired men back then were embarrassed by their long hair; philosophers wore it as a badge of honor, "barbarians" as a matter of course. The perspective of "dishonor" is from the standpoint of Greco-Roman society in the time of Paul; see below.

189. Paul plays on "glory" in contrast to dishonor elsewhere as well (15:43; 2 Cor. 6:8); in 1 Cor. 15:43, as here, "glory" alludes to his use of the same phrase not long before this in his discussion.

190. Paul's "divine passive" no doubt means, "by God."

191. The word used here for covering, in fact, usually denotes pinned-up hair, which was commonly how long hair was publicly worn; see Thompson, "Hairstyles," p. 112.

192. See Diog. Laert. *Lives* 7.1.88–89, 148–49; e.g., Epict. *Disc.* 1.19.7; Sen. *Ben.* 5.8.2, 5; 7.19.5; *Ep. Lucil.* 30:11; Marc. Aur. *Med.* 1.9.1, 17.5; 2.9, 11, 12, 16, 17; 3.1, 2.2, 9, 12; 4.1, 5, 9; etc. One can virtually flip through pages of Epictetus or Seneca at random and find it throughout.

193. Meeks, *World,* pp. 58–59. Seneca (*Dial.* 7.13.1) tries to harmonize the Stoic and original Epicurean positions on this matter.

194. Meeks, *World,* p. 60. One finds it often enough in Aristotle (e.g., *Pol.* 1.1.4, 1252b; 1.1.8–9, 1252b–52a; 7.15.11, 1337a), who also cites similar arguments made by others with whom he disagrees (*Pol.* 1.2.3, 1253b).

195. E.g., Orphic Hymn 10 (admittedly a hymn to *physiō,* not an argument); Juv. *Sat.* 10.300–301; 13.239; 14.31, 321; Hor. *Poet.* 108, 408; *Sat.* 1.1.50–51, 87; 2.111; 3.35–36; 5.102; 6.93; 10.12–14. I have not tried to draw a distinction here between the semantic ranges of the Greek *physis* and Latin *natura*; the senses are roughly equivalent, and the specific semantic range varies from one author to another. The one philosophical group which thoroughly subordinated nature to culture-based custom (the Skeptics; cf. Sext. Emp. *Out. Pyrr.* 3.220) is addressed in Paul's next argument.

196. E.g., Varro *Lat. Lang.* 5.5.31 ("all *natura* is divided into sky and earth" [LCL]); Sen. *Clem.* 1.9.1–2; Epict. *Disc.* 1.16.4 (on animals); Cic. *Par. Stoic.* 14; *Leg.* 1.5.16, 1.8.25 (the human mind); *Tusc. Disp.* 1.14.31 (nature proves the soul's immortality). Some of Epictetus' nature examples of animal practices show that one did not have to be biologically accurate to convince most hearers, who would not have known the difference anyway (e.g., *Disc.* 4.11.1–2).

197. Cic. *Nat. Deor.* 2.32.81; *Offic.* 1.33.120; *Re Publ.* 3.28.40; Epict. *Disc.* 1.17; Marc. Aur. *Med.* 2.17; Diogenes 25, to Hippon (*CynEp,* pp. 116–17). For a more detailed explanation, emphasizing the teleological character of nature, see Gilbert Murray, *The Stoic Philosophy* (New York: Putnam's, 1915), pp. 37–40; and especially A. A. Long, *Hellenistic Philosophy: Stoics, Epicureans, Sceptics* (New York: Scribner's, 1974), p. 148 (or more generally, pp. 147–78).

198. E.g., Diogenes 21, to Amynander (*CynEp,* pp. 114–15).

199. E.g., *Rhet. ad Herenn.* 3.22.35.

200. E.g., Sen. *Dial.* 6.7.3; 8.5.2; 9.2.11. Nearly all the examples above include ethical instruction. Contrast perhaps Hor. *Sat.* 1.3.113–17.

201. E.g., Zeno in Diog. Laert. *Lives* 7.1.87; Cicero *Tusc. Disp.* 5.28.82; Epict. *Disc.* 1.1.17; 1.2.34; 1.4.14, 29; 1.6.15, 20; 1.12.17, 19; 1.26.2; Sen. *Dial.* 1.4.8, 15; 6.7.1; 7.13.1; 8.5.1, 8. Marc. Aur. *Med.* 2.17 declares that "in the way of Nature there can be no evil" (LCL). For writers like Seneca, nature could be identified with God (*Ben.* 4.7.1; 8.1–3). Cf. Gerard Watson, "The Natural Law and Stoicism," in *Problems in Stoicism,* ed. A. A. Long (London: University of London, 1971), p. 233.

202. Epict. *Disc.* 4.11.9–18.

203. Plut. *Educ.* 5, *Mor.* 3C.

204. This is self-evidently true even though some philosophers, like the writer of Crates 28, to Hipparchia (*CynEp,* pp. 78–79), could argue that "Women are not by nature [*ephysan*] worse than men." Because "nature" could also mean "passion," an expression of human nature (probably Ach. Tat. *Clit.* 1.11.3 [this could be "Necessity" instead]; Test. Reub. 3:3; contrast Diogenes 47, to Zeno [*CynEp,* pp. 178–79]), 1 Cor. 11:14 could mean: the passion that makes long-haired women attractive warns you not to show off hair in church. But this interpretation requires a narrow reading of "nature," which is not demanded or implied by the context.

205. Cic. *Invent.* 1.24.34–35.

206. Epict. *Disc.* 1.16.10 (LCL).

207. Ibid., 1.16.14 (LCL).

208. Effeminate men make themselves "worse" than nature made them, according to Diogenes the Cynic in Diog. Laert. *Lives* 6.2.65. The Skeptic Sextus Empiricus notes that this is the prevailing opinion, but cites the example of the Amazons to prove that the opinion is not universally held (*Out. Pyrr.* 3.217).

209. Especially Jewish writers who confronted it in the Diaspora; Test. Naph. 3:4–5; Ps-Phocyl. 190. Cf. the fragment of Musonius Rufus in P. W. Van Der Horst, "Musonius Rufus and the NT," *NovT* 16 (4, Oct. 1974): 309. Artem. *Oneir.* 1.80 argues this for lesbian intercourse, but possibly means that it is difficult to accomplish; he does not believe that such dreams are inauspicious in all cases. A number of Roman writers, like Paul and all ancient Jewish sources, did not look favorably on homosexual practices, but our discussion here is only how that relates to the issue of "nature."

210. Bruce, *1 and 2 Corinthians,* pp. 107–8.

211. Meeks, *Urban Christians,* p. 125, noting that "Paul was not the first or the last moralist to conflate the two." Cf. Ramsay, *Cities of Paul,* pp. 202, 204–5, 233, who thinks that Paul assumes the oriental custom common to Tarsus but unusual in Corinth.

212. The idea might be arguable from *Rhet. ad Herenn.* 3.3.4; Cic. *Offic.* 3.6.30. Sen. *Dial.* 5.27.3 might have been helpful, except he does not use the term "natura."

213. Cic. *Invent.* 1.1.2; *Oratore* 2.21.89; *Rhet. ad Herenn.* 3.7.14, 3.16.28; Sen. *Dial.* 9.15.6; Epict. *Disc.* 1.11.5 with 1.10.6.

214. M. Cary and T. J. Haarhoff, *Life and Thought in the Greek and Roman World,* 4th ed. (London: Methuen, 1946), p. 99; Thompson, "Hairstyles," p. 104. Grown women's hair was generally long (ibid., p. 112); among the well-to-do, it was normally done up in coiffures (Cary and Haarhoff, *Life,* p. 99) (which were not counted as head coverings themselves; see above).

215. So also Robertson and Plummer, *1 Corinthians,* p. 236. Cf. C. R. Hallpike's essay, "Social Hair" (1969), as summarized by the editors in *Reader in Comparative Religion: An Anthropological Approach,* ed. W. A. Lessa and E. Z. Vogt, 4th ed. (New York: Harper & Row, 1979), p. 99, which argues that long hair on men transculturally stands for being outside societal norms.

216. Artem. *Oneir.* 1.18 (trans., p. 26); cf. 1.30 (beard). Long hair in a dream could be a good sign for them.

217. Sext. Emp. *Out. Pyrr.* 1.155; 3.204, claims that Plato rejected men's wearing feminine clothes, but Aristippus and, in Sextus' view, the Persians, accepted it.

218. Thompson, "Hairstyles," p. 104.

219. Arist. *Rhet.* 1.9.26, 1367a; Charillus 6 in Plut. *SSpart., Mor.* 232D.

220. Pomeroy, *Goddesses,* pp. 37–38.

221. Lucian *Alexander the False Prophet* 13.

222. Sext. Emp. *Out. Pyrr.* 3.217 speaks of Cybele's approval of effeminate men immediately after noting Amazonian sex reversals.

223. Petr. *Sat.* 63, 70, may imply this.

224. Apul. *Metam.* 7.6. Héring, *1 Corinthians,* p. 110, notes that "a man who lets his hair grow would pass (and actually did pass) as effeminate."

225. Epict. *Disc.* 3.1.27–28 (LCL). He is not, of course, speaking of hair on the top of one's head, but presumably the beard or (maybe more likely) the rest of the body.

226. Epict. *Disc.* 3.1.31.

227. Epict. *Disc.* 3.1.34.

228. Zeno in Diog. Laert. *Lives* 7.1.33.

229. Epimenides in Diog. Laert. *Lives* 1.109; Epicurus in Epict. *Disc.* 2.23.21 (beard); Cynics (Malherbe, *Exhortation,* p. 35); philosophers in general (Epict. *Disc.* 4.8.12; Artem. *Oneir.* 1.30 [beards]; Plut. *Isis* 3, *Mor.* 352C [beards]).

230. E.g., Diogenes the Cynic, in Diog. Laert. *Lives* 6.2.46 (LCL), who demanded that his interlocutor lift his robe to prove his gender.

231. Ps-Phocyl. 210–12 (*OTP* 2:581). *OTP* 2:581, n. b: "A man's wearing long hair was often considered as a sign of effemination, e.g. Philo, *Spec. Leg.* 3.37."

232. Num. 6; e.g., Sifre Num. 25.

233. Num. Rab. 10:10. Conversely, certain kinds of hair trimming were associated with paganism; see Goodman, *State and Society,* p. 49.

234. Moffatt, *1 Corinthians,* p. 154, "nature being regarded as supplying the norm even for such attire."

235. Meeks, *World,* p. 19, observes that Aristotle's ad hominem arguments appeal to "common experience, where 'common' means 'common to property-owning Athenian citizens.' " Fee, *1 Corinthians,* p. 530, notes that Paul elsewhere appeals to the practice of other churches (4:17; 7:17); the Corinthians seem to be acting as if they were independent from the other churches (cf. 14:33).

236. Quint. 1.5.72; 3.4.12 (*auctores plurimos*); cf. 5.11.36–37. The conduct of one's ancestors could also be used to extract principles (e.g., Isoc. *Panathenaicus* 164, *Or.* 12).

237. Isoc. *Demon.* 50, *Or.* 1 (LCL).

238. Theon *Progym.* 4.140–44. Cf. Mus. Ruf. *fr.* 12 (*On Sexual Indulgence*, in Malherbe, *Exhortation,* p. 154), who concludes his argument: "Everyone knows that."

239. E.g., b. Taan. 30b (local); p. R. H. 4:6, §1 (local); Bez. 3:6, §3d.

240. Malherbe, *Exhortation,* p. 33. The point is that custom varies from one culture to another (e.g., Sext. Emp. *Out. Pyrr.* 3.198).

241. See especially Liefeld, "Women," pp. 146–47; cf. the helpful points in G. Pella, "Voile et soumission? Essai d'interprétation de deux textes pauliniens concernants le statut de l'homme et de la femme," *Hokhma* 30 (1985): 3–20 (I know this article only through NTA 30:305).

# 2

# Questions about Questions—1 Corinthians 14:34–35

> For God is not the source of disturbances, but of peace, as in all the churches of the saints.[1] Let women remain silent in the churches, for it is not permitted for them to speak; rather let them remain submitted, just as the Law also says. And if they want to learn anything, let them ask their own husbands at home, for it is a shameful[2] matter for a woman to speak in church. Or did the word of God issue from you? Or has it come to you alone? (1 Cor. 14:33–36).

This chapter will be one of the shortest ones in this book, since it deals with the briefest passage we will cover: 1 Corinthians 14:34–35. But due to the overlap of its cultural context with the subject of our next chapter (on 1 Tim. 2:9–15), we will introduce here some of the background that will be important for both chapters.

After we have surveyed several problems for interpretation and some of the most significant interpretations of this passage, we will turn to what seems to be the most likely interpretation of 1 Corinthians 14:34–35: Paul was addressing relatively uneducated women who were disrupting the service with irrelevant questions. The immediate remedy for this situation was for them to stop asking such questions; the long-term solution was to educate them.

## PROBLEMS FOR INTERPRETATION

Paul's words in this passage have been interpreted and applied in many different ways mainly because his words, taken by themselves, can lend themselves to this bewildering array of interpretations. The following survey of problems is meant to show the need for an objective, contextual interpretation.

At first view, 1 Corinthians 14:34–35 would appear more restrictive toward women than nearly any church is today. Paul's language, if taken to mean all that it can mean, forbids *all* speaking in church and does not explicitly limit this to public exposition of Scripture. It appears that even a woman's leaning over to whisper a question to her husband is considered out of order. This goes even beyond the position required by most of today's strictest interpreters of the passage,[3] but if we are going to take the text to mean all that it can without regard to its specific situation, this is how we must read it. Is this passage as restrictive as it appears, or does the situation implied in the text narrow down the restriction it actually addresses?

Certain helpful points for answering that question can be noted simply from the context. Paul is carrying on the preceding argument concerning "order" in the use of spiritual gifts in the church service, and he inserts here a brief digression related to order: the women must stop disrupting the service.[4] This digression naturally suggests that women were disrupting the service.

But the probability that women were disrupting the church services in Corinth, and needed to stop, raises another question. Should we view the disruptiveness of women as a problem specific to the Corinthian church, or as a problem universal to all churches? (If the text addresses a specific situation yet is to be applied to all situations, the Corinthian situation must be universal.) And is Paul's solution particular to the church in Corinth, or could he have written it to any church in any period?

If Paul addresses all churches in all societies, not only his assessment of the problem but also his solution grates on modern ears. It would sound insulting enough to women to suggest that they are consistently disruptive in church; but the restrictions that Paul seems to impose in response sound even more offensive. Is Paul actually demanding the silence of all women, across the board, a silence so restrictive that wives could not even ask their husbands what was happening during the church service? Is such silence a necessary way to express their submission (14:34)? And does "submission" relate only to their husbands (cf. 14:35) or is it a general submissiveness to all church leaders (cf. 16:16)?

Compounding this apparent offense, if we ignore the situation and simply read the passage for all it could mean, it could also imply that Paul wants wives to learn only from their husbands at home, rather than being allowed to learn anything in the church services ("if they want to learn *anything*, let them ask their own husbands at home," 14:35). But this proposal, however supportable by the words of the text taken at face value, would unfairly ignore the context. If Paul did not want the women to learn in church, then when he suggests that "all" may "learn" from the prophecies (14:31; cf. v. 6), he means by "all" only the men, without bothering to point this out.

More likely, Paul could be saying, "If you can't learn it in church except *the way you're doing it,* you need to ask your husbands at home." In this case, he is not saying, "Let women learn only from their husbands at home, and not in the church services"; he is saying, "Don't learn so *loudly* in church!" He uses the same construction in 11:34: "If anyone is hungry, let him eat at home, lest you come together for judgment." In 11:34, Paul does not there mean that no one should eat at the Lord's Supper, or that it is wrong to be hungry when one gathers in church; his point is that it is better to eat at home than to disrupt the Christian community by the *way* one eats at church. Since he uses the same construction here, we may guess that his argument is roughly the same: the way women are trying to learn, rather than the learning itself, is problematic.

But how are these women disturbing the Corinthian worship services? The context is the best place to begin looking for clues. Women are not the only ones on whom Paul enjoins silence under certain circumstances. "Silence" is also preferred to using the gifts out of order (1 Cor. 14:28–29); if no interpreter were available, tongues-speakers were to pray in tongues only to themselves,[5] and prophets were to restrict their speech voluntarily if another arose with a message from God. In the context, "silence" thus relates to keeping the church service orderly. The context need not mean that Paul is demanding women's silence only with regard to spiritual gifts; Paul may be commenting on another kind of silence equally necessary to preserve order in the congregation. As we shall see below, it is unlikely that he is restricting women's participation in spiritual gifts at all, given the fact that he permits the activity in 11:4–5.[6] What is clear from the context is just that restricting one's own speech is sometimes necessary to preserve congregational order.

But once we have decided that the women are causing disturbances by their lack of appropriate silence, we still must ask what kind of disruptive speech Paul had in view when he dictated this passage. We shall argue in this chapter, in agreement with some other writers, that Paul does not address the preceding context of spiritual gifts here, but the immediate context of questions (14:35). Paul does not need to state this plainly at the beginning of the passage because both he and the Corinthians are familiar with the situation; we, however, have to infer it from clues in the text. We shall look for these clues and also try to show the specific cultural setting in which women's questions in the church service were likely to have been a problem.

No one takes this passage today to mean all that it could. Everyone allows that the text is somewhat more specific than its general injunction for all women always to be silent in church. Indeed, Paul's earlier permission to women to pray and prophesy publicly in church allows no way around it (11:5). The issue, then, is just what Paul specifically means here. Those who insist that this passage prohibits women from teaching must appeal to more than his general injunction to silence here; they must show that Paul had teaching specifically in mind. Unfortunately for their position, nothing in the context or situation indicates that the women were teaching.

Since Paul wrote this directive specifically to the Corinthians, we may assume that the problem was specific to Corinth and perhaps a few other cities like it.[7] After all, his other instructions in this chapter address specific abuses of the gifts at Corinth; had they obtained generally, we can be sure that Paul would have already given these regulations during his extended stay with them (Acts 18:11, 18).[8]

Whether the problem was specific to the Corinthian church because only they allowed women to speak at all, or because only they had a problem with women speaking in a certain way, must be decided by careful study of the text.

We shall argue below that Paul's solution, like the Corinthians' problem, is appropriate to a specific cultural context, and that it thus does not apply to every conceivable situation we face today. This is not to question the universal relevance of Paul's teaching; it is to say that we have to catch Paul's *real point* in addressing this situation before we try to apply his point to very different situations.

## INTERPRETATIONS

### Is 1 Corinthians 14:34–35 Paul's Passage After All?

Since 1 Corinthians 11:4–5 allows women to pray and to prophesy in church as long as their heads are covered, and since 14:34–35 sounds like it "silences" women and digresses briefly from its context, this passage has often been regarded as an addition to chapter 14 by a later editor rather than a teaching by Paul himself.[9]

A number of scholars hold this view, including Wayne Meeks,[10] Hans Conzelmann,[11] Robin Scroggs,[12] F. F. Bruce,[13] and the expert evangelical text critic Gordon Fee.[14] Although several of these scholars are among the world's best text critics, it seems to me that the textual evidence for this position is very weak.

A few manuscripts, mainly later Western texts with a narrow geographical distribution, admittedly relocate these verses, probably because they do not seem to fit their immediate context very well.[15] But there is no real evidence for omitting them entirely; those who hold them to be later additions must argue that they occurred too early in the text's history to leave evidence,[16] i.e., before subsequent manuscripts were copied from the original.

This idea of an early accidental addition of several verses is not easy to defend. It is not certain that Paul intended his letters to the Corinthians to be published and circulated,[17] but since Clement of Rome is familiar with 1 Corinthians in the 90s,[18] it is likely that 1 and 2 Corinthians had been in circulation for some years by his time. Unless only the wrongly edited text happened to survive the process of circulation, then a scribe added several verses to this Pauline letter, purporting to be instructions to the Corinthian church, when this document was still being read in its original form in Corinth. This proposal does not suggest a mere scribal mistake, but a deliberate change of the sort that ought to have been extremely rare in the earliest stage of the manuscript tradition.[19]

The main evidence adduced to prove that this is a later addition is not so much textual as contextual—the awkward way it fits its context. But such evidence is not very convincing; Paul frequently digressed, and digressions were a normal part of ancient writing.[20] Nor need we read this passage as a direct contradiction to 11:4–5; it is actually addressing a more specific issue than

11:4–5, as we shall observe below. To regard this as an addition on such slender evidence would lead us back to the scissors-and-paste approach so common in source criticism early in this century. Digressions and parenthetical notes can too easily become "interpolations" by "later editors." (I am grateful that my own works are not read so carefully, or I might not be thought the author of everything in my own books!)

Although I think that this passage is Pauline, I concede that some text critics far more capable than myself believe that it is a non-Pauline addition. I can only say that, if they are right, we may conclude quickly that Paul does not oppose women speaking in church. Because if Paul did not write it, this text clearly supplies no evidence for his position. I continue with this chapter, however, in the event that many of my readers, like myself, believe that these words are part of Paul's original letter to the Corinthians and must be understood in that context.

*A Refuted Quotation?*

Because Paul seems to cite and then to qualify or refute Corinthian positions earlier in his letter (e.g., 6:12–14; 7:1–5),[21] it has naturally been proposed that he is following the same procedure here. In other words, on this view Paul is citing the Corinthian position in 14:34–35 and then refuting it in v. 36.[22] This would mean that Paul actually disagrees with the apparently chauvinistic view reported in 14:34–35.

Paul's use of the Greek particle ἢ (*ē*) in verse 36 has led some scholars to see a disjunction in thought in verse 36; they point to the fact that Paul elsewhere begins with this particle when he wishes to challenge the Corinthian Christians' behavior. In 11:20–21, for instance, he states the situation in Corinth and then goes on to challenge their behavior in 11:22.[23] Some have further appealed to the masculine form of "alone" in verse 36 to suggest that Paul is reproving men in the congregation for trying to keep the place of power for themselves.[24] But Liefeld is right when he responds: "What Paul negates by his use of the adversative Greek particle ἢ is not the command in verses 34–35 but the assumed disobedience of it, just as in the structurally similar passage 6:18–19."[25] Nor does the masculine form help the case; masculine forms are used in Greek whenever a group includes even one male, so Paul's use of the masculine form of "alone" may refer as easily to the whole congregation as to the men in particular.[26]

What ultimately leaves this explanation most unconvincing is that Paul's citations of the Corinthian positions elsewhere are at least partly affirmed, though seriously qualified.[27] Ancient literature includes many cases of a writer or speaker correcting an imaginary interlocutor, but where Paul is completely correcting such a statement, as in Romans, he introduces the objection with a rhetorical question or another kind of rhetorical device (e.g., Rom. 2:3–4, 21–23; 3:1)[28] and often answers with "May it never be!" (e.g., Rom. 3:4).[29] The evidence that Paul is here correcting a Corinthian position seems strongly outweighed by the evidence that he is not. The burden of proof remains on those who argue that 1 Corinthians 14:34–35 do not reflect Paul's own position.

### *Segregated Church Services?*

Some readers have thought that Paul did not want women asking questions because they would have noisily disrupted the service even to question their husbands. These readers propose that husbands and wives met in separate parts of ancient synagogues,[30] and that the Corinthian church had carried this practice of gender segregation over into its own worship services. Although these scholars concede that the church normally met in homes, they suggest that the practice could have carried over from the Corinthian Christians' earliest meetings in the synagogue (Acts 18:4–8).

But the evidence for this practice is problematic at best. Although the temple in Paul's day did not allow women into the court of Israel,[31] there is no clear architectural segregation in the average local *synagogue*.[32] The custom of gender segregation in the synagogue seems to have first arisen in the Middle Ages, and earlier rabbinic literature presupposes that men and women met together there.[33] Most ancient sites provide no clear indication of galleries, and if they did it would still not be clear that these were reserved for women.[34] Still more problematic is the absence of architectural evidence that would allow any gender segregation in the homes; very unnatural dividers would have had to have been constructed.

We may therefore safely dismiss this suggestion, unless new evidence on behalf of the segregation of women in Diaspora synagogues (and architectural features that would permit it in Corinthian house churches!) is forthcoming.

*Abuse of Gifts of the Spirit?*

As noted in our introduction to the various interpretations of 14:34–35, some writers have argued that Paul is disturbed by how some women were using certain spiritual gifts. His call for silence could thus be a prohibition of women's participation in prophecy or tongues or both. This suggestion has the merit of dealing with the context of the whole chapter, which *does* deal with abuses of gifts of the Spirit.

The main weakness of this argument, however, is that Paul permits women to pray and prophesy publicly in chapter 11, and in this context appropriate public prayer would include praying in tongues if it is accompanied by an interpretation. The context of spiritual gifts in chapter 14 does not require us to suppose that Paul's words to women address their use of such gifts; the specific context of church order is sufficient reason for Paul to digress.

Then again, it is possible that the women could be using spiritual gifts improperly, and that Paul seeks merely to *regulate*, not terminate, their speech. A number of scholars have pointed out that women in the Dionysus cult were given to frenzied shouting and have suggested that this sort of raving may have carried over into the worship of Corinthian Christian women.[35]

This view cannot be rejected as impossible, but it has several weaknesses. The most obvious is that Paul enjoins silence and does not specify to what *extent* he might be regulating women's participation in the gifts. Another obvious objection is that Paul does not avail himself of the opportunity to condemn any associations with pagan cultic behavior their activity might have displayed (contrast 12:2). But other objections may also be raised against reading this passage in light of women's activity in the Dionysus cult.

It is true that women found cultic liberation[36] in the worship of Dionysus[37] and several other patron deities,[38] and that upper-class Roman men found such activities offensive.[39] It is not true that most of these cults were in actual practice limited to—or even predominantly composed of—women.[40] In the cult of Isis, a special protectress of women,[41] less than half the participants at Rome and Athens were women, and considerably smaller percentages obtained elsewhere.[42] Nor would ecstatic raving have characterized only women.[43] In the cult of Dionysus, which was no longer as prominent as it had been in an earlier period,[44] frenzied women called Maenads featured prominently;[45] but in the cult of the Asian mother-goddess Cybele, the main ecstatics were her castrated male priests called Galli.[46]

This is not to say that men did not think women were less emotionally stable than men; they usually did.[47] Nor is it to suggest that *outsiders* might not have been suspicious of frenzied women.[48] It is instead to question whether the cultural context of early Christianity really demands that we suppose that its women would have *actually* been more frenzied in their behavior than its men. Paul is not at this point addressing outside rumors about the Corinthian church; he is addressing the real behavior of women in the congregation. Typical ancient views on women's frenzy do not tell us how women acted; and texts on how women acted suggest that too many men acted in similar ways for us to apply this background only to female members of the Corinthian church.

In fact, 1 Corinthians 12:2–3 suggests that many of the Corinthians from pagan backgrounds had learned inappropriate forms of worship, forms which had carried over into their excesses in chapter 14. Paul in no way limits this background or its present consequences to the women, but assumes that this has affected many of his readers' ecstatic activity, whether they were women or men.

Those who believe that Paul here addresses an abuse of spiritual gifts like tongues or prophecy appeal to Paul's particular word for "speak" at this point, *laleō*. One writer points out that elsewhere in 1 Corinthians 14 this term usually refers to speaking in tongues.[49] But the meaning of *laleō* cannot be so limited; it sometimes refers to teaching or to preaching the gospel elsewhere in the same letter (2:6–7, 13; 3:1; 9:8), to prophecy (12:3; 14:3, 29),[50] to revelations (prophecies? interpretations? 14:6), to tongues (12:30; 13:1; 14:2, 4, 5, 6, 9, 11, 13, 18, 21, 23, 27, 28, 39), to anything except tongues (14:19), and to normal speech (13:11). The term "speak" does occur with tongues more frequently than with prophecy in this chapter, but for the simple reason that, in contrast to "prophesying," Paul had no single verb to express "speaking in tongues" without the word "speak."

We should note that Paul *nowhere* uses "speak" to mean "speak in tongues" without making it clear that he means "speak in tongues"—which he does not do in 14:34–35. Nor can the older, classical meaning of the verb "speak" here be used to support the theory that Paul is addressing ecstatic or babbling speech; by this period, it was an ordinary word for speaking and so occurs for ordinary speech throughout the New Testament.[51]

### *Judging Prophecies?*

In another effort to grapple with the context, some have related this passage about women to their right to "judge" prophecies in the assembly (14:29), since this would include an authoritative teaching as well as a prophetic function. Thus, though the context does not mention teaching, on this view Paul prohibits the women from doing anything authoritative *like* teaching.[52]

But "judging" prophecy is probably the spiritual gift earlier called "discernment of spirits" (12:10, cognate term),[53] and nothing in chapter 12 indicates that only men exercised this particular spiritual gift. Judging prophecy is no more authoritative than the prophetic gift itself, which is ranked second only to apostleship in 12:28, immediately above the gift of teaching. Why should women be permitted to prophesy but not to exercise a related spiritual gift to discern whether someone else was speaking by the same Spirit? Were not all those who prophesied to exercise this gift (14:29)?

Further, there is little reason to associate "asking questions" here with challenging prophecies. In Old Testament schools of the prophets, a presiding prophet may have sometimes "supervised" the prophetic activity of the other prophets, guiding them toward charismatic maturity (1 Sam. 19:20).[54] Paul seems to have envisioned a charismatic worship in his own day where all the prophets in a given church exercised the gift of discernment, testing prophecies and keeping young prophets in line (1 Cor. 14:29).[55] The New Testament offers no clear evidence that prophecies were tested with questions, nor any reason why a woman who wanted to challenge prophecies would profit by challenging them for her husband only after they returned home.

Thus it seems unlikely that judging prophecies is in view in this text.

### *Teaching?*

Although Paul may not be addressing women's abuse of prophecy or tongues, at least the suggestion that he is doing so could derive some support from the context. The same might be said for judging prophecies, unlikely as this proposal is on other grounds. But one view that has *no* support in the context is that Paul's requirement that women be silent just means that they are not allowed to *teach*. Nevertheless, some writers propound this view.

For instance, Knight interprets 1 Corinthians 14:34–35 in light of 1 Timothy 2:11–14 and says that the former passage therefore forbids women to teach men. Although he seems to think that this prohibition of women's teaching is universal, he believes that the prohibition of women asking questions in the service (1 Cor. 14:35) is directed only to the situation in Corinth.[56] Why he regards as universal a prohibition that is not even explicitly mentioned in the text, as against one that is, is not quite clear.

Since no contextual evidence favors this position, there is little more to say about it. But Paul here actually opposes something more basic than women teaching in public: he opposes them learning in public. Or put more accurately, he opposes them *learning* too loudly in public. This was, as we argue below, an issue related to ancient culture that no longer relates to women as a group.

## ASKING QUESTIONS IN CHURCH

It is true that Paul's language ("women may not speak in church") sounds more general than the specific example he goes on to give of women not being allowed to speak. But if Paul had in mind a specific situation that the Corinthians were experiencing, he could have stated it generally without having to explain it to his readers in Corinth. We might have to infer that situation from what he says, but the Corinthian Christians already knew it, so his argument would not suffer from any lack of clarity for them.

We can thus deduce only from clues in the text whether he is addressing a specific situation or all situations in general. On the one hand, Paul could be addressing a specific situation by applying a general principle, which would mean that he is saying: "Your women should stop asking questions, because women should always be silent." This universal silence cannot be what he means since, as we argued above, Paul did allow women in Corinth to pray and to prophesy. On the other hand, he could be making a general statement applicable only to certain types of conditions, for instance: "Your women should be silent because they are making too much noise."

We argue here that Paul's statement is meant to apply only to certain types of conditions. He does, of course, have a general principle in mind, and this principle has to do with church order: people should not disrupt worship services anywhere. But this does not mean that all women should always be silent in all churches; Paul tells these Corinthian women to be silent in church because he does not want them to interrupt the Scripture exposition with irrelevant questions anymore. Like the issue of head coverings, this activity could not have failed to create severe social tensions in the church.

It is doubtful that this particular problem obtained in most other churches in the Mediterranean world. Indeed, if this is the point on which Paul appeals to the custom of the other churches (14:33, contrary to our translation above), he may do so because women were not interrupting other churches' services.

The only kind of speaking *specifically* addressed in 14:34–35 is that the wife should ask her husband questions at home, rather than continuing what she is doing. Unless Paul changes the subject from women's silent submission (v. 34) to their asking questions (v. 35a) and then back again (v. 35b), this must be the issue he is addressing. (That Paul switches back and forth from one subject to another is made unlikely by the fact that he predicates v. 35a on v. 35b, "*for* it is inappropriate.") What she is doing, then, presumably, is speaking up, asking questions to learn what was going on during the prophecies or the Scripture exposition in church.[57]

If it is the *prophecies* that she is interrupting, her purpose is not to judge the prophecies (as some have suggested above), but to "learn" (14:35). This could mean that she wants to inquire of the word of the Lord through the prophets (cf. 14:31). The problem with this suggestion is that it would fail to explain Paul's alternative: she can get the same information from her husband at home. Will her husband necessarily be as prophetically endowed as the prophets at church, and will she necessarily be unendowed (cf. 11:4–5)?

What is almost certainly in view is that the women are interrupting the *Scripture exposition* with questions. This would have caused an affront to more conservative men or visitors to the church, and it would have also caused a disturbance to the service due to the nature of the questions. What is the cultural situation in which asking questions during an exposition would most naturally be a problem?

### *Why Were the Women Questioning?*

The women are asking questions to probe what the speaker is saying during the church service. Although questions could be used to teach as well as to learn,[58] the issue here is learning, because this is what these women can get as easily from their husbands at home (14:35). (Nearly all Greek women in Paul's day were married.) Questions were widely used in learning. They needed to be asked in an orderly way, as a Jewish source (probably second century) indicates:

> A sage who enters—they do not ask his opinion immediately, [but wait] until he has settled down. And so too a disciple who came in—he has not got the right to ask a question until he has settled down. [If] he came in and found them engaged in discussion of a law, he should not jump into their discussion until he has settled down and knows what they are talking about.[59]

Perhaps more relevant to the context of the Corinthian church is the way public lectures were conducted by teachers in the broader Greco-Roman world. Plutarch says that it is important to ask lecturers questions only in their field of expertise; to ask them questions irrelevant to their discipline is rude.[60] Worse yet are those who challenge the speaker without yet understanding his point:

> But those who instantly interrupt with contradictions, neither hearing nor being heard, but talking while others talk, behave in an unseemly manner; whereas the man who has the habit of listening with restraint and respect, takes in and masters a useful discourse, and more readily sees through and detects a useless or a false one, showing himself thus to be a lover of truth and not a lover of disputation, nor froward and contentious.[61]

This principle is particularly applicable to uneducated questioners who waste everyone's time with their questions they have not bothered to first research for themselves:

> For when they are by themselves they are not willing to give themselves any trouble, but they give trouble to the speaker by repeatedly asking questions about the same things, like unfledged nestlings always agape toward the mouth of another, and desirous of receiving everything ready prepared and predigested.[62]

So also those who nitpick too much, questioning extraneous points not relevant to the argument.[63] It was rude even to whisper to one another during a lecture, so asking questions of one another would also have been considered out of place and disrespectful to the speaker.[64]

Why would the women in the congregation have been more likely to have asked irrelevant questions than the men? Because, in general, they were less likely to be educated than men. Most Jewish women knew less of the law than most Jewish men, and most Greek women were less accustomed to public lectures than were their husbands.[65]

Of course, some Greek and Roman women studied philosophy,[66] but their numbers, in comparison with the men, seem to have been very small.[67] Further, few of the women in the Corinthian congregation would have belonged to the aristocratic class; and among the working classes, husbands might have generally been more likely to hear public philosophical lectures in the agora than their wives. Girls as well as boys were educated during this period,[68] but, among those who could afford it, older students who went on to study philosophy or rhetoric were normally men.

The contrast between men's and women's education is more dramatic, where we can examine it, in ancient Judaism. The case should not, of course, be exaggerated. Women must have heard some Torah teaching regularly in the synagogues (Acts 17:4; 18:26),[69] probably often learned some Bible teaching from their parents,[70] and were presumably sometimes expected to join the father in teaching the children, especially when they were young.[71] It was not unnatural for a wife or daughter of a rabbi to be able to cite Scripture accurately and effectively.[72]

But the rabbis did not normally feel that women needed Torah as much as men did. An early second-century rabbi wanted women to learn enough Torah at least to understand the procedure to be followed if they were suspected of adultery;[73] knowing this passage could serve as a good deterrent from giving your husband any reason to suspect you! One of his colleagues, however, taught, "Whoever teaches Torah to his daughter, it is as if he teaches her sexual satisfaction."[74] A later comment on this second rabbi's view charges that it is better for the words of Torah to be burned[75] than for them to be given to a woman.[76] This became the prevailing view among the later rabbis, and all our Jewish sources point in the direction that girls, unlike boys, did not receive much Torah training.[77]

Like minors and slaves, women were excluded from some obligations of the law,[78] such as the obligation to wear tefillin (phylacteries)[79] or to dwell in *sukkoth* ("booths" or "tents") during the Feast of Tabernacles.[80] They were exempt from study of the

Torah,[81] perhaps, as Wegner suggests, because the rabbis feared that too much education would liberate their women.[82]

Although occasionally a woman mastered the Scriptures (e.g., Beruriah, wife of R. Meir),[83] women who sought to expound Torah as authorities on it were usually not received by their male colleagues. The sages ruled that women were not to be appointed as officials,[84] and we never read of rabbis ordaining women disciples to be rabbis. We know of one rabbi who followed a different practice: Jesus had women among his disciples (Luke 10:39; cf. 8:1–3; Mark 15:41) and chose them as witnesses of his resurrection (Matt. 28:1–10; Luke 24:1–11; John 20:10–18). But we may suspect that most first-century Jewish men in Palestine agreed with what became the rabbinic consensus: as one first-century Jewish writer, Josephus, puts it, even the testimony of a woman is unacceptable, "because of the levity and temerity of their sex."[85]

We do not have to assume that Jewish women were equally repressed in all parts of the Mediterranean world, but Philo and Josephus, both Jewish authors writing in Greek, do not substantially improve our picture of the educational status of Jewish women.[86] Perhaps in traditional hellenistic areas like Egypt women would have been less educated, whereas more well-to-do Jewish women in places like Sardis would have been more educated. But our point is that we have good reason to believe that women were usually considerably less trained in the Scriptures than their husbands, and hence more prone to err or to ask irrelevant questions.

What then do Paul's directives mean in such a context? His instruction that they stop asking such questions would solve the immediate problem. But if a woman (or someone else) was less educated and could not ask proper questions, was she then to refrain from asking questions altogether? Assuming that the husbands generally had a better knowledge of what was going on because their background was normally better, Paul expected them to help their wives.

When Paul suggests that husbands should teach their wives at home, his point is not to belittle women's ability to learn. To the contrary, Paul is advocating the most progressive view of his day: despite the possibility that she is less educated than himself, the husband should recognize his wife's intellectual capability and therefore make himself responsible for her education, so they can discuss intellectual issues together. We find this perspective in Plutarch. In writing to Pollianus, he suggests that Pollianus learn philosophy well: "And for your wife you must collect from every source what is useful, as do the bees, and carrying it within your own self impart it to her, and then discuss it with her, and make the best of these doctrines her favourite and familiar themes."[87] Knowing philosophy, he contended, would make a woman virtuous.[88]

Of course, Plutarch's view is not entirely complimentary toward women; he believes that of themselves they produce base passions and folly, and need a man's input to straighten them out.[89] Here the comparison between Paul and Plutarch ends, since there is no indication that Paul regards women as more inherently incomplete than men are—indeed, earlier passages in his letter would suggest that he certainly believes otherwise (1 Cor. 7:32–35; 11:11). But Paul would surely agree with Plutarch that a woman can and should learn, and that her husband should take an active interest in her development as a mature person. Paul proposes teaching one's wife at home as a long range solution to the lack of biblical education that characterized the inappropriate questioning.

### *What Kind of Silence?*

As noted above, a prohibition of literally all speech by women here would keep us from being able to take the "all" of other verses in the context literally (e.g., 14:31), and would contradict 11:4–5. More reasonably, as we have argued above, Paul's words merely *limit* speech in public settings; Paul is opposing only the irrelevant questions some women have been asking during the teaching part of the church service.

Yet Paul's injunction to even a qualified silence for women might have appealed to his culture; a quiet demeanor was considered a necessary characteristic of a submissive wife in many ancient circles.[90] But if Paul recommends a quiet demeanor for women at Corinth, would he recommend it for all cultures? And does a quiet demeanor signify the same attitude in all cultures? Many men today would rather know what their wives are really thinking than be forced to speculate about it. Is quietness equivalent to submission if her husband prefers her to be more vocal in expressing her views?

The women's silence (14:34) does not mean that they could not be prophetically inspired in their speech (cf. 14:28). The point is rather that preserving church order (14:40) means preserving the common good by not scandalizing the culture. It was "shameful" or "disgraceful" for a woman to interrupt the service with her questions (14:35) the same way that it was "shameful" or "disgraceful" for a woman to have her head uncovered or hair cropped short (11:6): it offended the cultural sensitivities of those whom the church wanted to reach with the gospel.[91]

Silence, like asking questions, could be compatible with the attitude of a learner, if the learner was not yet in a place to ask questions. Silence was sometimes used as a moral discipline or a form of submissive demeanor for a student.[92] We will examine this issue in slightly more detail when we address 1 Timothy 2:11–12 in the following chapter.

### *"As Even the Law Says"*

Much discussion has focused on Paul's appeal to the law to substantiate his claim that wives should be submissive to their husbands and so be silent in church. Although very few people use Paul's biblical argument from creation in 1 Corinthians 11 to argue that all women should cover their heads today, many view the allusion to the law in 14:34 as transculturally binding.

Before we turn to the question of whether Paul would apply this allusion to all cultures, we should ask what text or texts he has in mind when he says "the law." Some writers feel that he is using rabbinic law, rather than biblical law, since no Old Testament passage says quite what Paul says here.[93] This interpretation might work if Paul is citing someone else's saying and then refuting it,[94] but we have discounted that idea above. Since Paul nowhere else refers to rabbinic law as "the law," and since it is unlikely that his readers would have assumed that he meant something different than what he usually meant by the phrase, this suggestion is improbable.[95]

The ambiguity of this possible reference to the law has been cited by those who feel that this text is an interpolation added by a later writer. Fee points out that Paul nowhere else appeals to the law absolutely, and that when Paul refers to the law, he always cites the text; therefore, this passage is not from Paul.[96]

But Paul sometimes does refer to the whole law as teaching something in a general way.[97] The term "law," or the combination "Law and Prophets," could be used rather loosely to refer to the Old Testament writings as a whole (e.g., 14:21, a quote from

Isaiah).[98] In this case, Paul might refer to the *general* subordination of women in the Old Testament period, which is probably how Josephus (another first-century Jewish writer) uses the term when he says that "the law" enjoins the wife's submission.[99] Earlier Paul said that he became "under the law" to those who were "under the law," to win everyone, to relate to everyone, and to avoid causing anyone to stumble (1 Cor. 9:20). It is not unreasonable to suppose that Paul's motives are the same here: even though he does not require believers to keep all the stipulations of the law, he expects them to respect standard customs that could derive support from the law.

If a specific text is in view, it is more likely that Paul is arguing again from the creation order (Gen. 1) than that he is arguing from the results of the Fall (Gen. 3:16), which he would not regard as the ideal of God's kingdom.[100] In this case, we would need to regard his argument the same way we understand the creation order argument for head coverings (as in our preceding chapter).

But whether Paul means the law in general, or the creation order in particular, he is probably calling upon the law to support the wife's submission rather than her silence. As we shall note in chapter 5 (on Eph. 5), the Christian ideal does not remove the common ancient ideal of the wife's submissiveness; it merely adds the requirement that the husband join her in it. In this case, the wives are to submit themselves by following the propriety required of them to maintain church order.

### *This Is How It Is Done*

Paul's final appeal (1 Cor. 14:36–38) is similar to his closing appeal in 11:16: This is just how it is done. To those who think the Spirit inspires them to challenge this injunction on church order, Paul points out that there are also people endowed with the prophetic gift on the other side of the question, including Paul himself. Indeed, Paul, the apostolic founder of their church, is certainly well endowed with the Spirit of prophecy, and his advice should thus be heeded (14:36–37; cf. 7:40).[101] The one who did not listen to Paul's injunctions would be in trouble not merely with Paul but with God (14:38).[102]

But as clearly as Paul's wisdom was God's wisdom for the situation in Corinth, applying it to situations for which it was not intended would be a misapplication of God's wisdom. Those who thought that they were spiritual enough to decide the case against Paul had to reckon with his spirituality. But the fact that Paul addresses his argument in this particular letter to the specific situation in Corinth, and that his injunction to silence cannot contextually mean more than that the women should not ask ill-conceived questions during public lectures, mean that the inspired principle he articulates calls us to order in worship, not to the silence of women. It also has certain other obvious applications—for instance, seminary students who did not do their homework should not ask silly questions in class—but it certainly does not apply today to women on the basis of their gender.

## CONCLUSION

Paul's point is that those who do not know the Bible very well should not set the pace for learning in the Christian congregation; they should instead receive private attention to catch them up to the basics of Christian instruction that the rest of the congregation already knows. In Corinth, the issue had come to a head with uneducated women interrupting the Scripture exposition with questions. Paul suggested a short-range and a long-range solution to the problem in his instructions on how to bring order back to the Corinthians' church services. The short-range solution was that the women were to stop interrupting the service; the long-range solution was that they were to learn the knowledge they had been lacking.[103]

## NOTES

1. "As in all the churches of the set-apart ones" may go with the following clause as easily as with the preceding one. In favor of it attending the following paragraph is what appears to be the citation of other churches' precedent in 14:36; but this could be intended to parallel a preceding argument (14:29–33) rather than to continue 14:33b–35. In favor of it attending the preceding paragraph, as we have translated it here, is the awkwardness of saying, "As in all the churches . . . let it be in the churches" (14:33–34). Of course, anyone who has wrestled with Paul's syntax in Greek recognizes that awkward constructions in Paul are always possible, so it is unlikely that the issue will be resolved by appeal either to "standard" Greek grammar or to the passage's structure. Paul elsewhere appeals to the example of other churches for specific activities meant only for his day (16:1), especially with regard to the covering of

women's heads (11:16); see above. But if the situation addressed in 14:34–35 is what we have proposed, Paul could have appealed to the example of the other churches, most of which probably did not even have the problem of women interrupting the speaker with uneducated questions. So in the end, it does not entirely matter which way one takes the clause. Since the issue must be decided on situational-contextual rather than grammatical grounds, it will depend on, rather than inform, our exegetical conclusions.

2. Cf. 11:5, which, we argued above, and most current readers agree, is culturally conditioned. It probably means "culturally inappropriate"; causes for "shame" vary from culture to culture, and most cultures of Mediterranean antiquity had a highly developed concept of "shame."

3. Cf. John Piper and Wayne Grudem, "An Overview of Central Concerns: Questions and Answers," in *Manhood and Womanhood,* p. 71.

4. Order and propriety were matters of major concern; cf. Diog. Laert. *Lives* 3.103–4; Plut. *T.-T.* 1.2.4, *Mor.* 617B (including ranks of distinction in seating arrangements) (contrast Menedemus in Diog. Laert. *Lives* 2.130, whose predilection in the other direction is considered unusual). Such a concern seems to have obtained, however informally, in Diaspora Jewish assemblies for prayer as well (3 Macc. 6:1). Among ancient rules relating to sitting or standing in different sacred settings (Pes. Rab. 15:9) and lecture settings (Ab. R. Nathan 6 A; b. Meg. 21a, bar.) were rules governing such actions (especially seating) according to rank (Apul. *Metam.* 10.7; Lycurgus 14 in Plut. *SSpart., Mor.* 227F; *T.-T.* 1.2.3–4, *Mor.* 616E, 617B; Gen. 43:33; Luke 14:7–11; t. Sanh. 7:8; 8:1; b. Hor. 13b, bar.; p. Ter. 8:7; Taan. 4:2, §§8–9, 12; Ket. 12:3, §6; Sanh. 1:2, §13; Gen. Rab. 98:11; Ps-Phocyl. 220–22; cf. p. R. H. 2:6, §9); the Essenes were especially particular about speaking according to rank and propriety (1QS 2.19–23; cf. 1QS 7.9–10; Jos. *War* 2.8.5, §132). While 1 Cor. 14:30–33 stresses order (apparently implying also that the inspired speaker should stand, taking the position of authority), its complete lack of emphasis on rank is significant.

5. It is possible that "to himself" is meant more literally, i.e., that the one who prays in tongues communicates divine messages to himself as if in prophecy (cf. 2 Sam. 23:2–3; Ps. 12:1, 5; 46:1, 10; 91:2, 14–16; Jer. 25:15; 27:2; Hos. 1:2); this depends primarily on whether we read "and to God" or "even to God" (in the latter case, "to himself" might mean he is the object of edification or that he is simply the only participant besides God).

6. Streeter, *Woman,* p. 60, points out: "It is remarkable with what persistency the Church and people in general are prepared to insist on literal application of texts in certain cases and absolutely disregard them in another."

7. Streeter, *Woman,* p. 62, emphasizes Paul's words, "let *your* women keep silence," implying (he argues) that the Corinthian women were particularly problematic.

8. As a charismatic student once told me, restricting utterances in tongues to three makes sense in a regular church service, but Paul surely

would not have enjoined it for an all-night prayer meeting! Given the purpose of the gifts (building up the believers in love, chs. 12–14), even prophecy, if practiced as in the NT, might cause division in many non-charismatic churches, so many readers would view even Paul's exhortations concerning prophecy as the most useful gift as also conditioned by the situation. (This is simply to reaffirm that various modern situations will be different from the one in Corinth, and that we need to take into account the situation when we apply the text; it is not to deny our need for the gifts today.)

9. That it is in some measure a Pauline fragment from another letter has also been proposed; cf. R. W. Allison, "Let Women be Silent in the Churches (1 Cor. 14:33b–36): What did Paul Really Say, and What did it Mean?" *JSNT* 32 (1988): 27–60, who argues also that Paul is refuting a Corinthian position.

10. Meeks, *Urban Christians,* p. 125 (although he does not commit himself to this position absolutely); cf. idem, "The Image of the Androgyne: Some Uses of a Symbol in Earliest Christianity," *HR* 13 (3, Feb. 1974): 203–4, again tentatively.

11. Conzelmann, *1 Corinthians,* p. 246.

12. Scroggs, "Woman," p. 284.

13. Bruce, "All Things," p. 94, notes its "textual doubtfulness"; in idem, *1 and 2 Corinthians,* pp. 135–36, he notes that if these verses are genuinely Pauline, they may refer to asking questions or discussing prophecies, but he thinks that they mean more than that.

14. Fee, *1 Corinthians,* pp. 699–705.

15. Cf. Metzger, *Textual Commentary,* p. 565.

16. E.g., G. M. M. Pelser, "Women and ecclesiastical ministries in Paul," *Neot* 10 (1976): 100.

17. Sometimes upper-class writers wished their letters to be published; e.g., Diog. Laert. *Lives* 1.122 (Pherecyded's letter to Thales); D. E. Aune, *The New Testament in its Literary Environment,* LEC 8 (Philadelphia: Westminster, 1987), pp. 171–72. This was much more often a Roman than a Greek trait (ibid., p. 170), but Corinth included Roman as well as Greek elements, and the custom would have been known to both Paul and the Corinthians. In practice, of course, most texts were passed along among individuals (cf. R. J. Starr, "The Circulation of Literary Texts in the Roman World," *CQ* 37 [1, 1987]: 213–23); only inscriptions were actually published for the public eye. This is not the place to investigate the old distinction drawn between letters and epistles (Deissmann, *Light,* pp. 229–34; idem, *Bible Studies* [Edinburgh: T. & T. Clark, 1923], pp. 3–59; cf. George Milligan, *St. Paul's Epistles to the Thessalonians* [London: Macmillan, 1908], p. 121; more nuanced, W. M. Ramsay, *The Letters to the Seven Churches of Asia* [London: Hodder & Stoughton, 1904], pp. 23–26; idem, *Teaching of Paul,* pp. 412–47; idem, "Roads and Travel [in the New Testament]," in *Dictionary of the Bible,* ed. James Hastings [Edinburgh: T. & T. Clark, 1904], 5:401; cf. R. P. Martin, "Approaches to New Testament Exegesis," in *New Testament Interpretation,* p. 232; see especially Stowers, *Letter Writing,* pp. 17–19; Aune, *Environment,* p. 160). Most of Paul's letters to congrega-

tions offer moral exhortation, like philosophers' letters to disciples and others (e.g., Diog. Laert. *Lives* 1.43–44, 64–67, 73, 81, 93, 99–100; *CynEp* passim [mostly or all pseudepigraphic]; cf. Stowers, *Letter Writing,* pp. 37–43; Aune, *Environment,* pp. 167–68; Malherbe, *Exhortation,* p. 79). They would have been publicly read to the congregations. Although the reading of Paul's letters would have been limited to their local congregation, their public use could have sped up the process of their collection and eventual scribal copying and publication.

18. Besides allusions; this is explicit in 1 Clem. 47.

19. There are, of course, many cases of marginal notes coming into the text through scribal misreadings; but we are again dealing with something early in the history of this text's transmission, and the naked imperatives are more naturally Pauline or willfully pseudonymous than a marginal note someone appended to the original autograph. Cf. also D. A. Carson, " 'Silent in the Churches': On the Role of Women in 1 Corinthians 14:33b–36," in *Manhood and Womanhood,* p. 142.

20. Rhetorical practice employed "dwelling on the point" (including returning to it) (*Rhet. ad Herenn.* 4.45.58), and digressions were standard even in historical works (see Aune, *Environment,* p. 30). A common rhetorical technique for transitions was one point reminding the writer of another (Quint. 9.2.60–61). Fiorenza, who also thinks that the grounds for exclusion are more theological than textual (*Memory,* p. 230), suggests that this passage, far from being a randomly placed digression, is meant to join 11:1–16 in framing Paul's discussion on church worship services (ibid., p. 226).

21. This is often pointed out; e.g., Bruce, "All Things," p. 89. For more material, cf. Keener, *And Marries Another,* pp. 184–85, n. 131, particularly on responses to imaginary interlocutors, which were frequent in what scholars traditionally called diatribe style (e.g., Dio Chrys. *21st Disc., On Beauty; 61st Disc., Chrys.; 67th Disc., Pop. Opin.*; Epict. *Disc.* 1.1.23–25, 28; Sen. *Ben.* 4.5.1, 21.6; *Dial.* 3.6.1, 8.6; *Ep. Lucil.* 14.1; 42.2; Hor. *Sat.* 101–2; *Rhet. ad Herenn.* 4.16.23–24; Cic. *Tusc. Disp.* 3.23.55; 5.36.103; Mek. Pisha 1.35; p. Sanh. 6:1, §1).

22. N. M. Flanagan and E. H. Snyder, "Did Paul Put Down Women in 1 Cor 14:34–36?" *BTB* 11 (1, Jan. 1981): 10–12; C. Ukachukwu Manus, "The Subordination of the Women in the Church. 1 Cor 14:33b–36 Reconsidered," *RAfT* 8 (16, 1984): 183–95; W. C. Kaiser, *Toward an Exegetical Theology* (Grand Rapids: Baker, 1981), pp. 76, 119; Bilezikian, *Roles,* pp. 150–53.

23. D. W. Odell-Scott, "Let the Women Speak in Church. An Egalitarian Interpretation of 1 Cor 14:33b–36," *BTB* 13 (3, July 1983): 90–91. He defends this position in idem, "In Defense of an Egalitarian Interpretation of 1 Cor 14:34–36. A Reply to Murphy-O'Connor's Critique," *BTB* 17 (3, July 1987): 100–103.

24. Odell-Scott, "Women Speak," pp. 91–92; Kaiser, *Exegetical Theology,* p. 77. Odell-Scott thinks that the opponents are Jewish legalists. Bilezikian, *Roles,* pp. 146–57, uses sets of parallel statements supposedly framing this passage to support the case, but the "framing" verses do not appear to me any more substantially linked to one another than they are

to other verses in the chapter. Birger Gerhardsson, *Memory and Manuscript,* ASNU 22 (Uppsala: Gleerup, 1961), pp. 275, 306, sees in 14:36 an allusion to the Torah going forth from Jerusalem, and reads this as a Jerusalem church tradition derived from Jesus himself; cf. Bruce, "All Things," p. 97; idem, *1 and 2 Corinthians,* p. 136; this seems to me unlikely. Peter Richardson and Peter Gooch, "Logia of Jesus in 1 Corinthians," in *The Jesus Tradition Outside the Gospels,* ed. David Wenham, GP 5 (Sheffield: JSOT, 1984), p. 45, suggest that it is a saying from the risen Lord; in this context, either prophecy (perhaps Paul's at that moment) or written Scripture seems the most likely meaning.

25. Liefeld, "Women," p. 149. In n. 40 he charges that Odell-Scott fails to discuss *ē* in 1:13; 6:2, 9, 16, 19; 9:6, 8, 10; 10:22.

26. D. A. Carson, *Exegetical Fallacies* (Grand Rapids: Baker, 1984), p. 39, points this out; it is a natural observation for all Greek readers, and one which deprives the use of the masculine here of any evidential value.

27. Cf. also ibid., p. 38.

28. Cf. e.g., Demosthenes *3d Philippic* 15; Epict. *Disc.* 1.6, 1.19.2–6; cf. Aune, *Environment,* p. 201; S. K. Stowers, "The Diatribe," in *Greco-Roman Literature and the New Testament,* SBLSBS 21 (Atlanta: Scholars, 1988), p. 75; Martin Dibelius, *James,* rev. Heinrich Greeven, trans. Michael A. Williams, Hermeneia (Philadelphia: Fortress, 1976), p. 150; Malherbe, *Exhortation,* p. 130.

29. Epict. *Disc.* 1.5.10, 8.15, 10.7, 11.24, 13, 19.7, 26.6, 28.24, 29.9; 2.8.2; 3.1.42 (besides his characteristic *mē genoito,* cf. his *oudamōs,* "by no means," e.g., 1.12.15); cf. S. K. Stowers, *The Diatribe and Paul's Letter to the Romans,* SBLDS 57 (Chico, Calif.: Scholars, 1981), pp. 153–54, for a correction of Bultmann on the nature of Paul's and Epictetus' use. Cf. J. B. Lightfoot, *St Paul's Epistle to the Galatians,* 3d ed. (London: Macmillan, 1869), p. 117; Robertson and Plummer, *1 Corinthians,* p. 126, for the LXX and Arrian (William Sanday and Arthur Headlam, *A Critical and Exegetical Commentary on the Epistle to the Romans,* ICC, 5th ed. [Edinburgh: T. & T. Clark, 1902], p. 72, allege that Paul here adopts "the mistranslations in LXX"). The opposite form could be used as a blessing formula (e.g., Jdt. 15:10).

30. Cf. E. M. Yamauchi, *The Stones and the Scriptures* (Grand Rapids: Baker, 1972), p. 102; Leonard Swidler, *Women in Judaism: The Status of Women in Formative Judaism* (Metuchen, N.J.: Scarecrow, 1976), pp. 89–90 (following Sukenik).

31. Jos. *War* 5.5.2, §§198–200; cf. b. Yoma 16a; S. Safrai, "The Temple," in *JPFC,* pp. 865–70; E. P. Sanders, *Jewish Law from Jesus to the Mishnah* (London: SCM, 1990), pp. 104–5. The distinction between Jewish women, proselytes, and slaves, on the one hand, and "Israel" on the other, may be significant (e.g., Sifre Num. 39.6.1); "the court of Israel" was holier than "the court of women" (m. Kel. 1:8).

32. H. G. May, "Synagogues in Palestine," *BA* 7 (1, Feb. 1944): 14, cites the balconies in the court of women (m. Mid. 2:6), but while this may offer a rationale for later segregation of genders, it offers no evidence of segregation of synagogues this early. His citation of Philo would be more helpful, but does not account for the lack of archaeo-

logical data to support the thesis. Ben Witherington, *Women in the Ministry of Jesus,* SNTSMS 51 (Cambridge: Cambridge University, 1984), p. 7, notes that there is no evidence before Trajan's time; the Trajanic evidence he cites (p. 135, n. 79, where he follows Sukenik but cites the reference differently) is from the Palestinian Talmud, which does not *necessarily* guarantee even an authentically Trajanic date.

33. S. Safrai, "The Synagogue," in *JPFC,* p. 939.

34. B. J. Brooten, *Women Leaders in the Ancient Synagogue* (Chico, Calif.: Scholars, 1982), pp. 103–38, dealing also with the side rooms. For Sardis, see A. R. Seager, "The Synagogue and the Jewish Community: The Building," in G. M. A. Hanfmann et al., *Sardis from Prehistoric to Roman Times,* ed. W. E. Mierse (Cambridge: Harvard University, 1983), pp. 170–71.

35. Catherine and Richard Kroeger, "Strange Tongues or Plain Talk?" *DSar* 12 (4, 1986): 10–13; Kroeger, "Cults of Women," p. 30; cf. Leonard, "Status of Women," p. 318. Longenecker, *Ethics,* p. 86, also sees charismatic excess here.

36. This is found in other societies, too, e.g., in the secret societies noted by Mircea Eliade, *Rites and Symbols of Initiation* (New York: Harper & Row, 1958), p. 79 (who, however, also notes the analogous behavior of male secret societies in the same cultures). It should be pointed out that Dionysiac "liberation" was not viewed by all social classes as liberation; Euripides may have been showing the destructiveness of the irrational impulse in Agave's tragedy (cf. Charles Segal, "The Menace of Dionysus: Sex Roles and Reversals in Euripides' Bacchae," in *Women in the Ancient World,* pp. 208–9).

37. See R. S. Kraemer, "Ecstatics and Ascetics: Studies in the Function of Religious Activities for Women in the Greco-Roman World" (Ph.D. diss., Princeton University, 1976), especially pp. 9–123 (though the imposition of the millenarian model is as external to the data as the psychoanalytic model); idem, "Ecstasy and Possession: The Attraction of Women to the Cult of Dionysus," *HTR* 72 (1, Jan. 1979): 55–80; idem, " 'Euoi Saboi' in Demosthenes de Corona: In Whose Honor Were the Women's Rites?" in *SBL 1981 Seminar Papers,* SBL Seminar Papers 20 (Chico, Calif.: Scholars, 1981), pp. 229–36, especially p. 233; cf. Otto, *Dionysus,* pp. 142, 171–80; Lefkowitz and Fant, *Women's Life,* pp. 114–15, 250–53. For implications of social disruption in the behavior of the Maenads, see Artem. *Oneir.* 2.37; Segal, "Menace," pp. 195–212 (with perhaps too much psychoanalytic theory); Henrichs, "Identities," pp. 137–60; cf. also the sexual warfare indicated in Plut. *T.-T.* 1.1.3, *Mor.* 614A; Sheila McNally, "The Maenad in Early Greek Art," in *Women in the Ancient World,* pp. 107–8, 119, 123.

38. Meeks, *Urban Christians,* p. 25, points out that Isis appears not only as liberator, but also as model spouse and protector of marital chastity; cf. also S. K. Heyob, *The Cult of Isis Among Women in the Graeco-Roman World,* EPROER 51 (Leiden: Brill, 1975), pp. 76, 80. Accusations against Isis-worshipers' morality (e.g., Juv. *Sat.* 6.489) came easily to ancient satirists given to slander (in *Sat.* 6.511–29 he mocks worshipers of Isis; in 542–47, Jewesses).

39. Especially Juv. *Sat.* 6.314–41 (frenzied women in the mysteries). Cf. the third/second century BCE Pythagorean treatise in Lefkowitz and Fant, *Women's Life,* pp. 104–5, §107.

40. Undoubtedly for socioeconomic reasons, there were few women in the cult at Samothrace (S. G. Cole, *Theoi Megaloi: The Cult of the Great Gods at Samothrace,* EPROER 96 [Leiden: Brill, 1984], p. 42); Mithraism excluded women altogether (J. G. Gager, *Kingdom and Community* [Englewood Cliffs, N.J.: Prentice-Hall, 1975], p. 133); the cult of Dionysus was open to both (L. H. Martin, *Hellenistic Religions: An Introduction* [New York: Oxford University, 1987], p. 93), although feminine participation was more prominent up through the late hellenistic period (Kraemer, "Ecstatics," pp. 48–57). This is not to deny their significant role in many such cults (cf. Pomeroy, *Goddesses,* pp. 75–78, 205–6, 217–26), but to argue that upper-class Roman men who produced much of our literary evidence reflect a chauvinistic bias that may not have reflected the reality experienced by the vast majority of Greco-Roman society.

41. See Heyob, *Isis,* pp. 37–52; for Greco-Roman women's perceptions, see pp. 53–80.

42. For percentages of men and women, see ibid., 81–110. Cf. similarly H. C. Kee, *Christian Origins in Sociological Perspective* (Philadelphia: Westminster, 1980), p. 91; cf. Robert Banks, *Paul's Idea of Community: The Early House Churches in their Historical Setting* (Grand Rapids: Eerdmans, 1980), p. 129.

43. Most feminine participation in Greek ritual was not ecstatic, if a survey of women's rituals in Greek and Roman religion in Kraemer, *Maenads,* pp. 11–42, is indicative of the general situation. This seems to include the second century CE rituals in Corinth described in Pausanias *Descr. Gr.* 35.6–8 (in ibid., p. 34).

44. Dionysus was popular by the sixth century BCE (Walter Burkert, *Greek Religion* [Cambridge: Harvard University, 1985], p. 166); most elements of the myth can be traced as early as the *Iliad* (Otto, *Dionysus,* pp. 54–55), but its prominence in the hellenistic period (Helmut Koester, *Introduction to the New Testament,* 2 vols. [Philadelphia: Fortress, 1982], 1:180–83) is not as easily documented in the NT period. The suppression of the cult in Rome after the excesses of 186 BCE (as reported by Livy 39.18; see Beryl Rawson, "The Roman Family," in *The Family in Ancient Rome* [Ithaca, N.Y.: Cornell University, 1986], p. 16) may have contributed to its decline. That it continued to exist, of course, is not in dispute; many Greek cities held Dionysiac festivals once every two years in the first century BCE (Diod. Sic. 4.3.2–5 in Kraemer, *Maenads,* p. 26), and we should not think that Romanization would have suppressed this entirely; we have evidence of its existence in second century CE Rome (M. P. Nilsson, *The Dionysiac Mysteries of the Hellenistic and Roman Age,* SUASIA 5 [Lund: Gleerup, 1957], p. 47, though noting that this woman had been introduced to this mystery in Asia Minor; it was perhaps more common elsewhere; cf. in Lefkowitz and Fant, *Women's Life,* pp. 252–53, §245). In the Roman period, it seems to have persisted especially in the east (Nilsson, *Mysteries,* pp. 45–66; cf. p. 147).

45. Plut. *R. Q.* 112, *Mor.* 291AB; *T.-T.* 4.6.1, *Mor.* 671C; cf. Lucian *Dionysus: An Introduction*; Plut. *Alex.* 2.5; Henrichs, "Identities," pp. 143–47; Burkert, *Religion,* pp. 164–65. Despite mythical associations, there were real Maenads; cf. the inscriptions cited by Lefkowitz and Fant, *Women's Life,* pp. 113–14, §115; pp. 252–53, §245.

46. Lucian *SyrG* 51 (Grant, *Religions,* p. 118); Lucr. *Nat.* 2.614–15; *Rhet. ad Herenn.* 4.49.62; Epict. *Disc.* 2.20.17, 19; Juv. *Sat.* 2.110–16; cf. Heraclitus 9, to Hermodorus (*CynEp,* pp. 212–13); Juv. *Sat.* 6.514–16; Hor. *Sat.* 1.2.120–21; G. S. Gasparro, *Soteriology and Mystic Aspects in the Cult of Cybele and Attis,* EPROER 103 (Leiden: Brill, 1985), pp. 26–28, 53; Walter Burkert, *Ancient Mystery Cults* (Cambridge: Harvard University, 1987), pp. 6, 36. Their castration did suggest to some that they were no longer fully male (M. J. Vermaseren, *Cybele and Attis: The Myth and the Cult* [London: Thames & Hudson, 1977], pp. 96–101; cf. Epict. *Disc.* 3.1.31; contrast 2.20.19); but the Maenads had similarly taken on traditionally masculine characteristics, so that gender reversal, rather than a limitation of frenzy to the ritual behavior of one gender, seems to be in view.

47. Plut. *R. Q.* 108, *Mor.* 289E; Apul. *Metam.* 7.8; Mus. Ruf. *fr.* 12 (Malherbe, *Exhortation,* p. 154); Ab. R. Nathan 9, §24 B; 4 Macc. 15:5 (where it is partly a compliment); Gardner, *Women,* pp. 21, 67; M. R. Lefkowitz, *Women in Greek Myth* (Baltimore: Johns Hopkins University, 1986), pp. 112–32; Wegner, *Chattel,* pp. 159–62; Pomeroy, *Goddesses,* pp. 150, 230; Peradotto and Sullivan, "Introduction," in *Women in the Ancient World,* p. 3; Moses Hadas, ed., *Aristeas to Philocrates,* JAL (New York: Harper & Brothers, 1951), p. 198. This judgment was sometimes meant as a call to protect women, rather than to repress them (Lefkowitz, *Myth,* pp. 134–36; b. B. M. 59a; cf. 1 Pet. 3:7 and the commentaries loc. cit.), and there were thought to be "exceptions" (4 Macc. 16:5, 14).

48. Cf. our own tentative suggestions on this matter in our treatment of the background of Eph. 5:21–31.

49. Boldrey, *Chauvinist,* p. 61. The Boldreys do agree that Paul does not allow forbidding to speak in tongues (14:39), but think that since this was the main cause of chaos in the assembly, the chaos caused by the women probably includes it.

50. Both references to prophecy in ch. 14 parallel glossolalic speech.

51. F. F. Bruce, *The Books and the Parchments* (Old Tappan, N.J.: Revell, 1963), p. 67; Liefeld, "Women," p. 150; Wayne Grudem, "Prophecy—Yes, but Teaching—No: Paul's Consistent Advocacy of Women's Participation Without Governing Authority," *JETS* 30 (1, March 1987): 20, n. 13.

52. Hurley, "Veils," p. 217; Carson, "Silent," p. 152; Liefeld, "Women," p. 150, following Grudem. Liefeld cites the analogy of Miriam judging Moses, but it was not his prophecy that was being judged, nor is it fair to exclude Aaron (though only Miriam was in this case punished, as he notes), nor is it likely that this analogy would have occurred to Paul's readers. David Hill, *New Testament Prophecy* (Atlanta: John Knox, 1979),

p. 135, suggests that some women may have abused the gift of prophecy, and that here their speech had to be tested.

53. C. E. B. Cranfield, *A Critical and Exegetical Commentary on the Epistle to the Romans,* ICC, 2 vols. (Edinburgh: T. & T. Clark, 1975), 2:620; cf. D. E. Aune, *Prophecy in Early Christianity and the Ancient Mediterranean World* (Grand Rapids: Eerdmans, 1983), pp. 220–21. Distinguishing good from evil could be lauded as a necessary and natural faculty (Marc. Aur. *Med.* 9.1.2; Antisthenes in Diog. Laert. *Lives* 6.1.5), but the distinguishing in 12:10 is a spontaneous manifestation of the Spirit testing prophecies of Christian prophets, not an application (in this case) of standard criteria for judging between valid and invalid prophets (contrast J. Martucci, "*Diakriseis pneumatōn* (1 Co 12,10)," *EgTh* 9 [3, 1978]: 465–71, using Did. 11.8). Aune, *Prophecy,* p. 32, argues that testing of oracles was rare in Greek circles; their interpretation, however, was more problematic until they were fulfilled (p. 51). But "evaluation," not "interpretation," of prophecies is what is in view here (Hill, *Prophecy,* pp. 133–34; Wayne Grudem, "A Response to Gerhard Dautzenberg on 1 Cor. 12.10," *BZ* 22 (2, 1978): 253–70; M. E. Boring, *Sayings of the Risen Jesus,* SNTSMS 46 [Cambridge: Cambridge University, 1982], p. 66, against Dautzenberg; though "judging dreams" could mean interpreting them, Artem. *Oneir.* 1.11). Plato could also affirm inspiration yet subordinate it to the interpretation of governors before implementation (cf. E. N. Tigerstedt, "Plato's Idea of Poetical Inspiration," *CHL* 44 [2, 1969]: 64–65), although his governors do not seem to have been acting charismatically.

54. Groups of prophets also appear in 1 Sam. 10 (probably under Samuel's influence; cf. 1 Sam. 3:1) and 2 Kgs. 2; 4:38–44; 6:1–7 (submitted to the leadership of Elijah and his successor, Elisha).

55. Perhaps the relative youth of the Christian movement had not permitted the maturation of local prophets to guide the others. What is significant, however, is not the lack of prophets but their abundance. As I argued in my dissertation, "The Function of Johannine Pneumatology in the Context of Late First-Century Judaism," the early Christians were "hyper-charismatic" compared to the rest of early Judaism, especially to what became the rabbinic movement. Since the average house church in Corinth may have held about fifty members, a plurality of members exercising the prophetic gift and an encouragement to others to seek this gift suggest a more active exercise of spiritual gifts than is seen even in many charismatic and Pentecostal churches today. As we see in Corinth, of course, this could also lead to the need for instruction and qualification.

56. Knight, "Teaching," p. 88.

57. That Paul's prohibition of women's speech here applies to the asking of questions has often been suggested, e.g., Williams, *Paul and Women,* p. 70; Kevin Giles, *Created Woman: A Fresh Study of the Biblical Teaching* (Canberra: Acorn, 1985), p. 56.

58. E.g., R. Akiba in Ab. R. Nathan 6 A. Cf. Luke 2:46 (perhaps), and Jesus' and Paul's use of rhetorical questions.

59. See t. Sanh. 7:10 (trans. Neusner, 4:221–22). S. Safrai, "Education and the Study of the Torah," in *JPFC,* p. 966, notes that rabbis taught in such a way as to encourage students' questions and participation; cf. also Goodman, *State and Society,* p. 79.

60. Plut. *Lectures* 11, *Mor.* 43BC. The same advice holds for questions asked of knowledgeable persons at dinner parties; cf. Plut. *T.-T.* 2.1.2, *Mor.* 630BC.

61. Plut. *Lectures* 4, *Mor.* 39CD (LCL).

62. Plut. *Lectures* 18, *Mor.* 48A (LCL).

63. Plut. *Lectures* 18, *Mor.* 48B.

64. Plut. *Lectures* 13, *Mor.* 45D.

65. On the other hand, more well-to-do Roman women in the congregation might have been more apt to speak out than their less educated, less well-to-do counterparts, and their speaking out may have created tension with the less educated women.

66. Hipparchia, Crates' wife, is the most famous (Diog. Laert. *Lives* 6.7.98; Diogenes 3, to Hipparchia [*CynEp,* pp. 94–95]), but others are reported, such as (possibly) Pythagoras' wife Theano and his daughter Damo (Diog. Laert. *Lives* 1.42–43); Eumetis or Cleobulina, who studied with Anacharsis (Plut. *Dinner of 7 Wise Men* 3, *Mor.* 148CE), or Cleobuline, daughter of Cleobulus (Diog. Laert. *Lives* 1.89); two pupils of Plato (Diog. Laert. *Lives* 4.1); Aristippus' daughter Arete (his other listed pupils are all male, Diog. Laert. *Lives* 2.72, 86). In a later period, we find "Magnilla the philosopher, daughter of Magnus the philosopher, wife of Menius the philosopher" (second/third century CE inscription in Lefkowitz and Fant, *Women's Life,* p. 160, §168). Most of these figures of earlier times were relatives of male philosophers, just as the few women who studied rabbinic law were. But there is evidence of other women who studied philosophy as well: the bride in Plutarch's *Advice to Bride and Groom* seems to be representative of upper-class women who had some training in philosophy. Even Hipparchia's abilities are later questioned by some, however (Crates 28–29, to Hipparchia [*CynEp,* pp. 78–79]). In theory women were often affirmed to be capable of learning philosophy (Crates 29, to Hipparchia [*CynEp,* pp. 78–79]; Mus. Ruf. *fr.* 3 [*That Women Too Should Study Philosophy,* in Malherbe, *Exhortation,* p. 134]; Epicurus [Stowers, *Letter Writing,* p. 39]; Cleobulus [Diog. Laert. *Lives* 1.90]).

67. R. A. Culpepper, *The Johannine School: An Evaluation of the Johannine-School Hypothesis Based on an Investigation of the Nature of Ancient Schools,* SBLDS 26 [Missoula, Mont.: Scholars, 1975], p. 129, notes (on Zeno's school): "In contrast to the Epicurean school, women were not admitted to the Stoic school." Meeks, *Moral World,* p. 46, observes: "Musonius argued that women, too, should study philosophy, but there is no record of any women among his own pupils." R. B. Ward, "Musonius and Paul on Marriage," *NTS* 36 (2, Apr. 1990): 288, observes that Musonius wanted women to be educated "specifically in Stoic philosophy, a philosophy that taught, above all, the virtue" of self-control (Mus. Ruf. *fr.* 3, 42.33, 23).

68. For the ideal in this period, cf. Quint. 1.1.6; (Ps)Plut. *A Woman, Too, Should be Educated, fr.* 128–33 (LCL); for the practice, see Meeks, *World,* p. 62. Arist. *Pol.* 2.4.6, 1266b had argued against educating everyone in the same way; they should be trained to fulfill their proper roles in society, not for anything else.

69. Cf. 1 Esd. 9:40. Brooten, *Women Leaders,* pp. 140–41, cites further evidence. She observes that women may have sometimes read Torah in Diaspora synagogues (ibid., p. 95); an argument to the effect that it was standard would be an argument from silence as much as its converse, but it seems to have been permitted in some cases (t. Ber. 2:12; b. Meg. 4a; cf. Witherington, *Women,* p. 7); G. F. Moore, *Judaism in the First Centuries of the Christian Era,* 2 vols. (reprint, New York: Schocken, 1971), 2:131, notes that a woman was permitted to read publicly, but states that "this was disapproved on grounds of propriety and no instance is reported." Probably most synagogues were more restrictive, but there were some exceptions in parts of the Roman Empire where local custom may have dictated otherwise, as in the case of certain synagogue officials Brooten mentions (see Brooten, *Women Leaders,* pp. 5–39; cf. also R. S. Kraemer, "A New Inscription from Malta and the Question of Women Elders in the Diaspora Jewish Communities," *HTR* 78 [3–4, 1985]: 431–38 [fourth or fifth century Malta]; S. J. D. Cohen, "Women in the Synagogues of Antiquity," *ConJud* 34 [2, Nov. 1980]: 23–29). It should be noted that what one learned in a synagogue was quite different from what disciples of sages were taught, however (at least according to second-century Palestinian practice; see Goodman, *State and Society,* p. 74).

70. This is extolled in Sus. 3; it should be admitted, however, that heroines in Greek literary works do not seem to have represented Greek men's normal ideal for Greek women, and this may be the case as well with Jewish works written under Greek influence.

71. 2 Tim. 1:5 (because the father was a Gentile, Acts 16:3); Tob. 1:8 (because his father had died); Verner, *Household,* p. 137 (noting that the father had the primary responsibility; cf. also 4 Macc. 18:9–19; Koh. Rab. 4:1, §1; Safrai, "Home and Family," p. 771; idem, "Education," p. 947; Moore, *Judaism,* 2:127); but contrast the evidence in Swidler, *Women,* p. 114, on their teaching other children. Later rabbis could claim that a woman could earn merit by sending her children and husband to places of study (b. Ber. 17a; Sot. 21a). The evidence is stronger, however, in Roman circles: Quint. 1.1.6; Plut. *Educ.* 20, *Mor.* 14B; cf. William Barclay, *Train up a Child: Educational Ideals in the Ancient World* (Philadelphia: Westminster, 1959), p. 157, but it must have been practiced to some degree in Jewish circles, for the law clearly mandated it (see the references in Nicole, "Authority," pp. 48–49).

72. Sifre Deut. 307.4.1; b. Ber. 10a (concerning a Tanna, though the tradition is later); Exod. Rab. 52:3 (later tradition about a Tanna). See Moore, *Judaism,* 2:128–29, for more references.

73. M. Sot. 3:4; p. Hag. 1:1, §1.

74. M. Sot. 3:4 (quoting from Neusner's translation in the Palestinian Talmud, 27:92). R. Joshua, often opposed to R. Eliezer, agrees here that it is not good to teach one's daughter much Torah.

75. Burning the Torah was a terrible offense, for which, Josephus tells us, a Roman soldier lost his life; only scrolls contaminated with heresy were not to be saved from the fire.

76. Num. Rab. 9:48.

77. Safrai, "Education," p. 955, citing the later OT writings, the Apocrypha, Philo, Josephus, and the Tannaim. I say "much," because in m. Ned. 4:3 it is clear that daughters as well as sons could be instructed, and we should not suppose that all men in all periods practiced the custom in exactly the same way. But while Christian apologists have sometimes overemphasized the chauvinism of early Judaism to make early Christian views look better (or at least normal for their day), some apologists for ancient Judaism have made it less chauvinistic than it was, and this is also not fair to a study of these documents in their historical context.

78. E.g., m. Hag. 1:1; t. Ber. 6:18 (where a parable explains that those who try to do the commandments, but cannot do them properly, will end up offending God); p. Hag. 1:1, §7; cf. b. Ber. 45b. This was because women were not included in the designation "Israel" (b. Men. 61b). For children's exemption from the commandments, cf. e.g., p. Hag. 1:1, §4.

79. See Mek. Pisha 17.160–61.

80. See m. Suk. 2:8; b. Suk. 2b (21b addresses slaves); p. Suk. 2:9. Cf. Bonsirven, *Judaism,* p. 119.

81. See b. Kid. 34a.

82. Wegner, *Chattel,* p. 161, suggests that the rabbis feared their sexual liberation; she documents that the legal aspects of women as chattel relate primarily to a wife's sexuality.

83. Witherington, *Women,* p. 195, n. 232, is right to point out that these exceptions involve women who could learn from scholars in their own homes, i.e., from husbands or masters. Swidler, *Women,* pp. 97–104, details Beruriah wife of R. Meir, but calls her "The Exception that proves the Rule"; on pp. 104–11 he argues that the other "exceptions" were not clearly learned in Torah.

84. Sifre Deut. 157.2.2.

85. Jos. *Ant.* 4.8.15, §219 (LCL).

86. Safrai, "Education," p. 955.

87. Plut. *Bride* 48, *Mor.* 145B (LCL).

88. Plut. *Bride* 48, *Mor.* 145C.

89. Plut. *Bride* 48, *Mor.* 145DE.

90. E.g., Sir. 22:5; 26:14; Num. Rab. 9:12. Women are said to be characteristically talkative (e.g., Deut. Rab. 6:11). A godly woman, according to Jewish tradition, was a gentle, peaceful woman (Jub. 36:23).

91. The language of something being "disgraceful" (v. 35) refers to decorum or order, which had to do with societal criticism in a specific cultural context (Liefeld, "Women," pp. 140–42, makes this case ably). Cf. similarly Nicole, "Authority," pp. 45–46.

92. Sen. *Ep. Lucil.* 52:10: Pythagoras made his disciples keep silence for five years.

93. Extrapolations of the law could be seen as law (t. Ber. 6:19), although the idea of oral Torah is probably only from a significantly later period.

94. Kaiser, *Exegetical Theology,* p. 76; Gundry, *Women,* p. 70. Although Paul elsewhere appeals to general custom (see Conzelmann, *1 Corinthians,* p. 246, n. 57), it is equally unlikely that this would be what he means here by "law."

95. Technically, of course, the body of "rabbinic law" did not yet exist, and even the concept of "oral law" may be considerably later (at the writing of this book, the matter is still debated). But we use the term here to include the possibility of interpretive legal traditions summarized as part of the law. (In this book I have tried to avoid discussion of the nature of "rabbinic" and other bodies of literature in the text itself, since most of the readers will not be familiar with current scholarly debates in Jewish or classical studies. Those readers who are aware of the nuances of scholarly debate will recognize at once the relative value and proper use of the different sources, without my further explanation.)

96. See Fee, *1 Corinthians,* pp. 707–8.

97. One may compare his use of "law" for the commandments in Galatians. For phrases like "Scripture says" or "the law teaches," cf. e.g., Sifra A. M. pq. 11.191.1.3.

98. "Law" (Sifre Deut. 32.5.12) and "Law and Prophets" (4 Macc. 18:10–18) naturally included other writings, and later rabbis could comment that "The Torah itself comes in three parts—Torah, Prophets, and Writings" (Pes. Rab Kah. 12:13, trans. Braude, p. 238).

99. Jos. *Ag. Ap.* 2.24, §§200–201.

100. Bruce, *1 and 2 Corinthians,* p. 136.

101. W. A. Grudem, *The Gift of Prophecy in 1 Corinthians* (Lanham, Md.: University Press of America, 1982), p. 71, notes on v. 36 that no one at Corinth spoke with absolute divine authority. Of course, the fact that Paul's authority was greater than theirs did not mean that they had no authority; OT prophets could make mistakes or could need to wait on God for an answer (2 Sam. 7:3–5; 2 Kgs. 2:16–17; Jer. 28:10–13), and apostles were likewise not always infallible (Gal. 2:11). As Bruce, *1 and 2 Corinthians,* p. 136, notes, the point is that "the Corinthians must not be a law to themselves." 1 Cor. 14:37 may well apply to the whole chapter, not just to the preceding verses (with Aune, *Prophecy,* pp. 257–58).

102. Perhaps this is only a harsh statement of Paul (cf. p. M. K. 3:1, §4, late second to early third century), but the passive probably implies a pronouncement of divine judgment: cf. G. P. Wiles, *Paul's Intercessory Prayers,* SNTSMS 24 (Cambridge: Cambridge University, 1974), pp. 119–21; Fee, *1 Corinthians,* p. 712; Aune, *Prophecy,* p. 258 (although I am not convinced that this need be oracular).

103. Even here, Paul makes a general statement covering only several verses; but in nearby Cenchraea, at least, we know of a woman who probably shared in the ministry of the word; see the discussion of Phoebe in Appendix A.

# 3

## Learning in Silence—1 Timothy 2:9–15

We now come to the only explicit prohibition in the entire Bible against women teaching, and one of only two texts that seem to appeal to the creation order to subordinate women in some manner (the other enjoins only that women cover their heads).[1] It would be surprising if an issue that would exclude at least half the body of Christ from a ministry of teaching would be addressed in only one text, unless that text really addressed only a specific historical situation rather than setting forth a universal prohibition. Since this passage seems to conflict with other passages where Paul commends the ministries of women, we will examine the cultural situation that may be addressed here.[2]

It should be noted in passing that the authorship of 1 Timothy is frequently debated in scholarly circles, and even more frequently simply assumed not to be Pauline. It is nearly impossible to be trained in biblical scholarship these days and not be forced to deal with this position, and my own training is no exception, although I stand among the minority of scholars who claim that 1 Timothy is Pauline.[3]

For the purposes of this book, however, the issue of authorship is not ultimately critical; although I will argue on the premise that 1 Timothy is written by Paul, those who hold that it was not written by him usually grant this letter less authority in church practice. Further, if it is not written by Paul, many of this book's arguments about historical situations would still hold true. Finally, the view that 1 Timothy was not written by Paul is rarely held by those who argue women's subordination from this passage anyway,[4] and it is the arguments of those subordinationists that this book is meant to address. The same may be said for Ephesians (see the following three chapters), whose authorship is challenged often but less frequently than that of 1 Timothy.

## THE CONTEXT: PUBLIC PRAYER

This passage, like 1 Corinthians 11, seems to assume women's right to pray in public. That Paul's instructions about women's apparel and teaching deal with women's role in public prayer is suggested by his admonitions to men about prayer in the preceding context.

The passage begins by exhorting public prayer for rulers and all who are in authority (1 Tim. 2:1–2).[5] This continued a standard Jewish custom practiced in the temple and synagogues. Throughout the Roman Empire people showed their loyalty to the emperor by offering sacrifices and prayers to him or on his behalf. To be sure, Rome exempted the Jewish people from having to pray *to* the emperor, but it nevertheless required that they pray *for* him.[6] Sacrifices and prayers for his health were offered in the temple until 66 CE,[7] and their cessation in that year signalled nothing short of revolt against Roman rule.[8] Naturally, Christians, eager to show that they were not anti-Roman,[9] would be inclined to demonstrate their loyalty by offering public prayer for Roman officials.[10] By doing this they hoped for the gospel to spread more freely (2:3–7);[11] proper behavior toward the state could function as part of one's witness (Titus 2:10–14; 3:1–8).

In this context of public prayer, Paul specifically calls on the men to pray in a certain way—forsaking anger and conflict. This could reflect conflict among the men in the church (1 Tim. 3:3; 6:4–5),[12] or a more widespread association of anger with the male gender.[13] The image of pure hands is common in Greek[14] and Jewish[15] texts, and hands were lifted for supplication and praise according to both Jewish[16] and Greco-Roman[17] texts and art. Paul requires that men "everywhere" pray with uplifted, pure hands. ("Everywhere" means either that this requirement is universally applicable,[18] or that he is addressing the rule to a number of different house churches in Ephesus.)[19]

Although the grammar is not clear on this point, the "likewise" of 2:9 probably suggests that Paul, who has just instructed the men how to pray, now turns to instructing the women in the same way.[20] As in 1 Corinthians 11, women are not silenced in church; they are permitted to pray. Since most synagogue prayers were offered by men,[21] this freedom is significant. But the fact that Paul's exhortations to them are more detailed than those given to men indicates that there are some special problems relating to the women in the Ephesian congregation, and these problems break down naturally into two categories of exhortation, one concerning dress codes, and the other concerning teaching. The women seem to be erring on these two points; the first error is inappropriate in the context of public worship,[22] and judging from Paul's language, the second error is worse than inappropriate.

## WOMEN'S DRESS CODE

Paul here seems to regulate women's dress, and multitudes of preachers have exploited this passage for a variety of fashion purposes (from requiring clothing in general, which is probably helpful, to requiring specific styles of clothes, often as antiquated as possible). But Paul is less concerned with prohibitions like our modern ones (such as no blue jeans in church) than he is with people adorning themselves to attract glances from congregants of the opposite gender or to show off their wealth or new fashions in church. While various churches have different cultural traditions of appropriate church clothing, the issues of intentionally suggestive attire and (particularly) of extravagantly expensive attire unfortunately receive considerably less attention in churches these days, and this is what Paul is addressing.

### Ancient Views on Adornments

Special adornments were not only permitted but blessed by Jewish teachers of the second century and later.[23] Rabbi Akiba, who permitted a husband to divorce his wife if he found someone more beautiful, said that wives could wear makeup and deck themselves out for their husbands.[24] Some later teachers said that God plaited Eve's hair before bringing her to Adam.[25] These teachers claimed that woman, being Adam's flesh, goes bad without adornment just as meat goes bad without spices.[26] Of course, it was recognized that the adornment was only for her husband (or perhaps for a marital prospect),[27] not for others. But, as we shall point out below, many earlier Jewish teachers looked on such adornment less favorably,[28] reflecting a tendency against excessive adornment found elsewhere in ancient Jewish and other Greco-Roman literature.

Physical beauty was emphasized and packaged in antiquity, just as it is today. It was treated as a "virtue" of the body.[29] Particular features sometimes associated with it in Greek literature are tallness,[30] thick, dark eyebrows,[31] and golden hair with pale skin,[32] though some writers who commented on the matter pointed out that standards of beauty varied from culture to culture.[33] But while a woman's beauty was a good thing in itself, a "virtue," it is often portrayed as a dangerous temptation to men.[34] In Greek romances, it induces love even involuntarily.[35]

Women who wanted to attract men would not settle for their natural beauty; those who could afford it would adorn themselves beyond their natural endowments with gold and other decorations,[36] especially adorning their hair.[37] Jewish traditions viewed these as tools of enticement to sexual sin.[38] According to one of these texts (of uncertain date), women used this evil ploy as the only way they could gain power over men.[39]

This was not, however, the only purpose of adornments, especially adornments of the hair. Well-to-do women in this period wore elaborate hairstyles, following the constantly changing, newest fashions.[40] This practice drew considerable criticism from the moralizing editorialists of the day.

Ostentation of wealth in general was commonly mocked by philosophers. For instance, Diogenes was said to have been invited to the house of a rich young man that was so richly adorned that the philosopher had nowhere to spit—except on his host.[41] Socrates was similarly said to have complained that he felt comfortable wearing the same cloak year-round, but that some changed garments more than once a day.[42] Plutarch said that it was not good for youths to wear gold,[43] and that men should set the example for their wives by avoiding all extravagance.[44] The Stoic Musonius Rufus declared that the wise man would live simply, seeking clothing that is useful rather than that which attracts attention.[45]

But the ostentatious extravagances of well-to-do women were especially criticized.[46] The satirists, who were an ancient combination of talk-show gossips and slanderous tabloids, portrayed such women as beating innocent slaves for making a mistake with their hair,[47] as spending themselves into poverty for luxuries,[48] and, worst of all, as decking themselves out splendidly only to keep their adulterous paramours happy.[49]

Some writers may have voiced other criticisms. One could have been that such glamorous dress would induce jealousy among other women, and since an honorable woman did not wish to be envied by other women,[50] this was dishonorable behavior. Excess clothing was part of well-to-do women's desire to flaunt their wealth. Plutarch modestly concludes that if women were not allowed to dress up so much they would stay at home as they ought to![51]

Paul's language here resembles that of other ancient writers on the subject, and Paul presumably means the same thing they did. (Otherwise his ancient readers would have had a hard time catching his point.) His problem with excessive adornment is that it is ostentatious and calls attention to its wearer. As David Scholer notes,

> there is no question that in the cultural context of the early church the rejection of external adornment was part and parcel of a woman's submission to her husband and a recognition of her place among men in general. External adornment was clearly seen as indicative of two most undesirable characteristics: (1) sexual infidelity; and (2) materialistic extravagance.[52]

The artificial augmentations of beauty Paul addresses here were the sort that only the wealthy could afford, and that turned men's heads as symbols of status inseparable from the cultural expressions of beauty they signified. In our day, contrary to what many might think, Paul's rebuke probably would have much more to do with church members' driving to church in BMWs or wearing the most expensive clothes than with their wearing blue jeans.

## The True Adornment

The warning in 1 Timothy 2:9–10 is undoubtedly against *excessive* adornment. The similar admonition in 1 Peter 3:3 advises against depending on external adornments like ornate hair designs, gold, and clothing, but it clearly does not prohibit the wearing of clothing or arranging of hair altogether. Braiding hair was not unusual,[53] so the reference in 1 Timothy may be to plaiting the hair with gold rather than to plaiting it and also wearing gold.[54] But that these women could be wearing gold at all suggests that they were well-to-do compared to most of the urban free.[55] This may even mean that they belonged to the class that ran the city or, more likely, that they were trying to pretend that they belonged in that social class.[56] This created the same sort of tension earlier initiated by uncovered aristocratic women in Corinth.

Paul's argument appeals to a common theme in ancient moralists: real beauty is that of one's character. This was true of men,[57] but even more so of women, who were expected to be "modest" in demeanor and dress.[58] A famous Spartan ruler was said to have "banished from the State all artificial enhancement of beauty" so that wives would be chosen only on the basis of true virtue.[59] One philosopher says that young women should realize that they are really honored for appearing "modest and self-respecting," not for their attempts to beautify themselves.[60] Other philosophical treatises exhorted women to dress in the simplest possible clothes.[61]

> The temperate, freeborn woman must live with her legal husband adorned with modesty, clad in neat, simple, white dress without extravagance or excess. She must avoid clothing that is either entirely purple or is streaked with purple and gold, for that kind of dress is worn by hetaerae when they stalk the masses of men. But the adornment of a woman who wishes to please only one man, her own husband, is her character and not her clothing. For the freeborn woman must be beautiful to her own husband, not to the men in the neighborhood.[62]

Modesty was often regarded as the true adornment.[63] Isocrates had long before exhorted:

> Consider that no adornment so becomes you as modesty, justice, and self-control; for these are the virtues by which, as all men are agreed, the character of the young is held in restraint.[64]

A later exhortation pretending to be from one woman to another advised:

> You should have a blush on your cheeks as a sign of modesty instead of rouge, and should wear nobility, decorum and temperance instead of gold and emeralds. For the woman who strives for virtue must not have her heart set on expensive clothing but on the management of her household.[65]

Diaspora (non-Palestinian) Jewish texts also came to reflect this ideal.[66]

It is thus relatively certain that the hearers in Timothy's congregation would have grasped Paul's point, had Timothy read the letter to them: dress and live simply and unenticingly, but be lavish in your spirit; decorate your heart with purity and humility. This may have irritated ostentatious members of the congregation then, just as it would irritate ostentatious members of our churches today if they understood it.

Some women today may feel that it was unfair for Paul to pick on extravagantly dressed, well-to-do women but not on men; but Paul no doubt did so because they were the ones normally addressed by this particular issue in this congregation and more generally in antiquity. This does not mean, however, that Paul would not have addressed the same counsel to the men had they been creating a similar disturbance (difficult as this would have been in that culture). Paul would certainly not want men to dress in a manner that caused women to stumble, either. After all, 1 Timothy 2:8 tells only men to avoid wrath and disputing when they pray, but Paul hardly wanted women to pray in wrath and disputing!

## WOMEN TEACHERS?

Paul gives several injunctions that could be taken to mean that he opposes women teaching. He calls on them to learn "quietly," and forbids them to teach in such a manner as to "take authority" over a man. But each of these statements must be understood in its own cultural context to be read the way Paul wanted his first readers to understand it.

### Silence

It is possible that Paul here imposes the same sort of silence on women that they faced in many other religious contexts of the day, including most synagogues for which we have evidence.[67] This would imply that he changed his mind after he wrote 1 Cor. 11:4–5. But it is also possible that he imposes on new learners the same spirit of quiet submission that was normally appropriate for novices in his day. He could even mean what he meant about learning quietly in 1 Corinthians 14:34–35: learn the basics before you try to challenge your teacher.

Silence was an appropriate way to learn except when one had a thorough knowledge of the subject.[68] Some teachers purportedly even required long periods of silence from their pupils, probably as a form of moral discipline.[69] When Paul admonished the women to be silent in 1 Corinthians 14:34, he used a stronger term than he uses here, but the same principle may apply to both:

they were to learn, but not by disrupting the whole assembly with unlearned questions. An admonition to learn in silence could also be an admonition to stop talking and pay attention to what was being said (cf. Acts 15:12; 21:40; 22:2), and need not mean that the person was forever to remain quiet (1 Cor. 14:28; cf. 14:30). This presumably relates to the specific situation in Ephesus suggested in 1 Timothy 5:13—many younger women were making the rounds with foolish talk, trying to teach but not knowing what they were talking about.[70]

The word used here for "silence" normally refers to respectful attention or a quiet demeanor.[71] The *whole* church is exhorted to this kind of quiet lifestyle with the same word in this very context (2:2), demonstrating that Paul refers to a certain attitude, not to complete muzzling. (Like the men's prayer without wrath or disputing in 2:8, this could have been applied equally strongly to either gender causing the problem.) Paul's reason for specifically addressing this admonition to the women is probably the same as his reason in 1 Corinthians 14:34–35: they were not yet taught.

**Usurping Authority?**

Paul warns against women "teaching in such a way as to take authority," but it is not exactly clear what the Greek term here translated "take authority" means. Does he mean "accept a position of authority"? Or does he mean "seize authority in an overbearing way"? Or could he mean even "to proclaim oneself originator"? Scholars are divided on the issue.

Kroeger finds evidence that the term can mean "to proclaim oneself the author or originator of something," and suggests that Paul here combats the Gnostic-type myth that woman is man's source.[72] While this does make excellent sense of the following context, most of her lexical evidence is from the patristic period (when it could also mean "have authority"; see below), as is the relevant myth. Her case works well if 1 Timothy is written by someone much later than Paul, but in Paul's period it is unlikely that his readers would have automatically understood the term so narrowly.

In contrast to the claims of some other writers,[73] Scholer observes that this term usually does carry a negative sense of "domineer" or "usurp authority."[74] We could thus read Paul's phrase as, "I am not allowing a woman to teach in such a way as to domineer over men." On this reading, Paul, who wants women to "learn quietly," does not want them to teach disruptively—something he also would have forbidden men to do.[75] This is not a new suggestion; it was proposed by evangelical supporters of the women's movement in the 1800s.[76]

Moo suggests that the term may mean either "have authority" or "usurp authority," but he contends that the idea of usurpation should only be read in it if it is suggested by the context.[77] It is difficult to evaluate what nuance readers would have attached to the term because the meaning of the term gradually changed, from associations with murder in classical usage to "domineer" and, by the patristic period, to "exercise authority."[78] If 1 Timothy was written by a second-century writer in Paul's name, the term *probably* just means "exercise authority" (or perhaps "proclaim oneself originator"). If the letter reflects the language of Paul or his amanuensis, it could well mean "domineer," since it is different from and probably stronger than the term he usually uses.

If we assume Pauline authorship, then, Paul may merely prohibit teaching done in a domineering way. But assuming that Moo is correct that only the context will really determine what nuance Paul intends, we may ask what sense the context suggests. That Paul wants women to learn submissively and shortly thereafter invokes the Genesis language about Eve probably indicates that these women are not submitting to their husbands but rather are seeking to lord it over them (cf. Gen. 3:16).[79]

The evidence is not entirely clear, as Scholer observes, but Scholer is right that this is not Paul's usual term for exercising authority.[80] The context, which helps us reconstruct the situation, suggests that Paul may here be warning against a domineering use of authority, rather than merely any use of authority.

## Specific Situation or General Rule?

First Timothy 2:11–12 clearly forbids women to teach in some sense, although most scholars, including those who think the passage disallows women elders, agree that it forbids them only to teach in such a way as to hold authority in some form.[81] Probably it only forbids them to teach in a way that usurps authority, and so seeks to domineer, although this is not absolutely clear. But even assuming that Paul's words actually prohibited women from teaching altogether, would he have applied this only to the women directly addressed by his letter (who were untaught),[82] or was he depending on a general principle applicable to all women in all times?[83]

Several arguments have been suggested to prove that Paul's instructions in this passage apply to all women in all cultures. Some of these arguments have nothing to do with the text of Scripture, for instance, the argument that the maleness of Christ is better represented through a male agent.[84] This argument reads like something out of Philo, who saw men as feminine before God, just as women were feminine before men, masculinity being the ideal spiritual state. But if Jesus' incarnation as a male means that ministers should be male, then it also means that they should be single, Jewish, give their teachings in Greek and/or Aramaic, and hang out with Galilean fishermen. I have never heard a persuasive argument for why Jesus' maleness must be represented by male ministers, but his singleness or Jewishness need not be.

Piper and Grudem argue that the well-educated Priscilla was in Ephesus when Paul wrote these words (2 Tim. 4:19),[85] so Paul forbade even well-educated women to teach authoritatively.[86] This point would certainly remove the force of our argument that Paul's injunction related only to the majority of uneducated women in Ephesus. It is not entirely clear, however, that Priscilla was already in Ephesus when Paul wrote 1 Timothy, since enough time had transpired between 1 and 2 Timothy for Paul to have been imprisoned in the interim.

But assuming that she was there, it is still hardly necessary to take Paul's general prohibition as applying to all cases. Paul no doubt means this as a general statement that might admit certain obvious exceptions. If that answer sounds too simplistic it should be remembered that most writers stated principles this way. Paul's requirement that an overseer be "husband of one wife" (1 Tim. 3:2) is a case in point: the statement could not apply to Paul and probably could not apply to Timothy, either.[87] Does his general prohibition nullify his own teaching and that of Timothy, whom no one was to despise (4:12)?

A more persuasive argument for the universal import of this passage is that it is stated in a universalistic manner. George Knight III says that 1 Timothy 2:11–12 and 1 Corinthians 14:34 "are clearly the didactic passages on the subject," so other passages should be interpreted in the light of them.[88] But to this we would respond that other passages which show the practice of early

Christians sanctioned by Paul (Appendix A) must qualify our understanding of anything else Paul says on the subject, since his "didactic" passages address specific churches and must be analyzed in the light of his whole teaching and practice.

Further, I believe that Knight is wrong in the way that he takes certain passages as didactic and other passages as not.[89] The author of 1 Timothy writes in another letter that *all* biblical texts are profitable for teaching (2 Tim. 3:16).[90] If Knight would object that some passages merely teach through concrete historical examples addressing specific situations (see 1 Cor. 10:11),[91] we reply that this is also how Paul's letters are to be read, for this is how they present themselves (e.g., Gal. 1:1–6; 1 Thess. 1:1–3). If "didactic" means that we can extract the passage from the situation it addresses, then *no* texts are didactic (including proverbs, which presuppose certain ancient Near Eastern customs and topics). If didactic means that the passage teaches us God's ways by illustrating how God has acted in concrete situations of the past, then all passages are didactic. Narrative, epistle, proverb, ethical admonition, prophecy, and apocalyptic are all genres with some degree of overlap, but "didactic" is not such a useful category, especially in the case to which Knight applies it, where one of his "didactic" passages and one of his nondidactic passages are from the same epistle.[92]

Against Knight and others who read this text as transcultural, arguments can be marshalled to demonstrate that this passage addresses a specific situation in the church at Ephesus. Several different reasons may be suggested for why women in this congregation must not teach. One is that church leaders in God's household exercised authority over different social groups in the household differently, as a householder would to members of his house (1 Tim. 5:1–2).[93] It would be much harder for a woman to fulfill this function in that society. Given the pressures the church was facing at this point, women who tried to hold a teaching office could thus contribute to outsiders' gaining a negative impression of Christianity, which is a major issue in 1 Timothy and the other letters ("Pastoral Epistles") written about this time. This is not to say that Paul would have therefore excluded women from this office, but to suggest that fewer women would have sought it and that Paul might have been more careful what kind of teaching role they would have been given.

A more important reason Paul may not have wanted these women to teach is that much of the false teaching in Ephesus was being spread through women in the congregation. This is not to say that women are more prone to lead others astray than men—the false teachers themselves seem to have been men. But in that culture the uneducated women seem to have provided the network the false teachers could use to spread their falsehoods through the congregations (1 Tim. 5:13; 2 Tim. 3:6–7). This is probably because the women were not as well learned in the Scriptures as men were, as we pointed out in the preceding chapter.

Presumably, Paul wants them to learn so that they could *teach*.[94] If he prohibits women from teaching because they are unlearned, his demand that they learn constitutes a long-range solution to the problem. Women unlearned in the Bible could not be trusted to pass on its teachings accurately, but once they had learned, this would not be an issue, and they could join the ranks of women colleagues in ministry whom Paul elsewhere commends.[95]

Some readers believe that Paul's wording also shows that this passage was meant only for the specific situation in Ephesus. The present indicative verb in the clause "I *am not allowing* a woman to teach" is contrasted with the more forceful command that follows, "let her learn." These readers take the first clause, forbidding a woman to teach, as situationally conditioned in contrast to the second clause, ordering her to learn, which they read as a universal command.[96]

What is most significant about the wording of the passage, however, is that Paul does not assume that Timothy already knows this rule. Had this rule been established and universal, is it possible that Timothy, who had worked many years with Paul, would not have known it already? Paul often reminds readers of traditions they should know by saying, "You know," or "Do you not know?" or "According to the traditions which I delivered to you." In his letters to Timothy Paul appeals to "we know" (e.g., 1 Tim. 1:8), "faithful sayings" (e.g., 1 Tim. 1:15), and cites Timothy's knowledge of Paul's own life (2 Tim. 3:10–11). He does give general moral counsel relating to Timothy's situation at Ephesus, but quite clearly not all his admonitions to Timothy are directly applicable universally (1 Tim. 5:11–14a, 23; 2 Tim. 4:13).

Since this passage is related so closely to the situation Timothy was confronting in Ephesus, we should not use it in the absence of other texts to prove that Paul meant it universally. In other words, we should not agree with Packer who suggests that, since there is doubt how Paul would apply this text in our culture, we should give him "the benefit of that doubt and retain his restriction on women exercising authority on Christ's behalf over men in the church."[97]

There are major problems with this writer's logic. First, if the matter is really in doubt, we should not be using it to pass judgment on other people's calls. A "fence around the law" interpretation was fine for the Pharisees, but Jesus' method of extrapolating from Scripture was to appeal to its intention and motive, not to let it mean all that it might legally mean for fear of contradicting it.

Second, this writer assumes that he is really giving the benefit of the doubt to *Paul*, an assumption that would need to be proved, and that is probably wrong. What if he is in fact contradicting what Paul believed by prohibiting women from authoritative positions of ministry? We cannot presuppose what Paul meant and then "give the benefit of the doubt" to this presupposed position.

Third, our evidence from elsewhere in Paul suggests that the matter is *not* in doubt; women are allowed to teach if they are adequately trained. Scandal would have arisen had Paul included women among his traveling companions, but once this fact is taken into consideration, the percentage of women colleagues Paul acknowledges is amazing by any ancient standards. (Because this evidence from elsewhere in Paul is important to our discussion, we provide a brief treatment of it in Appendix A.)

Perhaps if we do not know for certain whether we are right or wrong, we ought to give the "benefit of the doubt" to those who claim that God called them and who evidence the fruits of that call in their lives, rather than passing judgment on them.

## DAUGHTERS OF EVE: 1 TIMOTHY 2:13–15

It is easy to argue that Paul's injunctions against women teaching in this passage are directed to a specific situation, not to all situations. It is, in my opinion, impossible to take them any *other* way once one has examined those passages in Paul where women share in the ministry of God's word (see appendix A on that point).

But the nature of Paul's argument here complicates matters. As when he defends the use of head coverings for women, so here Paul bases his case on an interpretation of Scripture. That Paul bases his argument on the Old Testament creation narrative suggests that he is appealing to God's ideal plan, which ought to be followed by God's people throughout this age. This is not, however, the only way to read this passage, especially given his treatment of the same text in some of his other writings, particularly when he argues in favor of head coverings. "The woman's subordination from creation" is at any rate not the most obvious point of the text to which he alludes; it is in fact simply not what Genesis chapters 1–3 taken on their own terms teach, although this book is not meant to address those passages. Paul often makes his case by analogy, and when he cites Scripture does not always appeal to a universal principle to make his point, as we argued in chapter 1.

## Eve in Jewish Tradition

The rabbis clearly had it in for Eve.[98] Her sinful act was often rehearsed in rabbinic literature: women march ahead of the bier because Eve brought death to the world;[99] they menstruate because Eve shed Adam's blood;[100] they kindle the Sabbath lights because Eve extinguished Adam's soul.[101] A later rabbi even claimed that Eve was created so that Adam would sin.[102] Occasionally the resultant curse of Genesis 3, rather than her sin itself, was used as grounds for her subordination.[103] Nor were the rabbis the only Jewish male commentators on the subject, as a Diaspora Jewish text indicates: "But the woman first became a betrayer to him. She gave, and persuaded him to sin in his ignorance. He was persuaded by the woman's words, forgot about his immortal creator, and neglected clear commands."[104] Interestingly, this writer excuses Adam, not Eve, by the claim of ignorance, whereas 1 Timothy 2:14 takes the reverse approach.

Eve's deception was a special matter of comment in Jewish texts. In the related works, Life of Adam and Eve and Apocalypse of Moses (Heb. ca. first century CE), Eve appears as a well-meaning fool who is repeatedly deceived and keeps getting the wiser Adam in trouble with God. In this story, God, Adam, Eve, and the serpent all recognize that humanity's fall is Eve's fault.[105]

One tradition said that Satan disguised himself to mislead Eve sexually or in some other way besides the encounter described in Genesis 3.[106] As the story often goes, Satan or the serpent became jealous of Adam,[107] and so wished to kill him and take his wife.[108] Thus he entered Eden and corrupted Eve behind Adam's back.[109] But we cannot be sure how widespread this story was in Paul's day, and both Paul and his readers would have more likely thought of the account they knew from the Bible, namely, Eve's deception by the serpent at the tree. These other traditions merely reinforce the picture of Eve's gullibility and sinfulness.

Some of the rabbis did, however, explain Eve's sin at the tree as partly the fault of Adam. He had added to God's words when he relayed God's commandment to Eve; this was why she told the serpent that God had forbidden her not only to eat of the tree, but also to *touch* it.[110] In other words, the woman was deceived in part because she had not received the commandment directly from God, and the one who had passed it on to her had misrepresented it. This point may be significant to our discussion below.

Not only Eve but women in general were seen as more inclined to deception; it was usually assumed to be part of their weaker nature, according to general Greco-Roman[111] and Jewish[112] teaching. Of course, if one withholds education from a specific class of people on the assumption that they cannot learn, their subsequent lack of knowledge will be unjustly used to reinforce the conviction that they are not adept at learning; history is replete with examples of this practice. But 1 Timothy 2:14 bases the analogy on Eve's deception, not on the culture's low opinion of women's discernment; the context clearly shows that "the woman" in this passage refers to Eve, not to "woman" in a generic sense.[113]

## How to Interpret This Passage

Paul does not say, "Women in Ephesus, learn quietly and don't teach (in some sense) because of the situation in Ephesus." Paul says instead, "Women in Ephesus, learn quietly and don't teach (in some sense), for Eve was created after Adam and was deceived, and you could become like her." It is easy to see why many readers take this passage as forbidding all women to teach.

The matter is not necessarily this simple, however. The "for" ("for Eve was created") can be understood either as the reason for the impropriety of Ephesian women's teachings or as an explanation of it. If we read the clause as an explanation rather than a cause of the impropriety of their teaching, Paul could simply be drawing an analogy rather than making a universal argument.[114]

But if Paul is making arguments for why these women should not teach, it appears at first sight that he provides us with two of them here, rather than just one. The first is from the creation order: Eve was created second. The second is that Eve was deceived when she transgressed.

The creation order argument is the more problematic and difficult to fathom of the two, because it is hard to square with Genesis. The Genesis account, taken on it own terms, does not subordinate Eve because she was created second; it makes her an equal part of Adam—her creation was necessary for him to be complete. The Hebrew phrase "helper suitable for him," as is well known, denotes a role of strength ("helper" usually refers to God in the Hebrew Bible), and "suitable" may mean "corresponding to" or "equal to" (so that the woman is not viewed as a superior helper like God, nor as an unmatched creation like the animals).[115]

What then might Paul mean? There are at least three possibilities. The first is that Paul is exploiting the biblical account and twisting its meaning by ignoring its context. This suggestion would not appeal to most of us who think that Paul was writing under the Spirit's inspiration and those who hold this view would not accept Paul's case as a valid transcultural argument anyway. The second is that Paul is using the text in an ad hoc way to make a point but that, had he had more space, he would have qualified his point as he did in 1 Corinthians 11: woman was created second but she is really man's equal and interdependent partner.[116] Again, those who do not believe Paul's point to have been ad hoc in that passage must enforce women's wearing of head coverings in churches today (and perhaps explain why Paul does not explicitly appeal to "universal" head coverings to address the ornate hair of well-to-do women in 1 Tim. 2:9–10). The third possibility is that Paul intends to connect Eve's later creation to why she was deceived: she was not present when God gave the commandment, and thus was dependent on Adam for the teaching.[117] In other words, she was inadequately educated—like the women in the Ephesian church.

If we read Paul's injunction here as applying to all women in all cultures, then this passage must be understood to mean, "Eve was deceived, so all women are more easily deceived than all men." Otherwise he would not automatically exclude *all* women from teaching on this principle. On this reading of the text, Paul's argument is that any good man's teaching is better than any woman's (no matter how trained or devout), and that all women's teaching is necessarily invalid. But since Paul presupposes both male heretics and nonheretical women in the congregation, it is unlikely that he means this.

A better way to read this text is as an analogy, the kind Paul draws from Scripture throughout his letters. He often applies biblical examples just to analogous groups within particular local congregations in his own day (e.g., 1 Cor. 10:1–12). In this case, Paul is drawing an analogy between the easily deceived Eve and the easily deceived women in Ephesus. Since Paul elsewhere uses Eve as an analogy for the gullibility of the whole Corinthian church (2 Cor. 11:3)[118]—the men no less than the women—it is clear that he does not simply regard Eve as a standard symbol for women, any more than the consequences of Adam's fall apply only to men in other Pauline passages (Rom. 5:12–21; 1 Cor. 15:45–49).

At this point, we may complain that Paul should have qualified his case here, as he did in 1 Corinthians 11:11–12, if he wished us to understand that he was simply applying this illustration to the matter at hand. But Paul's illustration here covers the space of only two verses, and it may be too much to ask that such a brief illustration be qualified. If Paul was addressing only the issue in Ephesus, he was also writing the letter only to Timothy and the believers in Ephesus, and he would not have felt the need to explain to future generations that he was doing so. After all, if someone else later read the letter, Paul would assume that they would be smart enough to recognize that he was addressing his letter to a situation in Ephesus, as the letter as a whole claims to do. When we read Paul's message to our spiritual ancestors for its relevance to us, we ought to do so within the canon of his whole teaching and practice.

But, having said this, we should note that Paul may have qualified his point in this text after all. The only passage in his Bible that really spoke of women's subordination as a transcultural norm is the passage about Eve's judgment at the Fall. Eve's deception led to her subordination under man (Gen. 3:16). This is presented as part of the curse, and, like other aspects of the curse (labor pains, toil in the fields, sin, and death), does not need to be praised and enforced by church rules. But Paul may be saying in 1 Timothy 2:15, "Eve sinned and is a warning about what these women in Ephesus can do; but I must qualify my point: the curse that followed her sin is reversed for true followers of Jesus Christ."

*1 Timothy 2:15: Saved through Childbearing*

This passage is the climax of Paul's argument in 2:9–15,[119] and it must be related in some sense to what precedes it. The loose connective with the preceding verse may suggest that the image of Eve remains in 2:15.

There are at least three major ways to interpret this verse. The first is that women are saved because women are part of the plan of salvation, as evidenced in the great childbearing of Mary. Mary's childbearing reversed the effects of Eve's introduction of sin into the world.[120] The problem with this interpretation is that nothing in the context limits the childbearing to Mary's or suggests that Mary is in view.

The second is that despite Eve's sin, a woman can be saved if she lives righteously before God.[121] This verse can then mean either that she is saved through submitting to the curse of Genesis 3:16,[122] or that she is saved through fulfilling the roles necessary to be an appropriate witness in her culture. Given the specific language of this text (especially "propriety"), the latter view is more likely: they are saved "through the maternal and domestic roles that were clearly understood to constitute propriety (*sōphrosynē*) for women in the Greco-Roman culture of Paul's day."[123] This view makes good sense of the text and its context, and may be correct. I originally held this view, but reading ancient prayers for safety in childbirth eventually led me to concur with those who hold the third view.

The third position is that this verse refers to women being "brought safely through" childbirth. "Saved" means "delivered" or "brought safely through" more often in ancient literature than it means "saved from sin."[124] It is true that Paul nowhere else uses "saved" to mean "saved in childbirth," but it should be kept in mind that Paul nowhere else *speaks* of coming safely through childbirth. The most natural way for an ancient reader to have understood "salvation" in the context of childbirth would have been a safe delivery, for women regularly called upon patron deities (such as Artemis[125] or Isis[126]) in childbirth.[127]

Eve's sin was directly connected with the curse of a difficult childbirth in Genesis 3:16,[128] and in Jewish tradition this was developed to include death in childbirth.[129]

> Adam was the blood of the world. Because woman brought death upon him, she was put under obligation (to observe the law) of

> the blood of menstrual purity. Man was the dough offering of the world. Because she made him unclean, she was put under obligation (to observe the law) of the dough offering. Man was the light of the world. Because she caused him to be extinguished, she was put under obligation (to observe the lighting) of the (Sabbath) lamp. From this the Sages, blessed be their memory, said: For three offenses women die when they are giving birth: For carelessness in regard to menstrual purity, the dough offering and lighting the Sabbath lamp.[130]

Nor is this a strictly rabbinic reading of Eve's judgment; the very nonrabbinic Jewish work, Apocalypse of Moses, also indicates the view that she would "come near to lose [her] life from [her] great anguish and pains" at birth.[131] In the related Life of Adam and Eve, Eve's prayers in childbirth were not heard because of her sin, though Adam's prayers for her were heard.[132]

But as impiety delivered one over to the effects of the curse, so also piety could deliver one from certain effects of the curse.[133] The power to open barren wombs by prayer was sometimes attributed to pious men,[134] and priests were said to have fasted to prevent pregnant women from miscarrying.[135] An early Christian hymn even claims that Mary bore Jesus without any pain.[136]

It may thus be that Paul's promise that the women will be brought safely through childbirth is seen as a relief from part of the curse, from which believers will not be completely free until they share fully in the resurrection life of the second Adam, Christ (1 Cor. 15:45–49).[137] This would then qualify a connection between Eve's deception and the curse that might lead some of Paul's readers to assume that women must accept a subordinate role in the situation they faced in the Ephesian church because of Eve's sin.

At this point, someone could counter that Paul need not be qualifying the whole curse; Paul, after all, could still see the husband's rule over her (Gen. 3:16) as a valid part of God's plan until the curse is fully done away at the second coming of Christ. Paul's argument does not depend on this curse even to begin with, however, because the curse would have made a point much stronger than the one Paul wanted. Genesis 3:16 laments the effects of human sin as God's curse, but does not prescribe them as a normative rule we ought to follow, any more than the Fall's introduction of sin and death into the world is reason for us to promote sin and death. Paul does not appeal to the curse, but to Eve's sin; and here he merely makes plainer that the curse itself was never part of God's ideal plan for his people and that his appeal to the example of Eve's sin does *not* support the continuance of the curse.

Before the Fall, Adam and Eve together were to rule all things (Gen. 1:27–28). But after the Fall, Adam would rule his wife because, being stronger, he could force her to obey. She would desire to overcome him but be unable, and he would instead overcome and rule her. This is the best way to take the Hebrew of Genesis 3:16, given the parallel constructions in Genesis 4:7: sin's desire was toward Cain, but God told him to rule it, i.e., overcome it. This is a picture of marital strife, and Paul appeals instead to the creation order to establish his point: mutual harmony, which in this case mandates the woman's silence and submission. Creation order mandates harmony, but Paul wants no one to misunderstand his appeal to Genesis: the curse has been affected by Christ's triumph, and elements of it are passing away.

## CONCLUSION

There is a universal principle in this text, but it is broader than that unlearned women should not teach. If Paul does not want the women to teach in some sense, it is not because they are women, but because they are unlearned. His principle here is that those who do not understand the Scriptures and are not able to teach them accurately should not be permitted to teach others.[138] This text is unfortunately quite applicable today; there are all too many people teaching unhealthy interpretations of the Bible today, and most of them are men.

I have sometimes said tongue-in-cheek that this prohibition of incompetent teachers thus excludes from ministry those who prohibit women from teaching. This is, of course, an exaggeration; if God did not show mercy on us when our interpretations miss his point, none of us could count as competent (a warning not without merit; see Jas. 3:1–2). But in all seriousness, it *is* a dangerous thing to turn people from their call, or to oppose their call if it is genuinely from God. On what basis do any of us men who are called prove our call? We trust inner conviction and the fruit of holy lives and teaching and faithfulness to that call, and if these evidences are insufficient demonstration of divine calling in the case of our sisters, how shall we attest our own?

The logic of the case can be battled back and forth with ever-new arguments for years, but in the meantime, we are confronted with the issue of those who claim to be called by God, and with a harvest that is great but for which the laborers are few. My hope is that this chapter will open some minds and hearts to their own call from God, and other minds and hearts to receive the ministry of God's women servants whom God has anointed with his Spirit (Acts 2:18).

## NOTES

1. Eph. 5:31 also appeals to the creation order, but it does so in order to establish the opposite point, namely, the unity of husband and wife and therefore their mutual service and dependence. See chapter 5 below.

2. For a listing of divergent views on 25 major questions of interpretation in 1 Tim. 2:8–15, see Hull, "Difficulties," pp. 259–65.

3. I refer here to NT scholars in general, not to evangelical scholars (whose positions are sometimes ignored when less conservative scholars calculate majority opinions). Discussions of the issue from both sides are widely available, but I have chosen in this book to emphasize how the text should be read by those of us who believe it to be Pauline.

4. Meeks, "Androgyne," p. 208, and Scroggs, "Woman," p. 284, are among those who see a diminution of Paul's radical equality position in second- and third-generation Christianity.

5. The plural "kings" indicates client rulers as well as the Roman *princeps*.

6. A. M. Rabello, "The Legal Condition of the Jews in the Roman Empire," *ANRW* 2.13, pp. 703–4. The emperors paid for these sacrifices (Bonsirven, *Judaism*, p. 155). This practice of offering sacrifices on behalf of a ruler appears in Palestine quite early (1 Esd. 6:31–32); also among Egyptian Jews in the Ptolemaic period (Ep. Arist. 45), who felt that kings were to seek the peace of their subjects (Ep. Arist. 291–92); a Jewish ruler of the second century BCE asks the Spartans to remember his people at every time in their sacrifices and prayers (1 Macc. 12:11); a high priest was said to have sacrificed on behalf of an invader official's recovery (2 Macc. 3:32). Philo says that on Yom Kippur the high priest offers prayers for the peace of all humanity (*Embassy to Gaius* 306).

7. Philo, *Embassy to Gaius* 232; b. Yoma 69a (superimposed on Alexander of Macedon!); cf. James Parkes, *The Conflict of the Church and the Synagogue* (New York: Atheneum, 1979), pp. 9–10. A pre-70 teacher said to pray for the peace of the government (m. Ab. 3:2; cf. Jer. 29:7; Bar. 1:11; Ep. Arist. 45). This was within the bounds of acceptable Roman practice: Roman officials took vows for Augustus' health (Pliny *Ep.* 10.52; *Res Gestae* 9.1, in *The Roman Empire: Augustus to Hadrian*, ed. R. K. Sherk, TDGR 6 [New York: Cambridge University, 1988], p. 43, §26; cf. the sacrifice in the temple of Caesar in ibid., p. 58, §32); sacrifices could also be offered in honor of someone never deified (*I. Ital.* 13.1, p. 329, in ibid., p. 54, §28C).

8. Jos. *War* 2.17.2, §§409–10; cf. Bo Reicke, *The New Testament Era* (Philadelphia: Fortress, 1974), p. 256; Moore, *Judaism,* 2:115. The hoped-for restoration of this sacrifice was for the purpose of obtaining Roman favor (Reicke, *Era,* p. 287). It is possible, though not proved, that Jewish-Roman tensions in Palestine on the verge of revolt were affecting Diaspora synagogue communities, and through them some of Paul's churches; "peace" here could then refer to political stability (2 Macc. 12:2), and prayer could be seen as a pious alternative to Zealot-like violence (3 Macc. 1:23).

9. See ch. 4 below.

10. As in the Isis propaganda in Apul. *Metam.* 11.17. Oscar Cullmann, *State in the New Testament,* p. 85, says that this practice continued among the Christians even in times of harshest persecution; cf. e.g., Polycarp *Phil.* 12; Tert. *Apol.* 40.13–15.

11. The wording of v. 3 may suggest that some saw this as a compromise with the imperial cult; Paul saw it instead as good sense. It is also possible that God's wish for everyone to be saved in this text is more directly related to the prayers; the biblical teaching that kings' hearts could be turned by God's will also led to the possibility that prayer could affect rulers (e.g., Ep. Arist. 17); but Jewish prayers were for the emperor's well-being and behavior, not his conversion (Hans Conzelmann, *History of Primitive Christianity,* trans. John E. Steely [Nashville: Abingdon, 1973], p. 133). Cf. t. 'A. Z. 1:3: "They ask after the welfare of gentiles on their festivals for the sake of peace" (Neusner 4:311; cf. Pes. Rab Kah. 28:9). Richard and Catherine Kroeger, "May Women Teach? heresy in the pastoral epistles," *RefJ* 30 (10, Oct. 1980): 15 (also F. B. Martin, *Call Me Blessed* [Grand Rapids: Eerdmans, 1988], pp. 151–52), suggest that the following verses about women teaching relate to female mediator figures, given the context (cf. 1 Tim. 2:5); but this does not seem the most natural way to construe the context, nor are female mediatorial figures necessarily connected with women's teaching roles (cf. our discussion of the cult of Isis in ch. 4). The points of contact with Gnosticism that Catherine Kroeger notes in "1 Timothy 2:12—A Classicist's View," in *Women, Authority & the Bible,* pp. 232–42, are real, but I think the influence more likely flows from the NT to Gnosticism rather than the reverse. (She is careful to qualify that she does not see fully developed second-century Gnosticism in this text, p. 242.) Serpent veneration may be pre-Ophitic (ibid., p. 242), but this is not the element of Gnostic tradition that would be addressed in 1 Tim. 2, or even in Rev. 12 (where Gen. 3 could account for it, or Asclepius, Python, etc.).

12. A. B. Spencer, *Beyond the Curse* (reprint, Peabody: Hendrickson, 1989), p. 73, compares Josephus' report of a quarrel during synagogue prayer.

13. Cf. Plut. *Bride* 37, *Mor.* 143C, who praises the wife wise enough to remain silent until her husband has finished his fit of male rage; one of the terms for her silence is the same enjoined on women later in this passage.

14. See in A. D. Nock, *Early Gentile Christianity and Its Hellenistic Background* (New York: Harper & Row, 1964), pp. 18–19; in the

Homeric period, C. H. Gordon, *The Common Background of Greek and Hebrew Civilizations* (New York: Norton, 1965), p. 259. Martin Dibelius and Hans Conzelmann, *The Pastoral Epistles,* trans. Philip Buttolph and Adela Yarbro [Collins], Hermeneia (Philadelphia: Fortress, 1972), p. 44, point out that "holy hands" "in the Greek tragedians are hands which are ritually pure"; presumably 1 Tim. 2 refers to hands undefiled by angry use ("holy" meaning right behavior, as in Sib. Or. 1:170; see G. D. Fee, *1 and 2 Timothy, Titus,* NIBC [Peabody, Mass.: Hendrickson, 1988], p. 71).

15. E.g., Ep. Arist. 305–6; S. Safrai, "Religion in Everyday Life," in *JPFC,* p. 830. Of course, OT ritual purification, especially for the priests, developed further under later influences (e.g., Jub. 21:16).

16. Besides the biblical references (such as Isa. 1:15; Lam. 1:17; 2:19; 3:41), see Jub. 25:11; 1 En. 84:1; Ps. 155:2; 1 Esd. 9:47; 2 Macc. 3:20 (women); 14:34; 15:12, 21; 3 Macc. 5:25; 4 Macc. 4:11; Sib. Or. 3:559–60, 591–93; Test. Mos. 4:1; Mek. Pisha 1:38; t. M. K. 2:17; cf. 1 Clem. 29; Acts of John 43; cf. also the priestly blessing (m. Taan. 4:1; Sifre Num. 39.4.1; p. Taan. 4:1, §2). For the lifting of hands in earlier Near Eastern texts, see e.g., J. F. Ross, "Prophecy in Hamath, Israel, and Mari," *HTR* 63 (Jan. 1970): 3. The same practice is still followed in Islam (cf. Phil Parshall, *Bridges to Islam* [Grand Rapids: Baker, 1983], p. 81).

17. Epict. *Disc.* 4.10.14; Plut. *Cleverness of Animals* 17, *Mor.* 972B; Chariton *Chaer.* 3.1.8; Apul. *Metam.* 3:7 (to supplicate people); Suet. *Nero* 41; Deissmann, *Light,* p. 415; in Zoroastrianism, see Jack Finegan, *The Archeology of World Religions* (Princeton: Princeton University, 1952), p. 91.

18. This posture of prayer is also found in some societies unrelated to ancient Mediterranean culture, e.g., some African societies (J. S. Mbiti, *African Religions and Philosophies* [Garden City, N.Y.: Doubleday, 1970], p. 84). It is possible that Paul desires the raising of hands only because this is understood as pure worship in the culture he was addressing, using the imagery of worship standard in his culture.

19. The latter view is found in Fee, *1 Timothy,* p. 71; Verner, *Household,* p. 167, but the parallel examples cited by J. N. D. Kelly, *A Commentary on the Pastoral Epistles* (London: Adam & Charles Black, 1972), p. 65 (1 Cor. 1:2; 2 Cor. 2:14; 1 Thess. 1:8; also Mal. 1:11, cited also by Dibelius and Conzelmann, *Pastoral Epistles,* p. 45) suggest the former position. One could read "in every place" with the verb rather than with the noun that immediately precedes this phrase, meaning that prayer should be held in every place (cf. Pes. Rab Kah. 24:4), but this is not the most natural way to take the syntax.

20. Fee, *1 Timothy,* p. 70; Gundry, *Women,* p. 76; F. F. Bruce, "All Things," p. 94 (following Chrysostom); more tentatively, Verner, *Household,* p. 168; Williams, *Paul and Women,* pp. 110–11. Roger Nicole, "Authority," p. 47, n. 1; and D. J. Moo, "1 Timothy 2:11–15: Meaning and Significance," *TJ* 1 (1, Spring 1980): 63, cover the evidence for both positions fairly. Men's "pure hands" in prayer correspond to the true, spiritual adornment required of women in prayer.

21. Cf. Kelly, *Pastoral Epistles,* p. 65.

22. Cf. ibid., p. 66. D. M. Scholer, "1 Timothy 2:9–15 and the Place of Women in the Church's Ministry," in *Women, Authority & the Bible,* p. 198, sees this as the concern for propriety, for the church's reputation in Greco-Roman society, which is stressed quite often through the Pastorals (he cites 1 Tim. 3:4–5, 7, 12; 5:14; 6:1; Titus 1:6; 2:4–5, 8, 10).

23. They also seem to have been permitted in OT culture. Earrings *may* be a sign of paganism in Gen. 35:4; Jub. 31:2 (cf. Jos. & As. 3:6; Koh. Rab. 9:15, §4 [translator's interpretation]; Song Rab. 2:2, §2; Balch, *Wives,* pp. 101–2), but in Gen. 24:22 and Exod. 35:22 they appear to be acceptable (cf. the ornateness of the garment in Exod. 39).

24. See b. Shab. 64b; other references in Safrai, "Home and Family," pp. 761–62.

25. Ab. R. Nathan 4 A; 8, §22 B; and b. Ber. 61a (with an earlier attribution); Koh. Rab. 7:2, §2 (much later attribution).

26. Ab. R. Nathan 9, §24 B; Gen. Rab. 17:8.

27. Cf. Asenath after her conversion in Jos. & As. 18:6 (in some enumerations, 18:4–5); that ornaments for a rich bride included jewelry was commonplace, though in Roman society they were normally gifts of the groom (Ludwig Friedländer, *Roman Life and Manners Under the Early Empire,* trans. Leonard A. Magnus, J. H. Freese, and A. B. Gough, 4 vols. [New York: Barnes & Noble, 1907], 1:235).

28. See b. Shab. 64b, though it may refer to the menstrual taboo. The Dead Sea sect may have prohibited the wearing of finery or may not have been able to afford it (C. T. Fritsch, *The Qumran Community: Its History and Scrolls* [New York: Macmillan, 1956], p. 11); but since all property was held in common, such adornments were probably simply contributed into the wealth of the community.

29. Arist. *Pol.* 3.7.3, 1282b; *Rhet.* 1.6.10, 1362b; Jdt. 8:7; cf. t. Ber. 6:4; *OTP* 2:203, n. k. It is a subject for praise in encomium speeches, along with other bodily attributes like health and strength (Theon *Progymn.* 9.20). Although Callirhoe's nobility of character is stressed throughout Chariton's narrative, beauty is stressed as her central virtue (e.g., *Chaer.* 3.2.14); women were often renowned for beauty (e.g., Athen. *Deipn.* 13.608F). Plut. *Bride* 25, *Mor.* 141D, however, says that a woman is loved more for her character than for her beauty.

30. Ach. Tat. *Clit.* 4.5; Plut. *Div. Veng.* 33, *Mor.* 568A; Jos. & As. 1:4, 5/1:6, 8); Pes. Rab Kah. 17:6. For men: Arist. *Rhet.* 1.5.13, 1361b; Chariton *Chaer.* 2.5.2; Plut. *Lyc.* 17.4; Artapanus on Moses (Euseb. *Pr. Ev.* 9.27.37, in *OTP* 2:903).

31. Ach. Tat. *Clit.* 1.4.3; Artem. *Oneir.* 1.25.

32. Ach. Tat. *Clit.* 1.4.3; Chariton *Chaer.* 2.2.2; Apul. *Metam.* 5.22; Plut. *Theseus* 23.2. Artem. *Oneir.* 1.28 adds full cheeks.

33. Sext. Emp. *Against the Ethicists* 3.43.

34. Jdt. 10:7 (to Judith's advantage); Sir. 9:8; 25:21; cf. Sir. 11:2 (do not judge a man by beautiful appearance). A woman's beauty is again a good thing in Sir. 36:22. Plut. *Bride* 24, *Mor.* 141CD, says not to marry for beauty; it is more important to know how a woman will be to live with.

35. Chariton *Chaer.* 2.1.5; book 5, e.g., 5.5.3, 9; 6.1.9–12, 6.6.4.

36. Diog. Laert. *Lives* 6.1.10; Epict. *Encheir.* 40; Jdt. 10:4; Jos. & As. 18:6/18:4–5.

37. Apul. *Metam.* 2.9; Jdt. 10:3 (braided hair).

38. 1 En. 8:1–2; Test. Reub. 5:3, 5; Test. Jud. 12:3, 13:5; Test. Jos. 9:5. Tert. *Apol.* 6.4 says that things have become so bad that a matron and a prostitute dress the same way. Fee, *1 Timothy,* p. 72, sees 1 Tim. 2:9–10 as addressing women's seductiveness. C. D. Osburn, "*Authenteō* (1 Timothy 2:12), *RestQ* 25 (1, 1982): 11, is thus not correct to suggest that there are no sexual connotations because overdressing rather than underdressing was in view.

39. Test. Reub. 5:1–5.

40. Cary and Haarhoff, *Life,* p. 99.

41. Diogenes 38 (*CynEp,* pp. 162–63); cf. his criticism of an elaborately dressed youth in Diog. Laert. *Lives* 6.2.54; cf. also Epict. *Disc.* 3.1 (perhaps the elaborate dress is viewed as effeminate?). Men's adornments are also critiqued in 1 En. 98:2; cf. Mart. *Epig.* 4.36; 10.83; Sext. Emp. *Out. Pyrr.* 3.203, however, thinks that the nature of men's adornment is geoculturally determined.

42. Socrates 6 (*CynEp,* pp. 232–33). Naturally the Cynics opposed luxury, but so did Epicureans (Lucr. *Nat.* 2.20–53).

43. Plut. *Statecraft* 27, *Mor.* 820A.

44. Plut. *Bride* 48, *Mor.* 145AB.

45. Lutz, nos. 18AB, pp. 19, 20, in Meeks, *Moral World,* p. 49.

46. On ancient "luxury of dress and adornment," see Friedländer, *Life,* 2:173–85 (pp. 180–82 for pearls and jewelry); Plut. *Bride* 29, *Mor.* 142AB; Cary and Haarhoff, *Life,* pp. 98–99; Ramsay MacMullen, *Roman Social Relations: 50 B.C. to A.D. 284* (New Haven: Yale University, 1974), pp. 106–7; Aldo Massa, *The World of Pompeii* (Geneva: Minerva, 1972), p. 55; Jérôme Carcopino, *Daily Life in Ancient Rome* (New Haven: Yale University, 1940), pp. 164–70. The beautifying tools used included heated irons to arrange hair (Varro *Lat. Lang.* 5.29.129).

47. Mart. *Epig.* 2.66.1–8.

48. Juv. *Sat.* 6.352–65. Luxuries come under fire elsewhere, too, of course; Hor. *Ode* 1.38 (cf. 3.9.4) abhors Persian extravagance. In Jos. & As. 10:11/12 Asenath, upon her conversion, gives her expensive clothing to the poor, though she later dresses up to attract Joseph.

49. Juv. *Sat.* 6.457–73. Cf. Jos. & As. 4:1/2; Artem. *Oneir.* 1.78 for what could be a connection between expensive fineries and intercourse.

50. See the first century BCE Roman inscription in Lefkowitz and Fant, *Life,* p. 135, §138, and the third/second century BCE treatise attributed to Pythagoreans in ibid., p. 105, §107.

51. Plut. *Bride* 30, *Mor.* 142C, on the analogy of Egyptian peasant women who had no shoes.

52. Scholer, "Women's Adornment: Some Historical and Hermeneutical Observations on the New Testament Passages," *DSar* 6 (1, 1980): 5.

53. Artem. *Oneir.* 2.6; Kelly, *Pastoral Epistles,* pp. 66–67.

54. Hurley, "Veils," pp. 199–200, taking the construction as a hendiadys.

55. R. M. Grant, *Early Christianity and Society* (San Francisco: Harper & Row, 1977), p. 80 (who notes that much wealthier women existed); Verner, *Household,* p. 168.

56. Verner, *Household,* p. 180.

57. Diogenes 46, to Plato the sage (*CynEp,* pp. 176–77); Thales in Diog. Laert. *Lives* 1.37.

58. Cf. Malherbe, *Exhortation,* p. 82 (on the Pythagorean letters); Stambaugh and Balch, *Environment,* p. 111; Dibelius and Conzelmann, *Pastoral Epistles,* p. 46 (on inscriptions).

59. Plut. *Lyc.* 15, *SSpart., Mor.* 227B–228A (LCL); cf. *Lyc.* 19, *Mor.* 228B.

60. Epict. *Encheir.* 40 (LCL).

61. A third/second century BCE treatise attributed to the Pythagoreans, in Lefkowitz and Fant, *Women's Life,* p. 105, §107.

62. Ps-Melissa, *Letter to Kleareta* (in Malherbe, *Exhortation,* p. 83).

63. E.g., Plut. *Bride* 10, *Mor.* 139C; a third/second century BCE treatise attributed to the Pythagoreans, in Lefkowitz and Fant, *Women's Life,* p. 105, §107 (see also Balch, *Wives,* p. 101). For young men, "silence" was appropriate (Plut. *Lectures* 4, *Mor.* 39B).

64. Isoc. *Demon.* 15, *Or.* 1 (LCL).

65. Ps-Melissa, *Letter to Kleareta* (in Malherbe, *Exhortation,* p. 83). One may also compare Crates 9, to Mnasos (*CynEp,* pp. 60–61); Plut. *Statecraft* 27, *Mor.* 820A; Verner, *Household,* pp. 168–69; Kelly, *Peter,* p. 129.

66. 3 Macc. 3:5; 6:1; 4 Macc. 6:2. Sifre Deut. 36.4.5 reflects it as well, although the analogy there may have arisen naturally without direct influence from the milieu.

67. Kelly, *Pastoral Epistles,* pp. 67–68, cites the silence required of them in synagogues. This cannot have been true in all synagogues, since they exercised leadership roles in some of them (e.g., *CIJ* 2:10, §741); but our extant evidence (which seems to be a representative sampling) suggests that Jewish congregations with prominent roles for women were certainly in the minority. "Silence" was valued as part of women's submissiveness in various periods, especially in classical Athens (Pomeroy, *Goddesses,* p. 74), which is one of our most extreme examples.

68. Cf. Isoc. *Demon.* 41, *Or.* 1 (using a Greek term that was generally stronger than Paul's). Spencer, *Curse,* pp. 77–78, cites rabbinic texts advising silence for students.

69. Diog. Laert. *Lives* 8.1.10, claiming that Pythagoras required this of his disciples for their first five years, and using the same term as here.

70. See Fee, *1 Timothy,* p. 72.

71. Spencer, *Curse,* pp. 75–80; it is used for Abraham in Test. Ab. 1; A. Moo, "1 Timothy 2:11–15"; idem, "What Does It Mean Not to Teach or Have Authority Over Men? 1 Timothy 2:11–15," in *Manhood and Womanhood,* p. 183, prefers "silence" to "quietness" because the

context is teaching, but a verbal cognate of the same word is used in the same context (2:2) to mean "quietness," as is often pointed out.

72. Kroeger, "Classicist's View," pp. 231–32. Part of the problem is that the term occurs in extant literature especially in Christian documents (cf. Deissmann, *Light,* pp. 88–89).

73. G. W. Knight III, "*Authenteō* in Reference to Women in 1 Timothy 2.12," *NTS* 30 (1, Jan. 1984): 143–57, arguing that the normal Greek usage is simply "to have authority."

74. Scholer, "Ministry," p. 205; cf. Martin, *Blessed,* pp. 137–42. Osburn, *"Authenteō,"* pp. 2–4, favors "domineer" over the earlier sense of "murder." He sees "domineering" as applying to teaching vs. child-rearing and modest dress (ibid., pp. 11–12).

75. Spencer, *Curse,* pp. 86–88.

76. Hardesty, *Women,* p. 81.

77. Moo, "1 Timothy 2:11–15," pp. 66–67.

78. Cf. L. E. Wilshire, "The TLG Computer and Further References to *AUTHENTEŌ* in 1 Timothy 2.12," *NTS* 34 (1, 1988): 120–34.

79. Walter Lock, *A Critical and Exegetical Commentary on the Pastoral Epistles,* ICC (Edinburgh: T. & T. Clark, 1924), p. 32, bases his conclusion on very limited evidence, but adduces the helpful contrast with LXX Gen. 3:16.

80. Scholer, "Ministry," p. 205.

81. Piper and Grudem, "Overview," pp. 69–70, 85.

82. Gundry, *Women,* p. 70 (on 1 Cor. 14:34–35); Spencer, *Curse,* pp. 106–7; P. B. Payne, "Libertarian Women in Ephesus: A Response to Douglas J. Moo's Article, '1 Timothy 2:11–15: Meaning and Significance,' " *TJ* 2 (2, 1981): 169–97; Williams, *Paul and Women,* p. 112; J. Nolland, "Women in the Public Life of the Church," *Crux* 19 (3, 1983): 17–23; Alan Padgett, "Wealthy Women at Ephesus. I Timothy 2:8–15 in Social Context," *Interp* 41 (1, Jan. 1987): 19–31. Scholer, "Ministry," pp. 216–17, gives examples of Christian leaders holding this position as early as the 1600s, and examples from the 1800s including Catherine Booth and A. J. Gordon.

83. Moo, "1 Timothy 2:11–15," pp. 62–83.

84. J. I. Packer, "Let's Stop Making Women Presbyters," *CT* (Feb. 11, 1991): 20.

85. Though, unless they are reckoning the chronology of Paul's life so as to have him survive Nero's persecution, their date of 67 CE would make 2 Timothy post-Pauline. Their date is probably a typographical or editorial error.

86. Piper and Grudem, "Overview," p. 82.

87. This is treated more thoroughly in our chapter on 1 Tim. 3:2 in my *And Marries Another,* pp. 83–103. That book treats the unqualified statement of general principle, especially on pp. 23–28.

88. Knight, *The New Testament Teaching on the Role Relationship of Men and Women* (Grand Rapids: Baker, 1977), p. 45. Although I do not agree with his conclusions, it should be noted to Knight's credit that he does come up with an explanation for the difference. But the whole principle of "reading one passage in the light of another," as if the original

readers had the whole NT before them at once, seems problematic. Such a hermeneutic allows the privileging of theological agendas over exegesis; proper exegesis means trusting the Bible enough to do one's thorough exegesis on each passage first, then comparing the teaching of all the texts. If the Bible is inspired and our systems cannot accommodate diverse teachings within it, then we need to revise our systems, not proclaim the authority of one text of Scripture over against another. Knight would probably agree with me on this point, but I believe that his wording is seriously misleading here.

89. Cf. ibid., p. 46.

90. The size of unit is unspecified, but we may assume that it is best taught in the context that was available to its first readers or hearers, i.e., how a passage functions in the context of the particular book in which it was written (Genesis, Jeremiah, Mark, etc.).

91. Also Rom. 15:14. Some of what we call NT interpretation of the OT may be argument by analogy or argument from the lesser to the greater (cf. Arist. *Rhet.* 2.23.4–5, 1397b).

92. 1 Cor. 14:34 is laid against 1 Cor. 11:5. Knight is right that 1 Cor. 11:5 mentions the issue of women prophesying only "incidentally" (*New Testament Teaching,* p. 45). But while Paul does not specifically *expound* on the practice, he does plainly *accept* it (what is at issue here), and 1 Corinthians thus preserves for us his guidance on the matter.

93. Cf. the case in Verner, *Household,* pp. 158–59.

94. Spencer, *Curse,* p. 85, points out that learning was normally done so that one could teach (m. Ab. 6:6; cf. 2 Tim. 2:2). While this is probably the case here, given the context, in Judaism one also learned so one could obey; and in rabbinic literature, women were considered deprived of obeying certain commandments because they were deprived of learning them.

95. See Appendix A.

96. See Spencer, *Curse,* pp. 84–85; Fee, *1 Timothy,* p. 72.

97. Packer, "Presbyters," p. 20.

98. It is unlikely that the writer of the Pastorals is opposing the Gnostic view that Eve actually gave good knowledge (Kroeger, "Women Teach?" p. 17), unless 1 Timothy is dated in the mid-second century. One could argue for proto-Gnostic tendencies already in Paul's day (ibid., p. 18), but the actual *evidence* that he could be combatting this Gnostic position in the 60s of the first century is not good, and it is always precarious to extrapolate backward from Gnostic texts that show so much Christian (including NT) influence.

99. Ab. R. Nathan 9, §25, B; p. Sanh. 2:4, §2, citing Tannaitic tradition; Gen. Rab. 17:8 (R. Joshua).

100. Ab. R. Nathan 9, §25 B; 42, §117 B; Gen. Rab. 17:8.

101. Ab. R. Nathan 42, §117 B; Gen. Rab. 17:8.

102. Gen. Rab. 21:5, R. Berekiah (very late) in R. Hanan's name. Cf. a sightly earlier tradition in Lev. Rab. 18:2, R. Judah ben R. Simon in R. Joshua ben Levi's name ("his judgment and destruction are from himself" refers to Eve).

103. Ab. R. Nathan 1 A.

104. Sib. Or. 1:42–45 (*OTP* 1:336). Probably Sib. Or. 1 contains Christian interpolations but is in the main a pre-Christian Jewish document; the provenance may be Asian or Egyptian.

105. E.g., V. Adam 18:1, 35 (Apoc. Mos. 9); 38:1–2 (Apoc. Mos. 11:1–2); 44:1–5 (Apoc. Mos. 14); Apoc. Mos. 31–32, 42. Cf. Leonhard Rost, *Judaism Outside the Hebrew Canon* (Nashville: Abingdon, 1976), p. 154; the late Gr. Ezra 2:15–16 (ed. Wahl, p. 27; cf. Tischendorf's text, p. 26, on the textual variant). Cf. also Ab. R. Nathan 1 A: the serpent could not deceive Adam, so he went through Eve. But in the late Apoc. Sedrach 5:1 (same Greek word) Adam was deceived; in Sifre Deut. 323.6.2 the serpent led both astray; in Sib. Or. 1:40 the serpent deceitfully *(doliōs)* led them both astray, but in 1:42–43, the blame is especially placed on Eve.

106. V. Adam 10:1 (Apoc. Mos. 29:17). Given the confluence of the Corinthians' role as virgins betrothed to Christ (2 Cor. 11:2) and the mention of deceptive angels of light (11:14), it is not impossible that Paul has this in view in 2 Cor. 11:3. But deceptive angels also occur in other contexts (Apoc. Mos. 17:1; Test. Job 6:4, 17:2/1; 23:1; Pes. Rab Kah. 26:2; cf. Test. Abr. 16 A, 13 B [for Abraham's good]; cf. A. B. Kolenkow, "The Angelology of the Testament of Abraham," in *Studies on the Testament of Abraham,* ed. G. W. E. Nickelsburg, SBLSCS 6 (Missoula, Mont.: Scholars, 1976), p. 158; seductive gods as in Ach. Tat. *Clit.* 2.15.4 and often; Satan as a woman seeking to seduce Akiba and Meir in Urbach, *Sages,* 1:480), and the serpent of Gen. 3 was often held to be Satan or the angel of death in disguise (e.g. 3 Bar. 9:7, both recensions; Danielle Ellul, "Le Targum du Pseudo-Jonathan sur Genèse 3 à la lumière de quelques traditions haggadiques," *FV* 80 [6, Dec. 1981]: 12–25) (the earlier rabbinic traditions do not identify the serpent with Satan or other evil angels).

107. This element is presupposed as early as Wisd. 2:23–24; Jos. *Ant.* 1.1.4, §41; also in b. Sanh. 59b (later). In some versions, he refused to worship, e.g., Apoc. Sedrach 5:2–6. But this element can exist independently of other parts of the story.

108. Ab. R. Nathan 1 A; t. Sot. 4:17–18; Gen. Rab. 18:6; 20:4, 5.

109. There is probably an allusion to this in 4 Macc. 18:8; cf. 2 En. 31:6 J (if this recension was not influenced by the Bogomils here); Gen. Rab. 24:6. Philo speaks of the serpent as pleasure enticing Eve, who represents sense perception (*On the Creation* 157, 165; cf. *On Husbandry* 107), but this is common Philonic imagery for women in general.

110. Ab. R. Nathan 1 A. The point of the later tradition in Exod. Rab. 28:2 is less clear.

111. Plut. *Bride* 48, *Mor.* 145CE; Chariton *Chaer.* 1.4.1–2. Cf. Pomeroy, *Goddesses,* p. 150; cf. Spartans in Herod. *Hist.* 4.145.1 (in Gould, "Law," pp. 54–55). Pandora's role in Greek tradition is somewhat analogous to Eve's in developed Jewish tradition, though less prominent; cf. the survey of Hesiod summarized in L. S. Sussman, "Workers and Drones: Labor, Idleness and Gender Definition in Hesiod's Beehive," in *Women in the Ancient World,* p. 89.

112. Test. Job 26:6/7–8; b. Shab. 33b (the story of R. Simeon ben Yohai).

113. Cf. "the woman" for Eve in Jos. *Ant.* 1.1.4, §§40, 43, 48. On the other hand, "anyone like Eve" means "a woman" in Ab. R. Nathan 19, §41 B; her behavior affected all subsequent women in Ab. R. Nathan 9, §25 B.

114. Scholer, "Ministry," p. 208; Kaiser, *Exegetical Theology,* pp. 119–20. In contrast, Moo, "1 Timothy 2:11–15," p. 70, thinks that Eve's sin is at least "exemplary and perhaps causative" and affects the nature of women in general.

115. E.g., Swidler, *Women,* pp. 26–27; Giles, *Created Woman,* p. 15.

116. So also Scholer, "Ministry," p. 209; cf. Leslie, "Woman," p. 330, who sees this as "reminiscent of Paul's rabbinical-style argument in I Cor. 11:8f. for requiring women to wear a head-covering during worship." Knight, *Teaching,* pp. 40–41, suggests that the point is not chronology but derivation, on the analogy of 1 Cor. 11:8–9 (cf. also Moo, "1 Timothy 2:11–15," p. 68); but he fails to cite 1 Cor. 11:11–12, several verses down, which would have ruined his point. His argument (Knight, "Teaching," p. 85) on the creation order being determinative is flawed by his failure to come to terms with the real demand of 1 Cor. 11:1–16.

117. Cf. Kaiser, *Exegetical Theology,* p. 120. Spencer, *Curse,* p. 88–89, reads it as concessive: though Adam was created first, Eve transgressed first; this reading also connects the two elements mentioned in 1 Tim. 2:13–14.

118. Although I originally noticed this independently, it has been pointed out by many others, e.g., Scholer, "Ministry," p. 210; Spencer, *Curse,* pp. 89–90.

119. Also Scholer, "Ministry," p. 196.

120. Spencer, *Curse,* p. 92; idem, "Eve at Ephesus (Should women be ordained as pastors according to the First letter to Timothy 2:11–15)," *JETS* 17 (4, Fall 1974): 215–22; Williams, *Paul and Women,* p. 113; Lock, *Pastoral Epistles,* p. 33; P. K. Jewett, *Man as Male and Female* (Grand Rapids: Eerdmans, 1975), p. 60.

121. E. F. Scott, *The Pastoral Epistles,* MNTC (London: Hodder & Stoughton, 1936), p. 28.

122. Kelly, *Pastoral Epistles,* p. 69; Verner, *Household,* p. 170. J. H. Ulrichsen, "Noèn bemerkninger til 1. Tim. 2,15," *NTT* 84 (1, 1983): 19–25 (NTA 29:42), suggests that the text means she is saved because she raises her children to be good Christians. The term translated "childbearing" can also include "childrearing" (Moo, "1 Timothy 2:11–15," pp. 71–72).

123. Scholer, "Ministry," p. 197. The virtue of *sōphrosynē*, or self-control, sobriety, was often praised (e.g., Plato *Charmides* 159B–176C; Plut. *Poetry* 11; *Mor.* 32C; Acts 26:25, sometimes meaning also restraint from sinful desires (4 Macc. 1:31; cf. Ps-Phocyl 76), including sexual desires (Test. Jos. 4:1–2; Ach. Tat *Clit.* 1.5.6).

124. E.g., Exod. 14:13, 30; Sir. 46:1; Jdt. 8:17; 9:1; 11:3; 1 Macc. 4:25; Ps. Sol. 16:5; Jos. *Ant.* 2.16.2, §339; 3.1.1, §1; 11.6.12, §282; *War* 5.9.4, §415; 6.5.4, §310; Philo *The Decalogue* 53, 60, 155; 4 Macc. 15:8; Test. Job 19:2/1; Apul. *Metam.* 6.28; Chariton *Chaer.*

2.7.6, 2.8.1; cf. Plut. *Statecraft* 32, *Mor.* 824D; Apul. *Metam.* 3.27. It has a more "spiritual" sense in Tob. 12:9; Wisd. 9:18; 1 En. 50:3–4; Test. Job 3:5; Marc. Aur. *Med.* 12.29. Nigel Turner, "Second Thoughts—VII. Papyrus Finds," *ExpT* 76 (1964): 46, is right to point out that the specialized Christian usage is different from the connotations of some other religious environments, but Christians were not averse to using other senses of the term when the circumstances called for it (e.g., Acts 27:20, 31; cf. 27:43–28:1); and deliverance was the usual, not the specialized religious, use of the term.

125. Plut. *R. Q.* 2, *Mor.* 264B; cf. Otto, *Dionysus,* p. 171. It is not unlikely that the Ephesian Artemis also absorbed this function.

126. Heyob, *Isis,* pp. 70, 80, 128.

127. Cf. Test. Sol. 13:3, 6, where a particular demon was in charge of causing miscarriages and birth defects, but could be overcome by invoking a certain angel. Deities such as Zeus (inscription in Grant, *Religions,* p. 30; Epict. *Disc.* 1.22.16; Plut. *On Borrowing* 7, *Mor.* 830B; Athen. *Deipn.* 7.288.f), certain goddesses (Orphic Hymns 14.8; 27.12; 74.4), Ptolemies (*CPJ* 1:185–86, §38, 218 BCE; cf. a Jewish Alexandrian to the prefect in *CPJ* 2:31–32, §151), and deified emperors (*Empire,* ed. Sherk, pp. 57–59, §32, p. 61, §34B; Mart. *Epig.* 2.91) were seen as saviors; God was also addressed this way in Jewish tradition (1 Macc. 4:30; Sib. Or. 1:73, 152, 167; 2:28; 3:35; Otto Betz, *What Do We Know About Jesus?* [Philadelphia: Westminster, 1968], p. 109; Longenecker, *Christology,* pp. 142–43; Dibelius and Conzelmann, *Pastoral Epistles,* pp. 100–103).

128. This is the major emphasis of her punishment in Jos. *Ant.* 1.1.4, §49. Jub. 3:24 has both birthpangs and husband's rule (following Genesis very closely, except it deals with her nakedness before she gave the fruit to Adam, probably because Jubilees resents the hellenistic gymnastic nakedness of its day).

129. A third-century rabbi could nevertheless assert that man's suffering in toil is twice as difficult as women's labor in childbirth (b. Pes. 118a). Another rabbi, however, argued that the serpent was most cursed, then Eve, and Adam least (Gen. Rab. 20:3).

130. Ab. R. Nathan 42, §117 B (trans. Saldarini, p. 254); also 9, §25 B; cf. m. Shab. 2:6; Koh. Rab. 3:2, §2, with the same punishments but no mention of Eve. The pain of Gen. 3:16 is also extended to menstrual cramps (Ab. R. Nathan 1 A). We suggest that Paul here argues in a manner analogous to this, not that he knew this exact tradition.

131. Apoc. Mos. 25:1–2 (*OTP* 2:283).

132. V. Adam 19:2; 21:2. In Crates 33, to Hipparchia (*CynEp,* pp. 82–83), it is not piety but toil—the hard life of the Cynic philosopher—that provided a good birth.

133. Cf. the removal of women's birth pangs in the eschatological time of peace (2 Bar. 73:7). One may note, in contrast to this, the tendency in ancient Greek literature to parallel women's sufferings or death in childbirth with that of heroic men in war (Nicole Loraux, "Le lit, la guerre," *Homme* 21 [1, Jan. 1981]: 37–67).

134. Pes. Rab Kah. 22:2, a later story about the second-century rabbi Simeon ben Yohai.

135. See p. Taan. 4:3, §2. These particular stories are later but illustrate the way childbirth and piety were connected in Jewish thought.

136. Ode Sol. 19:7–9.

137. Christian women certainly suffer pain in childbirth, and have not always come safely through; but that Paul means that God hears the cries of one of his daughters in travail is as reasonable as James's promise that the sick will be healed (Jas. 5:14), even if readers must then explain why some of them are not.

138. Pointed out by others, e.g., Bilezikian, *Roles,* pp. 180–81.

# PART 2

## WOMEN'S ROLES IN THE FAMILY

In the first section of this book we examined texts in the Pauline corpus that address women's roles in public worship. In this section we focus on a text that addresses the role of women as wives in the home, Ephesians 5:22–31. Although the domestic role of women is also addressed in Colossians 3:18, 1 Timothy 5:14, and Titus 2:4–5, our discussion focuses on the most extended passage in Paul's writings, where Paul has more space to clarify precisely what he means. We have chosen to focus on only one passage because most of the background material relevant to this text also explains what we read in the other passages.

### INTERPRETATION ISSUES

In chapter 4 we try to reconstruct the situation that led Paul to emphasize the submission of women. As many scholars have pointed out, members of the Roman elite suspected Christianity, like several other non-Roman religions, of subverting Roman family values. By upholding what was honorable in Roman values, the Christians could try to protect themselves from undue persecution and from misunderstandings of the gospel. Paul's use of the three-part codes dealing with wives, children, and slaves followed a standard form used in antiquity, sometimes for this very purpose.

In chapter 5 we examine what Paul *means* by submission, and how his readers would have understood his point. In line with Paul's concern for an honorable Christian witness in ancient society, he clearly believes that it is right for wives to submit to their husbands. At the same time, he defines the wife's submission as respect rather than obedience, and he expects husbands to submit to their wives, something virtually unheard of in his day. Paul sometimes summarized only one side of this mutual submission formula, as in Colossians 3:18, probably for the reasons mentioned in chapter 4. But he argues for *mutual* submission when he explains his position more fully. Although Paul uses the standard form of household code, he significantly qualifies its meaning, earning himself a place among the most progressive of ancient writers.

Nevertheless, in his culture, Paul seems to have assumed that husbands would in some sense lead in the home, though they should submit to their wives' needs; men and women in his day both seem to have accepted this as the normal arrangement. Thus chapter 5 raises a question more problematic than the question raised in the first half of the book: Is Paul adopting the leadership structures of his day as a transcultural requirement, or does he just call us to live the Christian life within the framework of whatever leadership structures exist in our society?

With regard to the first half of our book, it is easy enough to say that the one passage unambiguously forbidding women to teach addresses a specific situation, since we have plenty of examples of women sharing with Paul in ministry. But it is more difficult to argue that Paul merely recognized husbands' leadership in his culture, rather than demanding it in all cultures, since the *whole* New Testament was written in a culture where men usually led in the home.

The case about husbands' leadership can be argued either way, depending on the assumptions one uses to interpret the passage. Was Paul trying to mandate roles in the home for all cultures or to deal with a pressing issue in his congregations? If, as I believe, he was doing the latter, we must ask whether Paul had even considered the question of cultures where wives could share equally with their husbands in the leadership of their homes. And if Paul had only his own culture in mind, how can we apply his principles in a completely different culture?

We grapple with this question in chapter 6. After Paul has addressed the relationship between wives and husbands in Ephesians 5, he moves on to the relationships between children and parents, and slaves and masters, in Ephesians 6, continuing to give a Christian reinterpretation of the traditional household codes. Probably most of us would be happy to maintain his instructions concerning parents and children, which have general Old Testament precedent. But most of us would also argue that in telling slaves to obey their masters as they would Christ, he is addressing slaves stuck in a less-than-ideal situation, not upholding the institution of slavery. As in the case of Paul's admonition to wives, his admonitions to slaves are significantly qualified by his corresponding instructions to masters.

Yet if Paul could call on slaves to submit without supporting slavery, we must allow that he could have asked wives to submit without supporting male dominance. The method of interpretation that leads some readers to uphold the husband's right to rule his family on the basis of Ephesians 5 would most naturally have led to the use of Ephesians 6 to uphold slavery a century and a half ago.

## PRACTICAL ISSUES

Mutual submission will be expressed in different ways from one culture to another, since husband and wife roles vary from one culture to another. The question of the nature of submission becomes most problematic in cultures in transition, where gender roles in a marriage are no longer clearly defined and divergent expectations about those roles become the basis for marital conflict. But where the culture leaves those roles undefined, mutual submission calls the wife and husband to communicate openly and to define their roles in dialogue together. Simply imposing the husband's "final word" does eliminate role confusion, but it may do so at the expense of the equal wisdom and leadership capability of the wife.

I am not saying that it is necessarily wrong for the man to lead in a household; I am suggesting that it is wrong for him to demand the position of leadership without his wife's consent. Given the educational and vocational status of women in our culture, an egalitarian marriage must be permitted as a viable option. This will require a great deal more communication and much more work in our marriages than a model where the husband's will is law; consensus requires discussion and ground rules for dialogue.

On the one hand, there are at least two disadvantages to the mutual-consent model of decision making: first, the husband may not agree to it; second, when the husband is definitely right and the wife is wrong, it will be more difficult for the husband to get his right way. On the other hand, the disadvantages of the husband-rules model of decision making are no less serious: first, in our culture, the wife may not agree to it; second, when the wife is definitely right and the husband is wrong, it will be more difficult for the wife to get her right way.

This book is written not to tell any couple which partner, if either, should lead in their home; it is written to argue that those who think they know which partner should always lead on the basis of Scripture have not read Scripture as clearly as they should have. One thing Scripture *clearly* demands, however, is mutual submission. We need to listen to our spouse and seek to serve him or her, and we need above all else to seek to please God. In marriages where both partners are bending over backward to outdo each other in love and service, the question of a "supreme authority" in the household other than God is surely less of an issue than some writers have made it. Due to the disobedience of one or both partners, not all marriages can attain that ideal; but Paul encourages us each to do our own part to strive for that ideal, to make our marriages a pure reflection of the loving service of our Lord Jesus Christ, that the world may be drawn to him.

## EPHESIANS 5:18—6:9: PROCEDURE FOR DISCUSSION

Many marriages today are troubled with the tension of openly conflicting wills. This situation is not necessarily worse than one partner's always getting his or her way and never realizing that the other partner would disagree if she or he could. But it is still hardly the picture of an ideal marriage. Biblically speaking, an ideal marriage would be one in which both partners cooperate in love, instead of either one seeking his or her own way.

Mutual cooperation seems to be the picture of relationships we find in Ephesians 5:21—6:9. Given the difficulty of loving and serving as radically as this text demands—Paul gives Christ's death as the standard for love, and our allegiance to Christ as the standard for submission—the context in which Paul places this discussion is significant: this is a kind of life that flows from being filled with Christ's Spirit (5:18–21).

Because this context is so important to the interpretation of "submission" in 5:21–22, we will survey the teaching of 5:18–21 before we examine 5:21–22. Because the instructions to husbands and wives are part of a larger section of household codes that also addresses father-child and master-slave relationships, we will also examine these texts, which will contribute to our understanding of how to apply what Ephesians teaches on husband-wife roles today. And because the whole passage can best be understood in the light of what was going on at the time, our discussion of Ephesians 5:18—6:9 is prefaced by a survey of the most likely social context of this passage.

# 4

# Why Paul Told Wives to Submit—The Social Situation of Ephesians 5:18–33

Because Ephesians 5:18—6:9 is the longest passage in the New Testament addressing household roles, and because most elements of the other passages are found here, we have devoted the second half of the book to an in-depth analysis of this passage.[1] The present chapter introduces the general social setting and issues that we will confront in our examination of the passage itself in the following chapter.

The question that this chapter on social setting addresses is, Why does Paul, who calls for mutual submission, deal more explicitly with the submission of wives than with that of husbands? The answer this chapter proposes is, in short, "Because he was smart." His social statements are among the most progressive of his day, but if he wanted the gospel to gain a strong hearing in the Greco-Roman world, he needed to temper his radicalism with prudent sensitivity to his culture. Assuming that Paul wrote this letter while imprisoned in Rome, we can well understand how sensitive he might have become to such issues.

## ARISTOCRATIC FEARS OF ANTITRADITIONAL GROUPS

The Roman aristocracy felt their power base increasingly threatened by social changes occurring around them. These changes included the upward mobility of socially inferior elements, such as former slaves, foreigners, and women. Foreign religions were sometimes suspected of aiding what the aristocrats viewed as a subversion of the appropriate moral order.

*Opposition to Foreign Cults*

The recognized guardians of traditional Roman values, Roman aristocratic men, were uneasy about the "new" religions from the east that seemed to challenge standard values like the honorable man's sober guidance of his family.[2] Juvenal's oft-cited complaint about the influx of foreign culture and superstition reflects the feelings of many well-to-do Roman men: "The Syrian Orontes has long since poured into the Tiber, bringing with it its lingo and its manners," and its music and religions.[3]

Xenophobia, or aversion to foreigners and foreign ways, was not limited to ancient society. In the United States of the nineteenth and twentieth centuries, the nonconformity of each new wave of immigration to U.S. societal standards has been viewed by established groups as a threat to social stability, no matter how loudly we may have simultaneously praised the virtues of pluralism. This should make it easier for us to understand the uneasiness of the conservative aristocracy when they were confronted with groups that not only seemed to hold "antisocial" beliefs, but began converting Romans to those beliefs.[4]

Roman mistrust of eastern cults is reflected in Roman literature. For instance, Apuleius writes of rogues who follow the "Syrian goddess"[5] but turn out to be guilty of temple robbery.[6] Especially significant, however, is his association of such cults with sexual perversity,[7] an accusation that also turns up in other texts: for instance, Petronius ridicules the sexual abnormalities of worshipers of Priapus.[8]

Although Roman policy tolerated foreign religions on their own soil, some religions were viewed as too disruptive for Rome itself.[9] Romans valued seriousness and duty, and emotionalistic cults threatened their very identity as respectable Romans. Only after such a cult's behavior became sufficiently tamed or Romanized by time would it be officially permitted in Rome. Roman citizens were thus officially restricted from the cult of Cybele until the time of Claudius,[10] i.e., within a decade or two before Paul arrived in Rome and wrote the letter we call Ephesians.

Egyptian cults, like the cult of Isis,[11] gained in popularity over time,[12] but became acceptable in Rome only shortly before the middle of the first century.[13] They gained *prominence* in Rome only in the period of the Flavians, i.e., after Paul's death.[14] Perhaps because Egyptians worshiped animals, and because most Greeks and Romans viewed them as socially inferior, Egyptian religion took some time to catch on in Greco-Roman cities.[15] But rarely would any city have offered worshipers of these cults as hostile a reception as Rome, where all secret meetings were suspect and where the Isis cult was persecuted as late as the early first century CE.[16]

All potentially questionable foreign religions came under the suspicion of upper-class Roman conservatives, who did not always bother to get their accusations straight. It was easy for enemies of various foreign religions to get them mixed up. Indeed, some people believed that Jews worshiped Dionysus, and associated Judaism with Dionysiac revelry.[17] Since Roman authorities would easily have viewed Christians as a special form of Jews in this period,[18] their attitude toward Judaism tells us much about their attitude toward Christians as well.[19]

In the eyes of the Roman elite, both Isis-worshipers and Jews in Rome represented a foreign superstition of the sort that could subvert the morals of virtuous Roman women. Earlier in the first century, scandals arose in regard to both religions that brought about persecution against both. The events are linked by those who report them,[20] and are linked by a certain important similarity: a male representative of the offending religion took advantage of a good Roman woman.

Josephus, a Jewish historian writing at the end of the first century, describes scandals that arose in relation both to the cult of Isis and to Judaism. A priest of Isis helped a deceiver to fulfill his adulterous designs on a virtuous Roman woman, and when the story got out, the authorities were enraged: the emperor banished the deceiver,[21] crucified the priests, and destroyed the temple of Isis. Although there is no evidence that all the priests were guilty, or that such behavior characterized the entire cult of Isis,[22] the religion as a whole suffered a great setback from the scandal.[23]

Josephus likewise tells us of a Jewish man who, pretending to teach the law, tricked a wealthy woman into giving him funds for the temple that he actually kept for himself. Josephus is quick to point out that this man was no proper representative of the rest of the Jewish community, but that this fact did not protect the rest of the Jewish community from the anti-Jewish sentiment aroused by the incident. The response of the emperor Tiberius was to banish the entire Jewish community from Rome.[24]

Nor did this mistrust of Judaism end with the expulsion under Tiberius. Juvenal, writing in the early second century, complains about the secrecy[25] and subversiveness[26] of the Jewish religion, and Tacitus devotes considerable space to slanders against it.[27]

Judaism and other foreign religions[28] were viewed with hostility by the Roman elite precisely because they were winning so many converts in Rome. The most virulent anti-Jewish attacks derived from Alexandria,[29] but Jewish rights were protected by legal precedent there and in most of the Roman Empire.[30] In Rome itself, however, the success of Jewish proselytism seems to have threatened the traditional Roman establishment.[31] It would not be long before the success of Christian evangelism would create a similar threat, but the Roman Christians, once they were distinguished from other Jews,[32] would quickly become an object of more outright persecution; they still had no politically powerful patrons.[33]

Judaism seems to have appealed especially to women—who did not have to contemplate the pain of circumcision at their conversion—and their willingness to convert seems to have irritated Roman men, who expected their wives to follow their own beliefs. The turning of a wife from her husband's religion was viewed as an especially subversive ploy on the part of foreign religions. Plutarch emphasizes the importance of the wife's worshiping her husband's gods:

> A wife ought not to make friends on her own, but to enjoy her husband's friends in common with him. The gods are the first and most important friends. Wherefore it is becoming for a wife to worship and to know only the gods that her husband believes in, and to shut the front door tight upon all queer rituals and outlandish superstitions. For with no god do stealthy and secret rites performed by a woman find any favour.[34]

Conservative writers like Plutarch, and especially the socially insecure satirist Juvenal, reacted against foreign cults which, they believed, were greatly strengthened through the gullibility of women.[35] The conversion of wives to Christianity thus posed a threat to upper-class men, and through them could provoke increased hostility toward Christians. Ephesians 5:22–33, unlike 1 Peter 3:1–7, deals only with Christian spouses; but the behavior of Christian families would no doubt affect public perceptions about Christianity. Paul did not want the church to be viewed as an immoral mystery cult.

### *Women and Upward Mobility*

The gains of women in ancient society had introduced new tensions into Greco-Roman life in general and probably into some marriages as well, due to the greater flexibility of possible role expectations now available. This meant that religions that were thought to ignore traditional roles for women would be viewed as threatening by the conservative male establishment.

Many scholars have commented on the gains in women's social status during the Roman imperial period. To say that women in later periods had more freedom than they had had in classical Athens is not to say very much; even if their poor status in classical Athens has been exaggerated, it was worse than we find it in most other societies in the ancient Mediterranean. But papyri from Egypt do indicate that women's status gradually improved over time,[36] especially in the Roman period.[37]

Roman laws in the New Testament period provided more independence for women than earlier laws had,[38] although the motives behind this stemmed from the advantage it would give the legislators, to whom the result of women's independence was a completely incidental matter.[39] Some women, such as the empress Livia,[40] became extremely powerful socially, and though such women may have been exceptions, their example could encourage other women to advance as much as their gender, social class, and especially economic status permitted.

Not only politically and legally, but also philosophically, women had received a greater hearing; even in very conservative circles, they were sometimes recognized to have moral and intellectual potential.[41]

### *Resistance to Social Change*

The perceived link between the growing social inversion and the religions from the eastern Mediterranean naturally bothered many members of the Roman elite, who sought to preserve the status quo and longed for more traditional times when their own power base was more secure.[42] The ideal figure of the Roman upper class was that of a "benevolent patriarch," who ruled fairly on behalf of those under him, but maintained his own superior rank and social status.[43] He thus viewed it as better for everyone if he wielded the power on everyone's behalf.

Thus the Senate passed laws to ensure that traditional boundaries for social classes were not transgressed; for example, members of aristocratic families were not to engage in nonaristocratic professions.[44] The Roman upper class also tried to protect its special prerogatives against the social advancement of freedmen.[45] The actual practice was, of course, quite different from the aristocratic ideal; as we have already observed, social mobility was occurring in the first century, to the consternation of the elite, who stood to lose most by it.

Maintaining the system as it was had long been emphasized by ideologists of the state: "Preserve the present order, and do not desire any change, knowing that revolutions inevitably destroy states and lay waste the homes of the people."[46] Thus it was commonly believed that earlier Roman society had had much "higher" morals, including much more severe discipline of unsubmissive wives. This idea became an important feature in Stoic and Augustan propaganda for proper aristocratic marriages.[47]

The increasing mobility of women drew fire from satirists like Petronius,[48] Martial, and especially Juvenal, satirists being among the first who were prone to criticize social trends. Juvenal complains that marriage might lead a man to suicide, since women were always wrangling and asking for more presents; a male bedfellow, he mocks, would be better than these women.[49] They love violence, delighting in their strength like men, while wishing to remain female for its superior joys.[50] The wife who lords it over her husband thus becomes a familiar object of his satire:

> "Crucify that slave!" says the wife. "But what crime worthy of death has he committed?" asks the husband; "where are the witnesses? . . . Give him a hearing at least; no delay can be too long when a man's life is at stake!" "What, you numskull? You call a slave a man, do you? He has done no wrong, you say? Be it so; but this is my will and my command; let my will be voucher for the deed." Thus does she lord it over her husband.[51]

Although some wealthy noble ladies were undoubtedly genuinely "spoiled," Juvenal's criticisms cannot be taken to reflect general social reality; the force of his satire is in the exaggeration. What bothered Juvenal and writers like him appears to have been the increase in women's social power, which threatened their own position of male dominance. This is presumably why Juvenal ridicules women who try to be educated in philosophy and rhetoric.[52]

So severe does the criticism seem to have become that one writer laughs:

> You do not know . . . how women dread satire. Lawyers may retreat and scholars may not utter a syllable before the flood of a woman's words, the rhetorician may be dumb and the herald may stop his cries; satire alone can put a limit to their madness, though it be Petronius' Albucia who is hot.[53]

Nor was such criticism an entirely new phenomenon.[54] Cato the Elder is quoted as complaining, "All mankind rules its women, and we rule all mankind, but our women rule us."[55] Cicero charged that a man who could not deny his wife anything was not a free man but the lowliest of slaves.[56] But the aristocratic discomfort was increasing by Paul's day, and this means that the antifeminist rhetoric of Roman aristocratic males was apparently getting hotter as well.

This dissatisfaction of men with freedoms they felt were increasingly being given to their wives led to marital conflicts. In modern society, wives are often more disappointed than husbands by the failure of marriages to conform to a romantic ideal; but in imperial Rome, husbands may have been the ones most dissatisfied by a failure of spousal role expectations, because their wives failed to emulate the legendary, submissive, domestic matrons of old.[57]

Different writers responded to this situation differently:

> For example, in Juvenal's case, bitter misogyny and nostalgia for an earlier, pure day; in Plutarch's, an attempt to subsume the new values under the old and so to preserve the essential structure of the old values by making certain minimal concessions to the times; and, in the case of Xenophon of Ephesus, easy acceptance of the new spirit of egalitarianism.

But those who did challenge the old traditionalism were opposing standard aristocratic opinion and "risked the charge of political subversion."[58]

The family was held to be the basic unit upon which society was built,[59] and ever since Aristotle political philosophy had outlined the proper family relationships necessary for the health of society as a whole.[60] This outline continued to be a standard format for defining proper family relationships in later writers.[61] Groups accused of undermining the moral fabric of Roman society thus sometimes protested that they instead conformed to traditional Roman values, by producing their own lists, or "household codes," fitting those normally used in their day.

## HOUSEHOLD CODES

Aristotle introduced three pairs of relationships into the household codes: the head of the family's relationship with wife, children, and slaves, in each case defining the nature of the father's rule.[62] As he puts it, "household management falls into departments corresponding to the parts of which the household . . . is composed . . . the primary and smallest parts of the household are master and slave, husband and wife, father and children."[63] This threefold format was preserved by Aristotle's philosophical followers and adopted by some other writers as well.[64] Given the relatively small percentage of families actually owning slaves in Roman antiquity, we may suspect that those who wrote such household codes had primarily other well-to-do people in mind as their readership.[65]

It was typical for ancient writers to think of families in these general terms of rank and duty; "family" was defined more by relationships of subordination than by blood relationship.[66] The man in charge of the household was often even compared to a king, since the family was viewed as a microcosm of society.[67]

It was important that propagandists for "suspicious sects" like Judaism and the cult of Isis emphasize their profamily orientation. They often did so, occasionally resorting specifically to three-part household codes. Thus, for example, an Isis aretalogy (a writing that celebrated a god's deeds or virtues), probably directed toward the average kind of family that did not have slaves, emphasizes proper child-parent and husband-wife relationships.[68]

It was likewise natural for Greek-speaking Jewish writers to dwell on the proper ways to act in various relationships.[69] To the extent that they needed to demonstrate their lack of subversiveness to Roman society, their use of household codes became all the more important.[70] If they could demonstrate the "orthodox" character of their family practices, they would have answered a critical charge leveled against them by powerful members of the surrounding society.[71] In fact, Josephus follows the three-part household code pattern in his defense of Judaism against Apion, one of its slanderers.[72]

Early Christian household codes[73] may serve the same apologetic purpose: to show that Christians were good members of society who did not seek to radically overturn Roman social structures.[74] Given Jesus' activism in Jewish Palestine, this apparent reticence of Paul to challenge many of the structures of his day is disappointing to some modern readers; but the rest of the Roman world required a different strategy for change than Jewish Palestine had. And, as we shall see, Paul's ethics were more revolutionary in function than they may appear on the surface.[75] Indeed, it may have been the socially liberating aspects of early Christianity that made it most vulnerable to the charges of subversion Christians ultimately would encounter despite Paul's precautions.[76]

## CONCLUSION

By adhering to certain societal standards, the early Christians could perhaps hope to distinguish themselves from traditional objects of Roman slander, "undignified" eastern Mediterranean religions, including such mysteries as the cult of Dionysus.[77]

This is not to suggest that Ephesians 5:18—6:9 is to be read as a direct defense of Christianity to Roman readership in the way that Josephus' tract *Against Apion* defends Judaism against the charges of its opponents. After all, this letter was no doubt sent to Asia, not to Rome; further, it was addressed to Christians, not to the opponents of Christianity.[78] But by encouraging Christians to live in a way that would silence some of the needless objections raised against the faith, as he had done in his previous letters,[79] Paul was contributing to a cultural defense of Christianity that would hopefully gain it a better hearing in Roman society. When he had written to the Romans, he had encouraged their support of civil authorities; now that he himself was in Rome, the issues that would contribute to a lifestyle defense of Christianity had no doubt become even clearer to him.

There is thus reason to think that Paul, awaiting trial in Rome, would have been contemplating strategies to appeal to the powerbrokers in Rome whose decisions could set precedents for policies toward Christians elsewhere in the empire. His household codes may represent a long-range response to basic Roman cultural objections to the gospel.[80] Stressing the wife's submission would be important for evangelizing resistant elements in the Roman world and for resisting progressive cultural temptations for wives to affirm too much independence at the expense of their marriage. This strategy makes sense if, as we suspect, it would not have alienated any other groups from the gospel; to my knowledge, no one was going around criticizing women for being too submissive.

But we are still left with a question. Let us say that Paul emphasized the wife's submission because it was an essential part of her witness in that culture. Would he have ignored her personal needs in favor of the church's witness? Would he have left "submission" undefined and ambiguous, so that she could theoretically be subordinated even more than most Roman women were in his day? Would he have ignored the gospel's equal demand for the husband's servanthood and submission? A brief examination of Ephesians 5:21–31 would suggest that he does not; he places her submission squarely in the context of mutual submission, and qualifies her husband's position of authority as one of loving service. To this point we will return in the next chapter.

## NOTES

1. This approach of concentrating on the more detailed passage is also followed by scholars holding the position we are challenging; see G. W. Knight III, "Husbands and Wives as Analogues of Christ and the Church: Ephesians 5:21–33 and Colossians 3:18–19," in *Manhood and Womanhood,* p. 165.

2. The most complete treatment of opposition to foreign cults with which I am familiar is D. L. Balch, *Let Wives be Submissive: The Domestic Code in 1 Peter,* SBLMS 26 (Chico, Calif.: Scholars, 1981), pp. 65–80 (ch. 5, "Greco-Roman Criticism of Eastern Religions"); see also p. 118.

3. Juv. *Sat.* 3.62. Although Juvenal refers to Eastern religions as a whole, it is interesting that Syrian Antioch, a major sending church in Paul's Gentile mission (Acts 13:1–3; 14:26–28), was situated on the Orontes.

4. M. Stern, "The Jews in Greek and Latin Literature," in *JPFC,* pp. 1150, 1157, citing Tacitus, Seneca, and Juvenal; cf. Meeks, *World,* p. 22. On the growing distrust of Roman aristocrats toward foreign elements in Rome in general, cf. e.g., Meeks, *World,* p. 25. The Roman elite's ethnocentrism may be exampled in Claudius' response to the Senate in 48 CE, preserved in inscriptions and paraphrased by Tacitus (see *Empire,* ed. Sherk, §55, pp. 97–98).

5. Apul. *Metam.* 8.27–28, where they cut themselves. The Phrygian music (8.30) could suggest the worship of Cybele, but 9.9–10 seem to distinguish her from the mother of the gods; this one claims to be her "sister."

6. Apul. *Metam.* 9.9–10.

7. Ibid., 8.29.

8. Petr. *Sat.* 16–26, including male prostitutes, aphrodisiacs, and the marriage of a seven-year-old girl. Petronius does not feel equally perturbed about men chasing boys.

9. Cf. Cic. *Leg.* 2.10.25, whose ideal laws exclude "the worship of private gods, whether new or alien" as disruptive to Roman religion (LCL). The necessity of preserving Roman religious custom is often heard, e.g., *Rhet. ad Herenn.* 3.3.4.

10. Grant, *Gods,* p. 33.

11. No doubt made a mystery only under Greek influence.

12. For its popularity, see H. C. Kee, *Miracle in the Early Christian World* (New Haven: Yale University, 1983), pp. 105–45.

13. In the 40s, under Caligula: see Françoise Dunand, "Les Mystères Egyptiens," in *Mystères et Syncrétismes,* EHR 2 (Paris: Librairie Orientaliste Paul Geuthner, 1975), p. 38; Cary and Haarhoff, *Life,* p. 343. It existed in Rome, with its own temple, from the first century BCE (Grant, *Gods,* p. 34), but the scandal in the reign of Tiberius had been a major setback (see p. 141 below).

14. Heyob, *Isis,* pp. 26–27. They increased again under the Antonines (ibid., pp. 28–33).

15. See Grant, *Society,* p. 60. Of course, Greeks had long touted their own cultural superiority (cf. Plato *Rep.* 5.470C; Diog. Laert. *Lives* 1, §33; 6.1.1, 10.117; Lucian *Dem.* 40; Diogenes 28 to the Greeks [*CynEp,* pp. 124–25]; contrast Anacharsis to Solon 2.1–2 [*CynEp,* pp. 38–39]), classifying other peoples as "barbarians" (Plato *Laws* 9.870AB; *Crat.* 409DE, 421D; *Alcib.* book 2, 141C; Isoc. *Pan.* 108, *Or.* 4; *Helen* 67–68, *Or.* 10; *Nic./Cyp.* 50, *Or.* 3.37; Dio Chrys. *1st Disc. on Kingship* 14; *12th Olymp. Disc.* 27–28; *31st Disc.* 20; *32d Disc.* 35; *36th Disc.* 43; Diog. Laert. *Lives* 6.1.2; Athen. *Deipn.* 11.461b; Plut. *Eum.* 16.3; *Ages.* 10.3; *Tim.* 28.2; *Bride* 21, *Mor.* 141A; Sext. Emp. *Out. Pyrr.* 3.267; *Against the Ethicists* 1.15; Strabo *Geog.* 13.1.1; 15.3.23; 16.2.38; Chariton *Chaer.* 6.7.12). Other peoples did not all take kindly to this (Jos. *Ag. Ap.* 1.3, §§15–18; 1.11, §58; Sib. Or. 3:171, 732; 4:70; cf. 4:1), although some accepted the typical Greek division of humanity into "Greeks" and "barbarians" as simply a standard way of speaking of all peoples (Rom. 1:14; Cic. *Invent.* 1.24.35; probably *Offic.* 3.26.99; Sen. *Dial.* 5.2.1; Jos. *Ag. Ap.* 1.22, §201; 2.39, §282; *War* 5.1.3, §17; *Ant.* 1.3.9, §107; 15.5.3, §136; 18.1.5, §20; Philo *On Drunkenness* 193; *On the Cherubim* 91; *On Abraham* 267; *On Joseph* 30; *Life of Moses* 2.18, 20; *The Decalogue* 153; *Special Laws* 2.44, 165; 4.120; *Every Good Man is Free* 94; *On the Contemplative Life* 21; 48; *Embassy to Gaius* 145; 292; Tatian 1, 21, 29). Although Jews were normally counted among non-Greeks (Strabo *Geog.* 16.2.38; Jos. *War* 1.preamble 1.3; contrast perhaps Philo *Special Laws* 2.165; 1 Cor. 10:32), educated Jews in Alexandria sometimes protested that they were culturally Greek.

16. Heyob, *Isis,* p. 36. Religious tolerance seems to have been higher in the period of the Republic; see Tenney Frank, *Aspects of Social Behavior in Ancient Rome* (Cambridge: Harvard University, 1932), p. 42. Judaism naturally despised Isis-worshipers, too; cf. Sib. Or. 5:484–91 (probably late first to early second century CE Egypt); the "thrice-

wretched goddess" (5:484; *OTP* 1:404) may be an allusion to the triple-goddess tradition applied to other composite goddess figures of antiquity.

17. Plut. *T.-T.* 4.6.1–2, *Mor.* 671C–672C, e.g., 6.2, *Mor.* 671DE (the Feast of Tabernacles is associated with Dionysus) and 672A (so also the Sabbath).

18. Lucian still has them mixed up in the second century in *Pereg.* 11. Outsiders recognized Christianity's Jewish roots well into the third century, no doubt to the embarrassment of many of the Jewish leaders (cf. R. L. Wilken, "The Christians as the Romans (and Greeks) Saw Them," in *Jewish and Christian Self-Definition,* ed. E. P. Sanders et al., 3 vols. [Philadelphia: Fortress, 1980–82], 1:119–23).

19. The sorts of charges cited against Judaism (cf. Tac. *Hist.* 5; Jos. *Ag. Ap.* 2) came to be leveled against Christians (cf. the ass's head in Tac. *Hist.* 5.4; and Tert. *Apol.* 16.1–4). They came to be accused especially of atheism (for rejecting the gods, Athenag. *Plea* 3; Justin *1 Apol.* 6; probably Marc. Aur. *Med.* 3.16.1), incest (probably based on brother-sister love in Christ; Athenag. *Plea* 3; Theoph. 3.4; Tert. *Apol.* 2.5, 20; 4.11; 7.1; cf. the story in B. J. Bamberger, *Proselytism in the Talmudic Period* [New York: KTAV, 1968], p. 235), infanticide and cannibalism (based on a literalistic misunderstanding of the Lord's Supper, Athenag. *Plea* 3; Theoph. 3.15; Min. Fel. *Oct.* 9.5; Tert. *Apol.* 2.5, 20; 4.11; 7.1); several of these charges recur in later Jewish sources (B. L. Vistozky, "Overturning the Lamp," *JJS* 38 [1, Spring 1987]: 72–80). Cannibalism (Otto, *Dionysus,* p. 113; Diog. Laert. *Lives* 7.1.121, 7.7.188) and child sacrifice (Tert. *Apol.* 9.2) may not have disgusted some marginal groups, but were generally among the greatest conceivable vulgarities, and figures such as Orpheus (Guthrie, *Orpheus,* p. 40) and Isis (Grant, *Religions,* p. 132) took credit for abolishing them.

20. Tacitus, who does not supply all the details provided in Josephus, nevertheless links the two events, and it almost sounds as if both the Egyptian and the Jewish communities were expelled by Tiberius at the same time (*Ann.* 2.85). The context is sexual offenses of upper-class women, but Tacitus seems only to be reporting discussions in the Senate. Perhaps because Judea was part of the Roman province of Syria, Jews and Syrians could be confused (possibly this explains Juv. *Sat.* 8.160).

21. As a Roman aristocrat, he received a lesser punishment, although he was more guilty than the priests. Class distinctions were part of standard Roman legal discrimination; e.g., Callistratus in *Digest* 47.21.2 (*Empire,* ed. Sherk, §160, p. 205).

22. Cf. Heyob, *Isis*; Meeks, *Urban Christians,* p. 25.

23. Jos. *Ant.* 18.3.4, §§64–80.

24. Jos. *Ant.* 18.3.5, §§81–83. Josephus adapts his narrative according to standard literary conventions for apologetic purposes (H. R. Moehring, "The Persecution of the Jews and the Adherents of the Isis Cult at Rome A.D. 19," *NovT* 3 [4, Dec. 1959]: 293–304), but this does not bring his basic story into question (Heyob, *Isis,* p. 118, thinks Josephus was just making Judaism look good at the expense of Isis devotees).

25. Juv. *Sat.* 14.102–3.

26. Ibid., 14.100–101.

27. Tac. *Hist.* book 5.

28. Cf. C. Salles, “Le monde gréco-romain du 1er siècle: une société interculturelle?” *Supplément* 156 (1986): 15–28 (NTA 31:85).

29. See Stern, “Literature,” p. 1118. For anti-Judaism in Greco-Roman antiquity, see e.g., *CPJ* 1:24–25; 2:36–55, §153; 3:119–21, §520; Philo *Flaccus* 1; 47; 85; Sib. Or. 3.271–72; Quint. 3.7.21; Hor. *Sat.* 1.5.100–101; Juv. *Sat.* 14.96–106; Persius *Sat.* 5.179–84; S. J. D. Cohen, *From the Maccabees to the Mishnah,* LEC 7 (Philadelphia: Westminster, 1987), pp. 46–49; J. C. Meagher, “As the Twig Was Bent: Antisemitism in Greco-Roman and Earliest Christian Times,” in *Anti-Semitism and the Foundations of Christianity,* ed. A. T. Davies (New York: Paulist, 1979), pp. 1–26; J. L. Daniel, “Anti-Semitism in the Hellenistic-Roman Period,” *JBL* 98 (1, March 1979): 45–65; E. R. Goodenough, *Jewish Symbols in the Greco-Roman Period,* 13 vols. (New York: Pantheon, 1953–68), 12:54. Nevertheless, Judaism was popular, as attested in the numbers of proselytes and God-fearers (J. G. Gager, *The Origins of Anti-Semitism* [New York: Oxford University, 1983], pp. 67–88; Cohen, *Maccabees,* pp. 49–58), though this only exacerbated the hostility of other outsiders (Gager, *Anti-Semitism,* pp. 59–61; cf. E. M. Smallwood, *The Jews Under Roman Rule,* SJLA 20 [Leiden: Brill, 1976], pp. 203–5).

30. Cf. e.g., Jos. *Ant.* 16.6.2, §§162–65; 19.5.2, §§280–85. The status of *religio licita* is often affirmed for Judaism (e.g., Meyer Reinhold, *Diaspora* [Sarasota: Samuel Stevens, 1983], p. 74; Selwyn, *Peter,* p. 51), though it may not be strictly accurate, since Judaism functioned as a *collegium* rather than a *religio* (Parkes, *Conflict,* p. 8; cf. Koester, *Introduction,* 1:365). Josephus’ evidence points not toward a *religio licita* status per se, but toward the use of precedents and appeals (Tessa Rajak, “Was There a Roman Charter for the Jews?” *JRS* 74 [1984]: 107–23). Precedent was important in Roman law (Augustus’ powers are cited in support of those of Vespasian in a law of 69–70 CE, in *CIL* 6.930, in *Empire,* ed. Sherk, pp. 124–25, §82), and Luke seems to appeal to as many legal precedents as possible in establishing the acceptability of Christianity in the book of Acts.

31. See especially the thesis of Gager, *Anti-Semitism,* who thinks that the main cause of antipathy toward Judaism in Rome was its popularity among others in Rome. Jewish proselytism does not appear in favorable light in our Roman sources: Hor. *Sat.* 1.4.141–44; see the full sampling in Molly Whittaker, *Jews and Christians: Graeco-Roman Views,* CCWJCW 6 (Cambridge: Cambridge University, 1984), pp. 85–91; cf. Parkes, *Conflict,* pp. 25–26. Of course, the foreignness and non-Roman exclusiveness of Judaism was also offensive, as may be attested in repeated criticisms of circumcision, Sabbath, and food laws (cf. Tac. *Hist.* 5.1–5; Gager, *Anti-Semitism,* p. 58; Smallwood, *Rule,* p. 123; J. N. Sevenster, *The Roots of Pagan Anti-Semitism in the Ancient World,* NovTSup 41 [Leiden: Brill, 1975], pp. 89–144); but Judaism’s popularity may be what made these threatening and more than objects of ridicule.

32. Judaism laid claim to protection partly on the basis of its antiquity (Jos. *Ag. Ap.* 1.1, §1); respect for the antiquity of tradition may

be one reason the Sibylline Oracles were placed in the distant past (H. W. Parke, *Sibyls and Sibylline Prophecy in Classical Antiquity* [New York: Routledge, 1988], p. 8). Although early Christians like Luke (who ties Christianity into the history of Israel in Luke-Acts) and Justin (*1 Apol.* 44) appealed to the antiquity argument, Roman magistrates did not initially grant recognition in their case.

33. We refer to the Neronian persecution of 64 CE, in Rome, reported by Tacitus and Christian tradition (Tac. *Ann.* 15.44; Tert. *Apol.* 5.3; Euseb. *Eccl Hist* 2.25.79–80). The objections of G. Fau, "L'authenticité du texte de Tacite sur les Chrétiens," *Cahiers du Cercle Ernest-Renan* 19 (72, 1972): 19–24 (NTA 16:218) are untenable; cf. Mattingly, *Christianity*, pp. 31–32; A. Giovannini, "Tacite, l''incendium Neronis' et les chrétiens," *Revue des Etudes Augustiniennes* 30 (1–2, 1984): 3–23 (NTA 29:307); M. J. Harris, "References to Jesus in Early Classical Authors," pp. 343–68 in *The Jesus Tradition Outside the New Testament*, ed. David Wenham, GP 5 (Sheffield: JSOT, 1984), pp. 348–50.

34. Plut. *Bride* 19, *Mor.* 140D (LCL). For an example of Plutarch's objections to foreign superstitions, cf. Plut. *Superst.* 2, *Mor.* 166AB (he includes Judaism as such in *Superst.* 8, *Mor.* 169C).

35. Meeks, *Urban Christians,* p. 25; cf. J. E. Stambaugh and D. L. Balch, *The New Testament in Its Social Environment,* LEC 2 (Philadelphia: Westminster, 1986), pp. 123–24. Pomeroy, *Goddesses,* p. 206, notes "the Romans' use of religious sanctions to promote socially desirable behavior," referring to the cults of *Fortuna*; for the Romans, religion should establish, not challenge, the social fabric.

36. Examples from the hellenistic period may be found in W. W. Tarn, *Hellenistic Civilisation,* 3d rev. ed. (New York: New American Library, 1974), pp. 99–100. Verner, *Household,* pp. 64–67, acknowledges improvements but notes that in hellenistic Egypt the same social restrictions obtained on wives; they were "expected to be domestic, socially retiring, chaste, and submissive to their husbands," lest they shame the household.

37. S. B. Pomeroy, "Women in Roman Egypt: A preliminary study based on papyri," in *Reflections of Women in Antiquity,* ed. H. P. Foley (New York: Gordon and Breach Science Pub., 1981), pp. 303–22; Verner, *Household,* pp. 68–70; cf. Meeks, *Urban Christians,* pp. 23–24. Some examples of powerful upper-class women—both respected and despised—are gathered, e.g., in Balsdon, "Women," pp. 24–31.

38. Carcopino, *Life,* pp. 84–85; cf. pp. 90–95, although the case may be exaggerated; cf. Friedländer, *Life,* 1:237–38.

39. See Hallett, "Elegy," p. 244.

40. Cf. Susan Treggiari, "Jobs in the Household of Livia," *PBSR* 43 (1975): 48–77; cf. also the Greek inscription of a message from Augustus in Karia, in *Empire,* ed. Sherk, p. 7, §3, where Livia's influence over her husband is evident even as early as shortly after 27 BCE.

41. Verner, *Household,* p. 81.

42. On Juvenal, see Tony Reekmans, "Juvenal's Views on Social Change," *AncSoc* 2 (1971): 117–61.

43. Martin, *Slavery,* p. 89; for Philo similarly, see ibid., p. 93.

44. E.g., the inscription cited in *Empire,* ed. Sherk, §35, pp. 61–63, in which no senator's descendant was allowed on stage, hence rejecting lower-class occupations (19 CE; one may contrast the socially "inappropriate" behavior in which Nero engages a generation later).

45. MacMullen, *Relations,* p. 105.

46. Isoc. *Nic./Cyp.* 55, *Or.* 3.38 (LCL). For the moralists' unitary view of society, see Malherbe, *Exhortation,* p. 88, and the excerpt from Hierocles he cites on pp. 100–104. Meeks, *World,* p. 21, shows how Creon's position in Sophocles' *Antigone* 663–77, from classical Athens, reflects the fear of women's disobedience disrupting the civic order.

47. Pomeroy, *Goddesses,* p. 154; on Stoics, see especially ibid., p. 230. See Val. Max. *Mem. Deeds* 6.3.9, first century CE (in Lefkowitz and Fant, *Women's Life,* p. 176), on an early Roman who cudgeled his wife to death for drinking some wine. Valerius Maximus need not be approving of beating one's wife to death, but he is appealing to the "higher" standards of earlier Rome concerning wifely submission.

48. He ridicules particularly Trimalchio's wife Fortunata, who controls her husband's money (Petr. *Sat.* 37).

49. Juv. *Sat.* 4.30–37 (although Juvenal also mocks male bedfellows).

50. Juv. *Sat.* 4.111–12; 6.246–67. The "joys" are probably sexual pleasures, as Teiresias the seer testified in the older Greek story. The violence no doubt refers to bickering savagely with her husband in bed, to which he refers in 6.268–85. This is, he complains, all due to the influx of luxury in recent times; the hard-working, humble wives of old Latium were chaste (6.286–305).

51. Juv. *Sat.* 6.219–24; he goes on to note that she also changes husbands frequently. In 6.474–85, he again charges that matrons will abuse the slaves unless the husbands are there to ensure their safety.

52. Juv. *Sat.* 6.434–56.

53. In Petr. *fr.* 6 (LCL).

54. Gould, "Law, Custom and Myth," p. 57, suggests that the men of ancient Athens appear to have been uncomfortable with women's potential for their own undoing as reflected in the myths.

55. Cato the Elder 3, in Plut. *SRom., Mor.* 198D (LCL). Of course, this fits Plutarch's own view, but this is not necessarily a reason to dispute the likelihood that he depends on prior tradition.

56. Cic. *Par. Stoic.* 36.

57. Rawson, "Family," pp. 26–27.

58. Verner, *Household,* p. 81.

59. Stambaugh and Balch, *Environment,* p. 123.

60. For his linking of household codes with the theory of the polis, the (city-) state, see Arist. *Pol.* book 1, e.g., chs. 1–3; connections between state and household precede him (e.g., Lycurgus 21 in Plut. *SSpart., Mor.* 228CD; or, more reliably, Soph. *Antigone* as cited in Meeks, *World,* p. 21). For the societal function of the household codes, see A. J. Malherbe, *Social Aspects of Early Christianity,* 2d ed. (Philadelphia: Fortress, 1983), p. 51.

61. Balch, *Wives,* p. 117; Dieter Lührmann, "Neutestamentliche Haustafeln und antike Ökonomie," *NTS* 27 (1, Oct. 1980): 83–97.

Balch, *Wives,* pp. 23–31, covers Platonic material and Stobaeus; pp. 33–49, Aristotelian and dependent writers; pp. 33–49, the "topos" in the imperial period; and pp. 51–59, the same in eclectic Stoics, hellenistic Jews, and Neopythagorean texts. Other kinds of social relations could be constructed, e.g., to one's body, to the divine, and to other people (Marc. Aur. *Med.* 8.27); but we can say without doubt that lists of social duties were at least common (Epict. *Encheir.* 30). For the household codes, in Seneca, see *Ben.* 2.18.1–2; 3.18.1–4 (D. L. Balch, "Household Codes," in *Greco-Roman Literature and the New Testament,* pp. 27–28); but the most convincing of the non-Peripatetic examples appears to be Hierocles (see in Malherbe, *Exhortation,* p. 85). For a treatment of previous research, see Verner, *Household,* pp. 16–22; Balch, *Wives,* pp. 1–20; idem, "Codes," pp. 47–50. Some commentators, noting that the Stoic and Jewish parallels (e.g., in Eduard Lohse, *Colossians and Philemon,* trans. William R. Poehlmann and Robert J. Karris, Hermeneia [Philadelphia: Fortress, 1971], pp. 154–57; Kelly, *Peter,* pp. 107–8) were not particularly close, and writing before the views of Balch, Lührmann, and Thraede on the Peripatetic roots of the structure became generally disseminated, thought that this was a spontaneous Christian form in the NT (C. L. Mitton, *Ephesians,* NCBC [Grand Rapids: Eerdmans, 1981], p. 194, is a notable example; cf. P. T. O'Brien, *Colossians, Philemon,* WBC 44 [Waco, Tex.: Word, 1982], pp. 215–26; G. E. Cannon, *The Use of Traditional Materials in Colossians* [Macon, Ga.: Mercer University, 1983], pp. 111–21. Leonhard Goppelt, *Theology of the New Testament,* trans. John E. Alsup, 2 vols. [Grand Rapids: Eerdmans, 1981–82], 2:169–70, regards it as a Stoic form but with roots in the Jesus tradition's affirmation of civil authority).

62. Slaves, like wives and children, were commonly considered part of the household; see Rawson, "Family," pp. 7–8; in Judaism, cf. *CPJ* 1:249–50, §135 (second century BCE); p. Ter. 8:1; Safrai, "Home," p. 750. It also included "freedmen, hired laborers, and other clients" (Aune, *Environment,* pp. 59–60); cf. m. Ab. 1:5, where a pre-Christian Jewish teacher is said to exhort his hearers to "let the poor be sons of your house," i.e., be (functional) dependents.

63. Arist. *Pol.* 1.2.1, 1253b (LCL). The three pairs also appear in Arist. *Pol.* 1.2.2, 1253b; 1.5.3–4, 1259b; 3.4.4, 1278b.

64. Balch, "Codes," p. 27. Even Artem. *Oneir.* 1.24 defines as classes subservient to a man, "wife, children, and slaves." Interestingly, Jewish legal literature typically classifies as dependents or as those incapable of full equality "women, slaves, and minors" (e.g., m. Suk. 2:8; p. Suk. 2:9), though other categories such as deaf mutes and imbeciles are also introduced; Swidler, *Women,* pp. 117–18, sees this as generally demeaning to women. Other philosophers, like the Cynics, completely ignored questions of transforming the social order (Meeks, *World,* p. 55). Post-Aristotelian Greek thinkers seem to have shared Aristotle's penchant for categorization.

65. Stambaugh and Balch, *Environment,* p. 123.

66. Meeks, *Urban Christians,* p. 30.

67. Arist. *N. E.* 8.11.2, 1161a (over son); 8.11.4, 1161a (over wife); Stowers, *Letter Writing,* p. 31. Aristotle held that the state was

composed of households (*Pol.* 1.2.1, 1253b), but disagreed with those who thought its government the same as that of the city-state (e.g., *Pol.* 1.1.2, 1252a).

68. In Grant, *Religions,* pp. 131–33, especially p. 132. This text is from second century CE Asia, probably copying an earlier one from Egypt.

69. E.g., Sir. 7:18–28.

70. Apologetic concerns could also be reflected in Palestinian Jewish community laws; cf., e.g., Sifre Deut. 344.3.2.

71. Malherbe, *Aspects,* p. 51; cf. Meeks, *Urban Christians,* p. 106.

72. Jos. *Ag. Ap.* 2.201–17; see especially the comments in Balch, "Codes," pp. 28–29. This is true despite the fact that Josephus is often partly defending himself (cf. Clemens Thoma, "Die Weltanschauung des Josephus Flavius. Dargestellt anhand seiner Schilderung des jüdischen Aufstandes gegen Rom [66–73 n. Chr.]," *Kairos* 11 [1, 1969]: 39–52). On the importance of apologetic in Greek-speaking Judaism, cf. e.g., C. R. Holladay, *Theios Aner in Hellenistic Judaism,* SBLDS 40 (Missoula, Mont.: Scholars, 1977), passim. While agreement has not been reached on whether many of our Greek-Jewish documents were meant to convert Greeks to Judaism, or Jews to a greater level of hellenization (e.g., Victor Tcherikover, "The Ideology of the Letter of Aristeas," *HTR* 51 [2, April 1958]: 60, 83; I think this much less likely, especially for Aristeas, whose readers would not have understood it had they not already had Greek education), or just as general propaganda showing that Jews were respectable citizens of Greek cities like Alexandria, I believe that it is fair to look for apologetic elements in most of this literature.

73. Besides those familiar to us from Colossians, Ephesians, 1 Peter, and possibly 1 Timothy, see Did. 4; Ign. *Antioch.* 9–10 (probably pseudonymous).

74. On 1 Peter, see Balch, *Wives,* pp. 81–116. Also Aune, *Environment,* p. 196, and others, following Balch.

75. Cf. Meeks, *World,* pp. 128–29 (on 1 Thessalonians).

76. See Balch, *Wives,* pp. 90–92, for data from ancient moralists that would strengthen this contention.

77. C. L. Rogers, Jr., "The Dionysian Background of Ephesians 5:18," *BibSac* 136 (543, July 1979): 257, suggests that the admonition of wifely submission in 5:22 is anti-Dionysiac. We acknowledge a possible connection with Dionysus, but the polemic is more likely to protect Christians from Roman perceptions of that cult than against any inroads that cult was likely to have been making into first-century churches.

78. One might also ask, if the use of the *Haustafeln,* or household codes, in Eph. 5 is apologetic, why he does not tone down possible astrological connotations to his language in Eph. 1 more explicitly, since some conservative Romans (like the later emperor Domitian) disliked astrologers. But there was widespread acceptance of divination, which was even part of state cults; and astrological beliefs, which had become standard fare in the imperial Mediterranean, were not the same as astrological predictions of an emperor's demise. And ultimately his language is anti-astrological anyway.

79. E.g., Rom. 12:17; 1 Cor. 6:6; 10:32; 14:23–25; 2 Cor. 8:2; 1 Thess. 4:12.

80. Cf. the similar argument of Alan Padgett, "The Pauline Rationale for Submission: Biblical Feminism and the *hina* Clauses of Titus 2:1–10," *EQ* 59 (1, Jan. 1987): 39–52; Johnson, "Response," in *Women, Authority & the Bible*, p. 157.

# 5

# Mutual Submission in Ephesians 5:18–33

In the last chapter we saw that it was important for ancient Christians not to be viewed as undermining the ethics that were holding Roman society together. They could go beyond those ethics—as we argue in this chapter that they did—but for the sake of their witness and their survival, Paul portrayed Christian ethics in terms that would best communicate to their culture the moral superiority of Christianity.

Paul understood the particular values of ancient society well enough to know how best to impact it. Those who thought most about morality in that culture called on wives to obey and husbands to govern them honorably. Paul avoids the nuances of "obedience" and "ruling," but he does not mind calling on wives to submit or husbands to love, because this was behavior that should indeed characterize all Christians. Paul does call children and slaves to obey; we shall examine the exhortations to them in the following chapter.

For all the social conservativism in Paul's words, there is yet a subversiveness he dares not play down. All believers were equal before God in Christ, regardless of race, social status, or gender (Eph. 2:11–22; 4:4–6; cf. Gal. 3:28; 1 Cor. 12:13). In this chapter we shall argue that, despite Paul's attempt to relate to the best values in Greco-Roman culture, his words differ from those values precisely where Paul believed those values fell short of the will of God.

Interestingly, when Paul calls on wives to submit in Ephesians 5:22, he presents this as a particular *example* of the submission of all believers to one another in 5:21. Paul uses the traditional form of household codes discussed above, but by grounding the wife's submission in general Christian submission, he qualifies the meaning of those codes. Yes, the wife should submit to her husband; but the husband, following Christ's example of self-sacrificial service for his wife, also must submit himself to his wife. This is even more explicit than that the wife should love her husband even as he loves her (cf. 5:2, 25).

In this chapter we will examine several features of the text under consideration. First, the text addresses the most practical question of how believers are able to live a submissive life: by depending on the Spirit. Second, to understand what Paul means by the wife's submission we must consider how and why wives were expected to submit in antiquity, so we will examine women's inferior status in society and inferior authority in the home. Third, we will look at how ancient readers might have read wives' "submission," if it were not placed in the context of mutual submission. Fourth, we will briefly examine the call for husbands to love their wives and the role models of Christ and his church. Finally, we will investigate the nature of mutual submission in this passage and consider the relevance of the nearest ancient parallels to this idea.

## THE SPIRIT AND SUBMISSION: EPHESIANS 5:18–21

Sometimes 5:21 is translated as if it begins a new section only incidentally related to the preceding section: "Submit to one another."[1] But it is more likely that the Greek phrase "submitting to one another" retains here its usual force in the context of the parallel phrases that precede it: a subordinate participial clause dependent on the preceding imperative.[2] In other words, the submission of 5:21, like the worship of 5:19–20, flows from being filled with God's Spirit (v. 18).[3]

Those who are filled with the Spirit, as opposed to being possessed by intoxication, show their inspiration by the Spirit in singing songs to one another[4] and worshiping God (5:19–20). This suggests that Paul views the charismatic, corporate worship of the community as a normative part of early Christianity, not just an aberration at Corinth that he was powerless to change (1 Cor. 14:26).[5]

The presence of the Spirit further leads believers to worship by confessing their faith that God is sovereign over the universe and will accomplish the purposes for which Christ came. When Paul says that the Spirit moves people to "give thanks in everything," this would no doubt have struck a resonant chord both in Jewish readers who knew of God's providence in the Bible[6] and in many Gentile readers influenced by common counsels of the time to be satisfied with God's or Fate's decrees.[7] In one list of virtues, for instance, Epictetus declares that the wise man will be "free, serene, happy . . . giving thanks for all things to God, under no circumstances finding fault with anything that has happened, nor blaming."[8]

But another expression of being filled with the Spirit affects one's relationships with others, particularly in the home. Those who are filled with the Spirit will also be "submitting to one another out of regard for Christ" (v. 21), and this mutual submission will be expressed in specific family relationships in the household (5:22—6:9).

This means that Christians cannot complain that what God asks in the following passage is too difficult for them because of their own background or emotional makeup. The power of the Spirit is sufficient in believers' lives to enable them to fulfill God's will in interpersonal relationships.

## WOMEN'S INFERIOR STATUS IN HOME AND SOCIETY

When Paul calls on wives to submit, his words, even taken in their strongest possible sense, do not call wives to further subjugation. At their strongest, his words merely fail to challenge the prevailing structures of authority in society, perhaps because challenging authority structures was not his purpose in this letter and would have accomplished little in his situation except to increase the persecution of Christians, as we suggested in the preceding chapter.

But before we can ask whether Paul meant submission the way his contemporaries meant it, we must ask exactly how his contemporaries did mean it, and ask what the "normal" roles for women were in his day. We shall first examine the general status of women in and around Paul's day, and then turn to the question of what wives' submission meant for most ancient men.

### *Non-Jewish Greco-Roman Sources*

The status of women was not constant through all periods of antiquity.[9] Women probably provided both skilled and unskilled labor in Mycenaean Greece,[10] but their status had declined significantly by the time of Plato and Aristotle,[11] at least in Athens.[12] Although women's seclusion there has been exaggerated, it seems that their opinion and even presence was not valued in discussions on moral matters.[13] Their position seems to have improved in the centuries before the spread of Christianity, at least where we have evidence.[14] This was not least true in Asia, the province where Paul's letter to the Ephesians was sent.[15]

But even by Paul's day, many men felt that women were morally weaker than men.[16] Among those who expressed such views were prominent philosophers and moralists. Earlier philosophers were credited with a prayer of gratitude that they were not born women,[17] and a century after Paul a Stoic emperor could differentiate a women's soul from that of a man.[18] Aristotle felt that virtue was different for women and men; just as it was the virtue of the master to command wisely, and of the slave to obey diligently, so the different natures of men and women required them to express virtue in different ways.[19]

The evidence is not always clear-cut: it is not all "for" or "against" women.[20] The moralist Plutarch is a case in point. He allows that women can acquire virtues,[21] and he praises the bravery of virtuous women throughout history.[22] But when Plutarch argues that women should learn philosophy from their husbands, it is in part because he believes that if left to themselves, apart from men, women will produce only evil passions and foolishness.[23]

Stoic philosophers likewise declare that women are capable of the same virtues as men.[24] But this was all too often a theory not translated into practice.[25] In theory, a man and a woman could be capable of the same virtues, but the different dispositions of their genders and other characteristics were thought to lead them to develop naturally in different ways.[26] While equality was good in theory, the same philosophers who advocated such a theory usually also maintained hierarchical roles in home and society.[27] This was not much of an improvement over Aristotle, who had argued that the virtue of men was different from that of women, and that men's courage was shown in commanding, whereas women's was shown in obeying.[28]

### *Jewish Sources*

Our Jewish sources also speak both positively and negatively of women. Properly behaved Jewish women were to be honored, but mistrust of women's moral character in Jewish texts is often stronger than what we find in the philosophers.[29] Since these Jewish texts were written by men and for men, women are usually viewed only in terms of their relationship to men, often as objects of sexual temptation in ethical admonitions, and as wives and daughters in wisdom and law.[30]

There is a striking preponderance of what would appear to us as negative evaluations of women in early Jewish literature. An early Jewish teacher whose work was undoubtedly known to Paul advised men not to sit among women, because evil comes from them like a moth emerging from clothes. A man's evil, this teacher went on to complain, is better than a woman's good, for she brings only shame and reproach.[31] The same teacher warns of the hardships of being married to an evil woman, developing a theme that also appears in Proverbs.[32]

The early Jewish teacher Hillel is said to have associated women with sorceries,[33] and some later rabbis expanded on this suggestion.[34] A still later rabbi points out that the initial letter of Satan's name first appears in the Bible at the creation of Eve, and draws from this the conclusion that Satan was created with woman.[35] Women are said, in a Diaspora Jewish document, to do their best to trick men into falling sexually,[36] and another such document declares that out of sixty thousand people led to destruction, only one woman had as many good deeds as bad deeds.[37]

There were other signs of a woman's inferior social status in early Judaism. One is the oft-cited[38] prayer of R. Judah:[39]

> A man must recite three benedictions every day: "Praised [be Thou, O Lord . . . ] who did not make me a gentile . . . a boor [ignoramus] . . . [or] a woman." A gentile—as Scripture states, All the nations are nothing before him. . . . A boor—for "A boor does not fear sin" [m. Abot 2:5]. A woman—for women are not obligated [to perform all] the commandments.[40]

This prayer was probably not in use as early as the first century, but it reflects a generally understood premise of social reality; it was not only the perspective of later rabbis[41] but a commonly cited Greek perspective as well.[42] The male privilege reflected in this specific case is the privilege of being able to keep all the commandments of the Torah; women were obligated only to keep certain ones.[43]

Although Palestinian Jewish women had some freedoms that their contemporaries lacked under Greek and Roman laws,[44] rabbinic law also suggests women's generally inferior social status in Palestinian Judaism.[45] That the woman was acquired as wife on the legal analogy of property[46] is not particularly significant; this just reflects the customary way of describing the husband's exclusive sexual rights to his wife under law[47] and does not mean that the wife was viewed by her husband as impersonal property.[48]

More significant, however, was her legal responsibility to obey her husband and surrender to him any income she might receive.[49] A second-century law also appears to place a higher priority on a man's life or property than on a woman's, and a higher priority on protecting a woman's sexual purity than that of a man.[50] Laws that reflect positively on women or offer them protection[51] do not change this indication that the husband had superior social status and power.

Old Testament rules about a woman's menstrual "uncleanness" were developed and extended by later Jewish legal authorities, which came to restrict the interaction of women and strict male observers of such rulings.[52] But from an earlier period, respectable Jewish men in Palestine avoided social contact with women for much less ceremonial reasons. It was argued that one should not sit among women;[53] indeed, sitting near another's wife could lead to desiring her and thus to destruction.[54]

A pre-Christian Jerusalem teacher and those who commented on him are reported to have said: "And do not multiply gossip with a woman; they said this concerning one's own wife—how much the more concerning the wife of one's companion." The end result of indulging in chatter with a woman, the Sages thus warned, was hell.[55] One rabbinic interpretation of this saying was that it referred to the danger of being seduced; another rabbinic interpretation was that it meant that trusting a woman would lead one to ruin.[56] Even conversing with a relative publicly was considered inappropriate for a scholar, since onlookers might not realize that she was a relative and could (presumably) suspect flirtation on his part.[57] Indeed, so important was this matter, later rabbis reasoned, that God himself avoided speaking with women.[58]

These later Jewish teachers normally regarded a woman's testimony as considerably less reliable than that of men,[59] and they were not alone. Josephus, an aristocratic Jewish writer familiar with broader currents of the Greco-Roman world, regards the prohibition of women's testimony as part of God's law, based in the moral inferiority inherent in their gender:

> Put not trust in a single witness, but let there be three or at the least two, whose evidence shall be accredited by their past lives. From women let no evidence be accepted, because of the levity and temerity of their sex; neither let slaves bear witness, because of the baseness of their soul.[60]

Many Jewish writers thought of women as unstable and overly talkative.[61] This is at least as true in most Jewish writings from outside Palestine as it is in Palestine.[62] Philo, our most productive example of a Jewish writer outside Palestine, indicates as a matter of common knowledge that women are "endowed by nature with little sense,"[63] and generally associates them with sense-knowledge, the opposite of masculine rationality.[64] The *Sentences* of the Syriac Menander warn a man—especially one seeking a prospective wife—to avoid the talkative woman.[65] Jewish women may have been somewhat better off in the Roman province of Asia,[66] but the evidence adduced for this indicates only that more women gained prominence there than in Palestine. The same evidence demonstrates that such upwardly mobile women remained in the minority even there.

For whatever reason—it may have often been economic[67]—male children also were often preferred to female children in Jewish Palestine.[68] (This attitude was, however, stronger elsewhere in the Mediterranean world. For instance, a Greek dream handbook predicts that a dream about male children is a favorable omen, but a dream about female children augurs bad luck.)[69] This is not to imply that daughters were less loved than sons, but it does reinforce the picture of their generally inferior social status in antiquity.

The picture is not wholly negative, of course.[70] Aside from literary texts, it seems that Jewish women outside Palestine (and possibly within Palestine as well) took part publicly in the life of their communities.[71] In Palestine women were not confined to the home and could work in local shops,[72] and the husband was required to allow his wife relative freedom of movement.[73] Further, the husband was always to respect his wife.[74]

That different views about women could exist side by side is illustrated by the dispute of several much later rabbis, whose conflicting opinions their followers felt compelled to harmonize:

> Rab also said: He who follows his wife's counsel will descend into *Gehenna*. . . . R. Papa objected to Abaye: But people say, If your wife is short, bend down and hear her whisper!—There is no difficulty: the one refers to general matters; the other to household affairs. Another version: the one refers to religious matters, the other to secular questions.[75]

Our point is not to argue that men did not care about women, but rather that they nearly always regarded them as suited to be followers, not leaders, by virtue of their disposition.[76] Some writers felt that this disposition was an innate part of their gender; most writers do not seem to have entertained the question either way. But the vast majority of male writers viewed women as socially subordinate, often ignoring those women who violated the stereotype, or sometimes honoring them as exceptions to the rule.

## THE MEANING OF WIFELY SUBMISSION

What then was the feminine ideal in antiquity, in light of these different views of women's character? And what would womanly submission have meant in the light of this ideal? Traditional Roman writers portrayed the feminine ideal as supportive and subservient.[77] Roman inscriptions similarly indicate that women were usually honored for their roles as mothers, wives, or daughters, even though they sometimes made other contributions to society.[78] Part of the male ideal of women's submission was that they be meek, quiet, and apparently what we would consider "shy" and "self-conscious" in the presence of men. This did not mean that a woman would never be valued or praised for her wisdom;[79] but the most standard womanly ideal included a quiet and reclusive demeanor,[80] and other elements were, for normal women, at best incidental.

This is partly because ancient male writers generally saw a qualitative difference between the character of men and that of women. "Manly" character could be expressed in negative ways like drinking too much,[81] but it normally had to do with strength or courage,[82] including courage in virtue.[83] When a woman acted with courage, she was thus said to act "manly."[84] This is not to imply that ancient people were offended by a woman's virtuous courage; it is to say rather that they were often surprised by it.[85] In a culture where a woman's timidity was a regularly practiced feminine virtue, it is not unnatural that the men thought this self-consciousness an innate feminine trait, despite the exceptions, and this anticipation perpetuated their expectations of women's normal unsuitability for societal leadership roles.

The submission of wives was standard in ancient culture. Roman law gave men binding authority over their wives and unmarried daughters.[86] Early Roman aristocrats were said to have believed that women themselves preferred submission to their husbands over freedom.[87] Marriage contracts from first and second century BCE Egypt stipulate specifically that the wife must be submissive to her husband.[88]

Philosophers had long extolled this virtue. Centuries before the New Testament period, Aristotle argued that the man was by nature superior to the woman and fit to rule her.[89] Plato described a woman's virtue as taking care of the home and being obedient to her husband.[90] In the Roman period, a Stoic writer thanks the gods for an "obedient" wife.[91] A Cynic moralist, pretending to give womanly advice to women, demands that doing whatever her husband wants must be the rule by which the virtuous woman lives her life.[92]

It appears in other writers as simply the expected norm of ancient society. Artemidorus in his dream handbook assumes that wives, like children and slaves, "obey" their men,[93] and in Apuleius' novel, Psyche promised to obey her unseen husband.[94]

As usual, the writings of Plutarch shed light on ancient moral thinking concerning the issue at hand. Plutarch insists on the wife's full submission in social and religious matters; she is to share her husband's friends, rather than to make her own, and thus she should also accept his gods and religion.[95] It is proper for a man to rule his wife, and a man who failed to do so would come under Plutarch's criticism.[96]

The few extant Jewish writers from the first century are at least equally insistent. The Jewish philosopher Philo assumes that the masculine rules the feminine,[97] and describes the wife's proper duty to her husband in the language of slave service.[98] Josephus attributes to "the Law" the view that the woman must submit to her husband: "The woman, says the Law, is in all things inferior to the man. Let her accordingly be submissive, not for her humiliation, but that she may be directed; for the authority has been given to the man."[99]

Most Jewish writers seem to have shared this view.[100] A pre-Christian work admonishes a man not to let his wife have authority over him while he lives.[101] The ideal wife in this work is silent, restrained, modest,[102] chaste, in a home that the husband rules well.[103] In one work, God disciplined Adam with death for listening to his wife, who should have been subject to him instead.[104] The later rabbis also recognized the husband's authority over his wife as standard.[105]

In other words, submitting to one's husband and other male relatives was part and parcel of what it meant to be a "good" woman in ancient society. This may give us some sympathy for the rarely told perspective of the "bad" women in antiquity, many of whom may have simply been normal wives struggling to deal with insensitive husbands. Some marriages may have been nearly equal, with husbands and wives working in the market together; but the ideal model propagated in ancient society was that wives should be submissive and obedient, often even slavishly so.

Paul urges submission, but by placing it in the context of mutual submission (see above), he defines it quite differently than most of his culture did, even at the risk of raising the charge of subversion he had worked so carefully to avoid. Paul does not call on wives to take charge of their husbands, but calls on husbands to love their wives in such a radical way that husbands become their wives' servants, too.

## HUSBANDS' LOVE FOR THEIR WIVES

That husbands and wives normally loved each other is, of course, almost a foregone conclusion; whatever else love might have meant in antiquity, it would naturally have been used to describe the ideal relationship between husbands and wives. Funerary inscriptions dedicated by widows or widowers to their deceased spouses testify to this affection among all social classes.[106]

Despite the likelihood that love between husband and wife might simply be assumed, some ancient moralists explicitly called for it. Some writers emphasized that the wife should love her husband.[107] Cicero declares that the most crucial natural bond is between husband and wife.[108] Some Jewish writers, both in Palestine and in the Diaspora, emphasized the responsibility of the husband to love and respect his wife.[109]

Nevertheless, the responsibility of the husband to love his wife is not explicitly stressed as much in ancient literature as the wife's responsibility to submit to him, though this may in part be because it was generally assumed. The household codes normally instructed the head of the household how to "rule" or "govern" his wife, rather than how to love her.

Paul is certainly among the minority of ancient writers in that he devotes more space to the exhortation of husbands to love in Ephesians 5 than to that of wives to submit. In our culture, his exhortation to wives to submit stands out more strongly; in his culture, the exhortation to husbands to love, rather than the normal advice to rule the home, would have stood out more strongly. Further, Paul does not address the husband's role in the wife's submission; he does not urge the husband to inculcate submission in his wife. Paul's only instructions to the husband are to serve her as Christ served the church, and, since husband and wife are "one flesh" (Gen. 2:24), to love her as he would his own body.

## ROLE MODELS: CHRIST AND THE CHURCH

Like any good ancient teacher, Paul was ready to cite authoritative role models to demonstrate how submission and love were to be expressed. Not settling for any secondary characters, Paul chooses for each the most authoritative models available to him: Christ as the lover and the church as submitter. Christ is also the example of love for the whole church (Eph. 5:1); the church is naturally enough not cited as the role model for its own submission in 5:21, but the parallelism is clear enough: all are to submit as part of the church, and all are to love as Christ did.

Husbandly love and wifely submission in this context thus become examples of those more general virtues, rather than statements that love is only the husband's role, and submission only the wife's. Indeed, Christ's love is explicitly defined in this passage in terms of self-sacrificial service, not in terms of his authority (5:25–27). Of course, authoritarian leadership on *any* basis conflicts with the teaching and example of Jesus throughout the Gospels, so those who advocate it today would do well to consider whether they grieve the Spirit of God.

The picture of Christ's relationship to his church as a husband to his wife has sometimes been associated with the "sacred marriage" of some Greek gods to their followers,[110] but most scholars[111] recognize a much more natural source for Paul's image.[112] Both Paul and his readers accepted the Old Testament as God's word, and found there plenty of examples of a certain "sacred marriage": God's covenant relationship with Israel is often portrayed in these terms.[113] This image continued to be used by Jewish people in Paul's time and later.[114]

Just as husband and wife became "one flesh" (Gen. 2:24), so Christ's church is his body, and those joined to him are one spirit with him (1 Cor. 6:17).[115] The emphasis here is not on hierarchy but on oneness, spiritual and sexual unity.[116] We have dealt with Paul's meaning of "headship" in chapter 1, but whatever Paul or others may have meant by "head" in general, Paul defines it by his usage here specifically as "Savior" (Eph. 5:23). The wife recognizes her husband as "head" in terms of submitting to his authority (5:22–23), but the husband recognizes his headship in terms of loving and serving his wife (5:28–30). The image of head and body here is meant to emphasize especially that the husband and wife should see themselves as one and work together with a common purpose and goal (5:31).

Many household codes were addressed as instructions only to the male householder,[117] but Paul addresses his instructions to each member of the household. He wants wives to do their part and husbands to do their part—not to use his letter to enforce the other person's part. Although Paul uses the most socially acceptable language of his day to present his case, his point is that both partners must seek to serve one another because of Christ's reign in their lives. It is likely that their roles will be different, according with their own background and cultural leadership models that develop different skills and preferences along gender lines. But Paul gives no instructions on transcultural role differences here, such as who does the cleaning or who works outside the home. He merely defines the marriage relationship in terms of mutual service.

## MUTUAL SUBMISSION

To call on wives to submit themselves to their husbands would not have been a radical statement in Paul's day. To "submit oneself" could mean to "give in" or "cooperate," and need not mean "obey";[118] the closest thing Paul gives to a definition of the term in this context, in fact, is the word "respect" in 5:33, where he plainly summarizes his whole exhortation to wives. This alone makes Paul's exhortation quite weak by ancient standards. But the context in which Paul places his exhortation qualifies it much more: it is an expression of the kind of submission all Christians render to one another, the kind that Christian husbands would thus also need to render to their wives.[119]

It is clear that the submission of verse 22 cannot be other than the submission of verse 21 from the simple fact that the word "submitting" does not even appear in the Greek text of verse 22: it has to be borrowed from verse 21. It is perfectly legitimate to read verse 22, "Wives, submitting to your husbands," as long as we understand that we must take verse 22 as an *example* of verse 21's mutual submission. Indeed, one commentator points out that verse 22 might be translated, "for example, wives to your husbands," and this is no doubt its force.[120] Wives should submit to their husbands because Christians should submit to one another.

Paul's argument here is both powerful and well crafted. If wives submit to their husbands, Roman moralists and others could not claim that Christianity subverted pagan morals. But if the husband also submits, and husband and wife act as equals before God, Paul is demanding something more than Roman moralists typically demanded, not less.

Further, Paul enjoins that submission must be done out of "the fear of Christ" (5:21).[121] Someone who keeps in mind that he or she has a Lord in heaven is not likely to lord it over others, but to take more willingly his or her place as a servant—whether the world views them as master or servant (6:7–9).

Would Paul's readers have caught the idea that he was trying to qualify what he said about wives' submission? Since some other writers in Paul's day also qualified such expressions, we may guess that they would have. For instance, the Stoic writer Hierocles assigns the husband the public duties and the wife the domestic duties, but he is not willing to separate these roles completely.[122] As mentioned above, many Stoics maintained both women's natural equality and the propriety of their social subordination to men.[123]

In a marriage relationship, Plutarch urges that the husband and wife act in harmonious consent—something like what we mean by mutual submission—but with the wife recognizing the husband's leadership.[124] The wife should not be afraid to joke around with her husband,[125] and the husband should respect no one as much as his wife.[126] But Plutarch also writes in no uncertain terms of the wife's duty to obey her husband, and that the husband should rule her with sensitivity:

> So it is with women also; if they subordinate themselves to their husbands, they are commended, but if they want to have control, they cut a sorrier figure than the subjects of their control. And control ought to be exercised by the man over the woman, not as the owner has control of a piece of property, but as the soul controls the body, by entering into her feelings and being kind to her through goodwill . . . it is desirable to govern a wife, and at the same time to delight and gratify her.[127]

This is one of the most "progressive" social models in Paul's day, and is similar to the one Paul advocates for his readers, although Paul, unlike Plutarch, does not explicitly call the wives to obedience (5:21–22).

But does Paul mean by mutual submission exactly what Plutarch means by his instructions? In this case, he would then have to mean that wives should always submit, and husbands should submit only in the sense that they lovingly look out for their wives' interests. If this is what Paul intends, we might even be led to think that Paul means the wife's submission in the complete and total sense in which Plutarch means it. Paul would then be saying that all Christians should submit to one another, but they should submit in different ways, as detailed in his list of duties in 5:22—6:9.

But while others speak of wives, slaves, and children submitting differently,[128] they do not speak in terms of *everyone* submitting: rare indeed is the ancient writer who would, with Paul, call *all* people, including the male heads of households, to submit to one another—other writers certainly would not have had them share the same verb as Paul does in 5:21–22. Other writers may have qualified traditional gender roles, but no one we know of qualified them as clearly as Paul did.[129]

It is most natural to read Paul as making a much more radical statement than Plutarch, both because of what Paul says and because of what he does not say. He subordinates wives so weakly, and emphasizes mutuality so strongly, that it is difficult to believe that he is arguing for their transcultural subordination.

Paul is responding to a specific cultural issue for the sake of the gospel, and his words should not be taken at face value in all cultures. Paul believes that Christians should be submissive and not seek their own interests, and thus that Christian women in his day should moderately conform to the general social ideal without fighting it. Although he explicitly defines the wife's submission only as "respect" (5:33), he emphasizes this duty from the wife more than from the husband to relate to the culture in which Christians were living out their witness. But would Paul expect Christian women today to conform to the forms of submission that were standard in Paul's day? Or would he expect Christian submission, both for the husband and the wife, to take a different form?

Interpreters who differ on this matter may read the same cultural background and interpret Paul's words to his own culture in the same way. But whether we believe that the nature of mutual submission will be different in our culture than it was then depends in part on how well we *know* ancient culture. It is unlikely that a wife today *could* perform the duties ancient cultures expected of wives and still submit to husbands in our culture, who would most likely find the cultural differences impossibly frustrating. It would not be possible for wives to submit in all other cultures in exactly the same way Paul was suggesting wives submit in his day.

Whether we believe that mutual submission must be practiced in the same form today as it was back then also depends in part on a different question: how we get from the "then" to the "now" in biblical interpretation. The question is not whether to apply and obey Paul's words, but rather how to apply and obey them in a new setting.[130]

Those of us who both study the Bible in the light of its culture and preach it to congregations face this question every time we preach, trying to apply the principles of the Bible in the way most relevant to our listeners. When we preach narrative, we look for the moral of the story and apply it, and we do the same when we read what Paul addressed to various situations in his churches. I am convinced that, in many cases except for the issue of women's submission, we simply unconsciously assume that this is the right way to read the Bible. But when it comes to an issue like women's submission, where a culturally informed reading of the text can challenge our church traditions, we are more reluctant to read the Bible on these terms.

One issue of debate in the nineteenth-century United States that is no longer a matter of much debate is the issue of slavery. Because I expect that all my readers will now agree with the abolitionists that slavery is morally wrong, I believe the way we read the Bible's teachings about slavery can be very instructive for how we read the Bible's teachings about women. This is especially the case since Paul goes on in the very context we have been discussing to address slaves in much the same manner that he has addressed wives. To this issue we turn in the next chapter of this book.

## CONCLUSION

As has often been pointed out, Ephesians 5:22–33 advocates mutual submission. The only explicit definition of the wife's submission in the text is that she respect her husband, and though Paul probably has more in mind than this, his call to submission was not at all radical. Paul defines the husband's submission in much greater detail, however, and defines it in terms of Christ's self-sacrificial service on behalf of the church. Paul's language seems to go considerably beyond his culture in this respect.

Some ancient writers did believe that husbands should nurture their wives as persons of equal worth, yet wives should obey their husbands. Their language concerning mutuality is not nearly as strong as Paul's, but for the sake of argument, we now raise the *possibility* that Paul was not as radical as he appears, and that he meant by wifely submission exactly what they meant.

Yet if we indeed read the husband-wife part of this household code in this way, we must also read the master-slave part of the household code in the same way. In the following chapter, I hope to show the parallels between the two issues, since Paul calls on slaves to obey their masters, no less plainly than he calls on wives to submit to their husbands. I also hope to demonstrate that Paul does indeed go beyond the most progressive elements of his culture and would not have mandated the continuance of the authority of the *pater familias* (the head of the Roman household) over either wives or slaves for all cultures.

## NOTES

1. Imperatival infinitives are rare in the NT, but they may be more customary for household codes; cf. Balch, "Codes," p. 45, especially on Arius Didymus. Imperatival participles (as this would be) occur in the papyri, although they tend to be rarer in the NT; cf. H. E. Dana and J. R. Mantey, *A Manual Grammar of the Greek New Testament* (Toronto: Macmillan, 1955), p. 229. Kelly, *Peter,* pp. 67–68, bases the use of the

imperatival participle on rabbinic Hebrew halakah (see W. D. Davies, *Paul and Rabbinic Judaism,* 4th ed. [Philadelphia: Fortress, 1980], p. 329, following Daube), but it is difficult to suppose that Paul's readers would have been familiar with such a form except as it had come to relate to Greek usages.

2. Cf. J. P. Sampley, *'And the Two Shall Become One Flesh,'* SNTSMS 16 (Cambridge: Cambridge University, 1971), pp. 114–16, although I do not share Robinson's appeal to patristic literature here.

3. Cf. e.g., the imperative (a prayer) in Ps. Sol. 17:22a that controls the infinitives in 17:22b–25.

4. Reciprocal use of the reflexive. Prayers like those in the Psalms could include exhortation; Tobit's written prayer in Tob. 13:6 includes even a call to repentance for Israel. Philo also reports male-female antiphonal singing among the Therapeutae. Talking with one another could educate one another, as some Greeks thought Jewish people did while engaging in philosophy (see Theophrastus, in Menahem Stern, *Greek and Latin Authors on Jews and Judaism,* 3 vols. [Jerusalem: Israel Academy of Sciences and Humanities, 1974–84], 1:10).

5. Cf. Mitton, *Ephesians,* pp. 190–91. The contrast with drunkenness in v. 18 suggests to J. A. Robinson, *St Paul's Epistle to the Ephesians,* 2d ed. (London: James Clarke, 1904), p. 122, that the social context is not public worship, but a common meal that took the place of public pagan feasts in the Greek cities. But the analogy should be with private religious meals rather than public here, and in early Christianity the communal meal seems to have been part of the gathering for worship rather than a distinct meeting (1 Cor. 11–14). Praise also seems to flow from being filled with the Spirit of understanding in Sir. 39:6.

6. Cf. Jub. 16:31; 1 En. 108:10. It is made explicit by Josephus, who repeatedly emphasizes terms used in the Greek world for "providence," though expressing them as manifestations of God's will, rather than as forces in themselves as in much Greco-Roman thought of this period.

7. Epict. *Disc.* 1.6.1, 14.16; Sen. *Dial.* 7.15.4, 16.1–3; 9.10.4; 11.4.1; Marc. Aur. *Med.* 6.16.

8. Epict. *Disc.* 4.7.9; as long as the wise man sees "good" and "advantage" as residing in his moral purpose and not in circumstances.

9. For a much more thorough and nuanced treatment than we have space for here, see Swidler, *Women,* pp. 7–25.

10. J.-C. Billigmeier and J. A. Turner, "The Socio-economic roles of women in Mycenaean Greece: A brief survey from evidence of the Linear B tablets," in *Reflections of Women in Antiquity,* pp. 1–18.

11. Gould, "Law," p. 43, observes that her legal status was that of a perpetual minor (which fits some other ancient laws, too), and that she was defined by law "as almost . . . an un-person" (p. 44). In drama, women's roles have both positive and negative features; cf. Foley, "Conception in Drama," pp. 127–68. Cf. Semonides *On Women* (sixth century BCE), who contended that women were made from a variety of garbage and were Zeus' worst curse on men (in Lefkowitz and Fant, *Women's Life,* pp. 14–16; for more examples, see pp. 12–20). Periander is said to have

killed his pregnant wife in anger (Diog. Laert. *Lives* 1.94), but this is also said of Nero in the imperial period, and the whole narrative portrays Periander as willing to treat human life cheaply, whether male or female.

12. For Sparta, contrast Gorgo 5, in Plut. *SSpartW., Mor.* 240E, and anonymous 22, *SSpartW., Mor.* 242B; and, closer to the period in question, Arist. *Pol.* 2.6.7, 1269b (Aristotle thinks the Spartan women's control while the men were away was bad).

13. See Banks, *Community,* p. 159.

14. Verner, *Household,* pp. 35–39. Early Roman law seems to have been much more positive than Greek law; see Frank, *Aspects,* pp. 22–23.

15. See Kraabel, "Judaism," p. 44. The textual variant in Eph. 1:1 may well suggest that this was a circular letter, but that our texts include Ephesus and no other city as a particular destination suggests that Ephesus was at least the major center in the region of the letter's circulation.

16. E.g., Juv. *Sat.* 6, passim (e.g., 6.242–43). This view seems to be assumed in direct narratives as well, e.g., the easily misled maid in Chariton *Chaer.* 1.4.1–2, though this may best apply to lower-class or slave women; or the wife in Ab. R. Nathan 3 A who is less generous than her husband.

17. See the references to Thales, Socrates, and/or Plato in Longenecker, *Ethics,* p. 70; Meeks, "Androgyne," pp. 167–68.

18. Marc. Aur. *Med.* 5.11. The implication seems to be that it is inferior, like that of a child, youth, tyrant, or animal.

19. Arist. *Pol.* 1.5.3–11, 1259b–1260b. He argues against Plato's portrayal of women's equality in the ideal society (*Pol.* 2.2.15, 1264b); of course, Plato himself elsewhere regarded women as inferior by nature (Meeks, "Androgyne," p. 170).

20. This is pointed out especially by the analysis of Boer, *Morality,* pp. 243–46 (evidence that women were badly treated), 246–51 (evidence that they were not so badly treated), 251–56 (Boer's intermediate standpoint); cf. especially his point on p. 269, that there was great variation even from one place to another in the same period.

21. Plut. *Bride* 48, *Mor.* 145C.

22. Plut. *Bravery of Women, Mor.* 242E–263C.

23. Plut. *Bride* 48, *Mor.* 145DE.

24. Sen. *Dial.* 6.16.1; this is true even though they are weaker, like the uneducated (6.7.3) (J. N. Sevenster, *Paul and Seneca,* NovTSup 4 [Leiden: Brill, 1961], pp. 192–96, points out that Seneca's opinion of them is usually poor). Also Antisthenes in Diocles in Diog. Laert. *Lives* 6.1.12; Crates 28, to Hipparchia (*CynEp,* pp. 78–79). Mus. Ruf. *fr.* 12, *On Sexual Indulgence* (Malherbe, *Exhortation,* pp. 153–54), demands the same morality of men as of women, but on the principle that it is unthinkable that men should be less moral than women.

25. See Meeks, *Urban Christians,* p. 23; idem, "Androgyne," p. 170. The Epicureans constituted an exception, treating women equally in the school (ibid., pp. 170, 172–73), although the Epicureans were nowhere as influential on popular thought as the Stoics in Paul's day.

26. Marilyn B. Arthur, "Classics" (review essay), *Signs* 2 (2, 1976): 402, summarizing C. E. Manning, "Seneca and the Stoics on the Equality of the Sexes," *Mnemosyne* 26 (2, 1973): 170–77.

27. Meeks, *World,* pp. 60–61. Lefkowitz and Fant, *Women's Life,* p. 104, §107, quote a treatise attributed to second/third century BCE Pythagoreans that differentiates external roles (in which women are to be domestic and husbands public), and internal qualities of virtue. Balch, "Codes," p. 31, speaks of the Roman Stoics as "egalitarian in theory but Aristotelian in practice." Because the same could naturally be said of Paul's argument in Eph. 5:21–22, where he moves from the principle of mutual submission into the household codes, we have included a discussion of master-slave roles, which is also part of this section, in chapter 6 to force modern interpreters to be consistent in their position on wives and on slaves. We offer two possible answers to this objection: first, whereas much of the Stoics' published teachings were meant to be widely disseminated, Paul's epistolary teaching is more occasional in nature and hence less likely to address questions of universality; second, *neither* source seems to have considered itself the originator of household codes, instead adopting codes that already existed; we cannot therefore assume the users' opinion of these codes' universal character except when they tie them into men's and women's "nature"; most thinkers probably did not consider the difference between their culture and other cultures' situations in this regard.

28. Arist. *Pol.* 3.2.10, 1277b.

29. Joachim Jeremias, *Jerusalem in the Time of Jesus,* trans. F. H. and C. H. Cave (Philadelphia: Fortress, 1969), pp. 359–76, provides a detailed study of the social position of women in rabbinic literature, although he overplays the negative elements. It may be that the already substantial negative elements came to predominate more in the later literature, just as one finds more misogyny in the church fathers than in the earliest Christian literature (cf. Swidler, *Women,* passim); others hold the opposite position (Witherington, *Women,* p. 10, suggests that the positive elements developed later, since many of our positive statements are also late; cf. Jacob Neusner, *Judaism in the Beginning of Christianity* [Philadelphia: Fortress, 1984], pp. 59–60). Women were prophets, queens, etc. in the OT, and remained important in Hasmonean times and in synagogue art; but the Essenes, the first-century priesthood, and the rabbis reserve such roles and most rights for men (Jacob Neusner, *The Tosefta: Translated from the Hebrew Third Division Nashim* [New York: KTAV, 1979], p. x).

30. In parts of the LXX and Pseudepigrapha; see Swidler, *Women,* pp. 29–55; in rabbinic literature, pp. 126–30. For different groups within early Judaism, see pp. 56–82; Swidler finds the views essentially negative. I have attempted to be as fair to the sources as possible in what follows, but my own research also suggests the preponderance of negative roles for women in Jewish wisdom traditions, though these may have been somewhat mitigated in practice. Swidler, *Women,* p. 167, concludes that a trend of increasing chauvinism in early Judaism ran counter to the increasing liberation in Greco-Roman antiquity, and thus did not simply

reflect the surrounding culture. Our point here, however, is not to pass judgment on early Jewish tradition, but simply to place Paul's admonitions in their proper context.

31. Sir. 42:12–14.

32. Sir. 25:12, 16–26. The point is no doubt true whether one refers to an evil husband or to an evil wife, but Proverbs appears more open to the availability of good wives than Sirach (though cf. Sir. 7:19, and 26:1–4, 13–18, forming an inclusio around the bad wife of 26:5–12).

33. See m. Ab. 2:7. Cf. the wife of Lucius' host in book 3 of Apuleius' *Metamorphoses.*

34. See b. Ber. 53a; Pes. 111a; cf. Moore, *Judaism,* 2:137.

35. Gen. Rab. 17:6, attributed to a third- or possibly fourth-century teacher.

36. Test. Reub. 5:1–5; 6:1; cf. the Egyptian woman on Joseph in 4:9.

37. Test. Abr. 9 B. Rec. A did not report that this soul was female, but neither did it record, as 10 B does, the doom to a wicked soul being a woman who murdered her daughter.

38. E.g., Bonsirven, *Judaism,* pp. 100, 134; Eduard Lohse, *The New Testament Environment,* trans. John E. Steely (Nashville: Abingdon, 1976), p. 150; Barth, *Ephesians,* 2:655–56.

39. Late second/early third century CE; an attribution to R. Meir would lower the date more generally to the second half of the second century.

40. See t. Ber. 6:18 (trans. Neusner, 1:40).

41. Most of the family and civil law in the Mishnah is not specifically Pharisaic and thus may derive from a wider body of Jewish custom, as Sanders, *Jesus to Mishnah,* p. 14, points out (against Neusner).

42. See Longenecker, *Ethics,* p. 70; Meeks, "Androgyne," pp. 167–68, cited above.

43. Cf. Fiorenza, *Memory,* p. 217.

44. Verner, *Household,* p. 45, although he notes that Greek and Roman laws also permitted certain rights not given under rabbinic law.

45. Fiorenza, *Memory,* p. 116, rightly appeals to the portrayal of Judith for a different model; but Judith belongs to an earlier period, and the rabbinic restrictions probably carry forward the basic male chauvinism that predominated in first-century Judaism, as exemplified in Philo and (more relevant for aristocrats in Palestine) Josephus. Both many of our later codices of Roman law and our collections of rabbinic law (and even the rabbinate itself) are significantly later than the time of Paul, introducing unavoidable complications into this discussion. We are here assuming that evidence of a sufficient commonality among diverse sources supports the general picture of women's inferior social status, even though the degree and nature of that inferiority varies considerably among specific bodies of data.

46. E.g., m. Kid. 1:1.

47. Wegner, *Chattel,* shows that a woman was regarded as chattel with regard to her sexuality (pp. 20–34, 40–70), but as a person in all other ways (pp. 34–38, 70–95, 114–20, 171). In terms of Jewish law, this

created a "legal hybrid," rather than an intermediate category between person and property (ibid., pp. 7–8). Man was thus the legal norm, woman the anomalous derivation, in the Mishnah; cf. idem, "Tragelaphos Revisited: The Anomaly of Woman in the Mishnah," *Judaism* 37 (2, Spring 1988): 160–72; Neusner, *Beginning,* p. 32. The husband's role can be compared to the Roman pater familias (Wegner, *Chattel,* pp. 3–4).

48. In other words, the rabbis could perpetuate and develop older legal categories, but such categories, like a gender-based language, do not render their users inherently more sexist if the *meaning* placed on them is not sexist.

49. See m. Ket. 6:1; Z. W. Falk, "Jewish Private Law," in *JPFC,* pp. 516–17.

50. See m. Hor. 3:7; cf. t. B. M. 2:32.

51. Women's status was in some regards higher than that of Gentiles or slaves (m. Naz. 9:1), and women, with minors and slaves, could say the blessings on behalf of the male householder if he could not (p. R. H. 3:10, referring back to the Tosefta). A girl was recognized to reach maturity before a boy, on natural biological grounds (cf. Wegner, *Chattel,* pp. 36–37, who associates this with personhood).

52. E.g., t. Shab. 1:14; cf. p. Hag. 2:6, §2. See especially Wegner, *Chattel,* pp. 162–65; Swidler, *Women,* pp. 130–39.

53. Sir. 42:12.

54. Sir. 9:9.

55. See m. Ab. 1:5 (my translation).

56. Ab. R. Nathan 14, §35 B, gives both interpretations; the second interpretation cites Samson as an example, and this interpretation is on the whole more likely, since one's own wife would not have been mentioned in the first case. This is true even though other texts cite the fear of seduction as a danger.

57. See b. Ber. 43b, bar.

58. See p. Sot. 7:1, §2; Gen. Rab. 48:20, 63:7, trying to minimize the biblical "exceptions." Cf. Swidler, *Women,* pp. 123–25, who also discusses the issue of men's conversation with women in Judaism.

59. Sifra VDDeho. pq. 7.45.1.1. They would use women when they had to, and regarded them as capable of giving truthful witness (Wegner, *Chattel,* pp. 120–23), but women normally would not testify; cf. Neusner, *Tosefta: Nashim,* p. xi. It is tempting to read Luke 24:11 (cf. Mark 16:11) in this light; even though it is not specifically stated that the male disciples disbelieved the women disciples on account of their gender, this could have augmented their perception that the women spoke "nonsense." A child was also unable to bear legal witness (t. Sanh. 9:11).

60. Jos. *Ant.* 4.8.15, §219 (LCL).

61. See b. Shab. 33b (Tannaitic attribution but undoubtedly later); Gen. Rab. 45:5; 80:5.

62. Most Diaspora writers in Greek areas were probably influenced by Greek chauvinism. We know that at least Jewish marriage customs in the Diaspora were shaped by Greeks laws rather than later-attested Palestinian Jewish ones (cf. Stambaugh and Balch, *Environment,* p. 50, following an article by Tcherikover).

63. Philo *Every Good Man Is Free* 117 (LCL). One suspects that he regards it as common knowledge since he uses this premise to make another point. For Philo, the man is more complete than and superior to the woman (see R. A. Baer, *Philo's Use of the Categories Male and Female,* AZLGHJ 3 [Leiden: Brill, 1970], p. 41. Baer's helpful work was brought to my attention by his daughter, my former colleague at Duke, ethicist Rebecca E. Baer).

64. See Baer, *Categories,* pp. 38–44, 65–66. Philo thus speaks of spiritual masculinity (which is essentially asexuality, femininity deviating from this norm; ibid., pp. 45–49). In comparison to the divine, however, even the male element in a person, the higher reason, is female, and the soul must become a passive and female receiver of divine impregnation in inspiration (ibid., pp. 55–64). Philo writes positively of women only such as those among the Therapeutae, whom he affirms to be living as virgins, thus seeing them (in his system) as ideals transcending sexual polarity (ibid., pp. 98–101).

65. Syr. Men. *Sent.* 118–21, 336–39.

66. Kraabel, "Judaism," pp. 46–48.

67. In Gen. Rab. 26:4 (attributed to a late second- or early third-century source), the preference for sons is based on the fact that the daughter is lost to the family who raised her when she is married. In ancient circles, a woman's changing families could mean that the economic investment in her was lost to her family of origin. But even a good brideprice could not recoup the cost of raising her, so marrying her off young was preferable to waiting.

68. Sifre Deut. 138.2.1; 141.2; cf. b. Ber. 5b; Pes. Rab Kah. 9:2; Safrai, "Home and Family," p. 750; J. D. M. Derrett, *Jesus's Audience* (New York: Seabury, 1973), pp. 31–32. Jews, unlike some Gentiles, forbade gender-based (or any other basis) infanticide, however (see Keener, *Marries Another*, p. 74 and notes); and Gentiles also loved daughters once they had them (Plut. *Bride* 36, *Mor* 143B).

69. Artem. *Oneir.* 1.15; 4.10.

70. For instance, Louis Finkelstein, *Akiba: Scholar, Saint and Martyr* (New York: Atheneum, 1970), pp. 187–91, portrays Akiba as a defender of women's rights, as over against the earlier patrician rabbis. If Finkelstein were correct on the chauvinism of the patrician rabbis, it would support our general thesis, but I am not convinced that his evidence for the class categories is sufficient to sustain that point.

71. R. S. Kraemer, "Non-Literary Evidence for Jewish Women in Rome and Egypt," *Helios* 13 (2, 1986): 85–101. P. W. van der Horst, "The Role of Women in the Testament of Job," *NedTT* 40 (4, 1986): 273–89 (NTA 31:212) (cf. Spittler in *OTP* 1:833) thinks that Testament of Job indicates a mystical Jewish community where women were prominent; this is possible, although it assumes a setting (especially for the final chapters) that precludes Christian influence.

72. Safrai, "Home and Family," p. 752, citing rabbinic evidence.

73. Ibid., p. 762, citing rabbinic texts.

74. Ibid., pp. 763–64.

75. See b. B. M. 59a (Soncino ed., p. 351).

76. Cf. similarly Swidler, *Women,* p. 168, who protests that cases of individual affection do not get us around the negative character of the "societal and religious *structures.*"

77. Hallett, "Elegy," pp. 241–44 (noting that some writers did portray freer women as a new ideal); Stambaugh and Balch, *Environment,* p. 111; cf. Malherbe, *Exhortation,* p. 82, for the Pythagorean letters; Epict. *Encheir.* 40 for a Stoic. Suzanne Dixon, *The Roman Mother* (Norman, Okla.: Oklahoma University, 1988), p. 3, points out that though the virtue of wives in a more ancient period had become a standard theme for later writers, "it was in the late Republic and early Empire that wives were prepared to die for or with their husbands." For classical Athens, see Pomeroy, *Goddesses,* p. 74; the inscription in Lefkowitz and Fant, *Women's Life,* p. 11, §22. Swidler, *Women,* p. 84, cites a midrash in which men are their wives' masters (Yalq. Shim. Sm. 78).

78. D. E. E. Kleiner, "Women and Family Life on Roman Imperial Funerary Altars," *Latomus* 46 (3, 1987): 545–54 (NTA 32:224); cf. Lefkowitz and Fant, *Women's Life,* pp. 147–55; Dibelius and Conzelmann, *Pastoral Epistles,* p. 46. See, e.g., *CIL* 6.10230 in *Empire,* ed. Sherk, p. 242, §184, where a son praises his mother for her domestic virtues, including obedience. Of course, honorary inscriptions, as opposed to funerary inscriptions, would not be as strongly weighted in this direction. Jewish tradition also strongly tied women's roles to the welfare of their husbands and home (Derrett, *Audience,* p. 33). The father as possessor of authority and benevolent patriarch also appears in Jewish piety (P. A. H. de Boer, *Fatherhood and Motherhood in Israelite and Judean Piety* [Leiden: Brill, 1974], p. 25), though the case in the OT may be overstated. When 1 Esd. 4:14 speaks of women "ruling" over men, it connects this to the fact that all men are born from women (4:15).

79. Jdt. 11:21.

80. Sir. 22:5; of course, "quietness" (1 Tim. 2:11–12) could also be applied to men (Test. Abr. 1 A). Cf. Val. Max. *Mem. Deeds* 8.3 (in Lefkowitz and Fant, *Women's Life,* p. 206, §205); Pomeroy, *Goddesses,* p. 74; the inscription in Lefkowitz and Fant, *Women's Life,* p. 11, §22. The Greek ideal of beauty was extended to male youths, who were also objects of adult male passion; Plato *Charm.* 158C notes that Charmides blushed and so "looked more beautiful than ever, for his modesty [bashfulness] became his years" (LCL).

81. Sir. 34:25.

82. 1 Macc. 2:64; Plato *Crat.* 413E–414A; Chariton *Chaer.* 7.1.8; Theon Progymn. 9.22. Arist. E. E. 3.1.2–4, 1228ab, defines *andreia* as the mean between rashness and cowardice.

83. Crates 19 to Patrocles (*CynEp,* pp. 68–69); see J. T. Fitzgerald, *Cracks in an Earthen Vessel,* SBLDS 99 (Atlanta: Scholars, 1988), pp. 87–90. In Wisd. 8:7 it appears as a superior attribute fostered by Wisdom, though perhaps this is meant only for men.

84. 2 Macc. 7:21; 4 Macc. 15:23, 30; 16:14; Apul. *Metam.* 5.22; cf. Arist. *Pol.* 3.2.10, 1277b. Philo, admiring the empress Livia, says that she became "male in her reasoning power" (*Embassy to Gaius* 319–20, in Meeks, *Urban Christians,* p. 24).

85. This surprise has exceptions, of course, even among the elite class; Pliny seems genuinely to appreciate the moral and intellectual sophistication of women peers; see E. S. Dobson, "Pliny the Younger's Description of Women," *CB* 58 (6, Apr. 1982): 81–85. For accomplishments of ancient women in various periods (more Roman than Greek), see Lefkowitz and Fant, *Women's Life,* pp. 21–25, 244–47. Honorably pious women are repeatedly praised in early Judaism, e.g., Sarah, Edna, and Anna in Tobit; the wives of rabbis, e.g., b. Taan. 23b; Lev. Rab. 5:4.

86. Gardner, *Women,* p. 5, including her exceptions and qualifications, which are for our purposes minor. Cf. also Verner, *Household,* pp. 33–34, 39; Carcopino, *Life,* pp. 80ff.; Pomeroy, *Goddesses,* pp. 150–52; Lefkowitz and Fant, *Women's Life,* pp. 191–93.

87. Livy 34.7.12, attributing a speech to Lucius Valerius in 195 BCE, although this is probably Livy's idealization of the past (I owe this reference to Marjorie Lightman and William Ziesel, "Univira: An Example of Continuity and Change in Roman Society," *CH* 46 [1, Mar. 1977]: 19–32).

88. Verner, *Household,* p. 38; also that she could not leave the home without permission, etc. A Samaritan marriage contract stipulates that the wife must obey her husband completely (in John Bowman, *Samaritan Documents Relating to Their History, Religion and Life,* POTTS 2 [Pittsburgh: Pickwick, 1977], p. 311).

89. In *Pol.* 1.2.12, 1254b.

90. Plato *Meno* 71 (from *Greek Philosophy: Thales to Aristotle,* ed. R. E. Allen [New York: Free, 1966], p. 98).

91. Marc. Aur. *Med.* 1.17.7, as well as loving. His term for "obedient" is listed in a lexicon as sometimes used for a horse's obedience to its reins.

92. Ps-Melissa, *Letter to Kleareta* (Malherbe, *Exhortation,* p. 83).

93. Artem. *Oneir.* 1.24.

94. Apul. *Metam.* 5.5. Her failure to do so brought her considerable grief, which suggests that the story's "moral" reflects Apuleius' views of a social norm, albeit one often violated.

95. Plut. *Bride* 19, *Mor.* 140D.

96. Plut. *Uneduc. Ruler* 2, *Mor.* 780C, critiquing the Persian king, who ruled everyone but his wife as a slave. Plutarch says he should have been his wife's "master" *(despotēs)*. Other writers have likewise cited other references for the obedience of wives; e.g. Stambaugh and Balch, *Environment,* p. 111; Barth, *Ephesians,* 2:611, n. 12; Dibelius and Conzelmann, *Pastoral Epistles,* p. 47; Gerhard Krodel, "The First Letter of Peter," in *Hebrews–James–1 & 2 Peter–Jude–Revelation,* Proclamation Commentaries (Philadelphia: Fortress, 1977), p. 73.

97. Cf. Baer, *Categories,* p. 69. Philo argues that the rational part of the person, which is masculine, should rule the feminine.

98. Meeks, "Androgyne," p. 177, citing Philo *Hypothetica* 7.3, 7.14.

99. Jos. *Ag. Ap.* 2.24, §§200–201 (LCL). That Josephus defends Judaism against Apion's charges in this work makes his statement all the more instructive for early Christianity, which faced intense suspicions of subversiveness in the Roman world.

100. It is, of course, anachronistic and culture-bound for modern readers to suppose that women raised in that culture would have found all expressions of submission objectionable; some expressions of submission seem to have been normal cultural role functions. The submission of Raguel's wife in Tob. 7:16 is as natural a fulfillment of cultural roles as the hospitality and marital preparations that accompany it. But it is difficult to believe that all or even most Jewish women would have been pleased by words like the above statement of Josephus.

101. Sir. 30:19 (also not one's son, brother, or friend).

102. Sir. 26:14.

103. Sir. 26:15–16.

104. V. Adam 26:2.

105. E.g., Sifra Qed. par. 1.195.2.2.

106. E.g., *Greek Anth.* 7.340; Verner, *Household,* pp. 62–63; and in Lefkowitz and Fant, *Women's Life,* p. 12, §26; *CIJ* 1:cxvi. It appears not only on tombstones but in family stories handed down from generation to generation and in poetry (Dixon, *Mother,* pp. 2–3). A surviving spouse could, of course, dedicate the inscription because that was the standard thing to do and nevertheless have been glad to get rid of the old boy. But we should guess that to be the exception rather than the rule, and the language of many of the inscriptions is touching even today. Standardized inscriptions and forms of grief expression no more make the monuments "artificial" than inscriptions on our tombstones or factory-made sympathy cards today (against Rawson, "Family," p. 26).

107. Dio Chrys. *fr.* (LCL). The young widow pining away for grief over her husband's death in Petr. *Sat.* 111 was widely respected, though in Petronius' satire at women's expense, she gives in (112). *CIJ* 1:118, §166; 1:137, §195, Jewish funerary inscriptions, praise wives for being "lovers of their husbands." A man's love could be understood in sexual terms (e.g., Gen. 26:8; Hieronymus' citation of Sophocles' reply in Athenaeus 13.557e), but we should not think that the term (the one in Athenaeus is used generally for love) is limited to this sense.

108. Cic. *Offic.* 1.17.54. Cf. *Rhet. ad Herenn.* 3.3.4.

109. Ps-Phocyl. 195 (this leads to lifelong mutual kindness, 196–97); *OTP* 2:581, note *s,* notes that this is a common paraphrase of Homer. The Babylonian Talmud calls on the husband to love his wife as he loves himself and to honor her more than himself (b. Yeb. 62b, bar., cited in Safrai, "Home and Family," pp. 763–64; Bonsirven, *Judaism,* p. 147; cf. the collection of material in C. G. Montefiore and H. Loewe, *A Rabbinic Anthology* [New York: Schocken, 1974], pp. 507–15). Love for wife is assumed in 4 Macc. 2:11, where the law comes before love toward one's wife, making one devout enough to challenge her wrongdoing.

110. E.g., Batey, *Imagery,* p. 11; cf. pp. 70–76. Richard Reitzenstein, *Hellenistic Mystery-Religions,* PTMS 15 (Pittsburgh: Pickwick, 1978), pp. 19–20, 25, 35–36, 118, 310–19, addresses this *hieros gamos* motif in the mysteries; while Reitzenstein was not always critical in how he interpreted his sources, his arguments are at least worthy of study. Cf. most older sources and some more recent ones: Ramsay, *Teaching,* pp. 291–96; Gilbert Murray, *Five Stages of Greek Religion* (New York: Co-

lumbia University, 1925), p. 32; W. L. Knox, *St Paul and the Church of the Gentiles* (Cambridge: Cambridge University, 1939), p. 183, n. 1, p. 201; Tarn, *Civilisation,* pp. 354–55; H. R. Willoughby, *Pagan Initiation* (Chicago: University of Chicago, 1929), p. 136; C. A. P. Ruck, "Solving the Eleusinian Mystery," in *The Road to Eleusis* (New York: Harcourt Brace Jovanovich, 1978), pp. 36, 40. But while the *hieros gamos* was a way to look at nature, it is not clear whether it was expressed ritually in Greek cults outside that of Dionysus (Burkert, *Religion,* pp. 108–9; cf. Gasparro, *Soteriology,* p. 81; Koester, *Introduction,* 1:177, 193; Günther Wagner, *Pauline Baptism and the Pagan Mysteries* [Edinburgh: Oliver & Boyd, 1967], p. 73); and there is no certain evidence for its practice in the Asian congregations (Meeks, "Androgyne," p. 206).

111. E.g., Barth, *Ephesians,* 2:669–70 (the differences he lists on pp. 670–72 I do not regard as significant).

112. After summarizing data on the sacred marriage in the mysteries (pp. 114–16), S. Angus, *The Mystery-Religions and Christianity* (New York: Scribner's, 1928), p. 116, notes that Eph. 5 gets the image from the OT picture of God and Israel, not from the mysteries. Cf. also Barth, *Ephesians,* 2:741–42.

113. Sampley, *One Flesh,* pp. 34–45, sees Ezek. 16:8ff. as a major source for Eph. 5. The image of Israel's marriage to Torah is later and secondary, and so need not be appealed to here (Num. Rab. 2:25; 12:4; Pes. Rab. 5:10).

114. Sifre Deut. 43.16.1; Sifra Shemini Mek. de-Miluim 99.2.2 (contrast 99.2.5); Gen. Rab. 52:5; Exod. Rab. 15:31; 19:7; 44:4; Deut. Rab. 2:37; 3:10, 12; Lam. Rab. 3:1, §1, 20, §7; Pes. Rab Kah. 12:11; 19:2, 4, 5; 22:5; Pes. Rab Kah. Sup. 6:5; Pes. Rab. 21:15; 31:3, 10; 33:11; 37:3 (many of these references occur in parables). The Song of Solomon was often allegorized to apply to Israel (Sifre Deut. 1.11.1; Deut. Rab. 2:37; Song Rab. 5:16, §6; Pes. Rab Kah. 5:6; 22:5; Pes. Rab Kah. Sup. 5:1; Pes. Rab. 5:5; 7:7; 15:6–15; 33:10; 35:1; 36:2), although this is not fully clear before we come to the rabbinic texts (W. W. Fields, "Early and Medieval Jewish Interpretation of the Song of Songs," *GTJ* 1 [2, Fall 1980]: 221–31). Goodenough, *Symbols,* 8:17–20, argues for erotic aspiration for God in pre-Christian Jewish mysticism, but while he has some evidence, he goes too far with too little of it; cf. also idem, *An Introduction to Philo Judaeus,* 2d ed. (Oxford: Basil Blackwell, 1962), p. 143.

115. Paul had used the analogy of marriage in less detailed form to describe the relationship between Christ and his church before (Rom. 7:1–4; 2 Cor. 11:2), and other Christian writers continued to use it after him, e.g., Rev. 21:2; 2 Clem. 14.

116. Cf. similarly Scanzoni and Hardesty, *Meant to Be,* p. 30.

117. Eduard Schweizer, *The Letter to the Colossians,* trans. Andrew Chester (Minneapolis: Augsburg, 1982), pp. 213–14; Balch, "Codes," pp. 38–39. Women were, however, addressed in Pythagorean moral texts such as *Ps-Melissa* and *Ps-Theano,* so we should not think this an absolute rule. That children are addressed may be more remarkable than that wives are addressed (Schweizer, *Colossians,* p. 223; cf. Andreas Lindemann, "Die Kinder und die Gottesherrschaft. Markus 10, 13–16 und die Stellung

der Kinder in der Späthellenistischen Gesellschaft und im Urchristentum," *WD* 17 [1983]: 77–104), although adult children are no doubt included in the admonition (see Safrai, "Home and Family," p. 771, for Jewish exhortation to adult children; in Roman life, cf. Dixon, *Mother,* pp. 211–12), and the responsibility of children is part of ancient household codes (Malherbe, *Exhortation,* p. 90).

118. Barth, *Ephesians,* 2:709–10, distinguishing between the active and middle/passive uses.

119. Sampley, *One Flesh,* p. 117; also most current Christian egalitarian authors; cf. Bilezikian, *Roles,* pp. 153–73; Hull, *Equal to Serve,* pp. 202–3; Gundry, *Women,* p. 71; Thompson, "Response," p. 92; Boldrey, *Chauvinist,* p. 53; Longenecker, *Ethics,* p. 79.

120. Barth, *Ephesians,* 2:610.

121. The "fear of God," central in biblical wisdom literature, remained important in later Jewish ethical admonition; e.g., Sir. 1:11–30; 25:10–11; 31:13–15; Tob. 4:21; 4 Macc. 15:8; Ep. Arist. 95, 159, 189, 200; Syr. Men. *Sent.* 9–10; Syr. Men. *Epit.* 2, 9, etc.; m. Ab. 1:3; p. B. M. 2:5, §2; cf. Test. Levi 13:1; Test. Jos. 10:6; 11:1; Test. Benj. 3:4. For the idea in hellenistic literature, cf. Pythag. *Sent.* 27 (Malherbe, *Exhortation,* p. 111).

122. Malherbe, *Exhortation,* pp. 97–98, citing Hierocles, *On Duties, Household Management* 4.28.21, which he quotes on pp. 98–99.

123. See especially Balch, *Wives,* pp. 143–49 (Appendix 5, "Roman Stoics and Plutarch on Equality between Husband and Wife").

124. Plut. *Bride* 11, *Mor.* 139CD. Peace between a husband and wife is emphasized also in b. Hul. 141a; b. Shab. 116a (attributed to R. Ishmael); Test. Sol. 18:15 (where the source of domestic disharmony is a demon).

125. Plut. *Bride* 29, *Mor.* 142A ("joking relationships" are distinguished from more respectful "avoidance relationships" in many cultures). The ideal of "mutual respect and affection" was more widespread, of course, and appears in Greek literature as early as Homer (see Marilyn B. Arthur, "Early Greece: The Origins of the Western Attitude Toward Women," in *Women in the Ancient World,* p. 15).

126. Plut. *Bride, Mor.* 144CD.

127. Plut. *Bride* 33, *Mor.* 142E (LCL). The language of the wife as the husband's "body" (some of which I have omitted for the sake of space) is strikingly similar to Paul's, although Paul's explicit citation of Gen. 2:24 makes it clear that this is his source for the concept.

128. Arist. *Pol.* 1254b3–1277b25, 1313b33–39, 1335a8–17 (Lefkowitz and Fant, *Women's Life,* p. 64, §86). Cf. Meeks, *World,* p. 36, citing Arist. *N. E.* 5.3.6. When Artem. *Oneir.* 1.8 speaks of "yielding to" or "submitting to" women, he refers specifically to intercourse and nothing more.

129. Ep. Arist. 257 does, but not in the context of household codes, which would apply the admonition to household relationships.

130. So also Johnston, "Authority and Interpretation," pp. 30–41; cf. Stanley Gundry's response that Johnston's solution may allow too much subjectivity here.

# 6

# A Model for Interpreting Wives' Submission—Slaves in Ephesians 6:5–9

Paul's admonitions to wives are similar to his admonitions to children and slaves, although wives, unlike children and slaves, are never summoned to "obedience."[1] Modern writers who argue that Paul's charge to wives to submit to their husbands "as to Christ" is binding in all cultures must come to grips with the fact that Paul even more plainly tells slaves to "obey" their masters "as they would Christ" (6:5). If one is binding in all cultures, so is the other.[2]

To interpret the whole passage consistently, therefore, we must insist that what we grant today concerning slaves (that Paul's call to submit is not a transcultural approval of the master's authority) we must grant concerning wives (that a call to submit is not a transcultural approval of the husband's authority). The arguments for the subordination of each were roughly the same in ancient household codes,[3] and a brief examination of the relevant New Testament passages will show that they are roughly the same there as well.[4] This is not to suggest that many wives today experience the same level of oppression slaves experienced; it is simply to require that we use the same principles of interpretation for both passages.[5]

Although this chapter will give attention especially to the question of Paul's treatment of the slavery issue, we must also briefly address his treatment of the obedience of children, since Paul treats that issue in the same context with wives' and slaves' submission, as do many other ancient household codes. Most of our culture values the obedience of children, and it is to this model, rather than to that of slavery, that advocates of modern wifely submission appeal.

But examining all three of these models of submission reveals the critical point: Paul advises his readers in the setting in which they lived; he does not make their setting valid for all times. He employs the standard household codes of his world, but these are not the standard codes of our world. His principles are illustrated by their concrete application in this letter, but need to be applied differently in different cultures and situations. In short, we must always submit to those in authority in Christian love, but Paul in no way requires the same authority structures for all cultures.

## CHANGING SOCIETY OR CHANGING HOUSEHOLDS?

Before examining Paul's views on children and slaves, we must ask why Paul addresses only the treatment of slaves, children, or wives in the household, and not the institutions of slavery and patriarchal authority over child and wife, in a broader societal way.

The only logical answer is that Paul simply had no reason to address the broader societal question in a letter of instructions to a local church. Paul was not in a position to change the social structures of his day; no one else was arguing for the abolition of slavery, including the very few who, like Paul, apparently considered enslaving people immoral.

The ancient world was not a modern democracy in which people of all classes could dissent and protest without anticipating violent suppression. In recent times, Gandhi and Martin Luther King, Jr., accomplished reforms by nonviolent protest, but the same tactic did not work so well in Beijing's Tiananmen Square, and it has failed to work in many cultures, particularly those with less respect for human life than our own.[6] Reformers who wished to accomplish the emancipation of all slaves in Roman antiquity could have sought to do so only by starting a bloody war they were certain to lose or by converting the rest of the empire to their beliefs in a God before whom all persons were equals.

Paul, a pastor and a missionary, was out to change the world by starting where he realistically and reasonably could: by spreading Christianity and demanding that all Christians love and respect one another as themselves. Whether he considered the possibility of Christians being able to radically alter even basic socioeconomic structures is uncertain; they were a small, persecuted minority in his day with no visible way to affect social structures controlled solely by the aristocracy. The radical implications of his teaching would ultimately be realized in a new kind of society after the return of the Lord, but if Paul ever considered that Christians might someday wield enough power in this present world to change all societal injustice, he had no reason to mention it in letters to congregations struggling with issues closer at hand. The few lines he did write, however, were among the most progressive words of his time, and he certainly wanted Christians to work for justice in the ways they had available to them—by transforming the relationships among and around them.

A writer to a small but growing Christian community in the first century cannot properly be faulted for not advocating a wholly impractical course in his letters, and to read him as if he wrote to people in our modern situation is to read him with an incredibly ethnocentric historical naïveté. Such naïveté may characterize the more faddish literary critics and some of the most radical feminists, but it is a tragedy when Christians read Paul in this same thoughtless way. It is especially tragic when Christians who read the Bible in this insensitive manner hurt other people by means of their interpretation, keeping them down and "in their place," as racist churches in the United States and South Africa have had a history of doing.

But because Paul's letters do not overtly recommend violent revolution does not mean that Paul did not care about the problems confronting his readers in their daily lives. Slavery was painful to slaves, and the insensitivity of authoritarian heads of households was painful to wives and children; these were issues that Paul as a pastor had to address. Paul addresses these issues not by recommending the immediate overthrow of existing structures, but by insisting that Christians act within those structures in a very different way than the world around them was acting.[7] Although Paul did not call for the violent overthrow of these structures, the principles Paul lays down for acting within them—mutual submission and equality—ultimately challenge the moral right of structures such as slavery to exist.

## THE OBEDIENCE OF CHILDREN: A BETTER MODEL?

Some writers have argued that if Paul would not have required wives in all cultures to submit, we must assume that children also do not need to submit to their parents in all cultures.

But this argument is not as consistent as it might appear to its proponents.

First, Paul explicitly bases wives' submission on mutual submission in 5:21–22, and defines submission in terms of respect rather than obedience. When he tells slaves to obey their masters as they would Christ, he turns this around by calling on masters to "do the same things for them" (6:9), even though his first readers might well have balked at taking him literally. But the analogy with parents and children is lacking at precisely this point; his call on parents to look out for their children is the closest he comes to reciprocal submission between parents and children.

Second, the situation Paul addresses compels him to use household codes in which wives, children, and slaves are called to be submissive. He does not tell us which of these instructions might be carried out in all cultures, because that is not the issue he is addressing in this text. But it is noteworthy that the Old Testament law clearly enjoined the submission of children under penalty of death, whereas the same was in no way true for wives or slaves.[8]

Third, it may also be pointed out that the common characteristics shared by wives, children, and slaves in antiquity were (1) they were in positions of inferior power; (2) they were viewed as economic dependents; (3) they were considered less knowledgeable in the matters in which the household head ruled.[9] All three of these assumptions can be challenged for women in our culture, but they remain to a much greater extent true of minors. The younger and less mature the child, the less independent the child can safely be.

Unlike women and slaves, children were reared with a view to eventual maturity and economic independence;[10] their subordination was more like a temporary apprenticeship than a lifelong servitude, and thus it ideally functions today. Unlike wives and slaves, children were not considered to be of a permanently inferior nature. Roman male children were always expected to honor their parents, but becoming old enough to enter society provided them a position of practical independence, in which the demands for obedience were less than they had been when the son lived at home. Further, many adult children no longer had adult fathers, who often passed away early in their children's adulthood. Submission to parents was a lifelong duty, but it demanded far less from an adult child than from a younger one; indeed, Aristotle's household codes specifically addressed *only* minors.[11]

Roman wives, however, remained subject to their husbands' legal control as long as their husbands remained alive, much as slaves did. As we pointed out in the last chapter, many men felt that women were by nature less rational than men, and thus men kept women in a state of social dependency, as if they were perpetual minors. But Paul nowhere paints the wife's or slave's submission in these "natural" terms. Ought we to suppose that women, who in our culture are usually as educated as men (and often more so), should be treated as permanent minors, while seeking for our male children to become independent?

The proper parallel for interpreting the wife text is not that of children, who attain more freedom as they grow older, but that of slaves, who remained under the direct authority of the head of the household until his death. If Paul teaches the permanent subordination of wives, we must accept that he also teaches the permanent subordination of slaves.

## SLAVERY AS A DIVINE CONCESSION IN THE OLD TESTAMENT

Those who wish to save this passage's power structure in the home regarding wives and children but not regarding slaves will have a difficult time. It is true that the Bible enjoins children's obedience more clearly than it does that of slaves; but it also *enjoins the submission of slaves more clearly than it does that of wives.*

### *Slaves as Property or People?*

Old Testament law, like other ancient Near Eastern law and that of later Roman society, had to address slaves from two standpoints: first, they were persons; second, they were bought and sold, and therefore functioned as a commercial commodity. If this strikes our ears uncomfortably today, it would be well for us to note that wives' sexuality, secured by the husband's brideprice, was likewise treated as a commodity as far as some aspects of law went. Law could proceed on an analogy of commercial exchange, without necessarily reflecting an assumption on the part of the legislators that slaves or wives were not human.

The Old Testament picture of Israelite slavery suggests that most slaves worked as household employees or, if field hands, labored alongside their masters.[12] The latter point has little in common with the way slaves were treated in the history of the United States. Israelite slavery also did not adopt the kind of racist ideology to perpetuate itself characteristic of slavery in the Americas. Still, a significant portion of the following data about the Israelite practice of slavery permitted by the Bible will be troubling to most of us.[13]

Slaves could be treated as less valuable than a son or daughter (Exod. 21:31–32), perhaps because, from a commercial standpoint, they were a more replaceable commodity.[14] Among the laws demanding proper treatment of slaves is one that today we find quite troubling:

> And if a man strikes his male or female slave with a rod and he dies at his hand, he shall be punished. If, however, he survives a day or two, no vengeance shall be taken; for he is his property (Exod. 21:20–21, NASB).

Examining this passage alone would give us an inaccurate picture of Israelite slavery. The harsh force of the above law calling the slave "property" is somewhat qualified by looking at related laws in the context:

(1) "Property" is qualified by the fact that the slave owner is to be punished by a civil court for killing his slave; no other "property" is treated accordingly.[15] The punishment implied here is probably corporal (Deut. 25:2) rather than capital,[16] since the slave owner presumably acted out of anger rather than lying in wait (i.e., it was not a premeditated murder; cf. Exod. 21:12–14).

(2) The "eye for eye" ruling that applied to free people did not help the person who lost the eye, except as a vindication of his or her honor (Exod. 21:24);[17] the slave does not get the same vindication, but gets a more practical benefit: his or her freedom (21:26–27).

(3) The owner is not punished if the slave survives a day or two; but the case may be the same here as with a free person (21:18–19).[18]

The broader context of Moses' laws[19] further qualifies this "property" view of slaves. The Sabbath laws show concern for slaves as well as for children[20] (Exod. 20:10; 23:12); they can also be placed alongside one's wife as well as one's possessions in such lists (20:17). In Exodus 21:7–11, a female slave who becomes a man's concubine is treated functionally as his wife; the law requires him to treat her fairly (even if she is a prisoner of war, as in Deut. 21:10–14).[21]

Israelite regulations about escaped slaves are also significant here. Although one who found his neighbor's stolen or lost property was to restore it or hold onto it for his fellow Israelite (Exod. 22:1–15; Deut. 22:1–4), and although other ancient Near Eastern laws applied this requirement to lost slaves as well,[22] the Bible does not mention slaves in this list of lost property. Slaves were people, volitional beings, who could leave in a way that other property could not. Israelite law in fact required escaped slaves to be given refuge (Deut. 23:15–16), just like foreigners in the land.[23] Someone who believed that slavery was a concession to human weakness, but that God's ideal demanded that we work against it, could certainly use such a passage to justify helping slaves escape to freedom. Harriet Tubman and others associated with the Underground Railroad in the history of our own country were well within the spirit of Israelite law.

But we still cannot get around the fact that this law calls the slave "property." The owner is disciplined—presumably beaten—if he or she in striking the slave causes the slave's death. But there is no law against *striking the slave* per se, just as there is no law against physically disciplining one's children. Whether the slave had entered servitude semivoluntarily, and so chose to put his or her life at risk (like volunteers for the Israelite army, Deut. 20:5–9), or whether the slave had been taken as a prisoner of war in lieu of being put to death, what the text does *not* say is more troubling than what it says. The *point* of the text is surely that the slave must be treated rightly, and that the master can be legally punished if the slave is abused; but this text still does not offer enough safeguards for the slave. The principle it states has to be extended to make it sufficient to cover all that is not stated.

An Israelite slave was to be treated rightly and released after a fixed period of time (Exod. 21:1–3; Lev. 25:34–43; Deut. 15:12; Jer. 34:8–22),[24] and given provisions to get on his own feet economically (Deut. 15:13–14).[25] This protection for the slave transforms slavery from a hereditary institution into a temporary period of economic dependence and hard labor in someone's life (Lev. 25:39–43). Like childhood, slavery could function as a temporary apprenticeship of sorts, with economic benefits to both master and servant.

Here, however, we run into other difficulties. If a male slave married while in slavery (Exod. 21:4), he would need to remain in slavery "voluntarily" to keep his family (21:5–6).[26] It is not so disconcerting that an individual's family bonds might take precedence over ideal justice; what bothers us is that the slave is forced to choose between family and freedom. The master may have permitted a freed slave to buy his family's freedom later, and probably would have; but this possibility is not required by law.

While this allowance may have seemed fair to the slave owner who paid for the male slave's wife when he bought her, it is fair only if the slave is viewed as property rather than as a person of value equal to that of his or her owner. History is replete with examples of slaves and masters who loved each other, where bonds of intimacy developed within the roles already established by society; yet nearly all of us would today agree that the very nature of a slave/master relationship was always far from God's ideal purpose. We have to live with all kinds of inequity and injustice today, but we also believe that it is God's will for us to work against that injustice.

Another weakness of Moses' "indentured servant" laws was that they applied only to Israelites. Israelite slaves had to be freed in the seventh year, or when the Jubilee year arrived; but this did not apply to foreign slaves (Lev. 25:44–46). Then again, one need not read the texts about foreign slaves as harshly as they could be read. What if this foreign slave converted and became an Israelite, a situation later Jewish interpreters of the law were forced to address?[27] And what happens when the principle behind one law is extended in such a way as to infringe upon another law (for instance, a slave as person in his or her own right versus a slave as property, a dependent of the owner)? But slave owners, like most people, act in their own economic interests and would probably take advantage of any opportunity afforded them in the law.

## *Interpreting and Applying Biblical Slave Law*

The spirit of some of the laws noted above seems to conflict with that of some of the other laws. This is no doubt true in slave laws in any society, since they must deal with the fact that the slave is a human being, but also with the economic reality that the slave is being treated as property. While Israelite law requires masters to treat their slaves benevolently, and what we gather from Israelite history suggests that this was the way the institution was generally practiced in Israel, we must still ask whether slavery in even its mildest form was ever God's ideal purpose.

Some of God's laws were concessions to human weakness, as Jesus clearly stated (Mark 10:5; Matt. 19:8).[28] One can see this, for example, in the institution of cities of refuge (Deut. 19:1–14). If one person killed another person accidentally, the slayer was not guilty of intentional murder and should not be put to death. But because in that culture a relative of the dead person might seek revenge, God provided the slayer a place of refuge. Ideally, the accidental slayer should have been able to remain safe in his own town; at best, the avengers of blood might serve as a good deterrent to negligence, but God did not institute them—God instituted instead a merciful way of coping with them.[29]

The law is clearly dealing with less than ideal situations. It takes the institution of slavery for granted, and never rules on the institution itself, merely on the most humane ways to practice it. Though its principles of humanity could ultimately undermine its cultural practice, that is easier seen in hindsight than in the time of the law itself. We have here a case in which God permits a measure of injustice so that at least some measure of justice and mercy could be required. But that slavery was not God's permanent intent we can learn from our equality as human beings created in God's image, just as God's original purpose for marriage shows that a husband and wife are to be one and that divorce was just a later concession in Mosaic law (Matt. 19:1–9).[30]

Indeed, certain principles in the law itself would militate against slavery if extended to their logical conclusions. As those who had been foreigners in the land of Egypt, Israelites were always to be kind and hospitable to foreigners in their own land (Exod. 23:9); they were likewise to give justice to the poor (Exod. 23:6; Deut. 24:14–15). By extension, we could argue that because Israelites had been slaves in Egypt, they were also to respect their slaves, whom God might also favor above their masters if they mistreated them. They were not to oppress hired servants (Deut. 24:14), and, remembering that they had been slaves in Egypt, they were not to oppress any of the poor (Deut. 24:17–18). Not only were they not to oppress them, but they were actively to provide for them (Deut. 24:19–22).[31] And they were to treat well and eventually free and provide for Israelite slaves because they had themselves been slaves in Egypt (Deut. 15:15), a principle that, if extended like the other principles in the law, could eventually demand the same treatment for all slaves. The law was so concerned with economic justice that it considered withholding a poor man's wages for even one night a form of robbery (Lev. 19:13); as an abolitionist preacher charged in 1835:

> If it was a sin against God, for one under the Mosaic economy to retain the wages of a hired servant for the space of one night only, how much more guilty must one be now, under the gospel dispensation, who compels a man to work during his whole life time, and pays him nothing for his hire?[32]

When Jesus healed the sick and proclaimed release to the oppressed, he was demonstrating the ideal purposes of God, which the law had been able to address only halfway because of its allowances for the fallen structures of this world order around us.

## Unbiblical Uses of the Bible in American Race-Slavery

Nevertheless, white slave owners in the United States used biblical texts about slavery and created a heretical interpretation of the Bible to support racism, to justify their own economic advantages. They valued the concessions addressing a certain culture above the principles that call Christians to advocate justice and mercy. Abolitionists, to the contrary, began with the principles of Scripture that showed how those concessions should be repealed by love and by the ethics of God's kingdom in Christ.[33] They demanded that slave owners explain how loving one's neighbor as oneself (Lev. 19:18; cf. Mark 12:31) was compatible with violently withholding a slave's liberty.[34] Abolitionists also pointed out that kidnaping (Exod. 21:16; 1 Tim. 1:19), and thus holding as property those who had been violently abducted, merited a death sentence under biblical law.[35]

Yet even many Christian abolitionists in the United States balked at full integration, usually due to fear of alienating society by being too radical for their day; after all, they were already going against the grain of their culture.[36] Only a few were willing to take a stand for full equality. When black and white abolitionists met together for the 1838 convention of the Philadelphia Female Anti-Slavery Society, their meeting hall was burned to the ground by rioters protesting that whites and blacks ought not to meet in the same building. Not only the mayor but also the male abolitionists pleaded with their female colleagues to exercise reason and to meet separately. Instead, these women met together again the next morning, issuing the following statement:

> Resolved,
>
> That prejudice against color is the very spirit of slavery, sinful in those who indulge in it, and is the fire which is consuming the happiness and energies of the free people of color.
>
> That it is, therefore, the duty of abolitionists to identify themselves with these oppressed Americans, by sitting with them in places of worship, by appearing with them in our streets . . . by visiting them at their homes and encouraging them to visit us, receiving them as we do our white fellow citizens.[37]

We may be glad today that these women chose to submit to God rather than to men in this case. Yet the truth they articulated remains difficult for many conservative Christians to live out a century and a half later; even after segregation was legally abolished, the cost in societal pressure remains too great for many Christians to cross the boundaries our history has created. May God grant us repentance.

It is all too easy for us to look back on the abuse of Scripture by white slave owners in the past and say, "It is good no one abuses Scripture like that today." Unfortunately, we are probably ignoring significant parts of the Bible in dealing with the history of slavery in the United States. In the wake of race-slavery and the continuing scourge of racism (originally advanced as its ideological justification), the Bible gives some clear and uncomfortable guidance to our nation as a whole, regardless of how many of its citizens descend directly from slave owners.

The Bible speaks of corporate[38] and transgenerational responsibility, even to the tenth generation (e.g., Deut. 23:3–8), and if our nation profited economically by enslaving another people (African-Americans) or from taking their land by force (Native Americans), and if the descendants of the profiting people had available better education and vocational opportunities for a number of generations than those they had oppressed, we cannot suppose that justice is done by simply saying now, "Let bygones be bygones." As noted evangelical leader John Perkins points out,

> The economic plight of American blacks today has its roots in slavery and in the center of oppression which followed emancipation. It is like a baseball game. In the ninth inning the team which

> is trailing 20 to 2 discovers that the winning team has been cheating all along. The leading team admits, "Yes, we were cheating, but we'll play fair now. Let's go out and finish the game."
>
> Now, it's good that the team is going to quit cheating, but with the score 20 to 2 the trailing team still has the feeling they're going to lose. When injustice has been done, establishing justice means something more than "playing fair from now on."
>
> In America today, one group has the capital, the other has the labor and the broken spirit. . . . Economic opportunity in capitalism depends on ownership of capital. . . . The oppressed among us know all too well that the oppressive forces which created their poverty in the first place keep them trapped in it.[39]

Scripture demands restitution, as costly as that will be. Slavery and its attendant and continuing sin, racism, are terrible evils that were practiced in this country in terrible ways that God's law never allowed.

Many readers would protest that economic, corporate restitution on a national level would bankrupt the economy, and many would question how the resources should be distributed; such protestations might be right. But there is no reason why we cannot take restitution seriously as a Christian church in ways that the needs themselves demand. If we value people more than possessions, we can forsake our personal economic objectives and move into the areas of need across this country, making our skills and incomes available to those who need them. Many of the horrors of drugs and violence that now plague our cities are the direct result of ghettoes spawned by economic discrimination southern blacks faced when they migrated to northern cities in our century. Many of these problems were intensified through the psychological damage of racism, including forced suppression and denial of beautiful aspects of one culture by another culture.

It is easy to say that we are against slavery today, because slavery is now more than unpopular in our culture. But the consequences of the abuse of biblical texts by some a century and a half ago still haunt the United States today, and even some biblical principles of justice are as ignored by our generation as they were by many preceding generations. Is it possible that some of us interpret Scripture as selectively as those who once used it to support slavery against the abolitionists?

*Cultural Concessions versus Eternal Purposes*

Most of us today will acknowledge that slavery was a concession and that treating other people justly is a command. But what rules can we use for separating "concessions" from "commands"? One way is to try to distinguish what is taken for granted in the law from what is explicitly commanded or prohibited with specifically attached penalties, especially the penalty of death.[40]

Examples could be offered concerning sexual offenses and authority relationships. Most sexual sins, because they defraud one's present or future spouse of the most important possession, his or her spouse's faithfulness, are listed as capital offenses (Deut. 22:13–30; Lev. 20).[41] This suggests the permanence of rules emphasizing sexual faithfulness to one's present or future spouse.

With regard to authority relationships, one dare not curse the king (Exod. 22:28; 1 Kgs. 21:10, 13) or one's parents (Exod. 21:17), and rebellion against parental authority could be punished with death (Deut. 21:18–21).[42] But nowhere is the "disobedience" of slaves or wives condemned. Sometimes wives like Abigail (1 Sam. 25), as well as sons like Jonathan (1 Sam. 20) and daughters like Michal (1 Sam. 19), might have to choose faithfulness to what was right over allegiance to a husband or father.

But while the law forbids disobedience to fathers except in such extreme circumstances, and assumes—and thus regulates—the institution of slavery, it neither mandates nor even explicitly assumes the necessary subordination of wives to their husbands. Abraham was called to hearken to Sarah as well as the reverse (Gen. 21:12); God could choose to reveal himself to a wife first (Judg. 13:2–23); his most prominent or trusted spokesperson in Josiah's time was a woman (2 Kgs. 22:13–20), and examples could be multiplied. The culture defined different roles for men and women, roles that changed from time to time and from culture to culture, and God worked with this aspect of the culture. But there is never any indication in the Old Testament that *God* mandated that men have sole authority over the home.

## SLAVERY IN ROMAN SOCIETY

Before we can examine Paul's comments on slavery, we must understand exactly what kind of slavery he was addressing. Because his comments to slaves occur within the context of household codes, we may be sure that he is addressing household slaves, members of his urban congregations whose situation was better in many ways than that of rural free peasants.

*The Roles and Position of Slaves in Roman Society*

Perhaps one-third of the inhabitants of early imperial Rome were slaves,[43] and many other cities of the Roman world boasted similar figures.[44] Probably only about one-quarter of the free families of Roman Italy actually owned any slaves (the same has been estimated for the U.S. South in slavery times).[45]

People had become slaves in a variety of ways. Some were enslaved by the Romans in wars, especially in earlier times,[46] while others were enslaved for violating certain laws,[47] were sold by poor parents,[48] etc.; most slaves, however, were born to enslaved parents.[49] But the way they had become slaves had less effect on their futures than the skills they could provide their owners.

There were many different kinds of slaves, and they found themselves in very different environments. The range of slave occupations, from land workers to managers, was roughly the same range one found among the free.[50] Their labor never quite replaced hired labor, although it competed with it. Free workers who were otherwise unemployed or underemployed had to be hired at harvest time, but slaves supplied a constant source of labor.[51] Slaves worked the massive estates as field hands[52] or household servants.[53] Petronius satirizes that one freedman was so wealthy that only one-tenth of his slaves had ever seen him.[54] There were also public slaves who served the state.[55]

Women slaves on estates and in households were employed domestically,[56] for instance, as weavers[57] or, less officially, as concubines or sexual objects;[58] other women slaves could be employed as prostitutes.[59] Male slaves could be employed as skilled professionals as well as laborers, though the latter were the great majority.[60]

Most slaves in the ancient world, like the nominally free peasants who made up most of the feudal, rural population, found little opportunity for social advancement. But the higher ranks of more skilled slaves could seek freedom or find upward mobility within slavery that brought social advancement beyond the ranks of many of the free.[61] To the chagrin of hereditary aristocrats, some freedmen (freed slaves) even became rich;[62] their chances to improve their conditions were better than those of the poor who were born free.[63]

This situation meant that many slaves in well-to-do households were better off than peasants outside those households; economically, socially, and even with regard to determining their future, such slaves held more options. Even field slaves were often fed better than free peasants in impoverished parts of the empire like Egypt;[64] hence the freer a person was politically from any patron, the closer he or she generally was to hunger.[65] In many peasant homes in Egypt, where twenty people would crowd into one-room dwellings and half their children died in infancy, a life of service to a well-to-do family in Italy may have seemed an appealing alternative.

If some ancient writer had attempted a modern social justice critique of oppression in antiquity, that writer would have had to have indicted the entire economic system of the Roman Empire—the feudal estates, the urban slums, and so on—and not simply slavery. Most writers, however, were concerned more with giving positive advice to those within the system than with entertaining the hypothesis of a social revolution. We must especially expect this attitude for a writer like Paul, who in a brief letter addresses various issues with which a congregation is struggling and devotes only a few verses to how slaves and masters are to treat one another. Successful social revolutions have to await a time and place where they can actually take root, and there was no point in Paul proposing such an unrealistic agenda in a letter to the churches in the vicinity of Ephesus.

The slaves whom Paul addresses in Ephesians 6 were not the most oppressed of the slaves, those in the mines, or the slaves working in the fields like the nominally free tenant farmers, but the household slaves who in most households were better off than free peasants, having more economic security and control over their own future than peasants did.[66] This is not to say that they were well off, but to say that, in general, probably most of the ancient world was worse off. If we expected from Paul a critique of ancient social injustice, we would perhaps need to look for it first in a critique of the oppression of the field and mine slaves (a closer parallel to the majority of slaves in the United States) and the oppression of the rural peasants and urban poor—something outside Paul's purview in this letter. That we expect a critique first of slavery as an institution is perhaps due to our *own* cultural limitations; we can easily denounce slavery as an institution because it is no longer practiced in our culture, while ignoring a similar critique of the poverty that continues in our country and in the world on a massive scale. Although it does not directly concern our point here, we may note in passing that Paul did address stifling poverty in situations where his readers could do something practical about it (Rom. 15:26; 1 Cor. 16:1–4; 2 Cor. 8–9; Gal. 2:10; Eph. 4:28).

Paul's lack of comment on the institution of slavery is thus no reason to assume that he supports it. But how can we know what view he would have taken, since he does not address this question directly? Whether he or other ancient writers would ideally like to have seen it abolished depends on two factors: (1) if they could have imagined circumstances that would have actually allowed its abolition; and (2) how the principles they do state would operate if such circumstances were realized. Many ancient writers emphasized the proper treatment of slaves and some argued for treating them as equal human beings. The idea that society would ever exist without slavery probably did not occur to them, but had the idea occurred to them, those who argued for human equality might well have appreciated the idea.

### *Ancient Slave Ideology*

Most people in antiquity took the institution of slavery for granted; some praised it. A few critiqued slavery, although these usually addressed the mistreatment of individual slaves rather than the institution of slavery as a whole. We shall first survey some general views on slavery among the people with power in antiquity, then turn to our closest parallels with Paul's statements, which critiqued the fundamental philosophical presuppositions on which slavery had been justified.

Despite the occupational commonalities between slaves and nonaristocratic free persons, there was a great distinction between slave and free in the minds of the traditional aristocracy.[67] Indeed, the difference was often perceived as one of character as well as one of status: "slavish" character was considered base,[68] the "bad" slave was an object of criticism,[69] slaves were sometimes thought distinguishable by their appearance,[70] and the genuinely free person would find slavery intolerable.[71] In other words, the most powerful in society felt that social stratification, including the institution of slavery, was the only proper way for society to work.

Many of these ideas go back to the original codes of Aristotle: he regarded the subordination of a slave as something as natural as that of body to soul and viewed it as being in the common interest of both master and slave.[72] Nature showed that some people were inferior to others, and it was to these people's advantage and security to be ruled by their superiors.[73]

Although the slave's subordination was rationalized as being "for his own good," the slave was legally considered a piece of his or her master's property. Roman and Jewish law portrayed slaves both as property[74] and as people,[75] as slave laws generally do. In practice, of course, household slaves were recognized as people; the polemic of some of the American slave owners about slaves as subhuman or members of another species was not necessary to assuage ancient consciences.[76] Bonds between masters and slaves sometimes were such that slaves had loyally saved their masters' lives.[77] Slaves could be addressed in the household codes precisely because domestic slaves were normally considered a part of the household.[78]

But Aristotle's theories of slavery also give us a harsh perspective of slaves as property. The master could have nothing in common with a slave, who was a living tool.[79] Slaves could have no real goals or purposes for their own lives.[80] Slaves simply had a different nature than free people, and only those with such a nature would make real slaves.[81]

> Hence there are by nature various classes of rulers and ruled. For the free rules the slave, the male the female, and the man the child in a different way. And all possess the various parts of the soul, but possess them in different ways; for the slave has not got the deliberative part at all, and the female has it, but without full authority, while the child has it, but in an undeveloped form.[82]

In a move that foreshadowed the racist slave ideology created by the economic interests of U.S. slave owners, Aristotle concurred with the typical Greek sense of Greek superiority by saying that barbarians were by nature meant to be slaves, whereas Greeks were by nature meant to be free.[83]

Slaves were legally treated as property and thus could be flogged.[84] This discipline was not limited to slaves, of course; it usually applied also to children, although it was applied to them more sparingly.[85] It seems to have been normal that slaves died young.[86] Slaves could also be examined under torture; for some reason the Romans believed this method was effective in exposing the truth rather than producing fabrications.[87]

Slave marriages were not legal under Roman law, although this did not always impose a practical obstacle to slaves' living as if they were married.[88] It became more problematic if the master desired sexual use of one of his female slaves, or when the husbands and wives were sold to different masters.[89] Slave children could be sold away from their parents at an early age, although some slave parents seem to have crossed household lines to try to keep in touch with their children.[90] In U.S. slavery, according to some estimates (the real figures must be lower, but nonetheless traumatize), as many as 50% of all slaves could expect to be sold away from their families, and the average slave would witness eleven sales of family members in a lifetime.[91] Since ancient slave owners were probably less wealthy than their modern counterparts, the breakup of families may have occurred even more often.[92]

Slaves were viewed as people as well as property, but the *law* normally treated them as people only at the master's discretion, rather than as a matter of policy.[93] Roman slave law continued to be used in other slavery codes throughout history, including in American slavery, although here it was modified further in favor of the slave owner against the slave.[94]

### *Ancient Critiques of Slavery*

Many ancient writers opposed the mistreatment of slaves. Epicurus reportedly said that wise men would not punish their servants.[95] He treated his servants with moderation and allowed slaves to be members of his philosophical school.[96] Another writer lists among virtues "not to be overbearing with slaves."[97]

In the early second century, Pliny boasts that he treats all his guests the same, including his former slaves; he could not afford to feed them as if they were on his social level, so he came down to their level instead.[98] But freed slaves were normally part of a well-to-do patron's clientele; for Pliny to treat them as social peers would have outraged traditional Roman aristocrats, but it was far from the same as treating his *slaves* as equals.

On the other hand, a Cynic writer notes that the Ephesians did not want slaves to dine with them, but replies that virtue, not social status, should be the criterion for seating arrangements.[99] The same philosopher argues that slavery is an injustice, and that the God who did not make dogs or sheep slaves would not have done so with people.[100] Of course Cynics, who did not believe in sporting any possessions except their cloak, wallet, staff, and (usually) cup, had no more love for slavery than they had interest in the economy of antiquity as a whole.

Stoics were not as otherworldly as Cynics, but calls for proper treatment of slaves also emanated from their circles. Epictetus, who had been a slave earlier in life, felt that the gods wanted masters to be merciful to their servants,[101] for servants were brothers by nature, fellow children of Zeus.[102]

The Stoic philosopher Seneca felt that slaves should be free to talk with their masters, and that their bad attitudes toward their masters were often the result of mistreatment by these masters.[103] Beatings were for animals alone; masters should lash servants only with their tongue.[104] He even exhorts slave owners to recognize slaves as their equals in humanity;[105] the master should keep in mind that he, too, may have a master someday.[106] The slave can act as a benefactor by giving his services to his master willingly, rather than by compulsion.[107] Seneca did not advocate the abolition of slavery, but argued that slaves should be properly treated.[108]

Seneca's views may not have been shared by all Stoics, of course; the founder of the Stoic school was said to have been beating a slave for stealing, when the slave objected, in good Stoic fashion, "It was my fate to steal." "Yes, and to be beaten too," the teacher is said to have replied.[109] This philosopher, like most men in antiquity, would presumably have beaten his son for the same offense, and Stoics in Paul's day seem to have accepted the equality of slaves as humans by nature.

The early Jewish teacher Joshua ben Sirach exhorted masters to love slaves and to grant good slaves their freedom.[110] The wise servant is praised and it is said—perhaps hyperbolically—that the free would render service to such a servant.[111] Indeed, a master was to treat his slave to some extent as he would treat himself:

> If you have a servant, let him be as yourself, because with blood you acquired him. If you have a servant, deal with[112] him as with a brother, because as your soul you need him; if you do him wrong and he runs away from you, where can you go to seek him?[113]

While this is not the same as freeing one's servant, it certainly demands more of slave owners than most slave owners were willing to give; the writer seems to advocate treating a slave as a voluntary member of the family. Other Jewish slave owners may not have been as gracious as this writer, but Joshua ben Sirach was not the only giver of humanitarian advice in Jewish circles,[114] and the Jewish slaves, at least, appear to have been generally well treated by Jewish owners.[115]

But arguing that slaves should be well treated was not the same as arguing that slavery should be abolished throughout the Roman Empire. Few ancient writers ventured to make sweeping demands of society that society would clearly not concede, demands that if followed would have demolished the ancient economy and left widespread poverty, especially for former slaves.[116] Slaves themselves seem not to have opposed slavery in principle; inscriptions tell us that slaves, once free, were more than happy to acquire slaves of their own.[117] As Dale Martin writes:

> The institution of slavery itself was never really questioned. Slaves may have resented their bondage, but given the chance they acquired slaves themselves. When freed, they simply moved up a notch in the system, becoming themselves masters and mistresses and pulling their dependents along with them. Almost no one, slaves included, thought to organize society any other way.[118]

To call for the universal abolition of slavery was to call for a widespread slave revolt, which was unlikely to happen. If such a revolt did happen, it was certain to result in much loss of life and equally certain not to succeed unless it could be renewed repeatedly, probably over several generations, with intense bloodshed.[119] Finley observes that the many outbreaks of slave violence in history have normally been

> minute in scale, shortlived and unanimously unsuccessful (apart from the success of a few slaves in escaping permanently from bondage). . . . Of the 250-odd outbreaks that have been identified in the history of the United States, the greatest and most famous, Nat Turner's Rebellion of 1831, was a purely local affair involving a few hundred men for a few months, with the actual fighting restricted to three days.[120]

Finley claims—perhaps slightly overstating the case—that in all history there were only four actual slave wars, three in Sicily and Italy in 140–70 BCE and the Haitian revolt led by free blacks in the wake of the French Revolution. Only the Haitian revolt was successful.[121] Thus, although many of the strongest Christian abolitionists in the United States believed that God would side with the slaves in a time of revolt, in general abolitionists (both black and white) prudently counseled nonviolence.[122]

The most practical, nonviolent way to abolish slavery in a society more permeated by slavery than nearly any other society in history[123] was to change the way the people in power looked at slaves.

Christianity, as a classless religion in which slaves became prominent church leaders and heroes of the faith,[124] was well equipped to ultimately abolish slavery by this long-term route. In the meantime, it had the moral power to give slaves self-esteem and strength for their task until slavery had been abolished. On a practical level, church funds were often used to free slaves, and sometimes Christians even became slaves themselves to ransom others; regarded as spiritual equals, slaves could rise to the position of bishop in the postapostolic church.[125]

Not everyone caught the liberating message present in the gospel; some church leaders like Augustine wanted to maintain the structures of society, including slavery, while arguing that slaves must be treated well.[126] Many of these writers argued only for treating slaves better; some even echoed their culture's prejudice against slaves' morals.[127] It was this element of social conservatism rather than the liberating power of the gospel that came to predominate in the centuries following Paul, and it is for this reason that Christianity did not become the decisive force of abolitionism that it could have been in late antiquity.[128]

But other Christian leaders, like John Chrysostom, had the insight to perceive the radical equality proclaimed in the Christian gospel; he argued that free Christians should buy, empower with skills, and then free slaves.[129] This strain of Christian pietism continued in the modern period through figures like Wesley and Wilberforce into the strongly evangelical abolitionist movements of Britain and the United States. Until proslavery polemic was created, most slaves and many masters in the United States recognized this truth of Christianity.[130] In my opinion, it is the abolitionist Christians who rightly captured the spirit of Paul's message; but it took a long time for their views to be heard above the din of tradition.[131]

## PAUL'S VIEW IN EPHESIANS 6:5–9

Although household codes regulated relations between masters and slaves, they rarely addressed slaves directly.[132] The fact that Paul addresses slaves in Ephesians 6:5–8 indicates that his letter is intended for a congregation that includes many slaves. No matter how interested Paul may have been in convincing the authorities that Christians were not subversive, he does not write as a philosopher or moralist whose work is meant to be read only by a social elite. He writes as a pastor to members of his congregation.

### *What Paul Does Say*

When Paul calls slaves to direct their service toward God, not toward their master, he is giving the same sort of advice he gives to anyone else under authority (Rom. 13:1) or in a hard situation (2 Cor. 12:7–10; cf. 1 Pet. 5:6–7).[133] As an abolitionist preacher pointed out in the nineteenth century, advocating submission to current masters no more means advocacy of slavery as an institution than commands to submit to the Roman government or to pray for persecutors meant that New Testament writers supported imperial policy or persecution against Christians.[134]

Paul is saying, do your best, recognize that God is sovereign, and know that your reward ultimately comes from God.[135] By making God and not the master the one to whom the slave directly answers, he relativizes the real authority of the master.[136] Seneca tells masters that they may have masters of their own someday;[137] Paul reminds masters that they already have a Master in heaven who regards their servants as highly as he regards them.[138]

By saying that slaves and masters are equal before God, *and* that masters should keep this in mind, Paul is saying that slavery is not part of God's purpose. To an ancient thinker like Aristotle, this position was unsatisfactory, for it declared that slavery as an institution was unjust.[139] This is the position that Paul articulates for equality in the community of God, the church, which models the future kingdom, God's ideal social order (1 Cor. 12:13; Col. 3:11)—for women's equality as well as slaves' (Gal. 3:28).

Those slaveholders who understood Paul's instructions as supporting the slaveholding system read into his words something that simply is not there; people who read Paul today and wish that he explicitly condemned slavery as an institution are asking Paul to have written something that would have had little practical value for his readers, while simultaneously missing that Paul's words imply the moral wrongness of slavery.

Slaveholders would indeed have profited from Paul's instructions. Many slaves in antiquity were regarded as slow and careless with their masters' property.[140] This makes good sense from the perspective of modern capitalism, of course: laborers who derive no profit from their labor have less incentive to work hard.[141] Paul's instructions could give the slaves a basis for self-respect and a motivation to excel in their work, and this would in the process also benefit the masters and restrain aristocratic charges of subversion, strengthening the church's witness to all levels of society.

While Paul commands slaves to submit to masters as they do to Christ (Eph. 6:5), his understanding of mutual submission is also at work here. His very brief command to masters is that they treat their slaves "in the same way" (6:9), literally, they should "do the same things to them." Although much of the rest of what he says is within the conceptual bounds of the other progressive writers in antiquity, the principle of mutuality on which he bases this exhortation calls for more than a measured application of authority. At the very least, even if taken figuratively, it includes looking out for the slave's interests in a nonpaternalistic way;[142] but if it means what it says, then Paul was even more radical than those whom Aristotle condemns for believing that slavery was against nature and therefore wrong. Paul not only holds that it is wrong in theory, but also that this wrongness should affect how Christians act, and this goes beyond the counsels of any other ancient writer whose work remains. Who else called for mutual submission between masters and servants?

### *Between the Lines: Would Paul Have Been an Abolitionist?*

Paul had no reason to tell local congregations to challenge the institution of slavery, as we have said, since the early church still had no power with which to challenge it. Paul also does not seem to have the recognized authority in his congregations to order the well-to-do members around, as we may gather from his reasonings with them in 1 Corinthians. Probably he could not even have expected the house-church sponsors to follow a unilateral order to free slaves.[143] But where Paul did have influence, he was willing to follow his convictions about human equality to their logical conclusion.

Trusted slaves were often sent on errands or to oversee business somewhere for their master. Sometimes one of these slaves would run off and seek a new life as a free person somewhere else in the empire. This may be how Onesimus escaped from Philemon.[144] But runaway slaves, when caught, would be taken back to their masters, to await whatever discipline their masters might impose on them.[145]

Sometimes, however, a slave might take refuge in another master's household. Pliny, who, as we noted above, was by ancient standards very sympathetic toward slaves, took in a slave and wrote on his behalf to the slave's master, pleading for clemency when he sent him back. It would not have been legal for Pliny to have held onto the slave indefinitely,[146] but he could at least successfully secure the master's mercy.[147]

Paul's letter to Philemon ranks among the most liberating documents of ancient times, in the same general category as Pliny's appeal for clemency. But Paul's writing goes beyond Pliny's,[148] in that he not only appeals to Philemon to have mercy on Onesimus, but he also uses the spiritual brotherhood of master and slave in Christ to argue that Philemon should free Onesimus (vv. 15–16, 21).[149] Nor is Paul simply asking for a transferral of Onesimus' slave title from Philemon to himself (vv. 13–14)—Paul really wants Onesimus back to labor with him as a fellow worker in the gospel, i.e., as a colleague.[150] And Paul, reminding Philemon that he owes him a favor anyway,[151] lays himself on the line and offers to make good any loss Philemon incurred when Onesimus escaped (vv. 18–19).[152] (The loss may refer to Philemon's loss of Onesimus' labor rather than implying that Onesimus had stolen anything.)[153]

Like Pliny, Paul had no formal, legal authority over the master on whose behalf he wrote.[154] But he did have significant influence, and he used it to achieve Onesimus' freedom. The fact that the letter is preserved would seem to testify that Philemon granted Paul's request. While Paul was in no position, even in the church, to require masters to free their slaves, it is clear that he believed that slavery was contrary to God's purpose and that, to the extent he could do anything about it, he would appeal for slaves' freedom.

## ABOLITIONISTS AND EGALITARIANS: A FAIR COMPARISON?

Those who today will admit that slavery is wrong but still maintain that husbands must have authority over their wives are inconsistent. If they were consistent with their method of interpretation, which does not take enough account of cultural differences, it is likely that, had they lived one hundred fifty years ago, they would have had to have opposed the abolitionists as subverters of the moral order—as many Bible-quoting white slave owners and their allies did. Many of the traditions which today use Scripture to subordinate women once did the same for slavery before that idea was anathema in our culture. In contrast, the method of interpretation we favor in this book is closer to the methods favored by the abolitionists.

George Knight III tries to avoid this conclusion by arguing that this is not a fair comparison. Slaves, he argues, had to submit to those in authority, but there was no indication that slavery was a God-ordained institution; marriage, by contrast, is God-ordained.[155] Knight is quite right that marriage and slavery differ in this regard, but his observation simply begs the actual question. The issue is not whether marriage itself is God-ordained, but whether a wife's submission to her husband is a permanently God-ordained part of marriage. It was the subordinationist link between the two that made them part of ancient household codes and forced Paul to address the issue in Ephesians. Knight assumes the very point he wishes to prove, which means that his argument is nothing more than an assertion.

This is the question our comparison between a wife's submission and that of a slave is meant to raise: Are all role relationships forever normative, or are we just to submit to *whoever* is in authority? And if we are just to deal with life "as is," as Knight suggests for the slaves, what would we do if we lived in a culture where wives could be their husbands' bosses (a situation not inconceivable in our own culture)? The issue is not whether it was right for slaves and wives to submit; the issue is whether it was also right to seek freedom for slaves and more rights for women.

It is true that there is no Old Testament support for slavery as an institution; it is assumed, not advocated. But a wife's submission to her husband is also not advocated in the Old Testament, and not even explicitly addressed as an institution. The wife's subordination is presented only as a result of the Fall—as a result of her husband's sinful abuse of power over her (Gen. 3:16). It is true that Paul argues from the creation order for wifely submission; he also derives from this the requirement for head coverings, and he also explicitly qualifies his argument, when he has used it most forcefully, to argue for mutual dependence and equality.

Nothing here supports the subordination of women any more than what was used to support the subordination of slaves, and those who appeal loudly to the several texts that they think demand women's subordination ignore quite a few other texts that demand subordination to slave masters, kings (1 Pet. 2:13, 17), etc. Knight rightly points out: "The principle is not that there must be kings and governors, but that Christians must submit to the human institution of government in whatever form or shape it may take and whoever the civil authorities may be." After all, 1 Peter 2:13 says to "submit to every human institution" before it says to submit to the king.[156] Despite Knight's wish to contend that the submission of wives is different from this submission, precisely the same method of application must be given to Ephesians 5:22—which prefaces the submission of wives with "submit to one another." Other civil authorities besides the king are mentioned in 1 Peter precisely because there *were* other civil authorities besides the king, and if we ignore the historical context of Scripture, we disrespect its own claims about itself and end up with a lot of "useless" texts left over—such as Paul's and Peter's claims that they were writing letters to specific audiences.

## CONCLUSION

Wives were to submit in a Christian way to those in authority over them in that culture, but neither the authority structures nor the expressions of submission are the same in all cultures. Although we respect governments and those in authority, we do not try to reinstitute the monarchy so we can obey New Testament demands that we submit to the king; nor would we reinstitute slavery so slaves can submit to their masters. Neither should we reinstitute old authority roles in marriage and thereby ignore the kinds of authority structures now standard in our culture. In a time of transition between old and new authority structures, we must choose structures most in harmony with the principles of God's kingdom; and given the fact that Paul was one of the most progressive writers in his day, I think that there is no question where we should stand today.

Should all women stay home cooking and cleaning and rearing children, or should they work in the fields as is customary for submissive wives in some cultures? Were women unsubmissive to demand the right to vote? Should they be allowed an education, and should they be allowed to use that education in the workplace? The implications of submission vary from culture to culture, and the most conservative of Americans would demand change in the nature of submission as it is required by some cultures.

Again, I believe that the Christian women's movement arose in the context of the Christian abolitionist movement because they both approached Scripture in an entirely different way than those who tried to take every commandment they could as binding on their own generation. Many readers today view only the chronologically later parts of the Bible as binding; but even among the later parts, they must concede that some matters are situationally conditioned (e.g., 2 Tim. 4:13, we wouldn't think to take Paul's cloak to him now!) or culturally conditioned (head coverings). Almost no one will try to duplicate the exact conditions of the ancient world so that the commandments can be fulfilled in precisely the same way as when they were first given. Yet many believers today unconsciously regard as commandments only those points that their traditions tell them to "keep."

I am arguing that, if we are genuinely to respect the authority of Scripture, we must know what all of it addresses in its own historical context. That means that we must understand how to apply all of its message to different cultural situations, and we must also understand the difference between what God has us put up with in less than ideal circumstances and the ideal for which we should strive if we have the opportunity.

The church has often simply sided with the most conservative and traditional social position rather than exploring the intention of Scripture, as Martin Luther King, Jr., pointed out to some of his colleagues in the clergy in a letter he wrote from the Birmingham jail:

> The contemporary church is often a weak, ineffectual voice with an uncertain sound. It is so often the arch-supporter of the status quo. Far from being disturbed by the presence of the church, the power structure of the average community is consoled by the church's silent and often vocal sanction of things as they are.[157]

One of the greatest tragedies of history is when God's holy Scripture, addressing one situation, is uncritically applied to another situation while ignoring the larger tenor of Scripture. It is doubly tragic because God's word is subverted to serve an unjust purpose, on the one hand, and God's word then is brought into disrepute for its unjust use, on the other.

Paul is addressing the authority structures of his day, not mandating the same authority structures for all periods. Paul does call on us to submit to those in authority, though he qualifies that authority by summoning those in authority to respect those under them as their equals. This is hardly the same as giving unqualified license to those in authority or saying that we must submit to the same structures in the same ways as people did in the Greco-Roman world, simply because that was the culture in which Paul happened to dictate his letter.

The earliest church was powerless to abolish slavery and to invert the social structures of its day, except by treating one another as equals and serving one another in their own homes. But the radical conception of self-sacrificial service was the seed that was bound to lead to abolitionism and other protests against human oppression. Through much of history, the true church's voice has been muzzled, as society's powerbrokers came to run the church; but the voice of our Lord, who came to serve and lay down his life for many, has never been and never will be silenced. May he speak to our hearts and our societies today.

## NOTES

1. Bilezikian, *Roles,* p. 171. 1 Pet. 3:6 notes that Sarah obeyed Abraham, but this hardly means that the reverse was not true: Gen. 21:12 says that God told Abraham to go ahead and obey Sarah, which he apparently would have done initially had her wish been less difficult (cf. 16:2). Peter emphasizes the wife's submission for the same reason Paul does, but nowhere excludes reciprocal obedience in the sense of listening to one another and supporting one another's wishes where they do not conflict with obedience to God.

2. This has been pointed out by others, e.g., Jewett, *Man,* pp. 138–41, 144, 148; Giles, *Woman,* p. 43. See also Clarice J. Martin, "The *Haustafeln* (Household Codes) in African American Biblical Interpretation: 'Free Slaves' and 'Subordinate Women,' " pp. 206–31, in *Stony the Road We Trod: African American Biblical Interpretation*, ed. Cain Hope Felder (Minneapolis: Fortress, 1990). Unfortunately I discovered this book only after completing the writing stage of the present work.

3. Arist. *Pol.* 1.2.12, 1254b, on women; it is a comparison brought into the context of Aristotle's discussion on slavery.

4. Giles's comparison between the bases listed for wives' submission and slaves' submission in the NT shows that the same bases are offered for each (*Woman,* pp. 44–46).

5. Even today, economic racial injustice is compounded intergenerationally in a way that gender discrimination cannot be (since most

economic or educational disadvantages of women progenitors affect both male and female descendants). If someone's parents, grandparents, and great-grandparents were denied educational opportunities and were unable to compete in a society that excluded them, this person may be starting with social and educational disadvantages that will require more work to overcome. But gender prejudice is still serious enough to affect very large numbers of women through various sorts of abuse, harassment, discrimination in certain areas of employment, and, unfortunately, discrimination in much of the church.

6. I do maintain that nonviolent protest is appropriate, but we must recognize that martyrdom often accompanies it and decide on which battlefront God calls each of us to lay down our lives, in view of the great need for martyrs in our world today. One brief biblical perspective on the issue is my article, "Nonviolence in the Face of Oppression: A Perspective on the Letter of James," *ESA Advocate* 12 (3, April 1991): 14–15.

7. Cf. D. M. Park, "The Structure of Authority in Marriage: An Examination of *Hupotasso* and *Kephale* in Ephesians 5:21–33," *EQ* 59 (2, April 1987): 123–24.

8. Deut. 21:18–21. On slaves in the OT, see below.

9. This is not to say that they were necessarily less educated: household slaves were often teachers or physicians. But aristocratic ideology portrayed low-born and slave-born people as unfit for proper authority roles. Greek women were usually much younger (often more than a decade) than their husbands.

10. Arist. *Pol.* 1.5.12, 1260b. Arist. *N. E.* 8.12.2–3, 1161b, says that parents love children from birth, but that children learn to love parents only as they grow to understand. Wives and slaves were to be ruled in different ways from one another, of course; Aristotle observed that barbarians failed to distinguish the two only because barbarians were fit to be enslaved themselves (*Pol.* 1.1.5–6, 1252b; Aristotle exemplified typical Greek intellectual imperialism and the best ancient equivalent of racist-based slavery ideology). Cf. Sext. Emp. *Out. Pyrr.* 3.211: children are "slaves" *(douloi)* of their fathers until attaining maturity, when they become like freedpersons.

11. Arist. *Pol.* 1.5.12, 1260b. The difference between what was owed a father by minor children and what was owed by adult children is implied in the Mishnah and Tosefta (see Boaz Cohen, *Jewish and Roman Law: A Comparative Study,* 2 vols. [New York: Jewish Theological Seminary, 1966], 1:174, for references).

12. This is frequent in narrative passages, many of the proverbs, etc. (e.g., Judg. 6:11, 27; Prov. 17:2; 30:10).

13. A comparison of different lists (those in Exodus and Deuteronomy and, where relevant, in Leviticus) indicate that we probably do not have all the slave laws that were used in ancient Israel. We do not know how Israelite laws developed into a full-scale legal code, debating ramifications and extensions of these laws, until the rabbinic period, although they must have been used for guidance earlier. We may use the common phrase "law codes," but "law collections" is no doubt more accurate technically, both for Israelite law and our other extant sources for ancient

Near Eastern laws (see N. M. Sarna, *Exploring Exodus* [New York: Schocken, 1986], pp. 168–70; John Bright, *A History of Israel*, 3d ed. [Philadelphia: Westminster, 1981], p. 59).

14. So also e.g., Laws of Eshnunna §§22–24. One may note that class distinctions (other than slave and free), which were natural in class-oriented societies' laws (Code of Hammurabi §§202–23; Roman law codes), are obliterated in the law of Moses. A nation of freed slaves had little need of class distinctions since they had had little time to develop them.

15. Indeed, under some *other* ancient Near Eastern laws, a master "could kill his own slave with impunity since he was considered to be a piece of property" (Yamauchi, *Stones and Scriptures*, p. 52, following Moshe Greenberg, "Some Postulates of Biblical Criminal Law," in *The Yehezkel Kaufmann Jubilee Volume*, ed. Menahem Haran [Jerusalem: Magnes, 1960], pp. 5–28, which I was not able to obtain).

16. Though cf. M. Stern, "Aspects of Jewish Society: The Priesthood and Other Classes," in *JPFC*, p. 629, who thinks Exod. 21:20 requires the owner's execution; this was also the opinion of some nineteenth-century U.S. abolitionist preachers, e.g., L. R. Sunderland (*The Testimony of God Against Slavery* [Boston: Webster & Southard, 1835], p. 22). Later Jewish law did mandate capital punishment for one who killed a Gentile slave (Bonsirven, *Judaism*, p. 148). Roman law charged a master in this position with murder only if he *intended* to kill the slave; see Cohen, *Law*, p. 4.

17. The *lex talionis* was standard legal practice in the ancient Near East and was executed by the court, not by individuals seeking personal vengeance; e.g., Code of Hammurabi §§196–205 (including in this context, as in Matt. 5:38–39, the insulting blow to the face); cf. Laws of Eshnunna §24; but these laws generally require monetary payment rather than lex talionis (§§42–43; likewise Hittite Laws §§1.7–8, trans. Goetze in *ANET*, p. 189).

18. In the law collection of Hammurabi, if one struck another, one needed to pay for the physician (cf. also Hittite Laws §1.10, in *ANET*, p. 189); if the other person died but this was not the striker's intention, he was not punished except for the fine (Code of Hammurabi §§206–7; the fine is less if the one killed is of lower societal rank, §208). This is analogous to the Israelite code, which must address the same legal categories of the period. The Laws of Eshnunna also list fines for injuries inflicted in a scuffle (§§44–47).

19. W. F. Albright, "The Antiquity of Mosaic Law," in *The Bible in Its Literary Milieu*, ed. Vincent L. Tollers and John R. Maier (Grand Rapids: Eerdmans, 1979), pp. 148–55, thinks that the law was edited into its present form around the sixth or seventh century BCE, but that the laws themselves date to the patriarchal period. His dating of analogous ancient Near Eastern law codes to 2100–1100 BCE suggests a date for Exod. 21–23 in the Mosaic period (*The Biblical Period from Abraham to Ezra* [New York: Harper & Row, 1963], pp. 17–18; cf. idem, *Yahweh*, pp. 101–5; cf. Moshe Weinfeld, "Deuteronomy—The Present State of the Inquiry," *JBL* 86 [3, Sept. 1967]: 249–62, who thinks traditions

compiled in Josiah's time were much older). Evangelical scholars have argued for a much earlier dating of Deuteronomy than most other scholars, based on the covenant form used in the final redaction of the book (K. A. Kitchen, *Ancient Orient and Old Testament* [Chicago: Inter-Varsity, 1966], pp. 90–102; idem, *The Bible in Its World* [Downers Grove, Ill.: InterVarsity, 1977], pp. 78ff.; M. G. Kline, *Treaty of the Great King* [Grand Rapids: Eerdmans, 1963], especially p. 43; for sample treaty forms from various periods, cf. *ANET,* pp. 199–206, and cf. especially the data in G. E. Mendenhall, "Covenant Forms in Israelite Traditions," *BA* 17 [3, Sept. 1954]: 58–60).

20. And, for that matter, animals and the land as well, as Christian environmentalists might happily point out.

21. Cf. Code of Hammurabi §170: if a free citizen ever calls children born to him by a slave "his children," they are counted as such. Even if he does not, the slave mother and the children she bore him are automatically freed upon his death (ibid., §171).

22. Laws of Eshnunna §50 charges an official who fails to return a lost slave or other property in seven days with stealing. In the law collection of Hammurabi, a free citizen or aristocrat who helps a slave escape is charged with a capital offense (§15, contextually linked with kidnaping a free person, §14; cf. Exod. 21:16; Deut. 24:7); so also with one who harbors any fugitive slave (Code of Hammurabi §16) or keeps him or her in his home instead of trying to return the slave immediately to the owner (§§17–19). Kidnaping, of course, warrants death in any case (Exod. 21:16; Deut. 24:7; Code of Hammurabi §14).

23. "Wherever he or she wants to dwell in your cities" could mean that this is a foreign slave, but the fact remains that no laws mandate the return of an escaped slave, and the only text addressing escaped slaves at all requires that they be given refuge.

24. This was naturally also pointed out by abolitionist preachers like Sunderland, *Slavery,* p. 22.

25. Some other ancient Near Eastern laws provided for the freeing of slaves whose labor had paid for their price at least twice over (cf. Deut. 15:18): Code of Lipit-Ishtar §14. Sunderland, *Slavery,* p. 28, used Deut. 15:12 to advocate economic restitution for slaves in his own day as a matter of justice.

26. In this text the drilling of a hole in the ear may not have been much more painful than what those who wish to wear earrings undergo today, but one may compare (by way of contrast) a severe judgment in the law collection of Hammurabi for a slave who denies that his master owns him: his ear is cut off (§282).

27. See b. Yeb. 47.

28. See the discussion of this point in my *And Marries Another,* pp. 42–43. 1 Sam. 8, 12 report the institution of the monarchy as another concession to Israel's wishes.

29. Another example like this may be the accidental killing of a fetus; the offender is fined as if he had caused the loss of property, rather than of a life. If a man strikes a woman and causes a miscarriage, he is liable for striking the woman, but not for intentionally killing the fetus,

since the death of the child was not his *intent* (Exod. 21:22–23). Many of us who oppose abortion today would still argue for the full personhood of the fetus, pointing out that the specific context of our passage addresses accidents, not intention, the same as with the slave above. This was a standard issue of discussion in ancient Near Eastern legal collections; cf. similarly Code of Hammurabi §§209, 211, 213 (fines levied against those who killed fetuses carried by women of different societal ranks; cf. also Hittite Laws §§1.17–18 in *ANET,* p. 190). But in the Code of Hammurabi, if the woman dies, instead of her striker being executed, as in Israelite law (Exod. 21:23), her striker's daughter is executed (§210; but it is only a fine if the deceased was of lower rank, §212, and a smaller fine still for a slave, §214; cf. Exod. 21:29–32). Moses seems to have a higher view of the dependent woman's worth and of personal responsibility. Middle Assyrian Laws (c. twelfth century BCE) imposed a stricter penalty for causing another free person's daughter to have a miscarriage, stricter yet if it is one's wife (i.e., his own wife's fetus is killed), and strictest of all if the other had no son to be a male heir (death) (§§A.21, 50–52, in *ANET,* pp. 181, 184–85); this law distinguishes these events from an abortion caused by the mother herself, the penalty for which was impalement on stakes (§A.53, *ANET,* p. 185).

30. Abolitionist preachers like Sunderland also argued that OT slavery was a concession, on the analogy of cities of refuge, levirate marriage, executing idolaters, and polygamy (*Slavery,* pp. 10–11), as I learned after completing my own study.

31. Albright, *Yahweh,* p. 181, asserts that the Mosaic law "is the most humanitarian of all known bodies of law before recent times," comparing favorably with other ancient Near Eastern collections, especially in defense of the poor.

32. Sunderland, *Slavery,* p. 24.

33. E.g., comparing the oppression of Israel in Egypt (ibid., pp. 12–17), subsequent biblical examples (pp. 29–37), God's favor for the oppressed in Psalms (pp. 37–43), the prophets' denunciations of comparable oppression (pp. 50–70), Jesus' teaching on showing mercy, loving enemies, etc. (pp. 70–79); Sunderland virtually promised God's judgment on the United States (pp. 36–37), which I believe came in the Civil War.

34. Ibid., p. 24.

35. Ibid., pp. 23, 27–28, 90–91.

36. Hardesty, *Women,* p. 118.

37. Sterling, *Sisters,* p. 115.

38. This was also understood elsewhere in the ancient Near East. With Deut. 21:1–9, cf. Code of Hammurabi §§23–24; Daniel's curse on Qiru-mayim in the Ugaritic Tale of Aqhat (*ANET,* p. 154); see Hittite regulations in J. C. Moyer, "The Concept of Ritual Purity Among the Hittites" (Ph.D. diss., Brandeis University, 1969), p. 120.

39. John Perkins, *With Justice For All* (Ventura, Calif.: Regal, 1982), p. 169. AME Bishop Henry McNeal Turner around the turn of the century proposed that the white churches could make restitution by supporting black missionary efforts (G. S. Wilmore, *Black Religion and Black Radicalism*, 2d ed. [Maryknoll, N.Y.: Orbis, 1983], pp. 123–24).

40. Another way—which is more difficult—is by comparing other ancient Near Eastern law codes and trying to see where Israel's laws differ. This will in some cases be successful, but while the similarities among categories reflect a related cultural matrix, there are differences among all the legal collections, and a great variety of situational factors must be taken into account.

41. Lev. 20 includes sins that would be almost universally agreed today to be sinful in evangelical circles. The most notable exception is the purity prohibition of intercourse during menstruation, though perhaps it should not be an exception; the "menstrual taboo" appears in many cultures.

42. Cf. Code of Hammurabi §195 (*ANET,* p. 175): "If a son has struck his father, they shall cut off his hand."

43. MacMullen, *Relations,* p. 103, suggesting that one-third to one-half may have been slaves or ex-slaves. M. I. Finley, *Ancient Slavery and Modern Ideology* (New York: Viking, 1980), p. 80, suggests around one-third, similar to the percentage in the U.S. South in 1860 (cf. also idem, *The Ancient Economy* [Berkeley: University of California, 1973], p. 71). Estimates are imprecise; Ladd, *Theology,* p. 529, cites an estimate that slaves outnumbered free people in Italy; but according to Cary and Haarhoff, *Life,* p. 130, free people outnumbered slaves even in urbanized areas. Nor would these statistics have been constant, even could we guess the numbers more closely; Mattingly, *Christianity,* p. 13; Koester, *Introduction,* 1:331, think that slave numbers had probably declined somewhat from an earlier period (though they were a small percentage in early Rome; Verner, *Household,* pp. 41–42). J. B. Lightfoot, *Saint Paul's Epistles to the Colossians and to Philemon* [reprint, Grand Rapids: Zondervan, 1959], pp. 320–21, claims that in "democratic" Athens there were probably three times as many slaves as citizens, and three times as many slaves as the whole free population, mostly employed in the fields, mines, or factories.

44. Verner, *Household,* p. 63, from Galen's report.

45. Verner, *Household,* p. 60, following M. I. Finley. He also gives other helpful statistics.

46. Tac. *Agric.* 31; Eustathius *Paraphrase of Dionysus Periegetes,* in *Geographi Graeci Minores* 2.253.8–10, in *Empire,* ed. Sherk, p. 37, §20; cf. F. C. Grant, "The Economic Background of the New Testament," in *The Background of the New Testament and Its Eschatology: In Honour of C. H. Dodd,* ed. W. D. Davies and D. Daube (Cambridge: Cambridge University, 1964), p. 104; W. W. Buckland, *The Roman Law of Slavery* (Cambridge: Cambridge University, 1908), pp. 1–21, 397; Koester, *Introduction,* 1:59.

47. Buckland, *Slavery,* pp. 401ff.

48. Cf. ibid., pp. 420ff. For various sources of slaves, see ibid., pp. 1–21, 397–436; S. S. Bartchy, *MALLON CHRĒSAI: First-Century Slavery and the Interpretation of 1 Corinthians 7:21,* SBLDS 11 (Missoula, Mont.: SBL, 1973), pp. 45–50; Francis Lyall, *Slaves, Citizens, Sons* (Grand Rapids: Zondervan, 1984), pp. 29–35.

49. Buckland, *Slavery,* pp. 397ff.

50. Finley, *Slavery,* pp. 81–82.

51. R. H. Barrow, *Slavery in the Roman Empire* (New York: Barnes & Noble, 1968), p. 97; Stambaugh and Balch, *Environment,* p. 72. Finley, *Slavery,* passim, sees the relation as essentially symbiotic; cf. idem, *Economy,* pp. 73–74, 79.

52. See Barrow, *Slavery,* pp. 65–97; Giuseppe Pucci, "Pottery and trade in the Roman Period," in *Trade in the Ancient Economy,* ed. Peter Garnsey, Keith Hopkins, and C. R. Whittaker (Berkeley: University of California, 1983), p. 116. I am inclined to think that the number of slaves in rural areas may be overestimated, given our stronger data for free peasant or bondsmen labor there (cf. Finley, *Slavery,* p. 79).

53. For the great diversity of specialization in the wealthy estates, see Treggiari, "Livia," pp. 48–77.

54. Petr. *Sat.* 37–38.

55. See the Greek stele from Lycia, 43–48 CE, in *Empire,* ed. Sherk, pp. 90–91, §48; at length, see Barrow, *Slavery,* pp. 130–50.

56. For the wide variety of occupations open to female servants in wealthy households, see Susan Treggiari, "Jobs for Women," *AJAH* 1 (1976): 76–104.

57. Cary and Haarhoff, *Life,* p. 130.

58. Mart. *Epig.* 1.84.1–5; Pomeroy, *Goddesses,* pp. 191–95. Women slaves have been used as wives, concubines, and sexual objects in most cultures where slavery existed, e.g., in some cultures in precolonial Africa; cf. J. K. Henn, "Women in the Rural Economy," in *African Women South of the Sahara,* ed. M. J. Hay and Sharon Stichter (New York: Longman, 1984), pp. 5–6. The racist ideology of slavery that generated opposition to interracial relationships in the United States made slaves' sexual treatment less public in this country than in some other cultures.

59. Mart. *Epig.* 9.6.7; 9.8; Apul. *Metam.* 7.9; Ab. R. Nathan 8 A; Dover, "Attitudes," pp. 147–48; Pomeroy, *Goddesses,* pp. 140–41, 192; Gardner, *Women,* p. 132.

60. Cary and Haarhoff, *Life,* p. 130; especially Martin, *Slavery,* pp. 11–15; on managerial slaves, pp. 15–22. For a survey of different uses of slaves in the empire, see Barrow, *Slavery,* pp. 22–150.

61. See Martin, *Slavery,* pp. 30–42, 49; *Empire,* ed. Sherk, p. 238, §178; cf. Meeks, *Urban Christians,* p. 20; Boer, *Morality,* pp. 83, 223. This is of course especially true of slaves of the emperors (Martin, *Slavery,* p. 7; Pomeroy, *Goddesses,* p. 196), although altogether they could have made up only a small percentage of the slave population. Slaves in the U.S. South had some possibilities of advancement within slavery (Fogel and Engerman, *Cross,* p. 149), but because slavery was racially based they could never move beyond a certain point, in contrast to ancient slaves who far more often achieved freedom.

62. Cf. Petr. *Sat.*, e.g., 38.

63. MacMullen, *Relations,* p. 124. Of course, freedpersons were still ill-regarded socially by many, including the later Jewish elite (e.g., Num. Rab. 6:1; for a fuller discussion, see Jeremias, *Jerusalem,* pp. 334–37).

64. Finley, *Economy,* p. 107.

65. Ibid., p. 108.

66. Cf. Apul. *Metam.* 8.15; C. L. Lee, "Social Unrest and Primitive Christianity," in *The Catacombs and the Colosseum,* ed. Stephen Benko and John J. O'Rourke (Valley Forge, Pa.: Judson, 1971), pp. 127–31. Most slaves in Palestine were domestic; see Goodman, *State and Society,* p. 37. Tacitus' report of slaves in Germany sounds more like serfs than Roman slaves (*Germ.* 25), although some slaves were used to cleanse sacred things and then were drowned (*Germ.* 40).

67. Gaius *Inst.* 1.9 (*Empire,* ed. Sherk, p. 236, §178A), lists this as the "principal distinction" among people. It was considered inappropriate for those of noble birth to be slaves (Chariton *Chaer.* 1.11.3).

68. Plato *Alcib.* book 1, 135C; Cic. *Acad.* 2.47.144; Jos. *Ant.* 4.8.15, §219; b. Men. 43b–44a; Moore, *Judaism,* 2:137. This pertains especially to such offenses as false speech (Chariton *Chaer.* 2.10.7; 6.5.5; Apul. *Metam.* 10.7 [even under torture, 10.10]; MacMullen, *Relations,* p. 116), insults to masters (Sen. *Dial.* 2.11.3), laziness (Sir. 33:24–30; b. Kid. 49b); gossip (Lucian *Lucius/Ass* §5), immorality (m. Sot. 1:6), cowardice (Ach. Tat. *Clit.* 7.10.5).

69. Syr. Men. *Sent.* 154–67.

70. Chariton *Chaer.* 1.10.7; 2.1.5, 2.3, 3.10; Test. Jos. 11:2–3.

71. Philo *Rewards and Punishments* 137; *Every Good Man Is Free* 36. For Philo's views of slavery laws and parallels with later rabbinic ideas, see Belkin, *Philo,* pp. 89–103.

72. Arist. *Pol.* 1.1.4, 1252a; 1.2.10, 1254a.

73. Ibid., 1.2.12, 1254b. The equality of unequals, he claimed, was not just (3.5.8–9, 1280a).

74. See m. Git. 1:6; Buckland, *Slavery,* pp. 10–38; Gardner, *Women,* pp. 209–13; John G. Gager, "Religion and Social Class in the Early Roman Empire," in *Catacombs,* p. 110; Lyall, *Slaves,* pp. 35–37. Cf. b. Ber. 16b, bar., R. Eliezer (early second century): One does not recite a funeral oration over a slave, but treats his death as if the owner had lost any other property. Under Roman law, all a householder's slaves and freedpeople (men, women, and children) would be executed if one slave killed him (Tac. *Ann.* 14.42, although the following context makes it clear how many people opposed this injustice; cf. 13.32; Apul. *Metam.* 10.12). Aristotle considers them humans, though different by nature than their masters (*Pol.* 1.5.3, 1259b), but also argues that they are property, on the analogy of animals (1.2.8–14, 1254ab); they are live tools (1.2.3–6, 1253b–54a).

75. Buckland, *Slavery,* pp. 73–130; Barrow, *Slavery,* pp. 151–72. Slaves could themselves own property; see Apul. *Metam.* 10.13; p. Yeb. 7:1, §2 (including other slaves!); Stern, "Aspects," p. 628; Martin, *Slavery,* pp. 7–11; Finley, *Economy,* p. 64; Buckland, *Slavery,* pp. 131–238; for a comparison of the *peculium* in Jewish and Roman law, see Cohen, *Law,* pp. 179–278. Slaves could be disfigured by beatings, but this was considered bad (Ach. Tat. *Clit.* 5.17.8–9; Mart. *Epig.* 2.64; 8.23; cf. 2.82).

76. See e.g., the examples in Carcopino, *Life,* p. 57; Cary and Haarhoff, *Life,* p. 132. Slaves usually did not worry about slavery per se but tried to perform well and work toward manumission (freedom) when

it was possible; see Bartchy, *Slavery,* pp. 67–72. Manumission was much rarer in the U.S. South (Fogel and Engerman, *Cross,* p. 150). Essene halakah mandated mercy toward slaves: they were not to be sold to Gentiles (CD 12.10–11).

77. Mart. *Epig.* 3.21; Sen. *Ep. Lucil.* 47:4. The loyalty of slaves who had been well treated appears also in Test. Abr. 15 A.

78. In Jewish circles, p. Ter. 8:1; Safrai, "Home and Family," p. 750; probably *CPJ* 1:249–50, §135 (second century BCE Egypt); in other Greco-Roman households, see Rawson, "Family," pp. 7–8; Dixon, *Mother,* p. 16; Meeks, *Urban Christians,* p. 30; Aune, *Environment,* pp. 59–60; Stowers, *Letter Writing,* p. 31. Dependents seem to have been called "sons of your house" (m. Ab. 1:5).

79. Arist. *N. E.* 8.11.6–7, 1161b; *E. E.* 7.9.2, 1241b.

80. Arist. *Pol.* 3.5.10, 1280a.

81. Ibid., 1.2.7–8, 1254a; 1.2.14–15, 1254b (even in soul).

82. Ibid., 1.5.6, 1260a (LCL).

83. Ibid., 1.1.4, 1252b; 1.2.18, 1255a; 3.9.3, 1285a. This was not, of course, based on skin tone; it was probably more analogous to the sort of intellectual elitism that characterizes some modern universities, except that many modern professors recoil at the suggestion of their racism or ethnocentrism, though all too often still looking down on "primitive" viewpoints that conflict with their dying strains of anti-supernaturalism, be they traditional African tribal religions, Islam, or orthodox Christianity. Aristotle's point was moot by Paul's day, of course; the Romans had recruited plenty of Greek slaves in the first century BCE.

84. Quint. 1.3.13–14 (who protests that it is not suitable for children, against the common practice). For a long list of examples of cruelties, see Barrow, *Slavery,* pp. 30–31; once one person "owns" another, tyranny is a common result. Fogel and Engerman, *Cross,* pp. 145–46, argue that its occurrence on U.S. plantations has been exaggerated; but the slave narratives provide ample evidence for its practice and the suffering it caused on countless estates.

85. Quint. 1.3.13–14 (citing it as the regular practice, of which he disapproves); Sir. 30:1; Pes. Rab Kah. 15:4; Ahikar 81.3; 82.4. Such instructions are qualified in Ps-Phocyl. 150; Quint. 1.3.13–14; 2.4.10.

86. Pomeroy, *Goddesses,* p. 194, notes the large number of wives even of imperial slaves who died between the ages of 20 and 25. There were, of course, exceptions, e.g., Hieron in *IGRR* 1.417 (*Empire,* ed. Sherk, p. 230, §173Y), and it is probable that the ages of those who died young figure more commonly on funerary inscriptions. Fogel and Engerman, *Cross,* p. 154, argue that 40% of U.S. slaves died before age 19, while pointing out that the mortality rate for young whites was also quite high.

87. *Rhet. ad Herenn.* 2.7.10; Tac. *Ann.* 3.67, 14.60; Chariton *Chaer.* 1.5.1; Apul. *Metam.* 3.8, 10.28; cf. Justin. *Digest* 48.18.1 (*Empire,* ed. Sherk, pp. 236–37, §178); Pes. Rab Kah. 15:7; Alan Watson, "Roman Slave Law and Romanist Ideology," *Phoenix* 37 (1, Spring 1983): 53–65. Quint. 5.4.1 (probably following Arist. *Rhet.* 1.15.26, 1376b) reports the existence of both views (torture yields truth or falsification), conveniently used in court according to which side is being argued.

88. In the strictest sense, only Roman citizens could contract "legal" Roman marriages (see data in my *And Marries Another,* p. 59, nn. 63–65 on p. 169), but the marital status of slaves was more problematic than that of other noncitizens, because masters had the legal right to split up families through the sale of one or both spouses and the children, and sometimes slaves were mated between households.

89. Justinian, *Codex* 9.23 (Lefkowitz and Fant, *Women's Life,* p. 183, §193); Gardner, *Women,* pp. 213–18; Rawson, "Family," p. 24; Pomeroy, *Goddesses,* p. 193; Martin, *Slavery,* pp. 2–3 (citing evidence that stable families could exist even when slaves belonged to different households). Slaves could be separated from their families and sold young; cf. e.g., the seven-year-old Sidonian girl in *CPJ* 1:119–20, §1, or the twelve-year-old Phrygian girl in *CPJ* 3:73, §490.

90. Dixon, *Mother,* pp. 17–18.

91. Finley, *Slavery,* p. 76. This is a high estimate; Fogel and Engerman, *Cross,* pp. 5, 49–50, place it considerably lower.

92. Finley, *Slavery,* p. 80.

93. Ibid., pp. 73–74.

94. Ibid., pp. 18–19.

95. Diog. Laert. *Lives* 10.118.

96. Ibid., 10.1.9.

97. Ps-Plut. *Educ., Mor.* 7DE (in Malherbe, *Exhortation,* p. 31).

98. Pliny *Ep.* 2.6.3–4, to Junius Avitus.

99. Heraclitus 9, to Hermodorus (*CynEp,* pp. 212–13).

100. Ibid.

101. Epict. *Disc.* 1.13.2. That many people viewed slaves as in some sense equals before the gods (Finley, *Economy,* p. 62) did not, however, generally lead to their better treatment, and certainly not to the equal treatment Paul commands in Eph. 6:9.

102. Epict. *Disc.* 1.13.4.

103. See Sen. *Ep. Lucil.* 47.4–5, 13; *Clem.* 1.16.1.

104. Sen. *Ep. Lucil.* 47.18–19.

105. Ibid., 47.10. *Clem.* 1.18.1 makes the principles of equity and right, rather than fear of retaliation, the proper limits for the master's treatment of slaves. Cf. Sevenster, *Paul and Seneca,* pp. 185–92, who wishes to contrast the motives of Seneca and Paul.

106. Sen. *Ep. Lucil.* 47.11. Likewise, another Stoic, Hierocles *On Duties. On Fraternal Love* 4.27.20 (Malherbe, *Exhortation,* p. 94), suggests that a master should think of how he would want to be treated if he and his servant reversed positions.

107. Sen. *Ben.* 7.4.4.

108. William Watts, "Seneca on Slavery," *DR* 90 (300, July 1972): 183–95.

109. Diog. Laert. *Lives* 7.1.23 (LCL).

110. Sir. 7:20–21; the question, of course, is whether this refers to freeing Israelite slaves in the seventh year or whether it is a general ethical admonition. As noted above, Israelite law provided for the ultimate freeing of all Jewish slaves. But it may simply refer to rewarding any industrious servant (cf. 7:18); cf. Syr. Men. *Sent.* 166–67 ("Love the

industrious servant"; in the context of the bad slave, vv. 154–65). Finkelstein, *Akiba,* pp. 191–94, cites Akiba's view on human equality for slaves.

111. Sir. 10:25.

112. The term could be taken in a variety of ways: lead, train, etc.

113. Sir. 33:30–31 (my translation; the enumeration varies in different texts). The "as yourself" is the same as in Lev. 19:18.

114. E.g., Ps-Phocyl. 223–27, especially 227 (accept the counsel of a wise slave).

115. Jeremias, *Jerusalem,* p. 316, and Bonsirven, *Judaism,* pp. 147–48, cite b. Kid. 20a, bar.: "Whoever purchases a Jewish slave actually purchases a master." For the unenviable social position of Gentile slaves in the later Jewish sources, see Jeremias, *Jerusalem,* pp. 345–51; Goodman, *State and Society,* p. 38, thinks that most slaves in Jewish Palestine were Gentiles.

116. Lohse, *Environment,* p. 213. Cf. Bartchy, *Slavery,* pp. 63–67, who argues that slavery was regarded in the Roman Empire as "an indispensable social institution" (p. 67).

117. E.g., *ILS* 7503, from Rome, in *Empire,* ed. Sherk, p. 229, §173. Although the racial injustice for slavery used in the United States usually prevented this from happening, it occasionally occurred even here (cf. the example in A. J. Raboteau, *Slave Religion* [Oxford: Oxford University, 1978], p. 141).

118. Martin, *Slavery,* p. 42.

119. Cf. Lightfoot, *Colossians,* p. 323. Slave revolts did occur in antiquity, but they were localized and never sufficient to challenge the institution as a whole, or people's ideas about the institution. Indeed, the threat of potential revolt could lead to greater repression: cf. the Spartans' treatment of their Helots, who outnumbered them (Arist. *Pol.* 2.6.2, 1269a, reports their attempted insurrections, like the serf class of Thessaly).

120. Finley, *Slavery,* p. 114.

121. Ibid., pp. 114–15.

122. Sunderland, *Slavery,* p. 26; similarly, he advocated submission to masters but demanded that slavery be abolished as quickly as possible (p. 88). Of course Turner, Brown, Vesey, Prosser, and other leaders of slave insurrections equally believed that God was with them and had even directed them to lead their revolts.

123. Finley, *Slavery,* p. 9, recognizes five slave societies in history, two (classical Greece and Italy) being in antiquity; he suggests (p. 67) that slavery as a major system originated in the Greco-Roman world. R. A. Padgug, "Problems in the Theory of Slavery and Slave Society," *ScSoc* 40 (1, Spring 1976): 3–27, especially pp. 21–22, sees only Greco-Roman antiquity as a slave society, but this may go too far.

124. See Lightfoot, *Colossians,* pp. 326–27.

125. K. S. Latourette, *A History of the Expansion of Christianity,* 5 vols. (Grand Rapids: Zondervan, 1970), 1:262–63, citing especially Apost. Const. 4.9; 1 Clem. 55.

126. Longenecker, *Ethics,* pp. 63–64.

127. A. W. Rupprecht, "Attitudes on Slavery Among the Church Fathers," in *New Dimensions in New Testament Study,* ed. Richard N.

Longenecker and Merrill C. Tenney (Grand Rapids: Zondervan, 1974) pp. 261–77. The prejudice is particularly apparent in the Alexandrian Fathers.

128. Finley, *Slavery,* pp. 123–49, looks for economic rather than ideological factors in the decline of slavery in late antiquity.

129. Longenecker, *Ethics,* p. 65.

130. Raboteau, *Religion,* pp. 103–16, 122–24, passim: many recognized that converted slaves were their "Christian" masters' spiritual siblings, and should thus be freed.

131. From the Catholic hierarchy through John Locke—defender of the doctrine of natural liberty—slavery was an accepted institution (Fogel and Engerman, *Cross,* pp. 30–31), and even well into the 1800s many professing Christians considered Christian abolitionism an extremist cause. That African slaves were first imported to Europe from Muslim countries or that slaves are still quietly held in some Islamic and other nations (cf. "Slavery," *Newsweek* [May 4, 1992]: 30–39) cannot keep modern Christians from wondering why so many who professed Christ in the past did not come to grips with the implications of the gospel. John Wesley lamented that Islamic slavery was more humanitarian than what was practiced in *allegedly* Christian lands (Sunderland, *Slavery,* p. 91). Yet many Christians today also interpret the Scriptures according to convenience and tradition rather than according to their spirit.

132. Balch, "Codes," p. 33, following Franz Laub, *Die Begegnung des frühen Christentums mit der antiken Sklaverei,* SB 107 (Stuttgart: Katholisches Bibelwerk, 1982); Balch, *Wives,* pp. 54, 97.

133. Acting from the right motives is stressed often in Jewish literature written in Greek: e.g., Ep. Arist. 270; Ps. Sol. 4:10. Paul's expression "singleness of heart" also appears: Wisd. 1:1; cf. also Test. Reub. 4:1; Test. Benj. 6:5–7; Test. Sim. 4:5; Test. Levi 13:1; Test. Iss. 3:1, 7–8; 4:1, 6; 5:1, 8; 6:1; 7:7; Test. Asher 6:1 (if the extant Testaments do not depend on Paul here).

134. Sunderland, *Slavery,* p. 11.

135. For the reward for serving God as Master, cf. Tob. 4:14, and the pre-Christian Jewish teacher Antigonus of Socho in m. Ab. 1:3.

136. Cf. Gen. 16:9, where God's angel tells Hagar to submit to her mistress's authority, but also 16:10–13, where this angel watches over her and cares for her.

137. Sen. *Ep. Lucil.* 47:11.

138. Cf. Laub, *Sklaverei,* p. 99, on "no respect of persons."

139. Arist. *Pol.* 1.2.3, 1253b.

140. Cary and Haarhoff, *Life,* p. 133.

141. Fogel and Engerman, *Cross,* repeatedly challenge this assumption for slavery in the United States, arguing that slaves were much harder workers and more efficient than free labor.

142. Contrast Gager, "Religion," p. 110, who sees Col. 4:1 as the only clear Pauline command to masters to treat their slaves fairly.

143. A poor modern analogy might be a reasonable insistence that since we ought to devote all our time and money to God's service, we should preach that members of a congregation put away their television

sets to save time, stop buying large houses, etc., to pour *all* their money, besides what they need to live on, into missions or serving the poor. It is, I believe, a good idea, and I have preached it; but I doubt that anything but persecution or judgment will shake up *most* of the church enough to think in these terms. We have to deal with even the redeemed community where it is before we can take it further in its obedience to God. On some issues, however, like racism (the Jewish-Gentile issue), Paul refused to make any compromise in his demands on the church, because the character of the gospel, as well as its spread and credibility, were directly at stake.

144. Stambaugh and Balch, *Environment,* pp. 40, 113. Cf. the aristocratic perspective in Chariton, *Chaer.* 4.5.5, where a runaway slave is identifiable by the extravagant manner in which he throws around money.

145. Lohse, *Philemon,* pp. 187, 196. Ancient literature could depict a runaway slave as having a hard time concentrating because of his fear of being arrested or meeting his master (Epict. *Disc.* 1.29.59, 63).

146. The illegality of harboring an escaped slave is fully documented in Barrow, *Slavery,* p. 54; see also Finley, *Slavery,* p. 111.

147. Pliny *Ep.* 9.21; cf. Lohse, *Philemon,* p. 196; R. P. Martin, *Colossians and Philemon,* NCBC (Grand Rapids: Eerdmans, 1981), p. 146. Cf. also the material on slave refuge in O'Brien, *Philemon,* p. 292. Interestingly, one tradition reports that Diogenes the Cynic had a slave, but he refused to pursue him when he escaped (Diog. Laert. *Lives* 6.2.55).

148. Martin, *Philemon,* p. 147, points out that Paul does not mention Philemon's right to be angry, in contrast to Pliny's plea to Sabinianus. The contrast of Lightfoot, *Philemon,* p. 318, lays too much emphasis on Paul's lack of rhetorical polish in the letter; this contrast with Pliny's letter of recommendation may be due to Pliny's higher education or to the different social level of the intended readers, more than with any contrast of ethics per se.

149. Martin, *Philemon,* p. 166. The possible play on Onesimus' name in v. 20, citing his new usefulness (cf. v. 11), does not militate against this interpretation; slaves were sometimes freed for services rendered (Chariton *Chaer.* 3.8.1–2). Some later Jewish teachers ruled that an escaped slave who returned was to retain his or her freedom (p. Git. 4:4, §2), but this was not true in Roman law.

150. Cf. Bruce, *Paul,* p. 406.

151. The reciprocal obligations prevent Paul from appearing as merely a client dependent on Philemon's mercy; Philemon must recognize that he himself owes Paul his own salvation, which is worth more than anything Paul could have asked in return. Paul uses the formal language of partnership in v. 17 (Meeks, *Urban Christians,* p. 66; cf. John Koenig, *New Testament Hospitality,* OBT 17 [Philadelphia: Fortress, 1985], p. 79).

152. His literary form here may be that of an acknowledgment of debt (Deissmann, *Light,* pp. 331–32; cf. O'Brien, *Philemon,* p. 300), but such acknowledgments of debt could be used in the reciprocal obligations

of ancient friendship; cf. P. Merton 62 in Stowers, *Letter Writing,* p. 157. One may compare many patronal letters of recommendation, e.g., P. Oxy. 32 in Stowers, *Letter Writing,* p. 157.

153. Lohse, *Philemon,* p. 204. Under ancient law, one who harbored a runaway slave could be liable for this loss of labor; see Martin, *Philemon,* p. 167.

154. Fiorenza, *Memory,* p. 215.

155. Knight, *Teaching,* pp. 21–24; idem, "Analogues," pp. 176–77.

156. Knight, *Teaching,* pp. 24–25. Knight further contends (p. 26) that we cannot simply let anyone be in charge, because this "overturns the very form which the apostles seek to establish and continue as a permanent element in marriage." Here again he assumes as a basis for his proof exactly what he hopes to prove.

157. Quoted in Haig Bosmajian, "The Letter from Birmingham Jail," in *Martin Luther King, Jr.: A Profile,* ed. C. Eric Lincoln, rev. ed. (New York: Hill & Wang, 1984), p. 138.

# 7

## Closing Words

Not every reader of this book will agree with all the arguments or conclusions presented here. The number of "mays" and "possibles" in my own arguments indicates that I myself am not settled on every detail of cultural background I have argued, although I am convinced that the case as a whole is sound.

But regardless of less crucial details, I trust that several basic themes have been argued persuasively. Because women are men's equals spiritually and intellectually, they are also capable of the same spiritual and intellectual roles. This means that they are capable of fulfilling the same calls as men and can serve alongside their husbands as equal partners in marriage and ministry. An increasing number of us men would, in fact, have it no other way. This method of arguing from clear principles in Scripture rather than from several proof-texts that are as easily interpreted another way is also the way evangelical abolitionists argued their case.[1]

This is not to play down the need for a wife's submission, but to emphasize that husbands are called to submit and serve no less. I think that most Christians would agree that a man who wants to imitate Jesus cannot be some epitome of macho masculinity with a beer in one hand and a television control in the other, snapping out orders while his wife is at his beck and call. The Jesus-like man will defend a Mary when a Martha challenges her for abandoning a traditional feminine role in favor of becoming a disciple (Luke 10:41–42)[2] and will lay down his life for his bride (Eph. 5:25–27). Such a man is secure enough in his own personhood and masculinity that he can serve without selfish self-assertion, respecting and nurturing his wife's relationship with God. Paul does not tell the husband to enforce his wife's submission; he tells him only to love sacrificially and thus submit to her. It is the wife, not the husband, who is reminded of wifely submission.

Nor is this book meant to argue that men and women are the same biologically[3] (as if both genders could become pregnant!)—a caricature of the egalitarian position that has sometimes been presented. There are also differences between men and women that are culturally based (i.e., they vary from one society to another). While some of these are harmful (e.g., withholding education from or abusing women), others (such as separate clothing styles) are no more hurtful than any other culturally defined distinctions and may simply acknowledge the biological differences on which gender is based to begin with.

Instead, this book is meant to proclaim that we should treat one another in marriage the way we should treat all believers: with dignity, respect, and support as fellow heirs of God's grace. Many, though not all, advocates of the more traditional "hierarchical" marriage actually come close to this position in practice because of their emphasis on mutual honor and Christian love.

Christian "submission" is not a dirty word. I have learned to delight in voluntarily submitting to my senior pastor with whom I work and to others in authority over me. I have also learned to delight in voluntarily submitting to my colleagues and students, seeking to minister to their needs. Submission need not imply hierarchy, and I consider myself blessed when those to whom I submit also submit to me, exemplifying the mutual love and unity that are meant to characterize the body of Christ. Submission in this sense is not blind obedience; it is desiring the honor and seeking the blessing of the other person above our own.

## IMPLICATIONS FOR MARRIAGE RELATIONSHIPS AND WORK OUTSIDE THE HOME

We noted earlier that an ideal marriage involved loving cooperation. Does cooperation require specific roles predetermined by gender, or can it be more flexible than that? Although the Bible provides some direct statements of principle, most of its examples are instead descriptions of ideal roles in given cultures, and we cannot glibly impose them on our own culture without thinking carefully how they should really be applied.

The nature of loving cooperation may vary from one culture to another: the matron may rule the domestic affairs as in a Greek context (1 Tim. 5:14, using standard ancient language for the wife's relative seclusion),[4] or she may be a smart businesswoman and real estate agent (Prov. 31:14–18, 24), highly respected by her husband and others (31:11, 28–31), well educated by the standards of the culture (31:26), who makes clothes for her family (31:19–22) and makes other clothes which she sells in the marketplace (31:34). This woman does not spend most of her time at home "rearing the children"; Israelite tradition demanded that both father and mother raise the children (e.g., Deut. 6:7; Prov. 1:8; cf. Eph. 6:4), and at a young age boys seem to have joined their fathers in their work (e.g., 2 Kgs. 4:18).

"Male" and "female" chores vary from one culture to another. One parent's staying home with the child all day has not marked most homes even in the history of Western culture—as important as a healthy amount of parental attention is. (The model of the wife staying home to engage mainly in childrearing while the husband is in the work force is an ideal of the relatively leisured, nineteenth-century U.S. middle class, and was not common through most of Western history, including recent Western history.)[5] Given the technological aids our society has provided to the homemaker, many homemakers do not find that homemaking consumes a whole day's schedule. Would not productive employment or ministry outside the home be healthier than time in front of a television set (cf. Prov. 31:27), in the cases where those are the main alternatives?

I would never suggest that being a homemaker or staying home to raise one's children is not an honorable profession; I am more than grateful to my mother, who sacrificed so much to spend time with me and my brothers and sister before we went to school. But I am challenging the position that I have heard some (certainly not all)[6] proponents of the traditional family model advocate, that a woman's proper place is necessarily in the home. I would not want to see *that* position imposed on my mother, sister, wife, or daughters as long as I live! Had my mother not been educated, and had she not also provided funds to help me with my schooling, I would probably be in no position to write this book today.

Since I have learned from women professors and ministers, studied alongside women colleagues in doctoral-level classes, worked alongside women colleagues in ministry, taught women students, and so on, the intolerance of those who pronounce judgment on women's calls strikes me as insensitive and demeaning. Spiritually, intellectually, and in leadership ability these women are complete equals of their male colleagues; biblical evidence for their subordination would have to appear much more compelling than it does for me to grasp how subordination could even reasonably be applied in their case.

I know all too many women who are forced to work to support their children because their husbands or boyfriends left them and are nowhere to be found. This situation was not created by feminism, as some allege;[7] it was created by male selfishness. Unless those who oppose women, especially mothers, working outside the home are willing to support the women who have no other way to feed their children, they ought to be quiet. If they admit that there are exceptions to their principle, then they must ask if there might be other exceptions besides those which they have already granted.

If we do not believe that a mother *must* make her own clothes for a family (Prov. 31:19–22)—indeed, if we believe that the emphasis on a woman's public role in the market (Prov. 31) and the emphasis on relative domestic seclusion (1 Tim. 5:14) do not conflict—we must allow that biblical principles are expressed in different ways in different cultures. If we do not allow differences for culture, we become the sort of rigid missionaries for our own culture (instead of the gospel) that Paul's opponents were in Galatia. They quoted Scripture and sought to impose its mandates on Paul's converts, without sensitivity to the situation or culture behind Scripture or to the people they were addressing.

Our world has seen enough "imposed liberation"—where a war for "rights" is forced on those who would rather have peace and food to eat—to make us rightly suspicious of anyone who demands that we "liberate" ourselves if we are happy with the way things are. This chapter is not meant to imply that only marriages based on absolute role equality are strong marriages. Each of us brings strengths and weaknesses to a marriage, and one partner may have leadership skills (including encouragement) that can help the other partner. But it is important for us to recognize our mutual dependence (1 Cor. 11:11–12) and mutual responsibilities (1 Cor. 7:3). None of us may take his or her spouse for granted; we need to care what the other person thinks and feels, and work together as God's servants.

In many traditional American marriages the husband and wife respected one another and looked out for one another's interests. Although specific roles of husband and wife may change from culture to culture and generation to generation, this version of traditional marriage is not in practice far from the sort of marriage based on equality that many of us advocate today.[8]

But the issue here is not just semantics, because others have abused the same "traditional" system to allow husbands to make all the decisions without their wives' counsel, to treat their wives and children as appendages of their own will, and often even to abuse them physically or sexually. Understanding what Paul teaches about mutual submission removes a supposedly biblical excuse some have used to justify their selfish and sinful behavior.

Of course, the egalitarian model of marriage, which affirms the full equality of both partners in a marriage, has been abused, too. When one or both partners perpetually clamor for his or her way, when division rather than unity of purpose marks the marriage, it means that selfish and sinful behavior has again entered in. The emphasis in Ephesians 5:18—6:9 is not so much on "equal rights" of the sort U.S. citizens are wont to demand; the emphasis is on mutual *submission*. Mutual submission means that we are each free to seek the other's good, to love and serve unselfishly, and to maintain these as a goal even when we feel our partner is not upholding his or her end of the contract. Both husbands and wives must love, and both husbands and wives must submit to one another's needs. Such a lifestyle is realized only through joint submission to the Holy Spirit.

Christian equality is different from worldly equality: we are equal servants, striving together to nurture one another in the service of our Lord. We thus find our true fulfillment in giving love, not in self-seeking indulgence; in commitment to a fellow person in God's image, not in satisfying fleeting passions. For the Christian, submission is not a burden, but a joy. Many a chauvinist and secular feminist alike cannot identify with the absolute security we have in Christ, a security that means that our self-esteem is not based on what others think: I can submit to others joyfully because I do it ultimately as an expression of love for my Lord Jesus Christ.

Before my conversion, I desired power over other people's wills; now I delight in serving, obeying, and submitting to the leadership of those God has placed over me. One of my greatest joys was working as associate minister under Pastor Carl Kenney at Orange Grove Baptist church. But Carl made it easy for me because he envisioned his own ministry as being a servant to the body of Christ, and we became intimate friends. In the Kingdom, leaders are servants, and we can lead without asserting our authority in a worldly way, because the only authority to which we need appeal in the body of Christ is the authority of Scripture and the law of love. If we present the Scriptures and present the current situation that guides our application, I believe that mature Christians can work through the details in love. Immature Christians may not respond to such an approach, but I am not sure they would respond to much else but the discipline of the corporate church anyway, and maybe not even that: "A rebuke goes deeper into the one who has understanding than a hundred blows into a fool" (Prov. 17:10, NASB).

I must add one caveat at this point: when we speak of "mutual submission," we are speaking in terms of submission under reasonably normal circumstances, not in cases of flagrant abuse or criminal behavior. Abigail was right to break with her husband Nabal and side with David; she saved the lives of many people by doing so (1 Sam. 25). Jonathan was likewise right to take David's side against his father, without breaking off his relationship with his father (1 Sam. 20). It has become increasingly common in our cities for wives to find their husbands selling drugs or engaged in other activities that could bring violence into the home. Both unfaithfulness and abandonment are given in the New Testament as grounds for dissolving the marriage if the erring partner refuses attempts at reconciliation. These are issues of pastoral concern for which the Bible offers us important guidelines (though not explicit rules for every conceivable situation), and they must be addressed with compassion and God's heart, directed by the principles of Scripture.[9] But the general rule is that, except under the most extreme circumstances, we must work to preserve and nurture our marriages.

Submission is a directive for husbands no less than for wives. History testifies that power corrupts, and that those in power have often used the Scriptures to maintain their power, whether over other peoples, slaves, or spouses. It is important for husbands not to be so quick to cite Paul's admonitions to wives; instead, we should pay attention to Paul's admonitions to ourselves. In most church circles with which I am familiar, wives have already heard their call to submit more than enough.

## THE ISSUE OF THE CHURCH'S WITNESS

Several of Paul's points treated in this book were meant to help the church to be a more viable witness in its own culture. In a culture where the submission of wives to their husbands was regarded by most as important and by others as acceptable, Paul could stress that wives should submit to their husbands, while still maintaining that Christian husbands should submit to their wives as well.

But in our day, what it takes to be a relevant witness has changed. Very few people would criticize a marriage in which a husband and wife lovingly submit to one another, but quite a lot of people have problems with a husband being his wife's master. An increasing number of people, in fact, have come to view Christianity as anachronistic and oppressive, since in their minds it is associated with the latter kind of marriage, even though Paul never taught this even in his own culture. Many feminists in the universities are becoming increasingly alienated from Christianity and drawn toward other religions, to the frustration of the Christian feminists who believe that Christianity is being misrepresented to them.

Although the focus of this book has been limited to what Paul meant and how that calls for a more biblical treatment of women in the church, our response to the issues addressed herein and to other issues mentioned in the introduction does affect our witness to society. At least in the segments of U.S. society I know best, a more egalitarian perspective in the church would substantially improve our witness.

This is especially true in how we respond to the concerns raised by the women's movement, which extend far beyond feminist circles themselves. That this statement needs to be made is tragic in view of the past century and a half of history. Most Christians will agree that the Bible elevated the status of women above what was available in surrounding cultures; many of us would argue that God might have elevated their status more but for a concession to human weakness.[10] But fewer U.S. evangelicals are aware of the evangelical roots of much of the women's movement in the nineteenth century, or its links with evangelical abolitionism we mentioned in our introduction.

Many in our society have chosen either to adopt or to reject uncritically all agendas touted as feminist, without recognizing the diversity among those who would consider themselves advocates for women's rights. Between a woman's right to vote and worshiping a mother-goddess are a wide variety of other causes that have come to be associated with feminism, and one does not have to support all those causes (most feminists do *not* worship the mother-goddess, and many are Christians) to work together with feminists on issues on which we can agree.

Most of us naturally think in reactionary rather than critical ways. But this is not helpful, and even when our reactionary attitudes get covered over with a rationalized Christian veneer, they are still not Christian. For example, evangelicals had been at the forefront of social justice issues until they reacted against liberal critics who played down the necessity of personal conversion. Although evangelicals have always done some of both, our witness has suffered because too many of us have withdrawn from genuine social justice agendas where Bible-believing Christians naturally belong.[11] The Bible commands us both to make disciples of all the nations and to defend the orphaned and needy. Those who claim obedience to the Bible dare not pick and choose which of these parts to obey.

In reacting against elements of the contemporary feminist movement that are objectionable from a Christian standpoint, we have often gone too far and repudiated our own heritage of being ahead of the world in seeking justice for all people. We have also alienated ourselves from some people for whom Christ died, and whom he calls us to love and call to himself.

We could be more effective witnesses to those who share some of our social justice agendas if we acknowledged and worked together with them on points with which we clearly agree, such as opposition to pornography and other forms of sexual exploitation. This is not to suggest that we compromise on matters of genuine disagreement, but dialogue is usually more productive than avoidance, when dialogue is possible. This is not to argue that we compromise truth; it is to argue that we expend more effort communicating it. Given the metamorphoses the women's movement has experienced in the past century, differences between many white feminist and black womanist thinkers (I am technically closer to the latter position), and so on, we may question whether the radical feminists who draw the most criticism necessarily have the right to set the agenda for the whole women's movement anyway.

Paul often used the dialogue approach in the book of Acts; he even had friends who were Asiarchs (Acts 19:31), officials who were, among other things, in charge of the cult of emperor-worship in Asia. Some Christians may be worried that they are not strong enough in their faith to begin to engage non-Christians in discussion. The ideal solution to their problem would be for them to spend more time reading their Bibles and to *become* strong enough. Like Paul, we must be willing to do whatever it takes to share Christ in relevant ways with all people (1 Cor. 9:19–23).

Indeed, most people in modern society who do not classify themselves as feminists would nevertheless be offended by an agenda that could suggest women's social, spiritual, or intellectual inferiority—and rightly so. My guess is that it would have offended Paul, too, especially to find out that his words were being used to advance such an agenda. This is not the best way to evangelize our culture or to be "above reproach" (1 Tim. 3:2, 7; 5:7, 14–15; 6:1; Tit. 2:5). It is necessary to challenge our culture where it departs from the values of the Kingdom; it is likewise necessary to relate to our culture where it has preserved some of the values of the Kingdom.

Yet, as important as communicating Christ to our culture is, we cannot simply guess which issues should be areas of common ground with our culture and which issues should be points of contention. We need an objective guideline in order to know where we should stand. Our best model for how we relate God's message to our culture is how God has always related his message to various cultures, and that model is available to us in the Bible. This was the model many of the first proponents of the women's movement in this nation followed, and it would certainly help our witness in society if we followed it better today.

Our witness is at stake, and this means that people's eternal destiny is at stake. This is no small issue, and those who loudly proclaim that the traditional view is the only proper biblical view would do well to reexamine their claims in the light of what is now at stake. A relevant witness to most of our society today should emphasize mutual submission, rather than just the submission of wives, as Alan Padgett points out: "Today, of course, we live in a different situation. If anything, the church is slandered because it continues to insist on the submission of women: quite the reverse of Paul's day."[12]

We would do well to consider such a critique. Christians must never compromise the truth of God's word. It seems to me that despite all our protestations that we honor God's word, we have dishonored it by failing to understand it, and therefore failing to obey it correctly. The church's disobedience has unfortunately always had disastrous consequences for the church's witness. May God in mercy send a fresh blowing of the Spirit among us , so that we may hear our Lord's voice in truth and be agents of revival in our generation.

## NOTES

1. Hardesty, *Women*, p. 82; on evangelical interpreters in the fledgling women's movement, cf. pp. 74–76, 81, 84–85. On the hermeneutics of nineteenth-century evangelical revivalism in general, especially of Charles Finney, see pp. 72–73.

2. People normally sat on chairs (Safrai, "Home and Family," p. 737), so Mary's posture at Jesus' feet (Luke 10:39) is significant. To "sit before" a teacher, at his feet, was to take the posture of a disciple (Acts 22:3; m. Ab. 1:4; Ab. R. Nathan 6, 38 A; 11, §28 B; b. Pes. 3b; p. Sanh. 10:1, §8; in m. Ab. 2:7, attributed to Hillel, "sitting" is schooling), i.e., of one in training to become a teacher.

3. Biological, including neurological, differences are presented capably in Gregg Johnson, "The Biological Basis for Gender-Specific Behavior," in *Manhood and Womanhood*, pp. 280–93 (Laura Shapiro, "Guns and Dolls," *Newsweek* [May 28, 1990]: 56–65, addresses biology and environment as factors). But none of these differences is so obvious as to suggest that average male leaders are better than all female leaders (which would need to be the case if females were inherently inferior leaders by virtue of creation); indeed, the indications that males are *usually* better at math after puberty and females are *usually* better in verbal skills (p. 290) could argue just the opposite conclusion; after all, which skills are more directly useful for Bible teaching?

4. Cf. especially Philo *Special Laws* 3.169–171. On the wife's domestic role in second-century Palestinian Judaism, see also Goodman, *State and Society*, p. 37.

5. See Rodney Clapp, "Is the 'Traditional' Family Biblical?" *CT* (Sept. 16, 1988): 26; J. D. Hunter, *Evangelicalism: The Coming Generation* (Chicago: University of Chicago, 1987), pp. 83–91 (with H. V. L. Stehlin as coauthor of the chapter). On the independence of Susannah Wesley, mother of John and Charles, see Scanzoni and Hardesty, *Meant to Be*, pp. 97–98. On the hardships for single, widowed, abandoned, and divorced women in the nineteenth-century U.S. setting, cf. B. L. Bellows, " 'My Children, Gentlemen, Are My Own': Poor Women, the Urban Elite, and the Bonds of Obligation in Antebellum Charleston," in *The Web of Southern Social Relations*, ed. Walter J. Fraser, Jr., R. Frank Saunders, Jr., and Jon L. Wakelyn (Athens, Ga.: University of Georgia, 1985) pp. 52–71. In ancient Israel, besides Prov. 31, see Song of Solomon 1:6; Gen. 29:9.

6. G. W. Knight III, "The Family and the Church: How Should Biblical Manhood and Womanhood Work Out in Practice?" in *Manhood and Womanhood*, p. 348, agrees that Titus 2:5 does not forbid work

outside the home (just as 1 Tim. 3:4–5 does not forbid it for men), though he says that the emphasis is on the home.

7. Ayers, "Failure," pp. 328–30, blames divorce on feminism. The prevalence of divorce in our society may be due to a move away from certain traditional values, but that does not make it dependent on feminism, and for a Christian the issue is not whether any given value is traditional, but whether it is biblical.

8. Piper and Grudem, "Overview," p. 62; Wayne Grudem, "Wives like Sarah and the Husbands Who Honor Them: 1 Peter 3:1–7," in *Manhood and Womanhood*, p. 195; Knight, "Family and Church," p. 349, qualify their position sufficiently that, while it remains different from the one advocated in this book, in practice two couples following the different approaches might not need to notice the difference between them.

9. Cf. my *And Marries Another,* passim, for a more detailed treatment of the NT texts on divorce.

10. See Hull, *Equal to Serve,* pp. 76–104; Bilezikian, *Beyond Sex Roles,* pp. 59–68.

11. A. F. Johnson, "Response," in *Women, Authority & the Bible,* p. 157, rightly points out that just as God's word would have been dishonored in NT times by wives not submitting to their husbands, it is dishonored today when outsiders come into male-dominated church services that seem to suppress women.

12. Padgett, "Rationale," p. 52.

# Appendix A: Women's Ministry Elsewhere in Paul

The biggest problem with interpreting 1 Timothy 2:11–15 as excluding women from teaching roles in the church is that Paul clearly commended women for such roles,[1] even though these roles made them far more prominent and equal to men than they would have been in Judaism in this period.[2] This poses a problem for those who believe that Paul wrote 1 Timothy but forbade all women to teach. It is also a problem, albeit a lesser one, for writers who deny Pauline authorship, since whoever wrote 1 Timothy would have to have known that Paul's genuine letters commended women as ministers of God's word.[3] The presence of these commendations, so striking in their culture, would not have been as easy to dismiss before church tradition had found ways to ignore Paul's explicit commendations of women's ministry.

## PHOEBE, SERVANT OF THE CENCHRAEAN CHURCH

Romans 16 lists a number of women in prominent positions of service in the church. Although some scholars have questioned whether Romans 16 was originally part of Paul's letter to the Romans (not whether it is genuinely Pauline),[4] the consensus is now that Paul wrote this chapter as the conclusion of that letter.[5] Most of those greeted seem to have been Paul's friends whom he met elsewhere in his journeys and who had settled, as many people did, in Rome.[6]

Phoebe is clearly the bearer of this important letter to the Romans, since she is coming from Paul to them. Aside from the mail service used for official imperial business, there was no postal system in Mediterranean antiquity. Letters would be carried by friends or travelers who happened to be going in a certain direction,[7] and thus letters could take months to reach the addressees.[8] Letters would sometimes include a praise of the bearer, as here;[9] at other times, the subject of the entire communication would be in praise of the bearer.[10] Letters introducing or commending certain people constituted a standard type of letter, the "letter of recommendation,"[11] normally written by a person of higher or equal social status (a "patron") to a peer, on behalf of someone of lower social status (a "client").

Romans 16:1–2 is clearly a statement of recommendation on Phoebe's behalf. Since she bears Paul's letter, she may be called upon to explain anything ambiguous in the letter when the Romans read it, and Paul wishes them to understand that she is indeed qualified to explain his writing. He argues this point by citing her church offices.

### *Phoebe as a Diakonos*

She is, first of all, a *diakonos,* variously rendered "minister," "deacon," or "servant," of the church at Cenchraea. (The church in Cenchraea was probably a daughter church started by Paul's work in Corinth.)[12] Although the term refers in some early Christian texts to a specific church office (where it is usually translated "deacon"), the nature of that office is never explained in the New Testament writings. Many churches today interpret the office in the light of the appointment of the overseers of tables chosen in Acts 6, who are said to "serve,"[13] even though the particular title *diakonos* is not used in Acts 6.[14]

If we think of Phoebe in this light, she certainly held a prominent role. In the synagogue community, those in charge of distributing help to the poor were highly regarded,[15] and sometimes were high officers in the religious community.[16] In Acts 6 these people play a prominent role in the community and are full of the Spirit and of wisdom (6:3, 5, 10); and the two examples that Luke articulates further become powerful preachers of the gospel, one of them a masterful expounder of the Scriptures (Acts 7–8).

Most New Testament texts that use this specific term, however, imply no definite office and apply the term generally to a minister of the word. Paul regularly applies the term to himself as an apostle of the true gospel (1 Cor. 3:5; 2 Cor. 3:6; 6:4; 11:23; Eph. 3:7; Col. 1:23, 25) and uses it also for his colleagues in the gospel (Eph. 6:21; Col. 1:7; 4:7; 1 Thess. 3:2; 1 Tim. 4:6).[17] He uses this term and its cognates in other ways as well, but he applies it most commonly to ministers of the gospel. Most readers would probably assume that meaning here if this passage did not refer to a woman and if it were translated the way it normally is in the New Testament. Based on the usual sense of the term in Paul, one scholar earlier in this century protested,

> It is quite clear that Phoebe was one gifted by the Holy Spirit for publishing the glad tidings, or preaching the Gospel. . . . Why is it that the translators, when interpreting it [*diakonos*] for men, used the word *ministers,* when for women, the word *servant*?[18]

"Deacons" even in the narrowest sense of a church office had to have sound teaching (1 Tim. 3:9) and the same proven *administrative* ability as pastor-elders (1 Tim. 3:12; cf. 3:4–5), although it is not clear that they regularly taught as elders did (1 Tim. 3:2; 5:17). F. F. Bruce is probably right to insist that the term normally be rendered "minister."[19]

The term appears in a Syrian inscription where it probably represents the Hebrew *hazzan,*[20] the synagogue official in charge of the building and Torah scroll and a salaried officer.[21] According to G. F. Moore, the *hazzan* sometimes lived in the same building where the synagogue met;[22] since owners of the homes in which house churches met would by definition be in charge of them, they may have filled the closest role to this office in the early church. Moore's rabbinic evidence is later than our period, and we cannot be sure that it held true for Diaspora synagogues, but if our Jewish evidence for *diakonos* points anywhere, it is in this direction. If so, it may be significant that in later times those who held this synagogue office were required to be knowledgeable in the Scriptures and humble, and that in later times regular teachers sometimes filled the post.[23] They also were the officials charged with administering corporal punishment.[24]

At the very least, then, Phoebe held a position of considerable responsibility, prominence, and authority in her congregation. She probably taught the Scriptures as well, but if she did not, she was at least trusted with sufficient regard theologically to be placed in this prominent authority role in the church, and to be recommended to those who might depend on her to help them understand Paul's letter to them.

*Phoebe as a Patroness*

Paul provides her with another title in v. 2, which the RSV badly translates "helper." The term means a patron, or a sponsor, one who supported the church or other group to whom the term is applied.[25] Jewish inscriptions testify that prominent and well-to-do individuals often served this function for the synagogues,[26] and that these individuals occasionally were women.[27] The title is one of authority and honor in antiquity, and those who wish to deny Phoebe prominence in the church at Cenchraea do a disservice to the natural sense of this text. Probably she was the owner of the home in which the Cenchraean church met, and thus its host.[28]

This need not mean that she was the teacher in this church, but it does indicate that she held a prominent and authoritative role, one in which Paul trusts and commends her. If an opponent of women's ordination concedes that a woman may hold a position of authority but argues that it is nonetheless wrong for her to teach the Bible (as opposed to secular matters), this person should be clear about what he or she is saying: it is not a woman's role of authority that bothers the objector, but her handling the Scriptures. It is thus her intellectual and spiritual reliability, not her position of authority, that is in question. If someone is actually willing to maintain the inferiority of women in their ability to interpret and expound Scripture, I would like to see this person debate the issue with some of my women colleagues—who, knowing them, would undoubtedly win the debate.

## PRISCILLA, A WOMAN MINISTER

Paul's greetings in Romans 16 contain other commendations as well. In fact, while Paul greets by name roughly twice as many men as women, he says something particular about as many of the women, and commends over twice as many of the women—nearly all of them he mentions—for their "work in the Lord" (16:1–2, 3, 6, 7, 12). Of the three men he commends for their work, two are mentioned in commendations alongside their wives (16:3, 7). It appears that Paul is aware of the prejudice against women's contributions in his society, and therefore works all the harder to make sure that the praiseworthy among them receive their due.

One of these women is Priscilla.[29] According to Luke, Paul first met Aquila and Priscilla when he came to Corinth. They had recently been expelled from Rome under Claudius (Acts 18:2),[30] and came to the city in nearby Greece that probably had the largest Jewish population[31] and the most obvious ties with Italy.[32] Since people of the same trade often lived near one another[33] and formed guilds that met together around the worship of a common deity,[34] Jewish people who worshiped the one God would have been more than happy to have found another Jew of the same trade. Aquila and Priscilla thus invited Paul in, and if they were not Christians already, it was not long before they became Christians (Acts 18:18). This couple eventually instructed even Apollos, a man mighty in the Scriptures (18:24–26), indicating that a woman could teach with her husband at least in a private setting.

That Priscilla's name is mentioned before her husband's in Romans 16:3 and twice in Acts is noteworthy, because the husband was nearly always mentioned first unless the wife was of higher social status or neither party had any concern for status.[35] That she should have such status in society is not particularly significant, but that Luke and Paul should recognize it is much more important for our purposes. It is also noteworthy that 2 Timothy 4:19 preserves this recognition of status; those who think that the Pastoral Epistles were written by a post-Pauline chauvinist may have more trouble demonstrating the author's chauvinism in texts not specifically related to the situation in Ephesus and Crete (2 Tim. 1:5; 3:15; 4:19, 21).

Aquila and Priscilla are praised for risking their lives for Paul,[36] and Paul indicates that they were sponsors of a house church in Rome, as Phoebe was in Cenchraea. Paul calls both of them his "fellow workers," indicating that they share in the same work of ministry in which he is involved (cf. Rom. 16:9, 21; 1 Cor. 16:16; Phlm. 1).

## JUNIA, A WOMAN APOSTLE

In Romans 16:7 Paul speaks of Andronicus and Junia, "who are of note among the apostles." "Andronicus" is a Greek name borne by some Diaspora Jews,[37] and "Junia" is a Latin name that was also sometimes used by Jews.[38] Both are said to be Paul's relatives (like Herodion in v. 11), and whether this means that they were close relatives[39] or only that they were Jewish,[40] they are certainly Jewish.

Since the text suggests that Junia was an apostle, some have debated whether "Junia" is really a feminine name; the RSV simply assumes that it is not by translating "men of note among the apostles"—even though there is little to support this translation but the opinion of the translators that a woman could not be an apostle. Although the name as it occurs here could be a contraction for the masculine Junianus,[41] there is no evidence for this in extant Roman inscriptions, and the most natural way to read the name is "Junia," a common enough woman's name.[42]

It is also unnatural to read the text as merely claiming that they had a high reputation with "the apostles."[43] Since they were imprisoned with him, Paul knows them well enough to recommend them without appealing to the other apostles, whose judgment he never cites on such matters, and the Greek is most naturally read as claiming that they were apostles.[44] Paul nowhere limits the apostolic company to the Twelve plus himself, as some have assumed (see especially 1 Cor. 15:5–11). Those who favor the view that Junia was not a female apostle do so because of their prior assumption that women could not be apostles, not because of any evidence in the text.

If Junia is a woman apostle traveling with Andronicus, a male apostle, certain scandal would result if they were not brother and sister or husband and wife. Since most apostles, unlike Paul, were married (1 Cor. 9:5), the early church was probably right when it understood them as a husband-wife apostolic team.[45] There were husband-and-wife teams in some other professions, for instance, physicians,[46] so there is no reason to think that a couple could not have functioned as apostles together.

## EUODIA AND SYNTYCHE

Paul's repeated exhortations to unity in his letter to the Philippians suggest some division within the Christian community there. Although a variety of factors may have been involved in this division, we know of personal strife between at least two individuals, Euodia and Syntyche. From their names it is possible that they were merchants, like Lydia (Acts 16:14–15), who were no doubt making a substantial livelihood in Philippi.[47]

Although Paul's words function as a letter of recommendation, it is to recommend the women as worthy of the church's efforts toward reconciliation, or to recommend a third party (the "loyal yokefellow" he addresses)[48] to mediate between the two women.[49] Paul mentions only incidentally that they were women who labored with him in the gospel; we may wonder how many other women ministers remain unnamed in his writings simply because their ministry was not normally at issue with him.

When Paul declares that they "contended with him" and Clement and Paul's other "fellow workers" (4:2), he employs a specific term that he earlier used to call the whole Philippian church to strive together in unity for the furtherance of the gospel (1:27). But the athletic imagery implied in the term is most frequently used for Paul's own labors, and this text specifically connects their ministry with his and that of his other "fellow workers," or ministers in the gospel. It is true that the specific nature of their ministry is not stated here, but the general nature is: they labored with him for the preaching of the good news, i.e., for the conversion of non-Christians to Christianity.

It is possible that Philippi allowed more prominence to women because of traditional customs in that region.[50] This would explain why women could help found this congregation and why Lydia plays a prominent role in Acts 16. Like many other women in this period[51] and some other women in Philippi, Lydia was a businesswoman, perhaps "the business agent for the luxury textile industry based in Thyatira in Asia Minor."[52] She was surely well-to-do,[53] since she sold purple fabrics,[54] which was associated with wealth throughout the history of the ancient Mediterranean world.[55] Like many other well-to-do women supporting dependents or hosting the meetings of religious associations,[56] Lydia probably fulfilled the role of patroness,[57] providing housing for the apostles and presumably later for the church there.[58] Although this still cast her in a lower social role than men, her role was analogous to that of a wealthy freedman: she wielded some measure of economic power, and hence respectability within nonaristocratic society.[59]

Women may have been accorded more prominent roles in Philippi than in some other parts of the Roman world, but Paul himself seems satisfied with the ministerial competence of the women so employed in this city. To admit that regional custom affected the roles of women is to admit that women are permitted leadership roles when the culture provides them the opportunities to become gifted leaders.

## PROPHECY AND OTHER GIFTS?

Paul plainly allowed women prophetesses (1 Cor. 11:5), and almost certainly commends a woman apostle (Rom. 16:7);

women also labored with him in sharing the good news of Christ (e.g., Phil. 4:2–3). Rarely does Paul note that any of his fellow workers, whether women *or men*, were involved in teaching, although it is nearly certain that most of his fellow workers were.

Despite this fact, many interpreters today say that Paul may have allowed women prophetesses or sharers of the gospel, but he did not allow women to teach the Scriptures because this would have given them a position of authority.[60] Is it possible that teachers had more authority than prophets and apostles in the local churches? Paul expressly ranks prophets higher than teachers in the one list where he explicitly ranks some of the gifts (1 Cor. 12:29),[61] although teachers are above most of the other gifts, which are lumped together after them (1 Cor. 12:29–30). Both prophecy and teaching are ranked higher than the gift of administration,[62] and thus both are distinguished from it. And is it merely coincidence that in two of his other three lists, Paul lists apostleship and/or prophecy before any other gifts (Rom. 12:6–8; Eph. 4:11)? Paul encourages the Corinthians that prophecy is the most useful gift for them and includes among its functions that those who hear it may *learn* (14:31). His whole contrast between prophecy and tongues is that prophecy, like teaching, communicates something intelligible.

Arguments that Old Testament prophetesses were less authoritative than Old Testament prophets (and thus than NT prophets and teachers) have no evidence in their favor. One writer who opposes women's ordination points out that people came to Deborah for judgment (Judg. 4:5), which makes her prophecy less authoritative than it would have been if she had gone to them.[63] The meaning of the text is quite the opposite, however; Deborah was not only a prophetess, but a judge of Israel (Judg. 4:4)—thus holding the highest position of authority in her time. That people came to her for judgment no more diminishes her authority than people coming to inquire of the Lord's word from Samuel (1 Sam. 9:6–10) diminished his.

The same writer protests that Huldah did not prophesy publicly, but only to messengers sent to her by the king (2 Kgs. 22:14–20).[64] But it seems odd to assume, on the basis of the only text we have which refers to her, that she did nothing other than what is stated in that one text. Is Ahijah less authoritative because Jeroboam I sent his wife to him (1 Kgs. 14:2)? Is Elisha less authoritative because a king wanted to inquire from him (2 Kgs.

13:14)? What about Isaiah, the inquiry to whom most strikingly parallels the one to Huldah (2 Kgs. 19:2)? That a king would send to her and then obey her instructions indicates her authority, not her lack of it; that she alone was chosen indicates that she was probably the most prominent prophetic figure in this part of Josiah's reign, even though Jeremiah had begun his early ministry (2 Kgs. 22:3; Jer. 1:2). Perhaps if the text had reported her prophesying in public, the same modern writer would have protested that she lacked the authority to prophesy to kings or the recognition to have messengers sent to her!

Arguments that the New Testament writers viewed prophecy as less authoritative than it had been in the Old Testament (and thus less authoritative than teaching) are unpersuasive.[65] Given Agabus' "Thus says the Holy Spirit" (Acts 21:11) and the formulas in Revelation 2–3, which are our clearest examples of prophecies in the New Testament (not exceptions, against some writers),[66] we cannot maintain Grudem's distinction between Old and New Testament prophecy (New Testament prophecy being understood as on a lower level and prophets being replaced by apostles).[67]

Nor does Paul feel free to disregard Agabus' prophecy in Acts 21:11 (cf. 11:27–30), which is a warning, not a command, in contrast to the position of some writers.[68] Agabus' prophecy may admit some poetic license, but this is typical of the writing prophets (e.g., Isa. 37:29).[69] Efforts to reduce New Testament prophets to a role subservient to New Testament teachers wrongly assume that only the latter would draw on the Bible—although even Old Testament prophets used the law and earlier prophets. This diminution of biblically-based early Christian prophets' authority flies in the face of explicit New Testament teaching to the contrary (1 Cor. 12:28; Eph. 2:20; 3:5; 4:11).

Admittedly there must have been different levels of prophecy; Agabus (Acts 11:27–28; 21:10–12) undoubtedly commanded more respect in practice than the disciples just beginning to prophesy in Acts 19:6. But while someone with less knowledge of Scripture and less experience in the prophetic gift must have functioned at a lower level of practical authority than a more mature prophet, the same contrast could be made between less informed and more mature teachers. Deborah and Huldah both demonstrate that women could qualify for the highest-level prophetic roles; the only barriers to such development in the gift in the early church would have been the same cultural obstacles women in Paul's day faced in becoming skilled teachers—lack of education in the Scriptures and culturally-defined male prejudice.

Although early Christian tradition is clear on the role of prophetesses (e.g., Acts 2:17–18; 21:9),[70] as is the Old Testament (Exod. 15:20; Judg. 4:4; 2 Kgs. 22:14; Isa. 8:3; Joel 2:28–29 ET), not all Jewish circles were so eager to admit women as prophets. A late rabbi suggests that the matriarchs were prophetesses,[71] and the prophetesses Deborah[72] and Huldah[73] were still respected in early Judaism. The end of the Testament of Job, which may reflect Christian influence, portrays Job's daughters as prophetically endowed.[74] But while Josephus calls Deborah a prophetess, he fails to inform his Greek readers that she was judging Israel;[75] and another late rabbinic tradition limits Huldah's prophesying to the women.[76]

Is it not more likely that women appear in teaching roles in the New Testament less frequently not because they were women but because teaching requires more training in the Scriptures than the other gifts, and this training was less frequently possessed by women? In addition, as we noted in passing above, Paul rarely designates *any* individual as a teacher, whether male or female; that he speaks of men and women laboring together with him in ministry, however, allows that some of both did so.

## FEWER WOMEN THAN MEN?

Some writers have objected that most apostles in the New Testament were men and most prophets in the Old Testament were men. From this they conclude that it is normative for men to lead.[77]

This position has two serious weaknesses. First, it fails to take into account cultural conditions that anyone who observes the modern church would have to take into account today. If the percentage of a given gender (or race, culture, etc.) in one period should determine the norm for all periods, some other periods of church history leave men (and certain races, cultures, etc.) in a rather bad light. Many of the mission fields opened in the late nineteenth and early twentieth centuries were pioneered by single women;[78] does this mean that men are less capable missionaries, able only to take over after women have done the initial work?

The same might be true if we pressed examples on race or culture. Unfortunately for Gentile Christians, most ministers in the biblical period were Jewish. Does this mean that only messianic Jewish believers should minister for Jesus today, or do we admit that culture and how God was working with people in that period of history may have had something to do with it?

Today I find most black American Christians far more aware of urban ministry needs than most white American Christians. Similarly, a larger percentage of white American Christians are involved in overseas missions than black American Christians (due in part to the lack of finances in the black church in the formative period of white American missionary expansion). Does this mean that God tends to call black Christians to U.S. cities, and white Christians overseas? This is doubtful. I do have white friends serving in the inner cities and black friends serving as foreign missionaries, and both are clearly called and used by God. Elward Ellis and other African-American missions specialists have repeatedly shown the need for more African-American missionaries overseas, who often can approach other cultures from a different perspective than white Christians do. But our different backgrounds affect the range of options we are likely to consider, and while the percentages are changing (Urbana 91 was an encouraging sign of this), it is still important to provide everyone with more options than their own cultural setting immediately brings to their attention.

In many cultures, the local Christians are now producing more cross-cultural missionaries than the West is—a fact which should not surprise North American and other Western Christians since the gospel did not originate with us. But in many countries, local Christians do not want to minister to certain other people groups, because their own culture makes it difficult for them to recognize this option. In some African tribes, African Christians conditioned by generations of intertribal hostility are convinced only slowly that a rival Muslim tribe is actually capable of being reached with the gospel. Generation gaps, education gaps, and culture gaps produce some of the same evangelical skepticism for reaching unreached people groups in Britain and North America as well.

The solution in these cases is not to throw up our hands and say, "God calls whom God wills, and many peoples never hear the gospel because God doesn't want them to." The solution is to recognize that God does want people to hear the gospel (e.g., 1 Tim. 2:4–5), and that we need to make it easier for God's servants to hear God's call to go to them. Engineers, doctors, teachers, and others cannot use their skills in urban or overseas missions unless they are made aware of the great need for their skills and of ways to get them there. U.S. Christians raised by parents who want them to "make it" may never consider forsaking "making it" in this life for the work of the Kingdom, unless they are made aware of the need. Young ministers having trouble finding positions in churches may never consider planting new churches unless someone starts them thinking about it.

Many of the women in the New Testament body of Christ were not mobilized for all the work of the Kingdom the way they could have been because their culture did not present this as a readily available option, and, as we discussed above, women usually did not have the same opportunities to learn the Scriptures as men did. In the Old Testament prophetesses were never portrayed as unusual, but they were rarer than male prophets probably in part because the traveling groups of prophets where individuals developed their charismatic skills did not mix genders and so were made up only of men.[79] In other words, it was not women's gender per se, but the place of their gender within their culture, that limited some of their ministry.

If someone replies that Jesus would not have given in to social constraints in choosing only male apostles,[80] we may point out that no slaves or Gentiles were among the apostles, either. If Jesus' choice of apostles was not influenced by social constraints, are Gentiles then forbidden to minister the word? He did, of course, see to it that the gospel was proclaimed to the Gentiles after his resurrection. But guess what gender the first messengers of his resurrection gospel were (Luke 24:1–11)?

The second problem with the view that male *dominance* in certain areas means that those are *exclusively* male areas is that its logic is severely distorted. No one would argue this analogy to make other points: for instance, to say that a certain mission field is dominated by Baptists but includes a few Christian and Missionary Alliance workers is not the same as saying that this field *ought* to include only Baptists.

If opponents of women's ministry concede Miriam, Huldah, and especially Deborah (a judge of Israel) as "exceptions" whose prophetic ministry also gave them authority in Israel, they have given away their own position; once they admit that "exceptions" to their rule exist, they have forfeited their right to pass judgment on any particular woman's call. Of course, they may then wish to institute quotas to provide that only a few women may be called, but if they use the same criteria to restrict the call of male ministers, we will have a leadership crisis of major proportions in a relatively short period of time!

Is it not possible that, even today, the fact that men outnumber women in many ministries of the church is due in part to the limitations we have placed on women? In ancient Rome equal education was normally denied women, and their resultant lack of eloquence in "male" disciplines reinforced male convictions that women were unfit for those disciplines. Similarly, in the nineteenth century even free blacks were denied equal education, but they argued that, if given the same opportunities whites had, they could achieve the same place in society. As Clarissa Lawrence, a black vice-president of the Salem Female Anti-Slavery Society, cried in Philadelphia's 1838 female antislavery convention:

> Faith and prayer will do wonders in the anti-slavery cause. Place yourselves, dear friends, in our stead. We are blamed for not filling useful places in society; but give us light, give us learning, and see then what places we can occupy.[81]

Perhaps some percentages remain skewed in the body of Christ only due to unequal opportunity. If so, justice as well as faithfulness to the Lord of the harvest demands that we find ways to make opportunities more widely available.

Appeals to biblical percentages based on ill-reasoned arguments would not be so tragic if they did not affect so many lives. But those who turn some people back from their call—whether some senior pastors who have crushed the spirits of young ministers, church leaders who have broken the will of their pastors, or officials or teachers who discourage women from ministry—will also be held responsible by God for the lives that went untouched because some people God called to touch them never obeyed the call. Meanwhile, those who turned their back on their call will also answer to God for obeying men rather than God. This is not a trifling matter. May the Lord of the harvest help us to understand and apply the word of God rightly.

## NOTES

1. This is especially the case in Rom. 16; see, e.g., D. M. Scholer, "Paul's Women Co-Workers in the Ministry of the Church," *DSar* 6 (4,

1980): 3–6. More broadly, E. Schüssler Fiorenza, "Women in the Pre-Pauline and Pauline Churches," *USQR* 33 (3–4, Spring 1978): 153–66.

2. Meeks, *Urban Christians,* p. 81.

3. Someone who wished to silence women might have been more likely to have chosen another apostle in whose name to write than Paul. Of course, a post-Paulinist could have appealed to a certain reading of 1 Cor. 14:34–35; Paul was certainly borrowed by other varied causes, including Valentinus and Marcion, and it is feasible that if the Pastorals are not written by Paul that they could be interpreted as excluding women from teaching ministry across the board. This could oppose Gnostic documents featuring or purportedly written by women (e.g., *The Questions of Mary* [see E. Hennecke, *New Testament Apocrypha,* ed. W. Schneemelcher, trans. A. J. B. Higgins et al., ed. R. McL. Wilson, 2 vols. [Philadelphia: Westminster, 1963–65], 1:338–40]), although other second-century works of more "orthodox" substance could advocate women's teaching (e.g., *Acts of Paul and Thecla* 3:41, 43, accepted by Hippolytus but rejected by Tertullian), and severer chauvinism surfaces in some Gnostic documents (e.g., *Gospel of Thomas* 114). Opponents of Irenaeus may have co-opted his name to have advocated the superiority of women (cf. J. M. Higgins, "Anastasius Sinaita and the Superiority of the Woman," *JBL* 97 [2, June 1978]: 256, if the document is early enough). The reader who opts for this approach, however, does need to be ready to address the resulting explicit conflict with the rest of genuinely Pauline teaching.

4. T. W. Manson, "St. Paul's Letter to the Romans—and Others," in *The Romans Debate—Revised and Expanded Edition,* ed. Karl P. Donfried (Peabody: Hendrickson, 1991), pp. 3–15; J. R. Richards, "Romans and I Corinthians: Their Chronological Relationship and Comparative Dates," *NTS* 13 (1, Oct. 1966): 30. J. I. H. McDonald, "Was Romans XVI a Separate Letter?" *NTS* 16 (4, July 1970): 369–72, argues on the basis of ancient epistolary forms that Rom. 16 could have been an independent letter.

5. K. P. Donfried, "A Short Note on Romans 16," in *Romans Debate—Revised,* pp. 44–52; L.-G. Lönnermark, "Till frågan om romarbrevets integritet," *SvExÅrs* 33 (1968): 141–48 (NTA 14:69); H. A. Gamble, Jr., *The Textual History of the Letter to the Romans: A Study in Textual and Literary Criticism,* Studies and Documents (Grand Rapids: Eerdmans, 1977); cf. also Malherbe, *Social Aspects,* p. 65; Meeks, *Urban Christians,* pp. 16–17, 201, n. 41; Stowers, *Diatribe,* p. 183; J. W. Drane, "Why Did Paul Write Romans?" in *Pauline Studies: Essays presented to Professor F. F. Bruce on his 70th Birthday,* ed. Donald A. Hagner and Murray J. Harris (Grand Rapids: Eerdmans, 1980), p. 223; A. M. Hunter, *The Epistle to the Romans,* Torch (London: SCM, 1955), pp. 128–29.

6. People commonly migrated to Rome from the east (Carcopino, *Life,* p. 55; cf. Friedländer, *Life,* 4:11), and this included both Palestinian (*CIJ* 1:282, §362; 1:287–88, §370; cf. 1:411, §556 [a captive]) and Diaspora (*CIJ* 1:365, §500) Jews (cf. H. J. Leon, *The Jews of Ancient Rome* [Philadelphia: Jewish Publication Society, 1960), pp. 238–40). Only six of the twenty-five names are Latin (Wolfgang Wiefel, "The

Jewish Community in Ancient Rome and the Origins of Roman Christianity," in *Romans Debate—Revised,* p. 95), and several of these clearly moved to Rome (Aquila and Junias); while it is true that only about half the Jews in Rome had Latin names (Leon, *Jews of Rome,* p. 107), it can be noted on the other side that *peregrini* and freedmen sometimes *assumed* Roman names (Friedländer, *Life,* 4:56–57).

7. Diogenes 6, to Crates (*CynEp,* pp. 96–97); cf. Ramsay, "Roads and Travel," pp. 379, 383, 387, 402; Stowers, *Letter Writing,* pp. 62–63; Stambaugh and Balch, *Environment,* p. 40. Sending it by a fellow Christian was probably considered safer; t. Shab. 13:11 allows sending letters by means of Gentiles, but notes that the very pious did not do so.

8. Sen. *Ep. Lucil.* 50:1; cf. M. P. Charlesworth, *Trade-Routes & Commerce of the Roman Empire,* 2d rev. ed. (New York: Cooper Square, 1970), p. 86.

9. Aune, *Environment,* p. 171.

10. Stowers, *Letter Writing,* p. 153.

11. Cf. e.g., Socratics 28, Aristippus to Philip (*CynEp,* pp. 284–85); 1 Esd. 4:61; p. M. K. 3:1, §2; Acts 9:2; Phil. 2:29–30; Philemon; C. H. Kim, *Form and Structure of the Familiar Greek Letter of Recommendation,* SBLDS 4 (Missoula, Mont.: SBL, 1972), p. 119; Malherbe, *Social Aspects,* pp. 102–3; Lionel Casson, *Travel in the Ancient World* (London: George Allen & Unwin, 1974), p. 188.

12. Cenchraea was Corinth's port on the isthmus; e.g., Philo *Flaccus* 155; Apul. *Metam.* 10, §35; Philostr. *V. A.* 4, §25. A. D. Nock, *Conversion* (Oxford: Oxford University, 1961), p. 56, points out from Apuleius that the Isis temple at Cenchraea had permanent professional clergy, which seems to indicate an openness to foreign religions there.

13. Cf. analogously Test. Job 15:1. This ministry was normally conducted from a position of wealth, as the exception in Test. Job 12:1–5/12:1–2 suggests.

14. The great patristic scholar J. B. Lightfoot, *St. Paul's Epistle to the Philippians* (reprint, Grand Rapids: Zondervan, 1953), pp. 188–89, also believes that the seven of Acts 6 were connected with the later diaconate.

15. Ab. R. Nathan 3 A. Josephus says that the Essenes "elect by show of hands good men to receive their revenues and the produce of the earth and priests to prepare bread and other food" (*Ant.* 18.1.5, §22 [LCL]; cf. Ep. Arist. 46.

16. This role is attributed to R. Gamaliel's court in t. Ber. 2:6. See especially S. Applebaum, "The Organization of the Jewish Communities in the Diaspora," in *JPFC,* pp. 491, 494–95, on the *archons* in various Jewish communities (distinct from the "servants").

17. Cf. also Epict. *Disc.* 3.26.28; on Jos. *War* 3, see Hill, *Prophecy,* p. 30.

18. Streeter, *Woman,* p. 63.

19. F. F. Bruce, *Commentary on the Book of the Acts,* NICNT (Grand Rapids: Eerdmans, 1977), p. 130.

20. *CIJ* 2:57, §805. The *hazzan* may appear in a third- or fourth-century Syro-Palestinian inscription in *CIJ* 2:94–95, §855 (the text is incomplete).

21. Moore, *Judaism,* 1:289. The term can also be rendered by other Greek words for "servant," as in Luke 4:20 (cf. Safrai, "Synagogue," p. 935).

22. Moore, *Judaism,* 1:289.

23. Alfred Edersheim, *The Life and Times of Jesus the Messiah* (Peabody: Hendrickson, n.d.), p. 200, cites b. Sanh. 92a; Hag. 5b; Git. 60a.

24. Applebaum, "Diaspora," p. 496, with notes.

25. Meeks, *Urban Christians,* p. 60; idem, "Androgyne," p. 197; Stambaugh and Balch, *Environment,* p. 140.

26. *CIJ* 1:71, §100; 1:284, §365 (see here Frey's note, and also in 1:xciv–xcv). The matter is spelled out in further detail in A. Kascher, *"M'srt hprwst'ts bqhylwt ysr'l btpwsh hhlnyst't-hrwmyt"* (The office of *prostatēs* in the Jewish communities of the Greco-Roman Diaspora) *Zion* 47 (4, 1982): 399–406 (NTA 28:66). The term was in wide use in Greco-Roman society, including for elected officials (Epict. *Disc.* 3.9.3, equivalent to patron in 3.9.18), and could even be applied to Zeus (Marc. Aur. *Med.* 5.27).

27. Brooten, *Women Leaders,* p. 151, citing a third- or fourth-century Diaspora inscription that also mentions the woman's charitable activities. In *Greek Anth.* 7.728, a priestess claims to have been patroness for many young women. Women were sponsors of other associations as well; see Meeks, *Urban Christians,* p. 24.

28. Malherbe, *Social Aspects,* p. 98. Banks, *Community,* p. 56, connects "sister" (16:1) with the family picture of the house churches; this is entirely possible, though not certain; "sister" naturally meant "fellow-Christian," as sibling language was used for fellow-Jews and members of religious associations.

29. On the shortened form "Prisca" in some texts, see Ramsay, *Cities,* p. 207. That she and her husband had Roman names may suggest that they were originally from Rome, where this was common, although it need not mean this (in Paul's case it indicated citizenship).

30. Cf. Suet. *Claud.* 25 (cf. *Tib.* 36), although inscriptions indicate that not all the Jewish community left (*CIJ* 1:lxxiii). The date (Leon, *Jews of Rome,* p. 24; Murphy-O'Connor, *Paul's Corinth,* pp. 130–31, 138–39; Robert Hoerber, "The Decree of Claudius in Act 18:2," *CTM* 31 [11, Nov. 1960]: 690–94; etc.) and cause ("Chrestus"; cf. Leon, *Jews of Rome,* pp. 25–26; Harris, "References to Jesus," pp. 353–54; George Howard, "The Beginnings of Christianity in Rome: A Note on Suetonius, Life of Claudius XXV.4," *RestQ* 24 [3, 1981]: 175–77; Stephen Benko, "The Edict of Claudius of A.D. 49 and the Instigator Chrestus," *TZ* 25 [6, Nov. 1969]: 406–18; Smallwood, *Rule,* p. 211; cf. Justin *1 Apol.* 4; Tert. *Apol.* 3.5) of the expulsion are debated, but that some were expelled (probably late in Claudius' reign) is in my opinion secure.

31. M. Stern, "The Jewish Diaspora," in *JPFC,* p. 159.

32. Theissen, *Setting,* p. 99; Malherbe, *Social Aspects,* p. 76.

33. MacMullen, *Relations,* pp. 69, 71–73, 129–35; Stambaugh and Balch, *Environment,* p. 118.

34. Meeks, *Urban Christians,* pp. 31–32; MacMullen, *Relations,* pp. 77, 82; Stambaugh and Balch, *Environment,* p. 125.

35. M. B. Flory, "Where Women Precede Men: Factors Influencing the Order of Names in Roman Epitaphs," *CJ* 79 (3, Feb. 1984): 216–24; MacMullen, "Women in Public," p. 210; Meeks, *Urban Christians,* p. 59; cf. p. 20. Mek. Pisha 1.17–34 has to argue (i.e., it cannot simply assume) that sequence of names is not always significant in the Hebrew Bible. Bruce, *Acts,* p. 369, suggests that Priscilla, if of higher social class than Aquila, may have belonged to the Roman noble family known as the *gens Prisca*. Wives sometimes formed business partnerships with their husbands, although the extent of their contribution is not entirely clear (Gardner, *Women,* p. 239).

36. "Laying down one's neck" (Acts 16:14) seems to have functioned idiomatically; cf. Deissmann, *Light,* pp. 117–18.

37. *CIJ* 1:436, §607; *CPJ* 1:149–50, §18.

38. The masculine form is attested in a Jewish inscription in Rome, *CIJ* 1:279, §357. E. A. Judge, *Rank and Status in the World of the Caesars and St Paul,* UCP 29 (Canterbury: University of Canterbury, 1982), p. 36, n. 18, observes that this is a Latin *nomen* and (unlike a mere Latin *praenomen*) should indicate Roman citizenship. Meeks, *Urban Christians,* p. 57, notes Eck's view that Junia must have been a freedwoman of the *gens Iunia,* since Andronicus was probably a freedman, but replies that "not every Jew with a Greek name [like Andronicus] in Rome was a former slave."

39. The term means "kinsman" in Diog. Laert. *Lives* 6.1.12 (citing Antisthenes in Diocles).

40. Meeks, *Urban Christians,* p. 216, n. 29; William Sanday and Arthur Headlam, *A Critical and Exegetical Commentary on the Epistle to the Romans,* ICC, 5th ed. (Edinburgh: T. & T. Clark, 1971), p. 423; Hunter, *Romans,* p. 131. A bond by office instead of kinship may be implied in Ep. Arist. 241–42, following Ptolemaic custom (Hadas, pp. 194–95), but the remoteness of context necessary to make that a plausible interpretation may safely rule it out here.

41. Sanday and Headlam, *Romans,* pp. 422–23, note that the name is feminine, but that it could be a contraction, like many other names in the list.

42. Judge, *Rank,* p. 36, n. 18; R. R. Schulz, "Romans 16:7: Junia or Junias?" *ExpT* 98 (4, Jan. 1987): 108–10; cf. V. Fàbrega, "War Junia(s), der hervorragende Apostel (Rom. 16,7), eine Frau?" *JAC* 27–28 (1984–85): 47–64 (NTA 30:175). This was also understood by the church fathers: see Spencer, *Curse,* p. 101; Bilezikian, *Roles,* p. 263, n. 54; cf. Fàbrega, "Junia(s)."

43. Against John Murray, *The Epistle to the Romans,* NICNT, 2 vols. (Grand Rapids: Eerdmans, 1965), 2:229–30. Despite his commentary's positive attention to theological concerns, it has hardly any cultural-historical sensitivity.

44. Also Bilezikian, *Roles,* p. 263; Spencer, *Curse,* p. 102; Sanday and Headlam, *Romans,* p. 423. That they were apostles is usually agreed; e.g., Ladd, *Theology,* p. 380; Walter Schmithals, *The Office of Apostle in*

*the Early Church,* trans. John E. Steely (Nashville: Abingdon, 1969), pp. 67, 81.

45. Martin Hengel, *Acts and the History of Earliest Christianity,* trans. John Bowden (Philadelphia: Fortress, 1980), p. 108; Meeks, *Urban Christians,* p. 57. Cf. n. 42 on their view.

46. Gardner, *Women,* p. 240.

47. Meeks, *Urban Christians,* p. 57. Sometimes one or the other of them has been identified with Lydia, "Lydia" in Acts 16 being taken as "the Lydian woman" (since Thyatira was in Lydia) (George Johnston, *Ephesians, Philippians, Colossians and Philemon,* Century Bible [Greenwood, S.C.: Attic, 1967], p. 46; F. W. Beare, *A Commentary on the Epistle to the Philippians,* 2d ed. [London: Adam & Charles Black, 1969], p. 144). Although her name is often linked with the Roman province of Lydia (Bruce, *Acts,* p. 331; Yamauchi, *Cities,* p. 53; cf. Kirsopp Lake and H. J. Cadbury, in *The Beginnings of Christianity,* vol. 4: *English Translation and Commentary* [reprint, Grand Rapids: Baker, 1979], p. 191), its occurrence is not limited to there, appearing especially also in Rome (e.g., Mart. *Epig.* 11.21; 11.71; Hor. *Ode* 1.8.1; cf. 1.25.8; 3.9.6–7, 20).

48. G. F. Hawthorne, *Philippians,* WBC 43 (Waco, Tex.: Word, 1983), p. 180, sees this title as addressed to the whole church. If a single individual is in view, that individual must have been prominent enough to have known that Paul addressed him (cf. Johnston, *Philippians,* p. 46, who also suggests that this may be the person's name ["Yokefellow"]).

49. For letters of recommendation used to reconcile relationships, see Stowers, *Letter Writing,* p. 155.

50. V. A. Abrahamson, "The Rock Reliefs and the Cult of Diana at Philippi" (Th.D. diss., Harvard Divinity School, 1986), argues that women were central in the cult of Diana, which was prominent in Philippi; see especially ch. 5, "Women's Roles in the Cult of Diana," pp. 108–30; for the application to Phil. 4:2–3, see idem, "Women at Philippi: The Pagan and Christian Evidence," *JFSR* 3 (2, 1987): 17–30. This may be in contrast with the situation in Ephesus; titles of magistracies and priesthoods were given to women in the eastern provinces, but usually did not reflect administrative power in this period (Gardner, *Women,* pp. 67–68). That some scholars have unfairly made a blanket contrast between the freedom of women in Pauline churches and the lack of it in the empire, without regard to geographical variations, has been pointed out by Averil Cameron, " 'Neither Male nor Female,' " *GR* 27 (1, April 1980): 61.

51. Gardner, *Women,* pp. 233–37, noting also minimal restrictions. Even in Egypt, a woman could own land, though her son might act for her legally (*CPJ* 3:9–10, §453; because the date is 132 CE, after the slaughter or expulsion of most of Egyptian Jewry, I am less convinced that the woman is Jewish).

52. E. A. Judge, *The Social Pattern of the Christian Groups in the First Century* (London: Tyndale, 1960), p. 36. Families of freedwomen retailers in the purple industry are attested; see Gardner, *Women,* pp. 238–39. The textile industry was strong in Thyatira (Charlesworth, *Trade-Routes,* p. 94), and Jewish people in Asia Minor were probably

commonly involved in it (see evidence in S. Applebaum, "The Social and Economic Status of the Jews in the Diaspora," in *JPFC,* pp. 716–17; A. Thomas Kraabel, "The Synagogue and the Jewish Community: Impact," in *Sardis from Prehistoric to Roman Times,* ed. G. M. A. Hanfmann [Cambridge: Harvard University, 1983], p. 181).

53. This would stand in contrast to most of the Macedonian population: see H. D. Betz, *2 Corinthians 8–9,* Hermeneia (Philadelphia: Fortress, 1985), p. 43.

54. On the murex shellfish from which the dye was extracted, see e.g., Athen. *Deipn.* 3.88; the legendary story of its discovery is recounted in Ach. Tat. *Clit.* 2.11. This had long been associated with the region of Tyre and is often called "Tyrian" (purple), e.g., Hor. *Sat.* 2.4.84; Mart. *Epig.* 2.29.3; 4.28.2; 8.48.1; Juv. *Sat.* 1.27; 10.334; Apul. *Metam.* 10.20; Petr. *Sat.* 30; Chariton *Chaer.* 6.4.2; 8.1.14, 6.7 (cf. "purple of the sea" in 1 Macc. 4:29; "Sidonian purple," Hor. *Ep.* 1.10.26); cf. L. B. Jensen, "Royal Purple of Tyre," *JNES* 22 (2, April 1963): 104–18. But cheaper (less "authentic") purple could be procured elsewhere (e.g., Hor. *Ode* 2.18.7–8), and much dyeing was done as nearby as Thessalonica (Meeks, *Urban Christians,* p. 46) and Corinth (Charlesworth, *Trade-Routes,* p. 125).

55. Besides the OT and older Greek classics like Homer, see Lucr. *Nat.* 5.1423; Hor. *Ode* 1.35.12; 2.18.7–8; Cic. *Senect.* 17.59; Athen. *Deipn.* 4.159d; Diog. Laert. *Lives* 8.2.73; 1 Macc. 10:20, 62, 64; 14:43–44 (royal); Gen. Apoc. 20.31; Sib. Or. 3.389, 658–59. In the imperial period, Petr. *Sat.* 38, 54; Epict. *fr.* 11; Mart. *Epig.* 5.8.5; 8.10; Juv. *Sat.* 1.106 (senatorial), 4.31; Apul. *Metam.* 10.20; Chariton *Chaer.* 3.2.17; Pes. Rab Kah. 2:7; 15:3; Test. Abr. 4 A; Jos. & As. 2:2/3, 8/14–15; 5:5/6; Sib. Or. 8.74 (senatorial); see Friedländer, *Life,* 2:175–76. Some writers complained that it was needlessly extravagant: Sen. *Dial.* 12.11.2; Plut. *T.-T.* 3.1.2, *Mor.* 646B; Ps-Melissa *To Kleareta* (Malherbe, *Exhortation,* p. 83); 1 En. 98:2 MSS (Knibb, p. 231); cf. the stench in Mart. *Epig.* 4.4.6; 9.62.

56. See the first century BCE inscription in Lefkowitz and Fant, *Women's Life,* p. 24, §48, and second century CE inscription, pp. 243–44, §232; Pomeroy, *Goddesses,* pp. 200–201; Gardner, *Women,* pp. 239–40.

57. Rosalie Ryan, "Lydia, A Dealer in Purple Goods," *BiTod* 22 (5, 1984): 285–89, suggests that she was probably a well-to-do widow. This may be correct (she seems to have been the head of the household; cf. F. F. Bruce, *The Acts of the Apostles: The Greek Text* [Grand Rapids: Eerdmans, 1951], p. 314), although we should not think that inheritance from her deceased husband was the source of her wealth; Stambaugh and Balch, *Environment,* p. 112, point out that Roman women normally could not inherit more than 10% of their husband's estates. She could, however, have accumulated substantial wealth from parental inheritance or other sources (Verner, *Household,* p. 39; for wealth independent of one's husband, e.g., *CIL* 6.10230, in *Empire,* ed. Sherk, p. 242, §184).

58. R. F. Hock, *The Social Context of Paul's Ministry* (Philadelphia: Fortress, 1980), p. 29, speculates on where Paul and his companions had stayed before; accommodations with her were substantially better.

59. Stambaugh and Balch, *Environment,* p. 115.

60. Cf. especially Grudem, "Prophecy—Yes," pp. 11–23.

61. "First . . . second . . . " normally carries this kind of meaning, e.g., 1QS 6.8–9.

62. Cic. *Offic.* 1.21.72, and Plut. *Statecraft* 17, *Mor.* 813C, recognize this gift as an endowment of nature; Cicero also notes that those who took this position at the helm of state without the endowment of wisdom encountered shipwreck (*Invent.* 1.3.4).

63. T. R. Schreiner, "The Valuable Ministries of Women in the Context of Male Leadership," in *Manhood and Womanhood,* p. 216.

64. Ibid.

65. Some Jewish circles believed that OT-style prophecy had ceased, others that it continued in some sense, but few used the language of "prophet"—which Paul uses freely (see my "Johannine Pneumatology," ch. 2, on early Jewish pneumatologies, especially pp. 77–91). Further, testing prophecy in a congregational setting was not a novel idea; Samuel presided over, and presumably evaluated and corrected, prophetic inspiration, and other schools of the prophets probably continued this practice (1 Sam. 19:20).

66. E.g., Aune, *Prophecy,* p. 320.

67. Grudem, "Prophecy—Yes," p. 11. I can agree with the distinction I believe that he *wishes* to make, between canonical revelation and other revelation that must be evaluated by it, but this is a theological distinction, not an exegetical insight into the change in the nature of prophecy.

68. Even Acts 21:4 is only said to be "through the Spirit," reflecting insight by the Spirit, and may mean no more than 20:23; attempts to dissuade from martyrdom appear also in Platonic dialogues on Socrates' last days and appeals to martyrs' age in Mart. Poly. 9; 2 Macc. 6:21–22. Paul knows what awaits him, and feels that God has called him to face it (Acts 20:23; 21:13–14).

69. Cf. the much stronger fulfillment in 37:36! The "inaccurate" language attributed to Agabus, supposedly reported to show that his prophecy was less authoritative than OT prophecy is reported in these words for other reasons, since it includes a typical Lukan parallel with Jesus (against Hill, *Prophecy,* p. 108; Grudem, *Prophecy,* p. 79).

70. Papias claimed to have received a tradition from Philip's prophetess daughters, in fr. 6 (Euseb. *Eccl Hist* 3.39). In Greek religion, see Aune, *Prophecy,* p. 28.

71. Gen. Rab. 72:6, R. Hanina bar Pazzi. Gen. Rab. 67:9 attributes the tradition to R. Haggai (fourth century) in R. Isaac's name (much earlier).

72. Ps-Philo 33:1–2.

73. Ab. R. Nathan 35 A; only her grave and that of David, present since the time of the early prophets (she actually is from the period of Jeremiah!), were allowed to remain.

74. Test. Job 46–50, especially the first daughter's angelic language in chs. 48–50.

75. Jos. *Ant.* 5.5.2, §201.

76. Pes. Rab. 26:1/2.

77. Knight, *Teaching*, p. 49, notes that men are mentioned in the ruling office of 1 Tim. 3:1–2, not women. He admits that some will object that these are also married men and fathers, but appeals to other texts (Matt. 19:11–12; 1 Cor. 7) to reply that single men are allowed and that Paul speaks of married men only because *most* of them were married (1 Cor. 9:5). But on his own logic, we can then appeal to Rom. 16:7 and other texts and say that Paul addresses only men in 1 Tim. 3:1–2 because most of the available leaders were men (or because of the situation addressed in chapter 3 of this book, on 1 Tim. 2:11–15).

78. R. A. Tucker, *From Jerusalem to Irian Jaya* (Grand Rapids: Zondervan, 1983), p. 16, observes that "women—single and married—constituted about two thirds of the North American missionary force."

79. 1 Sam. 10:5, 10; 19:20–24; 2 Kgs. 2:3–18; 4:38–44; 6:1–6. At least some of these prophets were, however, married, and owned their own homes (2 Kgs. 4:1–7); whether they stayed apart from their families for the training period or commuted is difficult to say. Our explicit examples cover only the periods of Samuel and Elijah/Elisha, but this is probably because these are the only eras where tales of prophets, possibly passed on orally in their schools, are told in sufficient detail to suggest anything about their organization. Most of the ministers Paul mentions by name as having traveled with him were men, but the ratios become less disparate when he names those ministering in local congregational settings.

80. Schreiner, "Valuable Ministries," p. 221.

81. Sterling, *Sisters*, pp. 116–17.

# Appendix B: Mysteries, Music, Women, and Wine—Ephesians 5:18–21 and the Threat of Subversive Religions

If Paul wished to distinguish Christianity from the wild rites associated with the less acceptable mysteries, he would need to encourage the Christians to avoid wrong impressions concerning the orderliness of their worship, the roles of women in their congregations, and perhaps the use of wine in the Lord's Supper.

Most of the exhortations he gives in Ephesians 5:18–21 could be directed just as easily against drunken banqueting, associated with exciting music and the availability of slaves as sexual partners of both genders, as they could against the excesses attributed to certain pagan cults. Lavish banquets were a prerogative only of those who could afford it, but those of lesser wealth could probably have found this same combination of wine, music, and sex in the taverns.

But while Paul's exhortation makes sense against the general backdrop of ancient life, it could have functioned particularly well in showing that Christians did not act like the drunken revelers in some of the mysteries. If this is Paul's point, his argument is the sort of reasoning followed by Christian apologists in the second century: if we will not even witness the carnage in the theaters, how shall we be accused of cannibalism? If we avoid all sexual activity outside marriage, how can we be accused of incest? In other words, Paul may highlight certain features of Christian ethics that would reduce external suspicions that Christianity was a subversive cult as the cults of Dionysus, Cybele, or Isis were thought to be.

In this appendix, we examine how some features of Ephesians 5:18–22 could have been read if Paul were seeking to distinguish Christianity from certain cults particularly troubling to the Romans. This is helpful in reinforcing the setting we proposed in chapter 4, since much of what Paul says here would make sense in that light. Of course, Paul's words here may be of more general import; but the cumulative weight of different motifs in one section of his letter may suggest that Paul is actively seeking to distinguish Christian gatherings from the more distasteful of the pagan religious associations.

## EPHESIANS 5:18 AND PERCEPTIONS OF "WILD" RELIGIONS

Ephesians 5:18–21 contrasts drunkenness with true spiritual worship and properly submissive relationships; this might suggest that the contrast is between true and false kinds of worship. Music, sexual liberation, and abuse of wine were not limited in any way to the mysteries, but if Paul is concerned to set Christianity apart from Roman perceptions of "foreign cults," these would be some issues that he would need to address. Paul is at least concerned in this context to distinguish Christians from those who perform pagan deeds in darkness (5:8–14). The darkness to which he refers surely contrasts with the true light of Christ (5:14),[1] but it could also point to the secretive (5:12),[2] nighttime initiations of most of the mysteries.[3]

Certain mystery cults were thought to give too much prominence to women.[4] Juvenal mocks frenzied women in the cult of Isis[5] and associates their devotion to Isis with their immoral behavior.[6] A chaste woman, it was often felt, would not participate in such ignoble cults.[7] Recent studies have indicated that, though women's participation was more offensive to Roman observers, they were in reality normally outnumbered by men in the cult.[8] The issue in this passage, however, is not how subversive many of the cults were (in contrast to our discussion in chapter 2, above), but how subversive the Romans *thought* they were. If Paul is distinguishing Christians from initiates to various mysteries, it is for the sake of popular opinion, not because Christians themselves did not know the difference.

One offensive cult in which women's frenzied participation had long been notorious[9] was that of Dionysus. This was the case although, again, men by this period participated as well,[10] as evidenced in public Dionysiac celebrations in Greece made every other year.[11] But women's roles were especially prominent in this cult, and, given Roman male views on property, this naturally led to social disturbances,[12] including a significant sexual scandal in Rome in 186 BCE.

Certain of the mysteries (though not the highly respected ones)[13] were associated with sexual immorality.[14] That this is especially true of the cult of Dionysus[15] is evidenced particularly by the example we have just mentioned, excesses associated with its presence in Rome in the second century BCE.[16] Perhaps the scandal was augmented by the association of Dionysus, the god of wine, with drunkenness. With or without the cult of Dionysus, wine was often associated with sexual immorality,[17] and the removal of inhibitions may have led to some of the early connections between Dionysiac revelry and women's participation in the cult. But whether or not drunkenness was stressed in the scandal, the connections between sexual license and the cult ritual itself are clear; if these diminished after their brutal Roman suppression in 186 BCE,[18] their reputation, at least, did not.

Some of the mysteries were celebrated with drunkenness,[19] and, as we have noted, the cult of Dionysus was no exception.[20] Frenzy, probably usually initiated through intoxicants and dance, was normally said to characterize his worship.[21] Indeed, frenzy or ecstasy characterized the cults of Dionysus and Cybele but not those of Demeter, Isis,[22] or later Mithras,[23] and this helps explain why the Romans were especially put off by the former groups. Dionysus' power was said to be irresistible,[24] and this also could trouble conservative Romans who wished to avoid all disorderly behavior.

Roman discomfort with Dionysian sexuality and frenzy was not eased by any reassurance that Dionysus wished to preserve the social order; to the contrary, worshipers of Dionysus symbolically overturned that order in their ritual. This applied not only to gender role reversal, but also to a breakdown of traditional social status categories. Wine, Dionysus' gift,[25] was to be provided at festivals across lines of social status, even to slaves.[26] This may suggest that Dionysus' ability to cut across social lines was significant; unlike formal initiations into more expensive mysteries, one could unofficially experience Dionysiac frenzy simply by getting drunk. Most worshipers of Dionysus were not official initiates into his cult, but the line between Dionysiac possession and Dionysiac initiation may not have been particularly important to those wishing to preserve order.

Dionysus' cult spread widely in hellenistic times,[27] and he was still worshiped in the eastern Mediterranean in the Roman period,[28] sometimes in the context of his mystery cult.[29] In a popular tradition, he was said to derive from Asia Minor, where Ephesus is located, and his first followers were said to have come from there.[30]

Although the cult spread widely, it took some time to become fully accepted in Rome.[31] The worship of Dionysus had even penetrated some upper-class Roman circles by the second century CE,[32] and this no doubt irritated conservative Romans all the more.[33] The cult had been stigmatized in Rome in an earlier period, probably including the first century, and it never gained the following in Italy that it held in the eastern Mediterranean. Any Christian worship that could be remotely compared to the worship of Dionysus would be quite a poor strategy for preventing scandal in Rome; and if Jewish worship had been compared to that of Dionysus,[34] the Christians could expect the comparison to be drawn with them, too.

If Christianity wished to dissociate itself from the popular perception of some of the wilder of the non-Roman religious groups, one front it could emphasize was its own disdain for drunkenness.

## EPHESIANS 5:18 AND DRUNKENNESS IN ANTIQUITY

In ancient literature,[35] including Jewish literature,[36] drinking wine in moderation was not considered evil. Of course, the alcoholic content of wine was lower then than it is today; while the lack of hermetic sealing or refrigeration meant that all grape juice after the grape vintage would have undergone some degree of fermentation, the lack of distillation meant that wine would not become more alcoholic than occurs by natural processes.

Furthermore, one could not have become drunk from a small amount of normal wine. It was customary in antiquity to water the wine down, often two parts water to one part wine;[37] to produce intoxication in Greco-Roman settings, one might add a variety of herbal toxins.[38] It was, of course, possible to become drunk from drinking large amounts of regular wine, but this would not occur in the ordinary quantities in which it was drunk at meals.

But drinking in excess came under attack from many circles.[39] Perhaps the most common problem associated with excessive drinking was the loss of one's self-control.[40] Sometimes drunkenness was said to lead to personal dangers. Just as Odysseus overcame the Cyclops Polyphemus by getting him drunk,[41] so Judith could kill a drunk Holofernes.[42] How did Delilah manage to keep Samson asleep on her lap while having someone cut his hair (Judg. 16:19)? One early Jewish writer explains that Delilah got him drunk first—an explanation that may actually have some merit.[43]

Likewise, drunkenness could lead a person to tell secrets unwittingly.[44] Other kinds of irresponsible[45] or silly talk also characterize the drunken person:

> For song, laughter, and dancing are characteristic of men who drink wine in moderation; but babbling and talking about what is better left in silence is at once the work of actual intoxication and drunkenness.

Hence Plato, too, holds that most men show their real natures most clearly when they drink.[46]

Drunkenness makes it more difficult to reason clearly;[47] thus a classical Greek orator warns that if one cannot avoid drinking parties, one ought at least to depart before becoming drunk, "for when the mind is impaired by wine it is like chariots which have lost their drivers."[48] A drunken man thus does things he would not have done in his right mind.[49]

It was also recognized that drunkenness normally led to lack of motor control, though a Stoic philosopher is reported to have said that it would not affect his fluency of speech,[50] and an Epicurean text charged that the wise man will not "drivel, when drunken."[51] A Jewish person who drank too much and vomited all over the place at a party would be considered disgusting and would be put out.[52] Like overeating, another form of immoderate behavior, drunkenness could "kill by giving pleasure."[53] And it could lead to trouble in bad company,[54] especially sexually loose company.[55]

Finally, we should observe that inspiration was sometimes compared with drunkenness (Acts 2:13).[56] Although Greek writers at times distinguished prophetic ecstasy from Dionysiac frenzy,[57] it is noteworthy at least in passing that drunkenness and divine frenzy are often linked in the worship of Dionysus,[58] and Dionysus[59] and his followers[60] could be said to be mantic, i.e., prophets. Interestingly, it is in the Jewish philosopher Philo that we find the most explicit connection between drunkenness and pneumatic inspiration.[61] It is possible that Philo was alluding to common concepts of Dionysiac inspiration.[62]

Does Paul allude here to the drunkenness of banquets and taverns, or to the drunkenness associated with pagan religious celebrations and perhaps inspiration? It may not be necessary for us to decide. There was no reason in antiquity to distinguish "secular" from "religious" drunkenness; these categories would not have made sense to the many people who would have believed that all intoxication was possession by Dionysus, deity of wine.[63]

Warnings against intoxication were, it is true, part of traditional moral exhortation, and need not have been associated directly with Dionysus.[64] But Paul's contrast between being "drunk with wine"[65] and being "filled with the Spirit"[66] (Eph. 5:18) may indicate that he is at least aware of the possession connotations many people in his day attached to drunken loss of control, and that he knows that some even saw it as an alternative source of inspiration.

## EPHESIANS 5:19 AND PAGAN MUSIC

Ephesians 5:19 refers to singing various kinds of songs as an expression of the Spirit's inspiration. It will therefore be helpful to comment briefly on the use of music in ancient cults. Music was not limited to cultic settings, of course; it was a regular part of Greek education;[67] it was standard fare with the wine at banquets;[68] it was sometimes used during labor or even rowing in the galleys,[69] and the heavens themselves were said to move in musical harmony.[70] Likewise, although dancing was appropriate in many religious settings,[71] it was also appropriate in other settings, including military training.[72]

But religious contexts were certainly one of the more important settings for music,[73] and the music of Ephesians 5:19 is explicitly religious music. Music and dancing were part of the Dionysiac and other cults.[74] Women's participation in the music may generally be assumed,[75] especially since we know that young girls were trained in music and dancing.[76] But the singing of "psalms and hymns and spiritual songs" for which Paul calls is far more like traditional Jewish worship[77] than the sort of frenzied worship that characterized the cults most troublesome to the Romans, especially those of Dionysus and Cybele.

Of course, all music characteristically involved emotion,[78] and some music could be thought to hold special powers. In the case of David, music had the power of exorcism (1 Sam. 16:23), perhaps implying prophetic anointing.[79] But emotionally or spiritually powerful music was not directly connected with the wild sort associated with the undignified cults; sometimes music could even be used to symbolize harmonious ideas.[80] Philosophical discourse could be substituted for music at the parties of the educated,[81] and a Jewish prophetic figure spoke of God's inspired law as "the hymn of the law."[82] Music could thus have a rational component as well as an affective one, and it could be used either positively or negatively from the Roman standpoint.

Paul does not take his case too far with regard to music; although drunkenness was always wrong, music simply needed to be done in an orderly manner to distinguish the Christians from other objects of Roman mistrust. Even though instruments such as cymbals were used in the cult of Cybele,[83] Paul does not exclude their use here, concentrating instead on the content of the music itself. Early Christian music may have been instrumental (especially with more readily available apparatus such as cymbals), as in temple worship and Jewish festal assemblies.[84]

The early Christians were less concerned to distinguish their worship from that of the synagogues than from that of certain pagan cults, although many of the gifts of the Spirit active in their congregations (1 Cor. 12–14) would have distinguished them from the synagogues well enough. But it is difficult to compare the house churches and the synagogues on the matter of worship, apart from the issue of charismatic gifts. We do not have clear evidence for corporate singing in the average first-century synagogue; the Essenes and the worship led by Levites in the Jerusalem temple included corporate singing, but we cannot say how prevalent this was in various synagogues throughout the Mediterranean world.[85]

It may be that the spontaneous worship of an Egyptian Jewish sect called the Therapeutae[86] is our closest parallel to ancient Christian worship.[87] But early Christian worship at least seems to have differed from *most* early Jewish communities for which we have evidence, with its emphasis on intensely corporate worship and especially on charismatic prayer. "Spiritual songs" may refer to such inspired prayers as sung prayers in tongues followed by interpretations (cf. 1 Cor. 14:13–15).

Music was often linked with inspiration,[88] as it is in Ephesians 5:18–19: "be filled with the Spirit, speaking to one another in psalms, hymns, and spiritual songs." The link can be found frequently in the ancient Near East,[89] including ancient Israel.[90]

The prophetic Spirit inspired people to sing in Jewish tradition,[91] which owned as part of its Bible an inspired hymnbook, the book of Psalms. The link between music and prophecy is clear in the Greek tradition in their consolidation in the person of Orpheus[92] or their joint patronage by Apollo;[93] similarly, the Muses are often entreated for poetic inspiration.[94] Indeed, the explicit transference between the musician Orpheus and the wine-god Dionysus,[95] and between Dionysus and the prophecy-god Apollo,[96] is remarkable.

Paul's emphasis on the *kind* of religious music generated by the Spirit's inspiration (psalms, hymns, and spiritual songs) may serve as an implicit contrast with the worship of certain pagan cults in his culture. This would be important in a climate where Christian house churches could still be mistaken for cult associations, which usually also met in homes.

## FEMALE ROLE MODELS IN ASIAN RELIGION AND TRADITION

The history that had been ascribed to Asia by Paul's day provided its inhabitants with various models for women taking on traditional masculine roles, models which would not appeal to conservative Romans if anyone ever acted on them. Such figures could be found in the Amazons, the mother-goddess, and the Ephesian Artemis. Greek writers had long been intrigued by traditions of the warlike Amazons in Asia,[97] and most ancient writers seem to have assumed that they actually existed.[98] These women warriors may have been modeled to some degree on the huntress Artemis, with whose Ephesian temple they are linked in Greek tradition.[99] They were seen as "manly" in their pursuits,[100] and were able to serve as a role model for philosophically minded women in Cynic exhortation.[101]

Mother-goddess worship was also easily associated with the Roman province of Asia and its environs. It was widely known that Cybele, the "Great Mother"[102] who induced frenzy and castration among her priests,[103] was of Phrygian origin.[104] Mother-goddess cults apparently had a long history in the area around Ephesus.[105] Because castration was a severe form of gender role reversal, Romans would be especially disturbed by this cult.

The cult of Artemis was of paramount importance in Ephesus,[106] although Acts 19:27 rightly reports the claim that both Asia[107] and the world[108] worshiped the Ephesian Artemis; her devotees had carried her cult with them elsewhere.[109] Her temple[110] was so impressive that it is listed first among the seven wonders of the ancient world.[111] Unlike the virgin huntress of Greek mythology, this Artemis is widely agreed to have been a fertility figure of some sort.[112] In the syncretism that had become typical of the hellenistic-Roman age, the Greek Artemis was identified with the original Great Mother and other female deities.[113]

Women were often praised in the inscriptions of the eastern provinces, although some of the titles may have been merely honorary.[114] Inscriptions especially from Ephesus indicate that many women were honored as priestesses.[115] Since there were also women of religious prestige in Rome, the Vestal Virgins, we need not suppose that this feature of Asian culture would have threatened Roman values.

But there was a sufficient distance between the Roman perception of women's religious and historical models in Asia and their own models to make them more cautious at the outset toward religious expressions emerging from this region. Political precedents in Rome, the heart of the empire, could affect the church in other parts of the empire. Paul, imprisoned in Rome but with many visitors from the Roman churches and Jewish community (Acts 28:14–16, 30), would be well aware of public perceptions of Christianity and would be interested in implementing strategies that would reduce unnecessary opposition to the gospel.

## CONCLUSION

Paul's words in Ephesians 5:18—6:9 make sense in the context of ancient religion, and especially in the context of Roman discomfort with certain expressions of non-Roman religion. Although other social factors were also at work, Paul was very concerned to be a relevant witness within Roman society for the sake of the gospel.

## NOTES

1. Cf. Eph. 1:18; 3:9; 4:18; 1 Cor. 4:5; 2 Cor. 4:2. Doing deeds in darkness to hide from the Holy One was not an unnatural Jewish charge; cf. e.g., Isa. 29:15 (cf. 45:3, 19); 1 Cor. 4:5; Num. Rab. 9:1.

2. E.g., Petr. *Sat.* 17; Wisd. 14:23; Burkert, *Cults,* p. 8. Sinning "in secret" is not an unnatural charge, and again need not relate to the

mysteries directly (Mus. Ruf. *fr.* 12, *On Sexual Indulgence,* in Malherbe, *Exhortation,* p. 153).

3. Apul. *Metam.* 11.21; Hor. *Epodes* 5.51–54; Petr. *Sat.* 17; Cic. *De Legibus* 2.14.35; cf. Epict. *Disc.* 3.21.13; a Pythagorean treatise, third/second century BCE, in Lefkowitz and Fant, *Women's Life,* p. 105, §107; Ramsay, *Teaching,* p. 294; Burkert, *Cults,* pp. 5, 8; G. E. Mylonas, *Eleusis and the Eleusinian Mysteries* (Princeton: Princeton University, 1961), pp. 243–85, et passim; Ruck, "Mystery," pp. 36–37; Koester, *Introduction,* 1:364; Lohse, *Environment,* p. 235.

4. For texts on women's participation in these cults and in witchcraft (alongside texts about goddesses), see Lefkowitz and Fant, *Women's Life,* pp. 113–26, 255–58; cf. Pomeroy, *Goddesses,* pp. 75–78, 205–6, 217–26.

5. Juv. *Sat.* 6.314–41. He mocks women in the Isis cult further in 6.511–29, shifting to attack Jewesses in 6.542–47.

6. Ibid., 6.489.

7. A Pythagorean treatise, third/second century BCE, in Lefkowitz and Fant, *Women's Life,* pp. 104–5, §107.

8. Cole, *Theoi Megaloi,* p. 42; Heyob, *Isis,* pp. 81–110; Banks, *Community,* p. 129. They were excluded from Mithraism (Gager, *Kingdom,* p. 133, who thinks this fact contributed to its ultimate demise!). Plut. *R. Q.* 3, *Mor.* 264C, shows that men could enter any shrine of Diana in Rome, except one.

9. Eurip. *Bacch.* passim; Plut. *Alex.* 2.5; cf. Otto, *Dionysus,* pp. 142, 171–80. Maenads were not just mythological figures; cf. e.g., the inscriptions in Lefkowitz and Fant, *Women's Life,* pp. 113–14, §115; pp. 252–53, §245; also Diod. Sic. 4.3.2–5, below. Kraemer argues that such cults provided outlets for women, who were generally marginalized in ancient society; see "Ecstatics and Ascetics," pp. 9–123, especially pp. 58–73; idem, "Ecstasy and Possession"; cf. idem, "Euoi Saboi."

10. Kraemer, "Ecstatics and Ascetics," pp. 48–57, argues that female participation is much more prominent than male at least until the late hellenistic period.

11. Diod. Sic. 4.3.2–5, in Kraemer, *Maenads,* p. 26.

12. Plut. *R. Q.* 112, *Mor.* 291AB (a spirit of madness in the ivy intoxicates them without wine); Artem. *Oneir.* 2.37. Symmachus speaks of Dionysus as "exciter of women" in his sacred rites (Plut. *T.-T.* 4.6.1, *Mor.* 671C). For the aggressive image of Maenads beating back attackers with their thyrsos wands, see e.g., Plut. *T.-T.* 1.1.3, *Mor.* 614A; cf. especially the analysis of paintings in McNally, "Maenad." For sex role reversal in the cult, see Segal, "Menace"; Henrichs, "Identities," pp. 138–39, 158. For Jewish hostility toward Maenadism, see Sib. Or. 5.55 (probably late first to early second century CE Egypt) (cf. 5.169, 184, 485).

13. Like the cult of Demeter and Persephone at Eleusis. Greco-Roman writers in general seem not to have been hostile to this cult; but Philo *Special Laws* 3.40, associates even this with sexual perversity.

14. Apul. *Metam.* 8.29; cf. P. Foucart, *Des Associations Religieuses chez les Grecs* (Paris: Klincksieck, 1873), p. 5. For sex symbols in Priapus

figures, see Nilsson, *Dionysiac Mysteries,* pp. 34–36; Plutarch also notes that the phallus was honored in Egyptian festivals, since Osiris' was eaten by a fish (*Isis* 18, *Mor.* 358B). Not all cults were guilty of such charges: the emphasis on sexuality in the propaganda of the Isis cult seems to have been on marital fidelity (Plut. *Isis* 2, *Mor.* 351F–352A; T. T. Tinh, "Sarapis and Isis," in *Jewish and Christian Self-Definition,* 3:107; Heyob, *Isis,* pp. 43, 111–27), even though outside writers repeatedly accuse it of immorality (ibid.).

15. Philost. *V. A.* 6, §20; Juv. *Sat.* 2.3; Philo *On Noah's Work as Planter* 148; cf. also Burkert, *Religion,* p. 109; Joscelyn Godwin, *Mystery Religions in the Ancient World* (San Francisco: Harper & Row, 1981), pp. 132, 142. The phallus was part of the traditional procession in the Attic festival of the Dionysia (Plut. *Love of Wealth* 8, *Mor.* 527D); cf. Otto, *Dionysus,* p. 164; Burkert, *Cults,* pp. 104–5; idem, *Religion,* p. 166. Diod. Sic. 4.3 distinguishes between the Dionysus of semiannual women's celebrations and the Dionysus worshiped by noctural drunkenness and sexual indecency (W. L. Willis, *Idol Meat in Corinth,* SBLDS 68 [Chico, Calif.: Scholars, 1985], p. 30). The association between Dionysus and drama could not have diminished suspicions of lewdness, which often characterized public pantomimes (Stambaugh and Balch, *Environment,* p. 134; cf. Friedländer, *Life,* 2:90–95; cf. Aristophanes *Lysistrata*). The orgies of the cult of Dionysus are often mentioned (Otto, *Dionysus,* p. 177; Guthrie, *Orpheus,* p. 117).

16. Nilsson, *Dionysiac Mysteries,* pp. 14–15, points out that Livy has embellished the details; but the event itself is not questioned. See Martin, *Religions,* pp. 96–98; Rawson, "Family," p. 16. For the Senate's decree, see the inscription in Lefkowitz and Fant, *Women's Life,* pp. 250–52, §243.

17. E.g., Hor. *Ode* 1.18; Ach. Tat. *Clit.* 2.3.3 (also connecting wine with Dionysus in this regard, and passion with Eros); Rom. 13:13; Gal. 5:21; 1 Pet. 4:3; Test. Reub. 3:13; Test. Jud. 11:2; 12:3; 13:5–6; 14:1–8; 16:1–4; Num. Rab. 10:10; perhaps Gen. 9:21.

18. Cf. e.g., Walter Burkert, "Orphism and Bacchic Mysteries: New Evidence and Old Problems of Interpretation," in CHSHMC 28 (Berkeley: Center for Hermeneutical Studies, 1977), p. 8. Willis, *Meat,* p. 30, points to the diversity in Dionysiac worship.

19. Epict. *Disc.* 2.20.17 alleges that madness and wine drive the Galli, priests of Cybele. For a Diaspora Jewish perspective on drunkenness and violence at pagan feasts in general, see Philo *On the Contemplative Life* 40–47, who contrasts this with the Therapeutae. Ruck, "Mystery," pp. 47–48; R. G. Wasson, Albert Hofmann, and C. A. P. Ruck, *The Road to Eleusis* (New York: Harcourt Brace Jovanovich, 1978), p. 80, seek to identify the hallucinogen used in the Eleusinian Mysteries; but, while intoxication was employed at Eleusis (Mylonas, *Eleusis,* p. 259), there are weaknesses in Wasson's "LSD" hypothesis (Burkert, *Cults,* pp. 108–9).

20. Cf. Athen. *Deipn.* 4.148bc (including Bacchic revels, music, and drinking). Plato is reported to have said that drinking in excess was becoming only at the feasts of Dionysus (Diog. Laert. *Lives* 3.39). Dionysus was the intoxicator (Plut. *T.-T.* 3.2.1, *Mor.* 648E). Cf. perhaps

Massa, *Pompeii,* p. 108, on Dionysus and wine at Pompeii (the usefulness of this purported connection may depend on the outcome of current analyses of Pompeii's viticulture).

21. Bacchic drunkenness is noted in *Greek Anth.* 4.3.132–33 (cf. 6.257); Orphic Hymn 50.8 speaks of Bacchic ecstasy, and 52.7–8 of omophagy, revel, and dance at triennial feasts; cf. the frenzy offered to Bacchus in Tert. *Apol.* 6.10. Cf. Otto, *Dionysus,* pp. 49–51, 54, 65, 101, 105–6, 127; Guthrie, *Orpheus,* pp. 159–60; Burkert, *Religion,* p. 110.

22. This is true even though devotees of Isis, proclaiming her universalism, identified her with the Phrygian mother of gods (Apul. *Metam.* 11.4–5); although mother-goddesses need not be linked with Cybele—cf. the Germanic tribes in Tac. *Germ.* 40, 45—Cybele was widely recognized as Phrygian, Diog. Laert. *Lives* 6.1.1.

23. Burkert, *Cults,* p. 112–13; cf. Grant, *Religions,* p. xxxvii.

24. Plut. *Par. Stories* 19, *Mor.* 310C; cf. Otto, *Dionysus,* p. 50. The classic example, of course, is the destruction of King Pentheus in Euripides' *Bacchants.*

25. Plut. *fr.* 54, below. Dionysus was commonly hailed as the source of wine, e.g., Orphic Hymn 47.1; 50.1; Ach. Tat. *Clit.* 4.18.5; and it always connoted his presence, according to Martin, *Religions,* p. 94.

26. Plut. *fr.* 54, from Scholia on Hesiod *Works and Days* 368–69, in Plutarch's *Moralia* (LCL).

27. Cf. e.g., the inscription from third century BCE Egypt in Grant, *Religions,* p. 14. This is widely observed, e.g., Nilsson, *Dionysiac Mysteries,* p. 147; Dieter Georgi, "Socioeconomic Reasons for the 'Divine Man' as a Propagandistic Pattern," in *Aspects of Religious Propaganda in Judaism and Early Christianity,* ed. E. Schüssler Fiorenza, UNDCSJCA 2 (Notre Dame: University of Notre Dame, 1976), p. 30; Koester, *Introduction,* 1:181–83 (rightly distinguishing between temples to Dionysus and his mysteries); I. M. Linforth, *The Arts of Orpheus* (Berkeley: University of California, 1941), p. 264; Michael Avi-Yonah, *Hellenism and the East* (Jerusalem: Hebrew University, 1978), p. 36; Stambaugh and Balch, *Environment,* p. 133.

28. Probably more than in Italy, where the Bacchic mysteries are known mainly from art, except for inscriptions set up by people from the Greek east (Nilsson, *Dionysiac Mysteries,* p. 66). On my reading, the evidence for the Bacchic mysteries in Italy (ibid., pp. 66–98) points less explicitly to the sort of religious activity encountered in the mystery cult proper (initiation, etc.) than does that in the Greek east; but this is not entirely relevant to our discussion, since we are here concerned with the region around Ephesus, and so only with the Greek east.

29. Athen. *Deipn.* 11.479c; Nilsson, *Dionysiac Mysteries,* pp. 45–66; cf. Ach. Tat. *Clit.* 2.2 (festival of Dionysus in Phoenicia, which need not be a mystery). For a text from the second century CE east, see Lefkowitz and Fant, *Women's Life,* pp. 252–53, §243.

30. Eurip. *Bacch.* 64, 462–64, 482–83, 604; cf. the connection with Cybele in 78–79. This alleged connection need not be true (cf. Otto, *Dionysus,* pp. 60, 64), but the cult certainly had gained a stronghold in the east; in the mid-first century, the emperor Claudius wrote followers

of Dionysus in Miletus in Asia Minor (Edwin Yamauchi, *The Archaeology of New Testament Cities in Western Asia Minor* [Grand Rapids: Baker, 1980], p. 119); cf. Plut. *Antony* 24.3, cited in Rogers, "Ephesians 5:18," p. 251, on the popularity of Dionysus in Ephesus in the first century BCE.

31. Cf. Grant, *Gods*, p. 39.

32. Stambaugh and Balch, *Environment*, p. 134, citing the second century CE inscription from a suburb of Rome, which includes the wife of a consul and some of her aristocratic relatives; a complaint of Seneca about highborns in Dionysiac shows; and second/third-century sarcophagi of the wealthy decorated with Dionysiac symbolism. Only the first reference necessitates mystery initiation, but it is quite clear. Nilsson, *Dionysiac Mysteries*, p. 147, gives the fullest display of evidence for this.

33. Cf. the reference to Seneca in first-century Rome in note 32 above.

34. Plut. *T.-T.* 4.6.1–2, *Mor.* 671C–672C, cited above. Jewish writers more than repudiated the association, reminding readers that they had resisted the imposition of this hellenistic cult in an earlier period (2 Macc. 6:7; cf. 3 Macc. 2:28–30). Dionysiac symbolism seems to have been transferred to Jewish art (perhaps including the ivy cluster in Ep. Arist. 70), but this need not mean that the original Dionysiac meaning was preserved; a Jew could adopt the name Dionysus as he could adopt any other Greek name (*CIJ* 2:445, §1538, from Egypt), and artistic representations in the Diaspora may have been no different (cf. Leon, *Jews of Rome*, pp. 213–15, who suggests that the sarcophagus may have been bought ready-made). For knowledge of Dionysus in Palestine, see D. Flusser, "Paganism in Palestine," in *JPFC*, pp. 1067–69, 1084–85.

35. Plut. *Educ.* 17, *Mor.* 13A; *Poetry* 11, *Mor.* 31C. Epictetus advises that one first learn abstinence, then test oneself with a little drink to see if one had yet gained self-control (*Disc.* 3.12.11).

36. Sir. 34:25–31; Syr. Men. *Sent.* 52–58; Ab. R. Nathan 37 A; Philo *On Flight and Finding* 32.

37. Mart. *Epig.* 1.56; Diog. Laert. *Lives* 7.7.184, 10.1.15; Apul. *Metam.* 7.12; Plut. *Poetry* 1, *Mor.* 15E; *Bride* 20, *Mor.* 140F; *T.-T.* 1.4.3, *Mor.* 621CD; Sifra Sh. par. 1.100.1.3; b. 'A. Z. 30a; Num. Rab. 10:8; Casson, *Travel*, p. 213; Cary and Haarhoff, *Life*, p. 95; Ruck, "Mystery," p. 41; Safrai, "Home and Family," p. 748. The level of dilution and kind of wine varied greatly; cf. e.g., b. 'A. Z. 30a; Num. Rab. 10:8; S. M. Paul, "Classifications of Wine in Mesopotamian and Rabbinic Sources," *IEJ* 25 (1, 1975): 42–45.

38. Ruck, "Mystery," p. 42; Wasson, Hofmann, and Ruck, *Eleusis*, pp. 89–90.

39. E.g., Sen. *Ep. Lucil.* 58.33; Avi-Yonah, *Hellenism*, p. 137, notes that the Greeks thought barbarians "drank unmixed wine to excess"; cf. Cary and Haarhoff, *Life*, pp. 148–49. The criticism was especially raised in Judaism: Tob. 4:15; Sir. 34:25–31; Syr. Men. *Sent.* 52–58; 1QpHab 11:13–14; 4QpNah 4:4–5 (interpreting Nah. 3:11a metaphorically); Sifra Sh. par. 1.100.1.2–3; Ab. R. Nathan 37 A; b. Ker. 13b; p. Ter. 1:6; Gen. Rab. 43:6; Lev. Rab. 12:1–5; Pes. Rab Kah. 4:4; Philo *Flaccus* 4 (in a religious context). For the idea that alcoholism as a disease

concept existed in late antiquity, see Mark Keller, "The Disease Concept of Alcoholism Revisited," *Journal of Studies on Alcohol* 37 (11, Nov. 1976): 1694–1717.

40. Cf. Hor. *Sat.* 1.3.90–91; Test. Iss. 7:3. One of the three wise men in 1 Esd. 3 says that wine is stronger than anything else (1 Esd. 3:17–24), though the wisest of the three says women and especially truth are stronger. Pittacus' law in Diog. Laert. *Lives* 1.76 probably suggests the recognition that certain offenses were more naturally committed under the influence of intoxication; cf. Sen. *Dial.* 4.20.2; 5.37.1.

41. Crates 10, to Lysis (*CynEp*, pp. 60–61), and Athen. *Deipn.* 1.10e, show that this tradition from Homer's *Odyssey* could be applied in later writers' day to those who drank immoderately. For wine's inducing sleep, see e.g., Hor. *Sat.* 2.1.9; for subduing people, Herod. *Hist.* 1, §§211–12.

42. Jdt. 13, especially v. 5.

43. Ps-Philo 43:6.

44. Chariton *Chaer.* 4.3.8; Jos. *Life* 225, §44. In Hor. *Ep.* 1.5.16–20 this occurs in a list of at least partly *positive* effects of drinking.

45. Cleobulus (c. 600 BCE) is said to have warned that one's words are taken less seriously when one has been drinking (Diog. Laert. *Lives* 1.92). Mart. *Epig.* 12.12 teases that Pollio makes drunken promises that he will not keep once sober.

46. Plut. *T.-T.* 3.intr., *Mor.* 645A. He argues that wine gets people to talk more, open up more, and thus get to know one another better (3.intr., *Mor.* 645AC). Wine changes one's character as it gradually warms the whole body (Plut. *Statecraft* 3, *Mor.* 799B) (the language of wine's "heating" was typical, e.g., Cic. *Tusc. Disp.* 5.41.118; Sen. *Dial.* 4.20.2, following Plato).

47. Anacharsis to Hipparchus 3.1–3 (*CynEp*, p. 41); Philost. *V. A.* 2, §36; Lucr. *Nat.* 3.476–83; Philo *On Noah's Work as Planter* 148. Plut. *Isis* 6, *Mor.* 353C, charges that drunkenness crazes men, driving them "out of their senses" (LCL). P. Ter. 1:6 links a drunken man's loss of sensibility to the inability of a blind person to distinguish kinds of produce.

48. Isoc. *Demon.* 32 (LCL), further complaining that the soul stumbles because the mind is impaired. Cf. Herod. *Hist.* 4, §84: the Spartans charge that Cleomenes became insane because "by consorting with the Scythians he became a drinker of strong wine" (LCL).

49. Jos. *Ant.* 1.6.3, §141; Jub. 7:7; and Gen. Rab. 36:4 (on Noah, with Gen. 9:21); Mart. *Epig.* 3.16.3; 68.5–10; cf. 82; Philo *Moses* 2.162; Sext. Emp. *Out. Pyrr.* 1.109. In b. Pes. 110b a man who drank too much lost track of his drinks and took an even number of cups; this, according to the superstition, delivered him into the power of the demons his ex-wife was trying to unleash on him.

50. Diog. Laert. *Lives* 7.1.26, citing Zeno according to Hecato. Cf. Philo *On Flight and Finding* 32, who also argues that the wise man, if compelled to become drunk, will maintain sobriety in his inebriation.

51. Diog. Laert. *Lives* 10.119 (LCL), citing Epicurus' *Symposium.*

52. Sifre Deut. 43.8.1 (a parable about a king's son). In Plato *Symp.* 176D, the physician Eryximachus declares that drunkenness is

harmful to the body; Jos. *Ant.* 13.15.5, §398, charges that Alexander Jannaeus "fell ill from heavy drinking, and for three years he was afflicted with a quartan fever" (LCL).

53. Sen. *Dial.* 1.3.2 (LCL); this naturally makes sense as a good Stoic thing to have said. On drunkenness as part of the pleasurable life of a foolish, nonvirtuous man, see Sen. *Dial.* 7.12.3.

54. Ahikar 2.9–10 (Syr. A; Arabic 2:12–13).

55. Test. Jud. 14:1–4; cf. Sir. 19:2; see the note above on wine and sexual immorality.

56. P. W. van der Horst, "Hellenistic Parallels to the Acts of the Apostles," *JSNT* 25 (Oct. 1985): 55, cites Plut. *R. Q.* 112, *Mor.* 291B; *Def. Orac.* 40, *Mor.* 432E; *Sep. Con.* 4, *Mor.* 150C; Lucian *Nigrinus* 5; Iamblichus *De mysteriis* 3.25; Philo *On Drunkenness* 146; wine could induce ecstasy in Eurip. *fr.* 265; Macrob. *Satur.* 1.18.1. That alcohol was used to induce the possession trance of some ancient Near Eastern ecstatics may even be suggested in Isa. 28:7 (cf. 29:9?); Mic. 2:11; cf. Amos 6:6 (for luxurious party habits of the wealthy priesthood in the north).

57. Plut. *Dial. on Love* 16, *Mor.* 758EF (expounding Plato); Burkert, *Religion,* p. 111. Despite this distinction, Aune, *Prophecy,* p. 21, observes, "the two were frequently confused in antiquity." Since Livy elsewhere reads prophecy into ecstatic speech, his account of prophetic activity in the Bacchic excess in second century BCE Italy may also reflect confusion of categories (ibid., p. 42). The fact that "confusion" could arise, however, means that not all people distinguished the two.

58. Burkert, *Religion,* pp. 109–10; cf. ibid., p. 292; Martin, *Religions,* pp. 93–94. In (Ps)Plut. *Par. Stories* 19, *Mor.* 310B, the offended Dionysus casts a man into a state of drunken rage that leads the man into an impious act that costs him his life. H. W. Parke, *A History of the Delphic Oracle* (Oxford: Basil Blackwell, 1939), pp. 335–46, points to the strong links between Dionysus and the Delphic oracle (cf. e.g., Plut. *E at Delphi* 9, *Mor.* 388E). Cf. Kroeger, "Cults," p. 34 (although I doubt that 1 Cor. 11:21 refers to ritual drunkenness; it is probably more related to the general custom of some people drinking too much at parties!).

59. Eurip. *Bacch.* 298 *(mantis).* Frenzy appears in the Orphic Hymns with other deities as well, such as Pan (11.21), Pluto (18.17), and the mother of the gods (27.13).

60. Eurip. *Bacch.* 299 *(mantikēn).* This particular language is used in earliest Christian tradition only of pagan inspiration (Acts 16:16).

61. E.g., Philo *On the Creation* 71; *Allegorical Interpretation* 3.82. See M. E. Isaacs, *The Concept of Spirit: A Study of Pneuma in Hellenistic Judaism and its Bearing on the New Testament,* HeyM 1 (London: Heythrop College, 1976), p. 50.

62. Philo *On the Contemplative Life* 84: the choirs of the Therapeutae sing antiphonally, and when they have finished their separate parts in this feast, having drunk "as in the Bacchic rites" of the strong wine of God's love, they join together as a single choir.

63. The point is especially stressed by Rogers, "Eph. 5:18," passim. A. D. Nock, "The Vocabulary of the New Testament," *JBL* 52 (1933): 134, is, of course, correct to note that the standard language for

divine possession in Greek paganism is never used in the NT; any comparison would be by way of contrast.

64. Barth, *Ephesians,* 2:580.

65. The language of this prohibition may derive from LXX Prov. 23:31 (the MT is quite different); see J. A. Robinson, *St Paul's Epistle to the Ephesians,* 2d ed. (London: James Clarke, 1904), p. 121.

66. The language of one being "filled with" a spirit, particularly the divine Spirit, appears elsewhere in early Jewish literature, e.g., Sir. 39:6; 48:12; cf. Sir. 35:15 (the Law); Test. Asher 1:9 (an evil spirit's venom).

67. Cary and Haarhoff, *Life,* p. 155; cf. Arist. *Pol.* 8.5.9–10, 1340b. It was less significant to the Romans, for whom it was primarily entertainment. For a survey of data on Greco-Roman music, see Friedländer, *Life,* 2:337–65.

68. Sir. 35:3, 5–6; cf. 40:20; Plut. *Bride* 38, *Mor.* 143D. Dio Chrys. *32d Disc.* §55, even suggests that being "intoxicated by song" is more dangerous than being "crazed by wine" (LCL). This could suggest that Eph. 5:18–19 is antibanquet rather than anticultic; banquets were often held at night, and could involve sexual excesses. It is mainly the contrast between drunkenness and being filled with the Spirit that leads us to see a religious context here, but the matter is admittedly open to question.

69. Quint. 1.10.16.

70. Plut. *On Music* 44, *Mor.* 1147A. Philo *On Creation* 126, compares the seven-stringed lyre to the choir of seven planets (of course, both he and Josephus relate the zodiac to the temple, etc.; astrological numerology was part of his scheme).

71. E.g., to Aphrodite and Dionysus; cf. Athen. *Deipn.* 14.631d. Ecstatic dance is associated with the Eleusinian Demeter (Orphic Hymn 40.15) and of Dionysian revelry (Orphic Hymn 52.7; cf. Burkert, *Religion,* p. 166, on vase paintings) and virtually all public celebrations of the mysteries (Martin, *Religions,* p. 61). The practice is far more ancient than our period; cf. "The Instruction of Ani," trans. John Wilson, *ANET,* p. 420.

72. Quint. 1.11.18–19. For a discussion of dancing forms, see Plut. *T.-T.* 9.15, *Mor.* 747A–748D.

73. See Cary and Haarhoff, *Life,* pp. 155, 177. J. T. Townsend, "Ancient Education in the Time of the Early Roman Empire," in *Catacombs and Colosseum,* p. 142, says that Romans distrusted too much musical education (Sallust 25.2, 5), but some training continued so school children could "supply choral singing in the various religious festivals." Rogers, "Eph. 5:18," p. 257, contrasts Eph. 5:19 with "the raving of drunken worshipers singing the praises of Dionysus." In a far earlier period, cf. A. F. Rainey, "The Kingdom of Ugarit," *BA* 28 (Dec. 1965): 124; O. R. Gurney, *The Hittites* (Baltimore: Penguin, 1972), pp. 153–55, 202.

74. Plut. *T.-T.* 1.5.2, *Mor.* 623B; cf. *Isis* 69, *Mor.* 378F *(bancheuontes).* For music in processions of Isis, e.g., Apul. *Metam.* 11.9; for Eleusis, cf. Mylonas, *Eleusis,* pp. 241, 261; for Cybele's drums, e.g., Lucr. *Nat.* 2.618–20; Orphic Hymn 27.11; Burkert, *Religion,* p. 178.

75. Lefkowitz and Fant, *Women's Life,* p. 30, record an inscription, 86 BCE, in which a female harpist is honored for her services to Delphi.

76. Friedländer, *Life,* 1:231.

77. E.g., 1 Esd. 5:59–60; 2 Macc. 10:38; Sir. 47:8; Jos. *Ant.* 11.3.8, §62; 20.9.6, §§216–18; Test. Job 43; m. R. H. 4:4; cf. 1QS 10 (10.10 associates it with entering the covenant and speaking God's decrees or precepts); 1QH passim. It is standard in pictures of angelic activity in heaven (e.g., Test. Abr. 20 A), and characterizes also the world to come (Sib. Or. 3:715, 726 [probably second century BCE]; t. Pisha 8:22; b. Taan. 31a; Sanh. 91b; Pes. Rab Kah. 27:5; Pes. Rab. 21:1; Num. Rab. 15:11; Koh. Rab. 1:11, §1). It is generally thought that some Christian hymns appear in the NT, though the extent and redaction of these are disputed (e.g., the Lukan infancy hymns in Hans Conzelmann, *History of Primitive Christianity,* p. 74; christological hymns in J. T. Sanders, *The New Testament Christological Hymns* [Cambridge: Cambridge University, 1971]); Barth, *Ephesians,* 2:582, sees hymns in Ephesians as modeling Paul's exhortation to the readers here. But the clearest examples, in my opinion, are in Revelation. Postbiblical psalms (such as Pss. 151–55 in *OTP* 2:609–24) bear many resemblances to the earlier biblical ones. Hymns were, of course, used in much Greek religion; e.g., the view attributed to Pythagoras in Diog. Laert. *Lives* 3.1.24; Cleanthes' Hymn to Zeus (Stobaeus *Eclogae* 1.1.12, in Grant, *Religions,* p. 154).

78. Jewish music seems to have often been joyful, inappropriate to a time of sorrow (Sir. 22:6).

79. Also Jos. *Ant.* 6.8.2, §§166–69; cf. Test. Job 14. In Ps-Philo 60.2–3, David's song directly addresses the demon, suggesting that this writer took the singing as prophetic. On the link between music and inspiration, which could carry over into prophetic inspiration, see below.

80. Diogenes the Cynic criticizes a musician for tuning an instrument while failing to provide harmony in his soul (Diog. Laert. *Lives* 6.2.65).

81. Ep. Arist. 286 (see the comments of Hadas, *Aristeas,* pp. 212–13); cf. Sir. 40:21; Epict. *Disc.* 1.16.15.

82. Sib. Or. 3.246, probably second century BCE. A much later rabbi in Pes. Rab Kah. 7:4 suggests that David's midnight harp playing (based on Ps. 119:62) was to stir everyone's hearts for Torah.

83. These were standard in the cult of Cybele (Lucr. *Nat.* 2.618–20; Mart. *Epig.* 14.204; cf. Eurip. *Bacch.* 59; Hor. *Ode* 1.18.14; Lucian *SyrG* 50; *Greek Anth.* 6.219–20; the "Syrian goddess" in Apul. *Metam.* 8.24, 30; probably the Egyptian letter, 245 BCE, in Deissmann, *Light,* p. 164, unless Isis is in view; perhaps Juv. *Sat.* 3.63) and perhaps Dionysus in contrast with calmer cults (Guthrie, *Orpheus,* p. 40; Priapus in Petr. *Sat.* 22–23), but were used in Jewish worship as well (e.g., 1 Esd. 5:59–60; 1 Macc. 4:54; Jos. *Ant.* 7.12.3, §305–6; cf. 1 Macc. 13:51).

84. Jdt. 16:2; 1 Esd. 5:59–60; 1 Macc. 13:51 (including hymns and songs); Jos. *War* 2.15.4, §321; m. Kel. 15:6; b. Suk. 50b, 51a; cf. 1QS 10.9. In heavenly worship, cf. 2 En. 17:1 A and J. Instruments were used in ancient Near Eastern music before the middle of the third

millennium BCE (Albright, *Yahweh*, p. 2). David played (*psallein*) on his harp in Jos. *Ant.* 6.8.2, §§166–69. Paul refers to musical instruments. 1 Cor. 13:1 could suggest the use of cymbals in Christian worship, but the allusion would also have made sense to the Corinthians without it (especially given Vitruvius' report on Corinthian bronze, *On Arch.* 5.5.1, 7–8 in Murphy-O'Connor, *Corinth*, pp. 75–76; but cf. William Harris, " 'Sounding Brass' and Hellenistic Technology," *BAR* 8 [1, 1982]: 38–41; W. W. Klein, "Noisy Gong or Acoustic Vase? A Note on 1 Corinthians 13.1," *NTS* 32 [2, April 1986]: 286–89).

85. We cannot be certain what instruments might have been in use in the average synagogue congregation, or whether corporate singing was ever practiced; our ancient reports of synagogues suggest that they were houses of study and lectures, personal prayer, and in some cases community centers, but corporate singing is not attested. E. P. Sanders even questions whether corporate prayers were recited in synagogues in this period (*Jesus to Mishnah*, pp. 72–76).

86. Philo *On the Contemplative Life* 84. Of course, Philo's depiction is no doubt colored by his thoroughgoing hellenistic cast; his representations of the Essenes, like Josephus' representations of Jewish sects, are filtered through a thoroughly hellenistic grid. Russell Spittler, in *OTP* 1:833, follows M. Philonenko in suggesting that the Testament of Job originated among the Therapeutae, though B. Schaller has criticized this position (see J. J. Collins, "The Testamentary Literature in Recent Scholarship," in *Early Judaism and Its Modern Interpreters*, SBLBMI 2 [Atlanta: Scholars, 1986], p. 276, siding with Schaller).

87. Epiphanius, following Eusebius (*Eccl Hist* 2.17), actually thought Philo was writing about Christians at this point (R. A. Pritz, *Nazarene Jewish Christianity*, SPB [Jerusalem: Magnes, 1988], p. 39).

88. Cf. Plato's "oracle-singers" (Aune, *Prophecy*, p. 38); cf. also the link between music and prophecy claimed for Dionysiac frenzies by Otto, *Dionysus*, pp. 143–45. Poetry is associated with inspiration (with the analogy of wine's frenzy) in Plut. *Poetry* 1, *Mor.* 15E; but oracles at Delphi were no longer given in verse (Plut. *Or. at Delphi*, *Mor.* 394D–409D). For a modern example concerning medium possession from the Shona people in what is now Zimbabwe, see Michael Gelfand, "Psychiatric Disorders as Recognized by the Shona," in *Magic, Faith, and Healing*, pp. 156, 162.

89. J. Lindblom, *Prophecy in Ancient Israel* (Philadelphia: Fortress, 1962), p. 99; H. B. Huffmon, "Prophecy in the Mari Letters," *BA* 31 (Dec. 1968): 112; cf. Albright, *Yahweh*, p. 252.

90. E.g., Kitchen, *Bible in Its World*, p. 119; S. M. Paul, "Prophets and Prophecy," *EncJud* 13:1156.

91. Ps-Philo 32:14; Mek. 14:31; 15:1 (as cited in Morton Smith, *Tannaitic Parallels to the Gospels* [Philadelphia: SBL, 1951], p. 64); p. Sot. 5:4, §1 ("the Holy Spirit" was a common rabbinic designation for the Spirit of prophecy). Pes. Rab. 9:2 asserts that God puts the praise in the mouths of his people. Music can be associated with joy (Sir. 22:6).

92. Linforth, *Orpheus*, pp. 165–66, 269–70; cf. Guthrie, *Orpheus*, p. 21; for his head making music posthumously, cf. e.g., Lucian *IgnBC*

11–12; *Dance* 51. On Orphism, see especially the hellenistic-Roman texts (mainly very late) in Grant, *Religions,* pp. 105–11; cf. reports on earlier figures in Leotychidas 3 in Plut. *SSpart., Mor.* 224E, *Notes on Empedocles, fr.* 24 (from Hippol. *Ref.* 5.20.5 [LCL]); Diog. Laert. *Lives* 6.1–4. Current scholarship speaks much more cautiously about Orphic mysteries, though it is clear that Orphic ideas spread in the hellenistic age (see Martin, *Religions,* p. 102; L. J. Alderink, *Creation and Salvation in Ancient Orphism,* APAACS 8 [Chico, Calif.: Scholars, 1981], p. 19; Linforth, *Orpheus,* pp. 172–73, 262–63, 266, 291–93; cf. the data in Guthrie, *Orpheus,* pp. 9–16; contrast Ugo Bianchi, "L'Orphisme a Existé," in *Selected Essays on Gnosticism, Dualism and Mysteriography,* SHRSN 38 [Leiden: Brill, 1978], pp. 187–95; cf. H. C. Sheldon, *The Mystery Religions and the New Testament* [New York: Abingdon, 1918], p. 18; E. R. Goodenough, *The Church in the Roman Empire* [New York: Cooper Square, 1970], p. 8). Orphic poetry may have been used in the Eleusinian mysteries (Orphic Hymn 18.19 [maybe used to summon Plouton back to Eleusis]; Victor Magnien, *Les Mystères d'Eleusis,* 3d ed. [Paris: Payot, 1950], p. 52; cf. the place of Persephone in the rites of Orpheus, in Linforth, *Orpheus,* p. 171) (though our present Orphic Hymns may date to the late third century CE; see A. N. Athanassakis in *The Orphic Hymns,* SBLTT 12, SBLGRRS 4 [Missoula, Mont.: Scholars, 1977], pp. vii–viii, xi).

93. Artem. *Oneir.* 2.35. For Apollo as god of music, cf. Lucian *Swans*; Dio Chrys. *32d Disc.* §§56–57; *Greek Anth.* §2, lines 266–70 (sixth century CE); associated with prophecy, Orphic Hymn 34.4 (cf. Hermes, 28.4). He is often linked with the Muses (e.g., Dio Chrys. *32d Disc.* §56; Marc. Aur. *Med.* 11.11).

94. E.g., Hor. *Ode* 1.26; cf. 2.12.13; 3.1.3–4 (cf. 3.3.69–72), 3.14.13–15; 4.8.29, 4.9.21. Though perhaps less prominent than in earlier texts, the Muses are still frequently praised in the imperial period; e.g., Juv. *Sat.* 7.1–10, 36–39; they also appear in literary allusions in some Jewish texts: Philo *On Noah's Work as Planter* 129; cf. *CIJ* 1:cxxiii (decorations on a pagan sarcophagus reused by Jews in Rome).

95. Guthrie, *Orpheus,* p. 113. For Orphic influence on the Dionysian cult (though not all the evidence is early or unambiguous), see Nilsson, *Dionysiac Mysteries,* pp. 133–43; cf. Burkert, "Orphism," p. 8; Guthrie, *Orpheus,* pp. 48, 258; for an older view, see Thomas Taylor, *The Eleusinian and Bacchic Mysteries: A Dissertation,* 4th ed. [New York: J. W. Bouton, 1891], p. 187; see the qualifications in Linforth, *Orpheus,* pp. 171 (not before 300 BCE), 264 (diversity of relationship). The issue of Dionysiac influences in the Eleusianian mysteries is still open to question (against: see Mylonas, *Eleusis,* pp. 241, 278; for: Wasson, Hofmann, and Ruck, *Eleusis,* pp. 123–26); probably they existed but were minimal (cf. Orphic Hymn 42.5–10) Cf. perhaps also Orphic Hymn 30.6–7, where Persephone is Dionysus' mother, but this may be due to the conflation of geographical variants of myths (Günther Zuntz, *Persephone: Three Essays on Religion and Thought in Magna Graecia* [Oxford: Clarendon, 1971], p. 80); in 29.6–7, she is mother of the Furies by Zeus. In Athen. *Deipn.* 1.30ab, Dionysus is said to be Priapus, whereas in

5.201d, Priapus stands at his side; linkage may have been more important than differentiation. So fluid was Orphic imagery that the Orpheus figure appears as a possibly soteriological symbol in third-century Jewish and Christian art, linked in the former with David and the latter with Christ (Bezalel Narkiss, "Pagan, Christian, and Jewish Elements in the Art of Ancient Synagogues," in *The Synagogue in Late Antiquity,* ed. Lee I. Levine [Philadelphia: American Schools of Oriental Research, 1986], pp. 184–85).

96. Between Apollo and Orpheus; see Guthrie, *Orpheus,* pp. 42–48; Otto, *Dionysus,* pp. 202–8; Marcel Detienne, "Un Polytheisme récrit. Entre Dionysos et Apollon: mort et vie d'Orphée," *ASSR* 30 (59–1, Jan. 1985): 65–75. Apollo is also called Dionysus, according to Plut. *E at Delphi* 9, *Mor.* 389A.

97. Plut. *G. Q.* 56, *Mor.* 303, has them sail from the land of the Ephesians; Isoc. *Panath.* 193, *Or.* 12, associates them with the Scythians, which is their usual approximate geographical setting (cf. Herod. *Hist.* 4, §§111–17). Strabo *Geog.* 11.5.1 gives different opinions on where they are said to live, and admits (11.5.4) that few reputable historians still knew where they were; but notes that Ephesus' founding was ascribed to them (ibid.).

98. Lefkowitz, *Women in Myth,* pp. 22–23; in Greek historians, see D. J. Sobol, *The Amazons of Greek Mythology* (South Brunswick: A. S. Barnes, 1972), pp. 81–90; for the question of their actual existence, see ibid., pp. 113–47 (with Tatian 32, I am skeptical that they existed). Isoc. *Panath.* 193, *Or.* 12, reports Athens' war with the Amazons as if it had happened. Plut. *Pericles* 31.4 claims that Pheidias portrayed Pericles fighting an Amazon; perhaps this is intended to parallel Pericles with Theseus in Athens (cf. Plut. *Thes.* 26–28). Cf. Pes. Rab Kah. 9:1, a late tradition that reports a place inhabited entirely by women (perhaps in Africa; not Lesbos), which dissuaded Alexander from waging war on them.

99. Sobol, *Amazons,* pp. 110–11; cf. Pomeroy, *Goddesses,* p. 5. For stories of women's bravery, including defending a city, see Plut. *Bravery of Women, Mor.* 242E–263C; for comments on a mythical woman warrior of the east (Assyria), see Juv. *Sat.* 2.108; for evidence of some women gladiators in Rome, see *Empire,* ed. Sherk, p. 226, §172E.

100. Sext. Emp. *Out. Pyrr.* 3.217.

101. Crates 28, to Hipparchia (*CynEp,* pp. 78–79).

102. E.g., *Greek Anth.* 6.220; as mother of Zeus (Jove), she was assimilated to Rhea (Eurip. *Bacch.* 59; *Greek Anth.* 6. 219–20; Mart. *Epig.* 9.39) of Greek myth.

103. *Greek Anth.* 6.220; Lucian *SyrG* 51; Lucr. *Nat.* 2.614–15; *Rhet. ad Herenn.* 4.49.62; Epict. *Disc.* 2.20.17, 19; Juv. *Sat.* 2.110–16; for further references, see above, ch. 2, on 1 Cor. 14:34–35.

104. E.g., Diog. Laert. *Lives* 6.1.1; Lucr. *Nat.* 2.611, 618–20. F. C. Grant, *Roman Hellenism and the New Testament* (New York: Scribner's, 1962), p. 40, says that the mysteries built around her were hellenistic, but that in Anatolia her cult relapsed into wild barbarism in the hellenistic age.

105. W. M. Ramsay, *Pauline and Other Studies in Early Church History* (New York: A. C. Armstrong, 1906), pp. 125–60; cf. G. B. Caird, *A Commentary on the Revelation of Saint John the Divine,* HNTC (New York: Harper & Row, 1966), p. 29.

106. Ach. Tat. *Clit.* 6.21.2. She may have had mysteries as well as the regular public worship; see Arnold, *Ephesians,* p. 26. For the images of Artemis and similar craftsmanship signifying her importance in Ephesus (Acts 19:24), see Jack Finegan, *Light from the Ancient Past* (Princeton: Princeton University, 1946), p. 267; Yamauchi, *Cities,* p. 88; Lake and Cadbury, *Commentary,* p. 245; and the appropriate material in R. Fleischer, *Artemis von Ephesos und verwandte Kultstatuen aus Anatolien und Syrien,* EPROER 35 (Leiden: Brill, 1973); for the economic ramifications of this cult and their relation to Acts 19, see e.g., R. Oster, "The Ephesian Artemis as an opponent of Early Christianity," *JAC* 19 (1976): 24–44; R. N. Longenecker, *The Ministry and Message of Paul* (Grand Rapids: Zondervan, 1971), p. 70; Reicke, *Era,* pp. 230–31; Lake and Cadbury, *Commentary,* p. 247; and the discussion of guild associations in this context in Judge, *Social Pattern,* p. 40; MacMullen, *Relations,* pp. 74–76. Those with vested economic interests were naturally the opponents in Acts 19, as in Pliny *Ep.* 10.96, or the Meccan opposition to Mohammed (Alfred Guillaume, *Islam* [New York: Penguin, 1956], p. 31). Barth, *Ephesians,* suggests that the Ephesian Artemis necessitated that the husband-wife section be as long as it is, but this is ultimately hard to say.

107. Cf. the inscription discussed in F. Sokolowski, "A New Testimony on the Cult of Artemis of Ephesus," *HTR* 58 (4, Oct. 1965): 427–31.

108. L. R. Taylor, "Artemis of Ephesus," in *Beginnings,* p. 251; Bruce, *Acts,* p. 399, n. 59 (following K. Wernicke).

109. See Stambaugh and Balch, *Environment,* p. 150; Grant, *Gods,* p. 28. Among the places is Corinth (Paus. *Desc. Greece* 2.2.6, in Murphy-O'Connor, *Corinth,* p. 23).

110. This temple was quite famous: Jos. *Ant.* 15.4.1, §89; Sib. Or. 5.293–94, 296–97 (probably late first to early second century CE); Strabo *Geog.* 14.1.20–22; cf. Herod. *Hist.* 1, §26, for the dedication of the whole city to Artemis.

111. Grant, *Gods,* p. 28; Yamauchi, *Cities,* p. 87; cf. pp. 103–4.

112. A variety of explanations for the bulbous appendages on her torso have been proposed (see Arnold, *Ephesians,* p. 25; Stambaugh and Balch, *Environment,* p. 150; Grant, *Gods,* p. 28; Yamauchi, *Cities,* p. 106), from breasts (Macrobius on Isis) to male genitals (though without the limb itself) to eggs to fruits, but all these explanations basically represent fertility; others have proposed an astrological significance, which seems less likely from their form, though it would fit her role as a cosmic savior deity. She could nevertheless remain associated with virginity (Ach. Tat. *Clit.* 6.21.2; a Greek perspective?); but that virgins could be associated with fertility has been shown in other cultures as well; cf. Eric Wolf, "The Virgin of Guadalupe: A Mexican National Symbol," *JAF* 71 (1958): 34–39 (in *Reader in Religion,* p. 114).

113. E.g., E. D. Reeder, "The Mother of the Gods and a Hellenistic Bronze Matrix," *AJA* 91 (3, 1987): 423–40; cf. F. V. Filson, "Ephesus and the New Testament," *BA* 8 (3, Sept. 1945): 75; Taylor, "Artemis," p. 253; Murray, *Stages,* p. 80; Tarn, *Civilisation,* p. 140. In contrast to Ramsay's view, some maintain that Artemis and Cybele were distinct (Yamauchi, *Cities,* pp. 68–69), but the great assimilation of deities that occurred in this era warns us not to press the distinction too strongly. She may also have become associated in this period with Agrippina; cf. L. J. Kreitzer, "A Numismatic Clue to Acts 19.23–41. The Ephesian Cistophori of Claudius and Agrippina," *JSNT* 30 (1987): 59–70.

114. Gardner, *Women,* pp. 67–68.

115. R. A. Kearsley, "Asiarchs, *Archiereis,* and the *Archiereiai* of Asia," *GRBS* 27 (2, Summer 1986): 183–92.

# Bibliography of Sources Cited


Abineno, J. L. C. "The State, According to Romans Thirteen." *South East Asia Journal of Theology* 14 (1, 1972): 23–27.

Abrahamsen, Valerie Ann. "The Rock Reliefs and the Cult of Diana at Philippi." Th.D. dissertation, Harvard Divinity School, 1986.

_________. "Women at Philippi: The Pagan and Christian Evidence." *Journal of Feminist Studies in Religion* 3 (2, 1987): 17–30.

Achilles Tatius. *Clitophon and Leucippe*. Translated by S. Gaselee. Loeb Classical Library. London: Wm. Heinemann; New York: G. P. Putnam's Sons, 1917.

Albright, William Foxwell. "The Antiquity of Mosaic Law." Pp. 148–55 in *The Bible in Its Literary Milieu*. Edited by Vincent L. Tollers and John R. Maier. Grand Rapids: Eerdmans, 1979.

_________. *The Biblical Period from Abraham to Ezra*. New York: Harper & Row, 1963.

_________. *Yahweh and the Gods of Canaan*. The Jordan Lectures 1965. Garden City, N.Y.: Doubleday & Co., 1968.

Alderink, Larry J. *Creation and Salvation in Ancient Orphism*. The American Philological Association, American Classical Studies 8. Chico, Calif.: Scholars, 1981.

Alexander, P. S. "The Targumim and Early Exegesis of 'Sons of God' in Genesis 6." *Journal of Jewish Studies* 23 (1, 1972): 60–71.

Alexander, William Menzies. *Demonic Possession in the New Testament: Its Historical, Medical, and Theological Aspects*. Grand Rapids: Baker Book House, 1980; Edinburgh: T. & T. Clark, 1902.

Allison, Robert W. "Let Women be Silent in the Churches (1 Cor. 14:33b–36): What did Paul Really Say, and What did it Mean?" *Journal for the Study of the New Testament* 32 (1988): 27–60.

Alsdurf, James and Phyllis. *Battered Into Submission*. Downers Grove, Ill.: InterVarsity, 1989.

_________. "Battered into Submission." *Christianity Today* (June 16, 1989): 24–27.

Angus, S. *The Mystery-Religions and Christianity*. New York: Charles Scribner's Sons, 1928.

*The Ante-Nicene Fathers: Translations of the Writings of the Fathers down to A.D. 325.* 10 vols. Edited by Alexander Roberts and James Donaldson. Revised by A. Cleveland Coxe. Grand Rapids: Eerdmans, 1975.

"Apocalypse of Adam." Translated by G. MacRae. 1:707–19 in *The Old Testament Pseudepigrapha.* 2 vols. Edited by James H. Charlesworth. Garden City, N.Y.: Doubleday & Co., 1983–85.

"Apocalypse of Moses/Life of Adam and Eve." Greek text. Pp. 1–23 in *Apocalypses Apocryphae.* Edited by Konstantin von Tischendorf. Hildesheim: Georg Olms Verlagsbuchhandlung, 1966.

Applebaum, S. "The Organization of the Jewish Communities in the Diaspora." Pp. 465–503 in *The Jewish People in the First Century: Historical Geography, Political History, Social, Cultural and Religious Life and Institutions.* 2 vols. Edited by S. Safrai and M. Stern with D. Flusser and W. C. van Unnik. Section 1 of Compendia Rerum Iudaicarum ad Novum Testamentum. Vol. 1: Assen: Van Gorcum & Co., B.V., 1974. Vol. 2: Philadelphia: Fortress, 1976.

_________. "The Social and Economic Status of the Jews in the Diaspora." Pp. 701–27 in *The Jewish People in the First Century: Historical Geography, Political History, Social, Cultural and Religious Life and Institutions.* 2 vols. Edited by S. Safrai and M. Stern with D. Flusser and W. C. van Unnik. Section 1 of Compendia Rerum Iudaicarum ad Novum Testamentum. Vol. 1: Assen: Van Gorcum & Co., B.V., 1974. Vol. 2: Philadelphia: Fortress, 1976.

Apuleius. *The Golden Ass.* Translated by W. Adlington. Revised by S. Gaselee. Loeb Classical Library. Cambridge: Harvard University, 1915.

*Aristeas to Philocrates: Letter of Aristeas.* Edited and translated by Moses Hadas. Jewish Apocryphal Literature. New York: Harper & Brothers, for The Dropsie College for Hebrew and Cognate Learning, 1951.

Aristotle. *Works.* 23 vols. Translated by G. Cyril Armstrong et al. Loeb Classical Library. London: G. P. Putnam's Sons; Cambridge: Harvard University, 1926–70.

Arnold, Clinton E. *Ephesians: Power and Magic: The Concept of Power in Ephesians in Light of its Historical Setting.* Society for New Testament Studies Monograph 63. Cambridge: Cambridge University, 1989.

Artemidori Daldiani. *Onirocriticon Libri.* V. Bibliotheca Scriptorum Graecorum et Romanorum Teubneriana. Leipzig: B. G. Tuebneri, 1963.

Artemidorus. *The Interpretation of Dreams (Oneirocritica).* Translated with commentary by Robert J. White. Noyes Classical Studies. Park Ridge, N.J.: Noyes, 1975.

Arthur, Marilyn B. "Classics" (review essay). *Signs* 2 (2, 1976): 382–403.

_________. "Early Greece: The Origins of the Western Attitude Toward Women." Pp. 7–58 in *Women in the Ancient World: The Arethusa Papers.* Edited by John Peradotto and J. P. Sullivan. SUNY Series in Classical Studies. Albany, N.Y.: State University of New York, 1984.

Athenaeus. *The Deipnosophists.* 7 vols. Translated by Charles Burton Gulick. Loeb Classical Library. London: Wm. Heinemann; New York: G. P. Putnam's Sons, 1927.

Aune, David E. *The New Testament in its Literary Environment.* Library of Early Christianity 8. Philadelphia: Westminster, 1987.

———. *Prophecy in Early Christianity and the Ancient Mediterranean World.* Grand Rapids: Eerdmans, 1983.

Avi-Yonah, Michael. *Hellenism and the East: Contacts and Interrelations from Alexander to the Roman Conquest.* Ann Arbor, Mich.: University Microfilms International; for Jerusalem: Institute of Languages, Literature and the Arts, The Hebrew University, 1978.

Ayers, David. "The Inevitability of Failure: The Assumptions and Implementations of Modern Feminism." Pp. 312–31 in *Recovering Biblical Manhood and Womanhood: A Response to Evangelical Feminism.* Edited by John Piper and Wayne Grudem. Wheaton, Ill.: Crossway Books, 1991.

*The Babylonian Talmud.* Edited by Isidore Epstein. London: Soncino, 1948.

Baer, Richard A., Jr. *Philo's Use of the Categories Male and Female.* Arbeiten zur Literatur und Geschichte des Hellenistichen Judentums 3. Leiden: E. J. Brill, 1970.

Balch, David L. "Household Codes." Pp. 25–50 in *Greco-Roman Literature and the New Testament: Selected Forms and Genres.* Edited by David E. Aune. Society of Biblical Literature Sources for Biblical Study 21. Atlanta: Scholars, 1988.

———. *Let Wives be Submissive: The Domestic Code in 1 Peter.* Society of Biblical Literature Monograph Series 26. Chico, Calif.: Scholars, 1981.

Balsdon, J. P. V. D. "Women in Imperial Rome." *History Today* 10 (1, January 1960): 24–31.

Bamberger, Bernard J. *Proselytism in the Talmudic Period.* Foreword by Julian Morgenstern. New York: KTAV, 1968. Original edition Cincinnati: Hebrew Union College, 1939.

Banks, Robert. *Paul's Idea of Community: The Early House Churches in their Historical Setting.* Grand Rapids: Eerdmans, 1980.

Barclay, William. *Train Up a Child: Educational Ideals in the Ancient World.* Philadelphia: Westminster, 1959.

Barker, Margaret. "Some Reflections upon the Enoch Myth." *Journal for the Study of the Old Testament* 15 (1980): 7–29.

Barrow, R. H. *Slavery in the Roman Empire.* New York: Barnes & Noble, 1968. First edition 1928.

Bartchy, S. Scott. *MALLON CHRĒSAI: First-Century Slavery and the Interpretation of 1 Corinthians 7:21.* Society of Biblical Literature Dissertation Series 11. Missoula, Mont.: Society of Biblical Literature, 1973.

Barth, Markus. *Ephesians.* 2 vols. Anchor Bible 34 and 34A. Garden City, N.Y.: Doubleday & Co., 1974.

Batey, Richard A. *New Testament Nuptial Imagery.* Leiden: E. J. Brill, 1971.

Bauckham, Richard J. *Jude, 2 Peter.* Word Biblical Commentary 50. Waco, Tex.: Word Books, 1983.

Beare, F. W. *A Commentary on the Epistle to the Philippians.* 2d ed. London: Adam & Charles Black, 1969.

Bedale, Stephen F. B. "The Meaning of *kephalē* in the Pauline Epistles." *Journal of Theological Studies,* n.s. 5 (1954): 211–15.

_________. "The Theology of the Church." Pp. 64–75 in *Studies in Ephesians.* Edited by F. L. Cross. London: A. R. Mowbray & Co., 1956.

Belkin, Samuel. *Philo and the Oral Law: The Philonic Interpretation of Biblical Law in Relation to the Palestinian Halakah.* Harvard Semitic Series 11. Cambridge, Mass.: Harvard University, 1940.

Bellows, Barbara L. " 'My Children, Gentlemen, Are My Own': Poor Women, the Urban Elite, and the Bonds of Obligation in Antebellum Charleston." Pp. 52–71 in *The Web of Southern Social Relations: Women, Family & Education.* Edited by Walter J. Fraser, Jr., R. Frank Saunders, Jr., and Jon L. Wakelyn. Athens, Ga.: University of Georgia, 1985.

Benko, Stephen. "The Edict of Claudius of A.D. 49 and the Instigator Chrestus." *Theologische Zeitschrift* 25 (6, November 1969): 406–18.

Benoit, Pierre. "Pauline Angelology and Demonology. Reflexions on the Designations of the Heavenly Powers and on the Origin of Angelic Evil According to Paul." *Religious Studies Bulletin* 3 (1, 1983): 1–18.

Best, Ernest. *1 Peter.* New Century Bible Commentary. Grand Rapids: Eerdmans, 1982; London: Marshall, Morgan & Scott, 1971.

Betz, Hans Dieter. *2 Corinthians 8 and 9: A Commentary on Two Administrative Letters of the Apostle Paul.* Hermeneia Commentaries. Philadelphia: Fortress, 1985.

Betz, Otto. *What Do We Know About Jesus?* Philadelphia: Westminster, 1968; London: SCM, 1968.

Bianchi, Ugo. "L'Orphisme a Existé." Pp. 187–95 in *Selected Essays on Gnosticism, Dualism and Mysteriography.* By Ugo Bianchi. Studies in the History of Religions (Supplements to Numen) 38. Leiden: E. J. Brill, 1978.

Bilezekian, Gilbert. *Beyond Sex Roles: What the Bible Says About a Woman's Place in Church and Family.* Grand Rapids: Baker Book House, 1986.

Billigmeier, Jon-Christian and Judy A. Turner. "The Socio-economic roles of women in Mycenaean Greece: A brief survey from evidence of the Linear B tablets." Pp. 1–18 in *Reflections of Women in Antiquity.* Edited by Helene P. Foley. New York: Gordon & Breach Science Publishers, 1981.

Boer, P. A. H. de. *Fatherhood and Motherhood in Israelite and Judean Piety.* Leiden: E. J. Brill, 1974.

Boer, W. Den. *Private Morality in Greece and Rome: Some Historical Aspects.* Mnemosyne: Bibliotheca Classica Batava, Supplementum Quinquagesimum Septimum. Leiden: E. J. Brill, 1979.

Boldrey, Richard and Joyce. *Chauvinist or Feminist? Paul's View of Women*. Foreword by David M. Scholer. Grand Rapids: Baker Book House, 1979.

Bonsirven, Joseph. *Palestinian Judaism in the Time of Jesus Christ*. New York: Holt, Rinehart & Winston, 1964.

Boring, M. Eugene. *Sayings of the Risen Jesus: Christian Prophecy in the Synoptic Tradition*. Society for New Testament Studies Monograph Series 46. Cambridge: Cambridge University, 1982.

Bosmajian, Haig. "The Letter from Birmingham Jail." Pp. 128–43 in *Martin Luther King, Jr.: A Profile*. Revised edition. Edited by C. Eric Lincoln. New York: Hill & Wang, 1984. Reprinted from "Rhetoric of Martin Luther King's Letter from Birmingham Jail." *Midwest Quarterly* 8 (January 1967): 127–43.

Bousset, William. *Kyrios Christos: A History of the Belief in Christ from the Beginnings of Christianity to Irenaeus*. Nashville: Abingdon, 1970.

Bowman, John, translator and editor. *Samaritan Documents Relating to Their History, Religion and Life*. Pittsburgh Original Texts and Translations Series 2. Pittsburgh: Pickwick, 1977.

Bright, John, *A History of Israel*. 3d ed. Philadelphia: The Westminster Press, 1981.

Brooks, Evelyn. "The Women's Movement in the Black Baptist Church, 1880–1920." Ph.D. dissertation, University of Rochester, 1984.

Brooten, Bernadette J. *Women Leaders in the Ancient Synagogue: Inscriptional Evidence and Background Issues*. Chico, Calif.: Scholars, 1982.

Brown, Raymond E. *The Gospel According to John*. 2 vols. Anchor Bible 29 and 29A. Garden City, N.Y.: Doubleday & Co., 1966–70.

Brownlee, William H. "Light on the Manual of Discipline (DSD) from the Book of Jubilees." *Bulletin of the American Schools of Oriental Research* 123 (October 1951): 30–32.

Bruce, F. F. *The Acts of the Apostles: The Greek Text with Introduction and Commentary*. Grand Rapids: Eerdmans, 1951.

_________. " 'All Things to All Men': Diversity in Unity and Other Pauline Tensions." Pp. 82–99 in *Unity and Diversity in New Testament Theology: Essays in Honor of George E. Ladd*. Edited by Robert A. Guelich. Grand Rapids: Eerdmans, 1978.

_________. *The Books and the Parchments*. Old Tappan, N.J.: Fleming H. Revell Co., 1963.

_________. *Commentary on the Book of the Acts: The English Text with Introduction, Exposition and Notes*. New International Commentary on the New Testament. Grand Rapids: Eerdmans, 1977.

_________. *1 and 2 Corinthians*. New Century Bible Commentary. Grand Rapids: Eerdmans, 1980; London: Marshall, Morgan & Scott, 1971.

_________. *The Message of the New Testament*. Grand Rapids: Eerdmans, 1981.

_________. "Myth and History." Pp. 79–99 in *History, Criticism and Faith*. Edited by Colin Brown. Downers Grove, Ill.: InterVarsity, 1976.

_________. "Paul and 'The Powers That Be.'" *Bulletin of the John Rylands Library* 66 (2, Spring 1984): 78–96.

_________. *Paul: Apostle of the Heart Set Free.* Grand Rapids: Eerdmans, 1977.

Buckland, W. W. *The Roman Law of Slavery: The Condition of the Slave in Private Law from Augustus to Justinian.* Cambridge: Cambridge University, 1908.

Burkert, Walter. *Ancient Mystery Cults.* Carl Newell Jackson Lectures. Cambridge: Harvard University, 1987.

_________. *Greek Religion.* Translated by John Raffan. Cambridge: Harvard University, 1985.

_________. "Orphism and Bacchic Mysteries: New Evidence and Old Problems of Interpretation." The Center for Hermeneutical Studies in Hellenistic and Modern Culture, 28th Colloquy. Berkeley, Calif.: The Center for Hermeneutical Studies in Hellenistic and Modern Culture, 1977.

Cadbury, Henry J. "A Qumran Parallel to Paul." *Harvard Theological Review* 51 (1, 1958): 1–2.

Caird, George B. *A Commentary on the Revelation of Saint John the Divine.* Harper's New Testament Commentaries. New York: Harper & Row, 1966.

Cameron, Averil. " 'Neither Male nor Female.' " *Greece and Rome* 27 (1, April 1980): 60–68.

Cannon, George E. *The Use of Traditional Materials in Colossians.* Macon, Ga.: Mercer University, 1983.

Caragounis, Chrys C. *The Ephesian Mysterion: Meaning and Content.* Coniectanea Biblica New Testament Series 8. Lund: C. W. K. Gleerup, 1977.

Carcopino, Jérôme. *Daily Life in Ancient Rome: The People and the City at the Height of the Empire.* Edited by Henry T. Rowell. Translated by E. O. Lorimer. New Haven: Yale University, 1940.

Carr, Wesley. *Angels and Principalities.* Cambridge: Cambridge University, 1981.

Carson, D. A. *Exegetical Fallacies.* Grand Rapids: Baker Book House, 1984.

_________. " 'Silent in the Churches': On the Role of Women in 1 Corinthians 14:33b–36." Pp. 140–53 in *Recovering Biblical Manhood and Womanhood: A Response to Evangelical Feminism.* Edited by John Piper and Wayne Grudem. Wheaton, Ill.: Crossway Books, 1991.

Cary, M., and T. J. Haarhoff. *Life and Thought in the Greek and Roman World.* 4th ed. London: Methuen & Co., 1946.

Casson, Lionel. *Travel in the Ancient World.* London: George Allen & Unwin, 1974.

Chariton. *Chaereas and Callirhoe.* Translated by Warren E. Blake. Ann Arbor: University of Michigan; London: Humphrey Milford, Oxford University, 1939.

*Charitonis Aphrodisiensis: De Chaerea et Callirhoe Amatoriarvm Narrationvm Libri Octo.* Oxford: Clarendon; London: Humphrey Milford, 1938.

Charlesworth, James H., ed. *The Old Testament Pseudepigrapha.* 2 vols. Garden City, N.Y.: Doubleday & Co., 1983–85.

Charlesworth, M. P. *Trade-Routes and Commerce of the Roman Empire.* 2d rev. ed. New York: Cooper Square Publishers, 1970.

Cicero. *Works.* 28 vols. Translated by Harry Caplan et al. Loeb Classical Library. Cambridge: Harvard University, 1913–.

Clapp, Rodney. "Is the 'Traditional' Family Biblical?" *Christianity Today* (Sept. 16, 1988): 24–28.

Clark, Elizabeth A. *Women in the Early Church.* Message of the Fathers of the Church 13. Wilmington, Del.: Michael Glazier, 1983.

"The Code of Hammurabi." Translated by Theophile J. Meek. Pp. 163–80 in *Ancient Near Eastern Texts Relating to the Old Testament.* Edited by James B. Pritchard. 2d ed. Princeton: Princeton University, 1955.

Cohen, Boaz. *Jewish and Roman Law: A Comparative Study.* 2 vols. New York: Jewish Theological Seminary of America, 1966.

Cohen, Shaye J. D. *From the Maccabees to the Mishnah.* Library of Early Christianity 7. Philadelphia: Westminster, 1987.

__________. "Women in the Synagogues of Antiquity." *Conservative Judaism* 34 (2, November 1980): 23–29.

Cole, Susan Guettel. *Theoi Megaloi: The Cult of the Great Gods at Samothrace.* Etudes Préliminaires aux Religions Orientales dans l'Empire Romain 96. Leiden: E. J. Brill, 1984.

Collins, John J. "The Testamentary Literature in Recent Scholarship." Pp. 268–85 in *Early Judaism and Its Modern Interpreters.* Edited by Robert A. Kraft and George W. E. Nickelsburg. Society of Biblical Literature Bible and Its Modern Interpreters Series 2. Atlanta: Scholars, 1986.

Cone, James H. *For My People: Black Theology and the Black Church.* The Bishop Henry McNeal Turner Studies in North American Black Religion 1. Maryknoll, N.Y.: Orbis Books, 1984.

Conzelmann, Hans. *1 Corinthians: A Commentary on the First Epistle to the Corinthians.* Translated by James W. Leitch. Bibliography and references by James W. Dunkly. Edited by George W. MacRae. Hermeneia Commentaries. Philadelphia: Fortress, 1975.

__________. *History of Primitive Christianity.* Translated by John E. Steely. Nashville: Abingdon, 1973.

Cope, Lamar. "1 Cor 11:2–16: One Step Further." *Journal of Biblical Literature* 97 (3, September 1978): 435–36.

*Corpus Inscriptionum Iudaicarum: Recueil des Inscriptions Juives qui vont du IIIe Siècle de Notre ère.* 3 vols. Edited by P. Jean-Baptiste Frey. Rome: Pontificio Instituto di Archeologa Cristiana, 1936–52.

*Corpus Papyrorum Judaicarum.* 3 vols. Edited by Victor A. Tcherikover, with Alexander Fuks. Vol. 3 edited by Victor A. Tcherikover, Alexander Fuks, and Menahem Stern, with David M. Lewis. Cambridge: Harvard University, for Magnes, The Hebrew University, 1957–64.

Crabb, R. W. "The *KEPHALĒ* Concept in the Pauline Tradition with Special Emphasis on Colossians." Th.D. dissertation, San Francisco Theological Seminary, 1966. (Dissertation Abstracts, 29.04A, pp. 1280–81).

Craigie, Peter C. *Ugarit and the Old Testament*. Grand Rapids: Eerdmans, 1983.

Cranfield, C. E. B. *A Critical and Exegetical Commentary on the Epistle to the Romans*. International Critical Commentary. 2 vols. Edinburgh: T. & T. Clark, 1975–79.

_________. "The Interpretation of I Peter iii.19 and iv.6." *Expository Times* 69 (12, 1958): 369–72.

Cullmann, Oscar. *Christ and Time*. Translated by Floyd V. Filson. Philadelphia: Westminster, 1950.

_________. *The Christology of the New Testament*. Philadelphia: Westminster; London: SCM, 1959.

_________. *Early Christian Worship*. Philadelphia: Westminster, 1953.

_________. *The State in the New Testament*. New York: Charles Scribner's Sons, 1956.

Culpepper, R. Alan. *The Johannine School: An Evaluation of the Johannine-School Hypothesis Based on an Investigation of the Nature of Ancient Schools*. Society of Biblical Literature Dissertation Series 26. Missoula, Mont.: Scholars, 1975.

*The Cynic Epistles: A Study Edition*. Edited by Abraham J. Malherbe. Society of Biblical Literature Sources for Biblical Study 12. Missoula, Mont.: Scholars, 1977.

Dalton, William Joseph. *Christ's Proclamation to the Spirits: A Study of 1 Peter 3:18–4:6*. Rome: Pontifical Biblical Institute, 1965.

_________. "Christ's Victory over the Devil and the Evil Spirits." *Bible Today* 1 (18, 1965): 1195–1200.

_________. "The Interpretation of 1 Peter 3,19 and 4,6: Light from 2 Peter." *Biblica* 60 (4, 1979): 547–55.

_________. "Proclamatio Christi spiritibus facta: inquisitio in textum ex Prima Epistola S. Petri 3,18–4,6." *Verbum Domini* 42 (5, 1964): 225–40. (NTA 9:372).

Dana, H. E., and Julius R.Mantey. *A Manual Grammar of the Greek New Testament*. Toronto: Macmillan Co., 1955.

Daniel, Jerry L. "Anti-Semitism in the Hellenistic-Roman Period." *Journal of Biblical Literature* 98 (1, March 1979): 45–65.

Daube, David. *The New Testament and Rabbinic Judaism*. New York: Arno, 1973; London: University of London, 1956.

Davies, W. D. *Paul and Rabbinic Judaism: Some Rabbinic Elements in Pauline Theology*. 4th ed. Philadelphia: Fortress, 1980.

"Defeating Date Rape." Staff Editorial. *The Chronicle* [Duke University] (Nov. 15, 1988): 8.

Deissmann, Adolf. *Bible Studies: Contributions Chiefly from Papyri and Inscriptions to the History of the Language, the Literature, and the Religion of Hellenistic Judaism and Primitive Christianity*. Translated by Alexander Grieve. Reprint. Winona Lake, Ind.: Alpha Publications, 1979; Edinburgh: T. & T. Clark, 1923.

_________. *Light from the Ancient East*. Reprint. Grand Rapids: Baker Book House, 1978.

__________. *Paul: A Study in Social and Religious History.* New York: Harper & Brothers, 1927; Torchbook edition, 1957.

Delcor, M. "Le mythe de la chute des anges et de l'origine des géants comme explication du mal dans le monde, dans l'apocalyptique juive. Histoire des traditions." *Revue de l'Histoire des Religions* 190 (1, 1976): 3–53.

Demosthenes. *Works.* 7 vols. Translated by J. H. Vince, C. A. Vince, A. T. Murray, N. W. DeWitt, and N. J. DeWitt. Loeb Classical Library. Cambridge: Harvard University, 1926–49.

Derrett, J. Duncan M. *Jesus's Audience: The Social and Psychological Environment in which He Worked.* New York: Seabury, 1973.

Detienne, Marcel. "Un Polytheisme récrit. Entre Dionysos et Apollon: mort et vie d'Orphée." *Archives de sciences sociales des religions* 30 (59–1, Jan. 1985): 65–75.

Dibelius, Martin. *From Tradition to Gospel.* Translated by Bertram Lee Woolf. Reprint. Cambridge: James Clarke & Co., 1971; Greenwood, S.C.: Attic, 1971.

__________. *James: A Commentary on the Epistle of James.* Revised by Heinrich Greeven. Translated by Michael A. Williams. Edited by Helmut Koester. Hermeneia Commentaries. Philadelphia: Fortress, 1976.

Dibelius, Martin, and Hans Conzelmann. *The Pastoral Epistles: A Commentary on the Pastoral Epistles.* Translated by Philip Buttolph and Adela Yarbro [Collins]. Edited by Helmut Koester. Hermeneia Commentaries. Philadelphia: Fortress, 1972.

Dillon, John. *The Middle Platonists: 80 B.C. to A.D. 220.* Ithaca, N.Y.: Cornell University, 1977.

Dio Chrysostom. *Works.* 5 vols. Translated by J. W. Cohoon and H. Lamar Crosby. Loeb Classical Library. Cambridge: Harvard University, 1932–51.

Diogenes Laertius. *Lives of Eminent Philosophers.* 2 vols. Translated by R. D. Hicks. Loeb Classical Library. Cambridge: Harvard University, 1925.

Dobson, Elizabeth Spalding. "Pliny the Younger's Description of Women." *Classical Bulletin* 58 (6, April 1982): 81–85.

Dodd, C. H. *The Bible and the Greeks.* London: Hodder & Stoughton, 1935.

Donfried, Karl P. "A Short Note on Romans 16." Pp. 44–52 in *The Romans Debate—Revised and Expanded Edition.* Peabody: Hendrickson, 1991.

Dover, K. J. "Classical Greek Attitudes to Sexual Behavior." Pp. 143–58 in *Women in the Ancient World: The Arethusa Papers.* Edited by John Peradotto and J. P. Sullivan. SUNY Series in Classical Studies. Albany, N.Y.: State University of New York, 1984.

Drane, John W. "Why Did Paul Write Romans?" Pp. 208–27 in *Pauline Studies: Essays presented to Professor F. F. Bruce on his 70th Birthday.* Edited by Donald A. Hagner and Murray J. Harris. Grand Rapids: Eerdmans, 1980.

Dunand, Françoise. "Les Mystères Egyptiens." Pp. 11–62 in *Mystères et Syncrétismes.* Etudes d'Histoire des Religions 2. Edited by

M. Philonenko and M. Simon. Paris: Librairie Orientaliste Paul Geuthner, 1975.

Dupont-Sommer, A. *The Essene Writings from Qumran*. Translated by G. Vermes. Gloucester, Mass.: Peter Smith, 1973.

Edersheim, Alfred. *The Life and Times of Jesus the Messiah*. Reprint. Peabody: Hendrickson, n.d.

Eliade, Mircea. *Rites and Symbols of Initiation: The Mysteries of Birth and Rebirth*. Translated by Willard R. Trask. New York: Harper & Row, 1958.

Ellis, E. E. "Christ and Spirit in 1 Corinthians." Pp. 269–77 in *Christ and Spirit in the New Testament: Studies in Honour of C. F. D. Moule*. Edited by Barnabas Lindars and Stephen S. Smalley. Cambridge: Cambridge University, 1973.

Ellul, Danielle. "Le Targum du Pseudo-Jonathan sur Genèse 3 à la lumière de quelques traditions haggadiques." *Foi et Vie* 80 (6, December 1981): 12–25.

Epictetus. *The Discourses as Reported by Arrian, the Manual, and Fragments*. 2 vols. Translated by W. A. Oldfather. Loeb Classical Library. London: Wm. Heinemann; New York: G. P. Putnam's Sons, 1926–28.

*The Ethiopic Book of Enoch: A New Edition in the Light of the Aramaic Dead Sea Fragments*. 2 vols. Edited by Michael A. Knibb, in consultation with Edward Ullendorff. Oxford: Clarendon, 1978.

Euripides. *Works*. 4 vols. Translated by Arthur S. Way. Loeb Classical Library. Cambridge: Harvard University, 1912.

*The Fathers According to Rabbi Nathan*. Translated by Judah Goldin. Yale Judaica Series 10. New Haven: Yale University, 1955.

*The Fathers According to Rabbi Nathan (Abot de Rabbi Nathan) Version B*. Translation and commentary by Anthony J. Saldarini. Studies in Judaism in Late Antiquity 11. Leiden: E. J. Brill, 1975.

Fàbrega, V. "War Junia(s), der hervorragende Apostel (Röm. 16,7), eine Frau?" *Jahrbuch für Antike und Christentum* 27–28 (1984–85): 47–64. (NTA 30:175).

Fau, G. "L'authenticité du texte de Tacite sur les Chrétiens." *Cahiers du Cercle Ernest-Renan* 19 (72, 1971): 19–24 (NTA 6:218).

Fee, Gordon. *1 and 2 Timothy, Titus*. New International Biblical Commentary. Peabody, Mass.: Hendrickson Publishers, 1988.

__________. *The First Epistle to the Corinthians*. New International Commentary on the New Testament. Grand Rapids: Eerdmans, 1987.

Feinberg, John S. "1 Peter 3:18–20, Ancient Mythology, and the Intermediate State." *Westminster Theological Journal* 48 (2, Fall 1986): 303–36.

Fields, Weston W. "Early and Medieval Jewish Interpretation of the Song of Songs." *Grace Theological Journal* 1 (2, Fall 1980): 221–31.

Filson, Floyd V. "Ephesus and the New Testament." *Biblical Archaeologist* 8 (3, Sept. 1945): 73–80.

Finegan, Jack. *The Archeology of World Religions*. Princeton: Princeton University, 1952.

__________. *Light from the Ancient Past.* Princeton: Princeton University, 1946.

Finkelstein, Louis. *Akiba: Scholar, Saint and Martyr.* New York: Atheneum, 1970.

Finley, M. I. *The Ancient Economy.* Sather Classical Lectures 43. Berkeley: University of California, 1973.

__________. *Ancient Slavery and Modern Ideology.* New York: Viking, 1980.

Fiorenza, Elisabeth Schüssler. *In Memory of Her: A Feminist Theological Reconstruction of Christian Origins.* New York: Crossroad, 1983.

__________. "Women in the Pre-Pauline and Pauline Churches." *Union Seminary Quarterly Review* 33 (3–4, Spring 1978): 153–66.

"1 (Ethiopic Apocalypse of) Enoch." Translated by E. Isaac. 1:5–89 in *The Old Testament Pseudepigrapha.* 2 vols. Edited by James H. Charlesworth. Garden City, N.Y.: Doubleday & Co., 1983–85.

Fitzgerald, John T. *Cracks in an Earthen Vessel: An Examination of the Catalogues of Hardships in the Corinthian Correspondence.* Society of Biblical Literature Dissertation Series 99. Atlanta: Scholars, 1988.

Fitzmyer, Joseph A. "Another look at *KEPHALĒ* in 1 Corinthians 11.3." *New Testament Studies* 35 (4, Oct. 1989): 503–11.

__________. "The Aramaic 'Elect of God' Text from Qumran Cave IV." *Catholic Biblical Quarterly* 27 (4, October 1965): 348–72.

__________. *Essays on the Semitic Background of the New Testament.* 2d ed. Sources for Biblical Study 5. Missoula, Mont.: Scholars, 1974.

__________. "A Feature of Qumrân Angelology and the Angels of I Cor. XI.10." *New Testament Studies* 4 (1, October 1957): 48–58.

__________. *The Genesis Apocryphon of Qumran Cave 1: A Commentary.* 2d rev. ed. Biblica et Orientalia 18 A. Rome: Biblical Institute, 1971.

Flanagan Neal M., and Edwina H. Snyder. "Did Paul Put Down Women in 1 Cor 14:34–36?" *Biblical Theology Bulletin* 11 (1, January 1981): 10–12.

Fleischer, R. *Artemis von Ephesos und verwandte Kultstatuen aus Anatolien und Syrien.* Etudes Préliminaires aux Religions Orientales dans l'Empire Romain 35. Leiden: E. J. Brill, 1973.

Flory, Marleen Boudreau. "Where Women Precede Men: Factors Influencing the Order of Names in Roman Epitaphs." *Classical Journal* 79 (3, February 1984): 216–24.

Flusser, D. "Paganism in Palestine." Pp. 1065–1100 in *The Jewish People in the First Century: Historical Geography, Political History, Social, Cultural and Religious Life and Institutions.* 2 vols. Edited by S. Safrai and M. Stern with D. Flusser and W. C. van Unnik. Section 1 of Compendia Rerum Iudaicarum ad Novum Testamentum. Vol. 1: Assen: Van Gorcum & Co., B.V., 1974. Vol. 2: Philadelphia: Fortress, 1976.

Fogel, Robert William, and Stanley L. Engerman. *Time on the Cross: The Economics of American Negro Slavery.* Boston: Little, Brown & Co., 1974.

Foley, Helene P. "The Conception of Women in Athenian Drama." Pp. 127–68 in *Reflections of Women in Antiquity*. Edited by Helene P. Foley. New York: Gordon & Breach Science Publishers, 1981.

_________, editor. *Reflections of Women in Antiquity*. New York: Gordon & Breach Science Publishers, 1981.

Foucart, P. *Des Associations Religieuses chez les Grecs: Thiases, Eranes, Orgéons*. Paris: Klincksieck, 1873. Reprint. New York: Arno, 1975.

France, R. T. "Exegesis in Practice: Two Examples." Pp. 252–81 in *New Testament Interpretation: Essays on Principles and Methods*. Edited by I. Howard Marshall. Grand Rapids: Eerdmans, 1977.

Frank, Tenney. *Aspects of Social Behavior in Ancient Rome*. Cambridge: Harvard University, 1932.

Friedländer, Ludwig. *Roman Life and Manners Under the Early Empire*. 4 vols. Translated by Leonard A. Magnus, J. H. Freese, and A. B. Gough. London: G. Routledge & Sons; New York: E. P. Dutton & Co., 1908–13.

Fritsch, Charles T. *The Qumran Community: Its History and Scrolls*. New York: Macmillan Co., 1956.

Gager, John G. *Kingdom and Community: The Social World of Early Christianity*. Prentice-Hall Studies in Religion. Englewood Cliffs, N.J.: Prentice-Hall, 1975.

_________. *The Origins of Anti-Semitism: Attitudes Toward Judaism in Pagan and Christian Antiquity*. New York: Oxford University, 1983.

_________. "Religion and Social Class in the Early Roman Empire." Pp. 99–120 in *The Catacombs and the Colosseum: The Roman Empire as the Setting of Primitive Christianity*. Edited by Stephen Benko and John J. O'Rourke. Valley Forge, Pa.: Judson, 1971.

Gamble, Harry A., Jr. *The Textual History of the Letter to the Romans: A Study in Textual and Literary Criticism*. Studies and Documents. Grand Rapids: Eerdmans, 1977.

Gardner, Jane F., editor. *Leadership and the Cult of the Personality*. The Ancient World: Source Books. London: Dent; Toronto: Hakkert, 1974.

_________. *Women in Roman Law & Society*. Bloomington: Indiana University, 1986.

Gasparro, Giulia Sfameni. *Soteriology and Mystic Aspects in the Cult of Cybele and Attis*. Etudes Préliminaires aux Religions Orientales dans l'Empire Romain 103. Leiden: E. J. Brill, 1985.

Gaster, Theodor H., editor. *The Dead Sea Scriptures*. Garden City, N.Y.: Anchor Books, Doubleday & Co., 1976.

Gelfand, Michael. "Psychiatric Disorders as Recognized by the Shona." Pp. 156–73 in *Magic, Faith, and Healing: Studies in Primitive Psychiatry Today*. Edited by Ari Kiev. New York: Free, 1964.

Georgi, Dieter. "Socioeconomic Reasons for the 'Divine Man' as a Propagandistic Pattern." Pp. 27–42 in *Aspects of Religious Propaganda in Judaism and Early Christianity*. Edited by Elisabeth Schüssler Fiorenza. University of Notre Dame Center for the

Study of Judaism and Christianity in Antiquity 2. Notre Dame: University of Notre Dame, 1976.

Gerhardsson, Birger. *Memory and Manuscript: Oral Tradition and Written Transmission in Rabbinic Judaism and Early Christianity.* Acta Seminarii Neotestamentici Upsaliensis 22. Uppsala: C. W. K. Gleerup, 1961.

Giles, Kevin. *Created Woman: A Fresh Study of the Biblical Teaching.* Canberra: Acorn, 1985.

Giovannini, A. "Tacite, l'"incendium Neronis' et les chrétiens." *Revue des Etudes Augustiniennes* 30 (1–2, 1984): 3–23 (NTA 29:307).

Godwin, Joscelyn. *Mystery Religions in the Ancient World.* San Francisco: Harper & Row, 1981.

Goodenough, Erwin R. *The Church in the Roman Empire.* New York: Cooper Square Publishers, 1970.

_________. *An Introduction to Philo Judaeus.* 2d ed. Oxford: Basil Blackwell, 1962.

_________. *Jewish Symbols in the Greco-Roman Period.* 13 vols. Bollingen Series 37. New York: Pantheon Books, 1953–65. Vol. 13: Princeton: Princeton University, 1968.

Goodman, D. "Do Angels Eat?" *Journal of Jewish Studies* 37 (2, 1986): 160–75.

Goodman, Martin. *State and Society in Roman Galilee, A.D. 132–212.* Oxford Centre for Postgraduate Hebrew Studies. Totowa, N.J.: Rowman & Allanheld, Publishers, 1983.

Goppelt, Leonhard. *Theology of the New Testament.* 2 vols. Translated by John E. Alsup. Edited by Jürgen Roloff. Grand Rapids: Eerdmans, 1981–82.

Gordon, Cyrus H. *The Common Background of Greek and Hebrew Civilizations.* New York: W. W. Norton & Co., 1965.

Gould, John. "Law, Custom and Myth: Aspects of the Social Position of Women in Classical Athens." *Journal of Hellenic Studies* 100 (1980): 38–59.

Grant, Frederick C. "The Economic Background of the New Testament." Pp. 96–114 in *The Background of the New Testament and Its Eschatology: In Honour of Charles Harold Dodd.* Edited by W. D. Davies and D. Daube. Cambridge: Cambridge University, 1964.

_________. *Hellenistic Religions: The Age of Syncretism.* The Library of Liberal Arts. Indianapolis: Bobbs-Merrill Co., 1953.

_________. *Roman Hellenism and the New Testament.* New York: Charles Scribner's Sons, 1962.

Grant, Jacquelyn. *White Women's Christ and Black Women's Jesus: Feminist Christology and Womanist Response.* American Academy of Religion Academy Series 64. Atlanta: Scholars, 1989.

Grant, Robert M. *Early Christianity and Society: Seven Studies.* San Francisco: Harper & Row, 1977.

_________. *Gods and the One God.* Library of Early Christianity 1. Philadelphia: Westminster, 1986.

*The Greek Anthology.* 5 vols. Translated by W. R. Paton. Loeb Classical Library. Cambridge: Harvard University, 1916–.

*Greek Philosophy: Thales to Aristotle.* Edited by Reginald E. Allen. Readings in the History of Philosophy. New York: Free; London: Collier-Macmillan, 1966.

*The Greek Versions of the Testaments of the Twelve Patriarchs, edited from nine mss. Together with the variants of the Armenian and Slavonic versions and some Hebrew fragments.* Edited by R. H. Charles. Oxford: Clarendon, 1908.

Green, Holly Wagner. "Wife Abuse: When Submission Goes Too Far." *Charisma* (July 1985): 44–54.

Grudem, Wayne A. "Christ Preaching Through Noah: 1 Peter 3:19–20 in the Light of Dominant Themes in Jewish Literature." *Trinity Journal* 7 (2, Fall 1986): 3–31.

_________. "Does *kephalē* Mean 'Source' or 'Authority Over' in Greek Literature? A Survey of 2,336 Examples." *Trinity Journal,* n.s. 6 (1, Spring 1985): 38–59.

_________. *The Gift of Prophecy in 1 Corinthians.* Lanham, Md.: University Press of America, 1982.

_________. "Prophecy—Yes, but Teaching—No; Paul's Consistent Advocacy of Women's Participation Without Governing Authority." *Journal of the Evangelical Theological Society* 30 (1, March 1987): 11–23.

_________. "A Response to Gerhard Dautzenberg on 1 Cor. 12.10." *Biblische Zeitschrift* 22 (2, 1978): 253–70.

_________. "Wives like Sarah, and the Husbands Who Honor Them: 1 Peter 3:1–7." Pp. 194–208 in *Recovering Biblical Manhood and Womanhood: A Response to Evangelical Feminism.* Edited by John Piper and Wayne Grudem. Wheaton, Ill.: Crossway Books, 1991.

Guillaume, Alfred. *Islam.* New York: Penguin Books, 1956.

Gundry, Patricia. *Women Be Free: The Clear Message of Scripture.* Grand Rapids: Zondervan Publishing House, 1977.

Gurney, O. R. *The Hittites.* Baltimore: Penguin Books, 1972.

Guthrie, W. K. C. *Orpheus and Greek Religion: A Study of the Orphic Movement.* 2d ed. New York: W. W. Norton & Co., 1966.

Hallett, Judith P. "The Role of Women in Roman Elegy: Counter-Cultural Feminism." Pp. 241–62 in *Women in the Ancient World: The Arethusa Papers.* Edited by John Peradotto and J. P. Sullivan. SUNY Series in Classical Studies. Albany, N.Y.: State University of New York, 1984.

Hanson, Anthony. "Philo's Etymologies." *Journal of Theological Studies* 18 (1, April 1967): 128–39.

Hanson, Paul D. "Rebellion in Heaven, Azazel, and Euhemeristic Heroes in 1 Enoch 6–11." *Journal of Biblical Literature* 96 (2, June 1977): 195–233.

Hardesty, Nancy A. *Women Called to Witness: Evangelical Feminism in the 19th Century.* Nashville: Abingdon, 1984.

Harrell, Pat Edwin. *Divorce and Remarriage in the Early Church: A History of Divorce and Remarriage in the Ante-Nicene Church.* Austin, Tex.: R. B. Sweet Co., 1967.

Harris, Murray J. "References to Jesus in Early Classical Authors." Pp. 343–68 in *The Jesus Tradition Outside the Gospels.* Gospel Perspectives 5. Edited by David Wenham. Sheffield: JSOT, 1984.

Harris, William. " 'Sounding Brass' and Hellenistic Technology." *Biblical Archaeology Review* 8 (1, 1982): 38–41.

Hawthorne, Gerald F. *Philippians.* Word Biblical Commentary 43. Waco, Tex.: Word Books, 1983.

Hengel, Martin. *Acts and the History of Earliest Christianity.* Translated by John Bowden. London: SCM, 1979; Philadelphia: Fortress, 1980.

Henn, Jeanne K. "Women in the Rural Economy: Past, Present, and Future." Pp. 1–18 in *African Women South of the Sahara.* Edited by Margaret Jean Hay and Sharon Stichter. New York: Longman, 1984.

Henrichs, Albert. "Changing Dionysiac Identities." Pp. 137–60 in *Self-Definition in the Greco-Roman World.* Edited by Ben F. Meyer and E. P. Sanders. Vol. 3 of *Jewish and Christian Self-Definition.* Philadelphia: Fortress, 1982.

Héring, Jean. *The First Epistle of Saint Paul to the Corinthians.* Translated by A. W. Heathcote and P. J. Allcock. London: Epworth, 1962.

Herodotus. *Histories.* 4 vols. Translated by A. D. Godley. Loeb Classical Library. Cambridge: Harvard University, 1920–25.

Heyob, Sharon Kelly. *The Cult of Isis Among Women in the Graeco-Roman World.* Etudes Préliminaires aux Religions Orientales dans l'Empire Romain 51. Leiden: E. J. Brill, 1975.

Higgins, Jean M. "Anastasius Sinaita and the Superiority of the Woman." *Journal of Biblical Literature* 97 (2, June 1978): 253–56.

Hill, David. *New Testament Prophecy.* New Foundations Theological Library. Atlanta: John Knox, 1979.

"Hittite Laws." Translated by Albrecht Goetze. Pp. 188–97 in *Ancient Near Eastern Texts Relating to the Old Testament.* Edited by James B. Pritchard. 2d ed. Princeton: Princeton University, 1955.

Hock, Ronald F. *The Social Context of Paul's Ministry: Tentmaking and Apostleship.* Philadelphia: Fortress, 1980.

Hoerber, Robert G. "The Decree of Claudius in Act 18:2." *Concordia Theological Monthly* 31 (11, November 1960): 690–94.

Hoffner, Harry A., Jr., "Symbols for Masculinity and Femininity: Their Use in Ancient Near Eastern Sympathetic Magic Rituals." *Journal of Biblical Literature* 85 (3, September 1966): 326–34.

Holladay, Carl R. *Theios Aner in Hellenistic Judaism: A Critique of the Use of This Category in New Testament Christology.* Society of Biblical Literature Dissertation Series 40. Missoula, Mont.: Scholars, 1977.

Hooker, Morna D. "Authority on her Head: An Examination of I Cor. XI.10." *New Testament Studies* 10 (3, April 1964): 410–16.

_________. *A Preface to Paul.* New York: Oxford University, 1980.

Horace. *The Odes and Epodes.* Translated by C. E. Bennett. Loeb Classical Library. Cambridge: Harvard University; London: Wm. Heinemann, 1914.

_________. *Satires, Epistles and Ars Poetica.* Translated by H. Rushton Fairclough. Loeb Classical Library. New York: G. P. Putnam's Sons; London: Wm. Heinemann, 1926.

Howard, George. "The Beginnings of Christianity in Rome: A Note on Suetonius, Life of Claudius XXV.4." *Restoration Quarterly* 24 (3, 1981): 175–77.

Huffmon, Herbert B. "Prophecy in the Mari Letters." *Biblical Archaeologist* 31 (December 1968): 101–24.

Hull, Gretchen Gaebelein. "Biblical Feminism: A Christian Response to Sexism." *ESA Advocate* (October 1990): 14–15.

_________. *Equal to Serve: Women and Men in the Church and Home.* Old Tappan, N.J.: Fleming H. Revell Co., 1987.

_________. "Under the Yoke: Facing the Challenge of Global Oppression." Pp. 16–19 in *World Christian Summer Reader 1990.* Pasadena, Calif.: World Christian, 1990.

Hull, Sanford Douglas. "Exegetical Difficulties in the 'Hard Passages.' " Pp. 251–66 in *Equal to Serve: Women and Men in the Church and Home.* By Gretchen Gaebelein Hull. Old Tappan, N.J.: Fleming H. Revell Co., 1987.

Hunter, Archibald M. *The Epistle to the Romans.* London: SCM, Torch Bible Commentaries, 1955.

_________. *The Gospel According to St. Paul.* Philadelphia: Westminster, 1966.

Hunter, James Davison, and Helen V. L. Stehlin. "Family: Toward Androgyny." Pp. 76–115 in *Evangelicalism: The Coming Generation.* By James Davison Hunter. Chicago: University of Chicago, 1987.

Hurley, James B. "Did Paul Require Veils or the Silence of Women? A Consideration of I Cor. 11:2–16 and I Cor. 14:33b–36." *Westminster Theological Journal* 35 (2, Winter 1973): 190–220.

"The Hypostasis of the Archons." Introduction by Roger A. Bullard. Translated by Bentley Layton. Pp. 152–60 in *The Nag Hammadi Library.* Edited by James M. Robinson. San Francisco: Harper & Row, 1977.

"India's Lost Women." *World Press Review* (April 1991): 49.

"The Instruction of Ani." Translated by John Wilson. P. 420 in *Ancient Near Eastern Texts Relating to the Old Testament.* Edited by James B. Pritchard. 2d ed. Princeton: Princeton University, 1955.

Isaacs, Marie E. *The Concept of Spirit: A Study of Pneuma in Hellenistic Judaism and its Bearing on the New Testament.* Heythrop Monographs 1. London: Heythrop College, 1976.

Isbell, Charles D. *Corpus of the Aramaic Incantation Bowls.* Society of Biblical Literature Dissertation Series 17. Missoula, Mont.: Scholars, 1975.

Isocrates. *Works.* 3 vols. Translated by George Norlin and Larue van Hook. Loeb Classical Library. London: Wm. Heinemann; New York: G. P. Putnam's Sons, 1925–61.

Jensen, Lloyd B. "Royal Purple of Tyre." *Journal of Near Eastern Studies* 22 (2, April 1963): 104–18.

Jeremias, Joachim. *Jerusalem in the Time of Jesus.* Translated by F. H. and C. H. Cave. Philadelphia: Fortress, 1975; London: SCM, 1969.

Jewett, Paul K. *Man as Male and Female: A Study in Sexual Relationships from a Theological Point of View.* Grand Rapids: Eerdmans, 1975.

Johnson, Alan F. "Response." Pp. 154–60 in *Women, Authority & the Bible.* Edited by Alvera Mickelsen. Downers Grove, Ill.: InterVarsity, 1986.

Johnson, Gregg. "The Biological Basis for Gender-Specific Behavior." Pp. 280–93 in *Recovering Biblical Manhood and Womanhood: A Response to Evangelical Feminism.* Edited by John Piper and Wayne Grudem. Wheaton, Ill.: Crossway Books, 1991.

Johnston, George. *Ephesians, Philippians, Colossians & Philemon.* Century Bible. Greenwood, S.C.: Attic, 1967.

Johnston, Robert K. "Biblical Authority and Interpretation: The Test Case of Women's Role in the Church & Home Updated." Pp. 30–41 in *Women, Authority & the Bible.* Edited by Alvera Mickelsen. Downers Grove, Ill.: InterVarsity, 1986.

"Joseph and Asenath." Translated by C. Burchard. 2:177–247 in *The Old Testament Pseudepigrapha.* 2 vols. Edited by James H. Charlesworth. Garden City, N.Y.: Doubleday & Co., 1983–85.

*Joseph et Aséneth: Introduction, Texte Critique, Traduction et Notes.* Edited by Marc Philonenko. Studia Post-Biblica tertium decimum. Leiden: E. J. Brill, 1968.

Josephus. *The Jewish War.* Edited by Gaalya Cornfeld with Benjamin Mazar and Paul L. Maier. Grand Rapids: Zondervan Publishing House, 1982.

_________. *Works.* 10 vols. Translated by H. St. J. Thackeray, Ralph Marcus, Allen Wikgren, and Louis H. Feldman. Loeb Classical Library. Cambridge: Harvard University, 1926–65.

"Jubilees." Translated by Orval S. Wintermute. 2:35–142 in *The Old Testament Pseudepigrapha.* 2 vols. Edited by James H. Charlesworth. Garden City, N.Y.: Doubleday & Co., 1983–85.

Judge, E. A. *Rank and Status in the World of the Caesars and St. Paul.* The Broadhead Memorial Lecture 1981. University of Canterbury Publications 29. N.p.: University of Canterbury, 1982.

_________. *The Social Pattern of the Christian Groups in the First Century: Some Prolegomena to the Study of New Testament Ideas of Social Obligation.* London: Tyndale, 1960.

Juvenal. *Satires.* Rev. ed. Translated by G. G. Ramsay. Loeb Classical Library. Cambridge: Harvard University, 1940.

Kaiser, Walter C., Jr. *Toward an Exegetical Theology: Biblical Exegesis for Preaching and Teaching.* Grand Rapids: Baker Book House, 1981.

Kascher, A. *"M'srt hprwst'ts bqhylwt ysr'l btpwsh hhlnyst't-hrwmyt"* (The office of *prostatēs* in the Jewish communities of the Greco-Roman Diaspora). *Zion* 47 (4, 1982): 399–406. (NTA 28:66).

Kearsley, Rosalinde A. "Asiarchs, *Archiereis,* and the *Archiereiai* of Asia." *Greek, Roman and Byzantine Studies* 27 (2, Summer 1986): 183–92.

Kee, Howard Clark. *Christian Origins in Sociological Perspective: Methods and Resources.* Philadelphia: Westminster, 1980.

_________. *Miracle in the Early Christian World: A Study in Sociohistorical Method*. New Haven: Yale University, 1983.

Keener, Craig S. *And Marries Another: Divorce and Remarriage in the Teaching of the New Testament*. Peabody, Mass.: Hendrickson Publishers, 1991.

_________. "The Function of Johannine Pneumatology in the Context of Late First-Century Judaism." Ph.D. dissertation, Duke University, 1991.

_________. "Is Paul's Teaching 'Sexist'?" *The Crucible* 1 (1, Fall 1990): 4–11.

_________. "Nonviolence in the Face of Oppression: A Perspective on the Letter of James." *ESA Advocate* 12 (3, April 1991): 14–15.

Keller, Mark. "The Disease Concept of Alcoholism Revisited." *Journal of Studies on Alcohol* 37 (11, November 1976): 1694–1717.

Kelly, J. N. D. *A Commentary on the Epistles of Peter and Jude*. Thornapple Commentaries. Grand Rapids: Baker Book House, 1981.

_________. *A Commentary on the Pastoral Epistles*. London: Adam & Charles Black, 1972.

Kim, Chan-Hie. *Form and Structure of the Familiar Greek Letter of Recommendation*. Society of Biblical Literature Dissertation Series 4. Missoula, Mont.: Society of Biblical Literature, 1972.

Kitchen, Kenneth A. *The Ancient Orient and the Old Testament*. Chicago: Inter-Varsity, 1966.

_________. *The Bible in Its World: The Bible and Archaeology Today*. Downers Grove, Ill.: InterVarsity, 1978.

Klausner, Joseph. *From Jesus to Paul*. Translated by W. Stinespring. New York: Menorah, 1979; London: Macmillan Co., 1943.

Klein, William W. "Noisy Gong or Acoustic Vase? A Note on 1 Corinthians 13.1." *New Testament Studies* 32 (2, April 1986): 286–89.

Kleiner, D. E. E. "Women and Family Life on Roman Imperial Funerary Altars." *Latomus* 46 (3, 1987): 545–54. (NTA 32:224).

Kline, Meredith G. *Treaty of the Great King—The Covenant Structure of Deuteronomy: Studies and Commentary*. Grand Rapids: Eerdmans, 1963.

Knight, George W. III. "*Authenteō* in Reference to Women in 1 Timothy 2.12." *New Testament Studies* 30 (1, January 1984): 143–57.

_________. "The Family and the Church: How Should Biblical Manhood and Womanhood Work Out in Practice?" Pp. 345–57 in *Recovering Biblical Manhood and Womanhood: A Response to Evangelical Feminism*. Edited by John Piper and Wayne Grudem. Wheaton, Ill.: Crossway Books, 1991.

_________. "The New Testament Teaching on the Role Relationship of Male and Female with Special Reference to the Teaching/Ruling Functions in the Church." *Journal of the Evangelical Theological Society* 18 (2, Spring 1975): 81–91.

_________. *The New Testament Teaching on the Role Relationship of Men and Women*. Grand Rapids: Baker Book House, 1977.

Knox, Wilfred L. *St Paul and the Church of the Gentiles*. Cambridge: Cambridge University, 1939.

Kobelski, Paul Joseph. "Melchizedek and Melchiresa: The Heavenly Prince of Light and the Prince of Darkness in the Qumran Literature." Ph.D. dissertation, Department of Theology at Fordham University, 1978.

Koenig, John. *New Testament Hospitality: Partnership with Strangers as Promise and Mission*. Overtures to Biblical Theology 17. Philadelphia: Fortress, 1985.

Koester, Helmut. *Introduction to the New Testament*. 2 vols. Hermeneia Foundations and Facets Series. Vol. 1: *History, Culture, and Religion of the Hellenistic Age*. Vol. 2: *History and Literature of Early Christianity*. Philadelphia: Fortress, 1982.

Kolenkow, Anitra Bingham. "The Angelology of the Testament of Abraham." Pp. 153–62 in *Studies on the Testament of Abraham*. Edited by George W. E. Nickelsburg. Society of Biblical Literature Septuagint and Cognate Studies 6. Missoula, Mont.: Scholars, 1976, from a 1972 Society of Biblical Literature seminar.

Kraabel, Alf Thomas. "Judaism in Western Asia Minor Under the Roman Empire, with a Preliminary Study of the Jewish Community at Sardis, Lydia." Th.D. dissertation, Harvard Divinity School, 1968.

_________. "The Synagogue and the Jewish Community: Impact." Pp. 178–90 in *Sardis from Prehistoric to Roman Times: Results of the Archaeological Exploration of Sardis 1958–1975*. Edited by George M. A. Hanfmann. Assisted by William E. Mierse. Cambridge: Harvard University, 1983.

Kraemer, Ross Shepard. "Ecstatics and Ascetics: Studies in the Functions of Religious Activities for Women in the Greco-Roman World." Ph.D. dissertation, Princeton University, 1976.

_________. "Ecstasy and Possession: The Attraction of Women to the Cult of Dionysus." *Harvard Theological Review* 72 (1, Jan. 1979): 55–80.

_________. " 'Euoi Saboi' in Demosthenes de Corona: In Whose Honor Were the Women's Rites?" Pp. 229–36 in *SBL 1981 Seminar Papers*. Society of Biblical Literature Seminar Papers 20. Edited by Kent Harold Richards. Chico, Calif.: Scholars, 1981.

_________. *Maenads, Martyrs, Matrons, Monastics: A Sourcebook on Women's Religions in the Greco-Roman World*. Philadelphia: Fortress, 1988.

_________. "A New Inscription from Malta and the Question of Women Elders in the Diaspora Jewish Communities." *Harvard Theological Review* 78 (3–4, 1985): 431–38.

_________. "Non-Literary Evidence for Jewish Women in Rome and Egypt." *Helios* 13 (2, 1986): 85–101.

Kreitzer, Larry J. "A Numismatic Clue to Acts 19.23–41. The Ephesian Cistophori of Claudius and Agrippina." *Journal for the Study of the New Testament* 30 (1987): 59–70.

Krodel, Gerhard. "The First Letter of Peter." Pp. 50–80 in *Hebrews–James–1 & 2 Peter–Jude–Revelation*. Proclamation Commentaries. Philadelphia: Fortress, 1977.

Kroeger, Catherine. "The Apostle Paul and the Greco-Roman Cults of Women." *Journal of the Evangelical Theological Society* 30 (1, Mar. 1987): 25–38.

_________. "The Classical Concept of *Head* as 'Source'." Appendix 3, pp. 267–83 in Gretchen Gaebelein Hull, *Equal to Serve: Women and Men in the Church and Home*. Old Tappan, N.J.: Fleming H. Revell Co., 1987.

_________. "1 Timothy 2:12—A Classicist's View." Pp. 225–44 in *Women, Authority & the Bible*. Edited by Alvera Mickelsen. Downers Grove, Ill.: InterVarsity, 1986.

Kroeger, Catherine Clark, and Richard Kroeger. "May Women Teach? heresy in the pastoral epistles." *Reformed Journal* 30 (10, Oct. 1980): 14–18.

_________. "Strange Tongues or Plain Talk?" *Daughters of Sarah* 12 (4, 1986): 10–13.

Kürzinger, Josef. "Frau und Mann nach 1 Kor 11,11f." *Biblische Zeitschrift* 22 (2, 1978): 270–75.

Ladd, George Eldon. *The Last Things*. Grand Rapids: Eerdmans, 1978.

_________. *A Theology of the New Testament*. Grand Rapids: Eerdmans, 1974.

Lake, Kirsopp, and Henry J. Cadbury. *English Translation and Commentary*. Vol. 4 in *The Beginnings of Christianity*. 5 vols. Edited by F. J. Foakes Jackson and Kirsopp Lake. Grand Rapids: Baker Book House, 1979.

Latourette, Kenneth Scott. *A History of the Expansion of Christianity*. 5 vols. Vol. 1: *The First Five Centuries*. Grand Rapids: Zondervan Publishing House, 1970; New York: Harper & Row, 1970.

Laub, Franz. *Die Begegnung des frühen Christentums mit der antiken Sklaverei*. Stuttgarter Bibelstudien 107. Stuttgart: Verlag Katholisches Bibelwerk, 1982.

"The Laws of Eshnunna." Translated by Albrecht Goetze. Pp. 161–63 in *Ancient Near Eastern Texts Relating to the Old Testament*. Edited by James B. Pritchard. 2d ed. Princeton: Princeton University, 1955.

Lee, Clarence L. "Social Unrest and Primitive Christianity." Pp. 121–38 in *The Catacombs and the Colosseum: The Roman Empire as the Setting of Primitive Christianity*. Edited by Stephen Benko and John J. O'Rourke. Valley Forge, Pa.: Judson, 1971.

Lee, Jung Young. "Interpreting the Demonic Powers in Pauline Thought." *Novum Testamentum* 12 (1, 1970): 54–69.

Lefkowitz, Mary R. *Women in Greek Myth*. Baltimore: Johns Hopkins University, 1986.

Lefkowitz, Mary R., and Maureen B. Fant. *Women's Life in Greece and Rome*. Baltimore, Md.: Johns Hopkins University, 1982; London: Gerald Duckworth & Co., 1982.

Leon, Harry J. *The Jews of Ancient Rome*. Morris Loeb Series. Philadelphia: Jewish Publication Society of America, 1960.

Leonard, Eugenie Andruss. "St. Paul on the Status of Women." *Catholic Biblical Quarterly* 12 (1950): 311–20.

Leslie, William Houghton. "The Concept of Woman in the Pauline Corpus in Light of the Social and Religious Environment of the First Century." Ph.D. dissertation, Northwestern University, 1976.

Lessa, William A., and Evon Z. Vogt, editors. *Reader in Comparative Religion: An Anthropological Approach.* 4th ed. New York: Harper & Row, 1979.

Liefeld, Walter L. "Women, Submission & Ministry in 1 Corinthians." Pp. 134–54 in *Women, Authority & the Bible.* Edited by Alvera Mickelsen. Downers Grove, Ill.: InterVarsity, 1986.

"Life of Adam and Eve." Translated by M. D. Johnson. 2:249–95 in *The Old Testament Pseudepigrapha.* Edited by James H. Charlesworth. Garden City, N.Y.: Doubleday & Co., 1983–85.

_________. "Greek text of the Vita of Adam and Eve, and the Apocalypse of Moses." Pp. 1–23 in *Apocalypses Apocryphae.* Edited by Konstantin von Tischendorf. Hildesheim: Georg Olms, 1966.

Lightfoot, J. B. *St Paul's Epistle to the Galatians.* 3d ed. London and Cambridge: Macmillan & Co., 1869.

_________. *St. Paul's Epistle to the Philippians.* Grand Rapids: Zondervan Publishing House, 1953; London: Macmillan & Co., 1913.

_________. *Saint Paul's Epistles to the Colossians and to Philemon.* Grand Rapids: Zondervan Publishing House, 1959; London: Macmillan & Co., 1879.

Lightman, Marjorie, and Zeisel, William. "Univira: An Example of Continuity and Change in Roman Society." *Church History* 46 (1, Mar. 1977): 19–32.

Lincoln, Andrew T. *Paradise Now and Not Yet: Studies in the role of the heavenly dimension in Paul's thought with special reference to his eschatology.* Society for New Testament Studies Monograph Series 43. Cambridge: Cambridge University, 1981.

Lincoln, C. Eric, and Mamiya, Lawrence H. *The Black Church in the African American Experience.* Durham, N.C.: Duke University, 1990.

Lindblom, J. *Prophecy in Ancient Israel.* Philadelphia: Fortress, 1962.

Lindemann, Andreas. "Die Kinder und die Gottesherrschaft. Markus 10, 13–16 und die Stellung der Kinder in der Späthellenistischen Gesellschaft und im Urchristentum." *Wort und Dienst* 17 (1983): 77–104.

Linforth, Ivan M. *The Arts of Orpheus.* Berkeley: University of California, 1941.

"Lipit-Ishtar Lawcode." Translated by S. N. Kramer. Pp. 159–61 in *Ancient Near Eastern Texts Relating to the Old Testament.* Edited by James B. Pritchard. 2d ed. Princeton: Princeton University, 1955.

Lock, Walter. *A Critical and Exegetical Commentary on the Pastoral Epistles.* International Critical Commentaries. Edinburgh: T. & T. Clark, 1924.

Lohse, Eduard. *Colossians and Philemon.* Translated by William R. Poehlmann and Robert J. Karris. Edited by Helmut Koester. Hermeneia Commentaries. Philadelphia: Fortress, 1971.

_________. *The New Testament Environment.* Translated by John E. Steely. Nashville: Abingdon, 1976.

_________. *Die Texte aus Qumran.* Munich: Kösel-Verlag, 1971.

Long, A. A. *Hellenistic Philosophy: Stoics, Epicureans, Sceptics.* New York: Charles Scribner's Sons, 1974.

Longenecker, Richard N. "Authority, Hierarchy & Leadership Patterns in the Bible." Pp. 66–85 in *Women, Authority & the Bible.* Edited by Alvera Mickelsen. Downers Grove, Ill.: InterVarsity, 1986.

_________. *The Christology of Early Jewish Christianity.* Studies in Biblical Theology 2/17. London: SCM, 1970.

_________. *The Ministry and Message of Paul.* Grand Rapids: Zondervan Publishing House, 1971.

_________. *New Testament Social Ethics for Today.* Grand Rapids: Eerdmans, 1984.

Lönnermark, L.-G. "Till frågan om romarbrevets integritet." *Svensk Exegetisk Årsbok* 33 (1968): 141–48. (NTA 14:69).

Loraux, Nicole. "Le lit, la guerre." *Homme* 21 (1, January 1981): 37–67.

Lucian. *Works.* 8 vols. Translated by A. M. Harmon and M. D. Macleod. Loeb Classical Library. Cambridge: Harvard University, 1913–67.

Lucretius. *De Rerum Natura.* 3d rev. ed. Translated by W. H. D. Rouse. Loeb Classical Library. Cambridge: Harvard University, 1937.

Lührmann, Dieter. "Neutestamentliche Haustafeln und antike Ökonomie." *New Testament Studies* 27 (1, 1980): 83–97.

Lyall, Francis. *Slaves, Citizens, Sons: Legal Metaphors in the Epistles.* Grand Rapids: Zondervan Publishing House, 1984.

McDonald, J. I. H. "Was Romans XVI a Separate Letter?" *New Testament Studies* 16 (4, July 1970): 369–72.

MacMullen, Ramsay. *Roman Social Relations: 50 B.C. to A.D. 284.* New Haven: Yale University, 1974.

_________. "Women in Public in the Roman Empire." *Historia* 29 (1980): 209–18.

McNally, Sheila. "The Maenad in Early Greek Art." Pp. 107–41 in *Women in Ancient World: The Arethusa Papers.* Edited by John Peradotto and J. P. Sullivan. SUNY Series on Classical Studies. Albany, N.Y.: State University of New York, 1984.

McNamara, Martin. *Palestinian Judaism and the New Testament.* Good New Studies 4. Wilmington, Del.: Michael Glazier, 1983.

McNeil, Brian. "Asexuality and the Apocalypse of Zosimus." *Heythrop Journal* 22 (2, 1981): 172–73.

Magnien, Victor. *Les Mystères d'Eleusis: leurs origines le Rituel de leurs initiations.* 3d ed. Paris: Payot, 1950.

Malherbe, Abraham J. *Moral Exhortation, A Greco-Roman Sourcebook.* Library of Early Christianity 4. Philadelphia: Westminster, 1986.

_________. *Social Aspects of Early Christianity.* 2d ed. Philadelphia: Fortress, 1983.

Manning, C. E. "Seneca and the Stoics on the Equality of the Sexes." *Mnemosyne*, 4th ser., 26 (2, 1973): 170–77.

Manson, T. W. "St. Paul's Letter to the Romans—and Others." Pp. 3–15 in *The Romans Debate—Revised and Expanded Edition.* Edited by Karl P. Donfried. Peabody: Hendrickson, 1991.

Manus, Chris Ukachukwu. "The Subordination of the Women in the Church. 1 Cor 14:33b–36 Reconsidered," *Revue Africaine de Théologie* 8 (16, 1984): 183–95.

Marcus Aurelius. *The Communings with Himself of Marcus Aurelius Antoninus, Emperor of Rome, together with his speeches and sayings.* A revised text and translation by C. R. Haines. Loeb Classical Library. Cambridge: Harvard University, 1916.

Martial. *Epigrams.* 2 vols. Translated by Walter C. A. Ker. Loeb Classical Library. New York: G. P. Putnam's Sons; London: Wm. Heinemann, 1920.

Martin, Clarice J. "The *Haustafeln* (Household Codes) in African American Biblical Interpretation: 'Free Slaves' and 'Subordinate Women.' " Pp. 206–31, in *Stony the Road We Trod: African American Biblical Interpretation.* Edited by Cain Hope Felder. Minneapolis: Fortress, 1990.

Martin, Dale B. *Slavery as Salvation: The Metaphor of Slavery in Pauline Christianity.* New Haven: Yale University, 1990.

Martin, Faith McBurney. *Call Me Blessed: The Emerging Christian Woman.* Grand Rapids: Eerdmans, 1988.

Martin, Luther H. *Hellenistic Religions: An Introduction.* New York: Oxford University, 1987.

Martin, Ralph P. *Colossians and Philemon.* New Century Bible Commentary. London: Oliphants, 1974; Grand Rapids: Eerdmans, 1974.

Martin, William J. "1 Corinthians 11:2–16: An Interpretation." Pp. 231–41 in *Apostolic History and the Gospel: Biblical and Historical Essays Presented to F. F. Bruce on his 60th Birthday.* Edited by W. Ward Gasque and Ralph P. Martin. Exeter: Paternoster; Grand Rapids: Eerdmans, 1970.

Martucci, J. "*Diakriseis pneumatōn* (1 Co 12,10)." *Eglise et Théologie* 9 (3, 1978): 465–71.

"The Martyrdom and Ascension of Isaiah." Translated by M. A. Knibb. 2:143–76 in *The Old Testament Pseudepigrapha.* 2 vols. Edited by James H. Charlesworth. Garden City, N.Y.: Doubleday & Co., 1983–85.

Massa, Aldo. *The World of Pompeii.* Geneva: Minerva, 1972.

Mattingly, Harold. *Christianity in the Roman Empire.* New York: W. W. Norton & Co., 1967.

May, Herbert Gordon. "Synagogues in Palestine." *Biblical Archaeologist* 7 (1, February 1944): 1–20.

Mbiti, John S. *African Religions and Philosophies.* Garden City, N.Y.: Doubleday & Co., 1970.

Meagher, John C. "As the Twig Was Bent: Antisemitism in Greco-Roman and Earliest Christian Times." Pp. 1–26 in *AntiSemitism and the Foundations of Christianity.* Edited by Alan T. Davies. New York: Paulist, 1979.

Meeks, Wayne A. *The First Urban Christians: The Social World of the Apostle Paul.* New Haven: Yale University, 1983.

_________. "The Image of the Androgyne: Some Uses of a Symbol in Earliest Christianity." *History of Religions* 13 (3, February 1974): 165–208.

_________. *The Moral World of the First Christians.* Library of Early Christianity 6. Philadelphia: Westminster, 1986.

*Mekilta de-Rabbi Ishmael.* 3 vols. Translated by Jacob Z. Lauterbach. Philadelphia: Jewish Publication Society of America, 1933–35.

Mendenhall, George E. "Covenant Forms in Israelite Traditions." *Biblical Archaeologist* 17 (3, September 1954): 50–76.

Metzger, Bruce M. *A Textual Commentary on the Greek New Testament.* 2d edition. New York: United Bible Societies, 1975.

Mickelsen, Alvera, editor. *Women, Authority & the Bible.* Downers Grove, Ill.: InterVarsity, 1986.

Mickelsen, Berkeley and Alvera. "What Does *Kephalē* Mean in the New Testament?" Pp. 97–117 in *Women, Authority & the Bible.* Edited by Alvera Mickelsen. Downers Grove, Ill.: InterVarsity, 1986.

"Middle Assyrian Laws." Translated by Theophile J. Meek. Pp. 180–88 in *Ancient Near Eastern Texts Relating to the Old Testament.* Edited by James B. Pritchard. 2d ed. Princeton: Princeton University, 1955.

*The Midrash Rabbah.* 5 vols. Edited by Harry Freedman and Maurice Simon. Foreword by I. Epstein. London: Soncino, 1977.

Milligan, George. *St Paul's Epistles to the Thessalonians: The Greek Text with Introduction and Notes.* London: Macmillan & Co., 1908.

*The Mishnah.* Translated by Herbert Danby. London: Oxford University, 1933.

*The Mishnah.* 7 vols. Pointed Hebrew text, introductions, translations, notes, and supplements by Philip Blackman. New York: Judaica, 1963.

Mitton, C. Leslie. *Ephesians.* New Century Bible Commentary. Grand Rapids: Eerdmans, 1981.

Moehring, Horst R. "The Persecution of the Jews and the Adherents of the Isis Cult at Rome A.D. 19." *Novum Testamentum* 3 (4, December 1959): 293–304.

Moffatt, James. *The First Epistle of Paul to the Corinthians.* Moffatt New Testament Commentary. London: Hodder & Stoughton, 1938.

_________. *The General Epistles: James, Peter, and Judas.* Moffatt New Testament Commentary. Garden City, N.Y.: Doubleday, Doran & Co., 1928.

Montefiore, C. G., and Herbert Loewe. *A Rabbinic Anthology.* New York: Schocken Books, 1974; London: Macmillan, 1938.

Moo, Douglas J. "1 Timothy 2:11–15: Meaning and Significance." *Trinity Journal* 1 (1, Spring 1980): 62–83.

_________. "What Does It Mean Not to Teach or Have Authority Over Men? 1 Timothy 2:11–15." Pp. 179–93 in *Recovering Biblical Manhood and Womanhood: A Response to Evangelical Feminism.*

Edited by John Piper and Wayne Grudem. Wheaton, Ill.: Crossway Books, 1991.

Moore, George Foot. *Judaism in the First Centuries of the Christian Era.* 2 vols. Reprint. New York: Schocken Books, 1971.

Moyer, James Carroll. "The Concept of Ritual Purity Among the Hittites." Ph.D. dissertation, Brandeis University, 1969.

_________. "Hittite and Israelite Cultic Practices: A Selected Comparison." Chapter 2 in *Scripture in Context II: More Essays on the Comparative Method.* Edited by William W. Hallo, James C. Moyer, and Leo G. Perdue. Winona Lake, Ind.: Eisenbrauns, 1983.

Murphy-O'Connor, Jerome. "1 Corinthians 11:2–16 Once Again." *Catholic Biblical Quarterly* 50 (2, April 1988): 265–74.

_________. "The Non-Pauline Character of 1 Corinthians 11:2–16?" *Journal of Biblical Literature* 95 (4, December 1976): 615–21.

_________. "Sex and Logic in 1 Corinthians 11:2–16." *Catholic Biblical Quarterly* 42 (4, 1980): 482–500.

_________. *St. Paul's Corinth: Texts and Archaeology.* Introduction by John H. Elliott. Good News Studies 6. Wilmington, Del.: Michael Glazier, 1983.

Murray, Gilbert. *Five Stages of Greek Religion.* New York: Columbia University, 1925. Reprint. Westport, Conn.: Greenwood, 1976.

_________. *The Stoic Philosophy.* New York: G. P. Putnam's Sons, 1915.

Murray, John. *The Epistle to the Romans: The English Text with Introduction, Exposition and Notes.* 2 vols. New International Commentary on the New Testament. Grand Rapids: Eerdmans, 1965.

Myers, Steven. "Crown of Beauty Instead of Ashes." Pp. 20–25 in *World Christian Summer Reader 1990.* Pasadena, Calif.: World Christian, 1990.

Mylonas, George E. *Eleusis and the Eleusinian Mysteries.* Princeton: Princeton University, 1961.

Narkiss, Bezalel. "Pagan, Christian, and Jewish Elements in the Art of Ancient Synagogues." Pp. 183–88 in *The Synagogue in Late Antiquity.* Edited by Lee I. Levine. Philadelphia: American Schools of Oriental Research, 1986.

Neusner, Jacob. *Judaism in the Beginning of Christianity.* Philadelphia: Fortress, 1984.

Newman, Robert C. "The Ancient Exegesis of Genesis 6:2, 4." *Grace Theological Journal* 5 (1, Spring 1984): 13–36.

*New Testament Apocrypha.* Edited by Edgar Hennecke and Wilhelm Schneemelcher. Translated by A. J. B. Higgins et al. Edited by R. McL. Wilson. Vol. 1: *Gospels and Related Writings.* Vol. 2: *Writings Related to the Apostles; Apocalypses and Related Subjects.* Philadelphia: Westminster, 1963–65.

Nickelsburg, George W. E. "Apocalyptic and Myth in 1 Enoch 6–11." *Journal of Biblical Literature* 96 (3, September 1977): 383–405.

Nicole, Roger. "Biblical Authority & Feminist Aspirations." Pp. 42–50 in *Women, Authority & the Bible.* Edited by Alvera Mickelsen. Downers Grove, Ill.: InterVarsity, 1986.

Nilsson, Martin P. *The Dionysiac Mysteries of the Hellenistic and Roman Age*. Skrifter Utgivna Av Svenska Institutet I Athen, 8°, V. Lund: C. W. K. Gleerup, 1957.

Nock, Arthur Darby. *Early Gentile Christianity and Its Hellenistic Background*. New York: Harper & Row, 1964.

_________. *Conversion: The Old and the New in Religion from Alexander the Great to Augustine of Hippo*. Oxford: Oxford University, 1933.

_________. "The Vocabulary of the New Testament." *Journal of Biblical Literature* 52 (1933): 131–39.

Nolland, J. "Women in the Public Life of the Church." *Crux* 19 (3, 1983): 17–23.

O'Brien, Peter T. *Colossians, Philemon*. Word Biblical Commentary 44. Waco, Tex.: Word Books, 1982.

Odell-Scott, David W. "In Defense of an Egalitarian Interpretation of 1 Cor 14:34–36. A Reply to Murphy-O'Connor's Critique." *Biblical Theology Bulletin* 17 (3, July 1987): 100–103.

_________. "Let the Women Speak in Church. An Egalitarian Interpretation of 1 Cor 14:33b–36." *Biblical Theology Bulletin* 13 (3, July 1983): 90–93.

*Die Oracula Sibyllina*. Edited by Johannes Geffcken. Griechische christliche Schriftseller 8. Leipzig, 1902.

*The Orphic Hymns: Text, Translation and Notes*. Translated by Apostolos N. Athanassakis. Society of Biblical Literature Texts and Translations 12. Graeco-Roman Religion Series 4. Missoula, Mont.: Scholars, 1977.

Osborne, Grant R. "Hermeneutics and Women in the Church." *Journal of the Evangelical Theological Society* 20 (4, December 1977): 337–52.

Osburn, Carroll D. "*Authenteō* (1 Timothy 2:12)." *Restoration Quarterly* 25 (1, 1982): 1–12.

Oster, R. "The Ephesian Artemis as an opponent of Early Christianity." *Jahrbuch für Antike und Christentum* 19 (1976): 24–44.

_________. "When Men Wore Veils to Worship: the Historical Context of 1 Corinthians 11:4." *New Testament Studies* 34 (4, October 1988): 481–505.

Otto, Walter F. *Dionysus: Myth and Cult*. Translated by Robert B. Palmer. Bloomington: Indiana University, 1965.

Packer, J. I. "Let's Stop Making Women Presbyters." *Christianity Today* (February 11, 1991): 18–21.

Padgett, Alan. " 'Authority Over Her Head.' Toward a Feminist Reading of St. Paul." *Daughters of Sarah* 12 (1, 1986): 5–9.

_________. "Paul on Women in the Church: The Contradictions of Coiffure in 1 Corinthians 11.2–16." *Journal for the Study of the New Testament* 20 (1984): 69–86.

_________. "The Pauline Rationale for Submission: Biblical Feminism and the *hina* Clauses of Titus 2:1–10." *Evangelical Quarterly* 59 (1, January 1987): 39–52.

_________. "Wealthy Women at Ephesus. I Timothy 2:8–15 in Social Context." *Interpretation* 41 (1, January 1987): 19–31.

Padgug, Robert A. "Problems in the Theory of Slavery and Slave Society." *Science and Society* 40 (1, Spring 1976): 3–27.

Park, David M. "The Structure of Authority in Marriage: An Examination of *Hypotasso* and *Kephale* in Ephesians 5:21–33." *Evangelical Quarterly* 59 (2, April 1987): 117–24.

Parke, H. W. *A History of the Delphic Oracle.* Oxford: Basil Blackwell, 1939.

_________. *Sibyls and Sibylline Prophecy in Classical Antiquity.* Edited by B. C. McGing. New York: Routledge, 1988.

Parkes, James. *The Conflict of the Church and the Synagogue: A Study in the Origins of Antisemitism.* New York: Atheneum, 1979.

Parshall, Phil. *Bridges to Islam: A Christian Perspective on Folk Islam.* Foreword by J. Christy Wilson, Jr. Grand Rapids: Baker Book House, 1983.

Paul, Shalom M. "Classifications of Wine in Mesopotamian and Rabbinic Sources." *Israel Exploration Journal* 25 (1, 1975): 42–45.

_________. "Prophets and Prophecy (in the Bible)." 13:1160–64 in *Encyclopaedia Judaica.* 16 vols. Edited by Cecil Roth and Geoffrey Wigoder. Jerusalem: Keter Publishing House, 1972.

Payne, Philip Barton. "Libertarian Women in Ephesus: A Response to Douglas J. Moo's Article, '1 Timothy 2:11–15: Meaning and Significance.' " *Trinity Journal* 2 (2, 1981): 169–97.

_________. "Response." Pp. 118–32 in *Women, Authority & the Bible.* Edited by Alvera Mickelsen. Downers Grove, Ill.: InterVarsity, 1986.

Peake, A. S. "Colossians." 3:477–547 in *The Expositor's Greek Testament.* 5 vols. Edited by W. Robertson Nicoll. Grand Rapids: Eerdmans, 1979.

Pella, G. "Voile et soumission? Essai d'interprétation de deux textes pauliniens concernants le statut de l'homme et de la femme." *Hokhma* 30 (1985): 3–20. (NTA 30:305).

Pearson, Birger A. *The Pneumatikos-Psychikos Terminology in 1 Corinthians: A Study in the Theology of the Corinthian Opponents of Paul and Its Relation to Gnosticism.* Society of Biblical Literature Dissertation Series 12. Missoula, Mont.: Scholars, 1973.

Pelser, G. M. M. "Women and ecclesiastical ministries in Paul." *Neotestamentica* 10 (1976): 92–109.

Peradotto, John, and J. P. Sullivan. "Introduction." Pp. 1–6 in *Women in the Ancient World: The Arethusa Papers.* Edited by John Peradotto and J. P. Sullivan. SUNY Series in Classical Studies. Albany, N.Y.: State University of New York, 1984.

Perkins, John. *With Justice For All.* Foreword by Chuck Colson. Ventura, Calif.: Regal Books, 1982.

*Pesikta de-Rab Kahana: R. Kahana's Compilation of Discourses for Sabbaths and Festival Days.* Translated by William G. Braude and Israel J. Kapstein. Philadelphia: Jewish Publication Society of America, 1975.

*Pesikta Rabbati.* 2 vols. Translated by William G. Braude. Yale Judaica Series 18. New Haven: Yale University, 1968.

Petronius. *Satyricon, Fragments, and Poems.* Translated by W. H. D. Rouse. Loeb Classical Library. London: Wm. Heinemann; New York: G. P. Putnam's Sons, 1913.

Philo. *Works.* 12 vols. Translated by F. H. Colson, G. H. Whitaker, and R. Marcus. Loeb Classical Library. Cambridge: Harvard University, 1929–62.

Philostratus. *The Life of Apollonius of Tyana.* 2 vols. Translated by F. C. Conybeare. Loeb Classical Library. Cambridge: Harvard University, 1912.

Pickthall, Mohammed Marmaduke, translator. *The Meaning of the Glorious Koran: An Explanatory Translation.* New York: New American Library, n.d.

Piper, John, and Wayne Grudem. "An Overview of Central Concerns: Questions and Answers." Pp. 60–92 in *Recovering Biblical Manhood and Womanhood: A Response to Evangelical Feminism.* Edited by John Piper and Wayne Grudem. Wheaton, Ill.: Crossway Books, 1991.

Plato. *Works.* 12 vols. Translated by Harold North Fowler, et al. Loeb Classical Library. Cambridge: Harvard University, 1914–26.

Pliny. *Letters and Panegyricus.* 2 vols. Translated by Betty Radice. Loeb Classical Library. Cambridge: Harvard University, 1969.

Plutarch. *Lives.* 11 vols. Translated by Bernadotte Perrin et al. Loeb Classical Library. London: Wm. Heinemann; New York: G. P. Putnam's Sons, 1914–.

_________. *Moralia.* 15 vols. Translated by Frank Cole Babbitt et al. Loeb Classical Library. London: Wm. Heinemann; New York: G. P. Putnam's Sons, 1927–69.

Pomeroy, Sarah B. *Goddesses, Whores, Wives, and Slaves: Women in Classical Antiquity.* New York: Schocken Books, 1975.

_________. "Women in Roman Egypt: A preliminary study based on papyri." Pp. 303–22 in *Reflections of Women in Antiquity.* Edited by Helene P. Foley. New York: Gordon and Breach Science Publishers, 1981.

Prince, Raymond. "Indigenous Yoruba Psychiatry." Pp. 84–120 in *Magic, Faith, & Healing: Studies in Primitive Psychiatry Today.* Edited by Ari Kiev. New York: Free, 1964.

Pritchard, James B., editor. *Ancient Near Eastern Texts Relating to the Old Testament.* 2d ed. Princeton: Princeton University, 1955.

Pritz, Ray A. *Nazarene Jewish Christianity: From the End of the New Testament Period Until Its Disappearance in the Fourth Century.* Studia Post Biblica. Jerusalem: Magnes; Leiden: E. J. Brill, 1988.

"Pseudo-Philo." Translated by D. J. Harrington. 2:297–377 in *The Old Testament Pseudepigrapha.* 2 vols. Edited by James H. Charlesworth. Garden City, N.Y.: Doubleday & Co., 1983–85.

*Pseudo-Philo's Liber Antiquitatum Biblicarum.* (Latin text.) Edited by Guido Kisch. Publications in Mediaeval Studies, University of Notre Dame. Notre Dame: University of Notre Dame, 1949.

"Pseudo-Phocylides." Translated by P. W. van der Horst. 2:565–82 in *The Old Testament Pseudepigrapha*. 2 vols. Edited by James H. Charlesworth. Garden City, N.Y.: Doubleday & Co., 1983–85.

Pucci, Giuseppe. "Pottery and trade in the Roman Period." Pp. 105–17 in *Trade in the Ancient Economy*. Edited by Peter Garnsey, Keith Hopkins, and C. R. Whittaker. Berkeley and Los Angeles: University of California, 1983.

Quintilian. *The Institutio Oratoria*. 4 vols. Translated by H. E. Butler. Loeb Classical Library. London: Wm. Heinemann, 1969.

Rabello, Alfredo Mordechai. "The Legal Condition of the Jews in the Roman Empire." Pp. 662–762 in *Aufstieg und Niedergang der Römischen Welt* 2.13. Berlin: Walter de Gruyter, 1980.

Raboteau, Albert J. *Slave Religion: The "Invisible Institution" in the Antebellum South*. Oxford: Oxford University, 1978.

Rainey, A. F. "The Kingdom of Ugarit." *Biblical Archaeologist* 28 (December 1965): 102–25.

Rajak, Tessa. "Was There a Roman Charter for the Jews?" *Journal of Roman Studies* 74 (1984): 107–23.

Ramsay, William M. *The Cities of St. Paul: Their Influence on his Life and Thought*. Reprint. Grand Rapids: Baker Book House, 1979; London: Hodder & Stoughton, 1907.

_________. *The Letters to the Seven Churches of Asia*. Reprint. Grand Rapids: Baker Book House, 1979; London: Hodder & Stoughton, 1904.

_________. *Luke the Physician and Other Studies in the History of Religion*. Reprint. Grand Rapids: Baker Book House, 1979; London: Hodder & Stoughton, 1908.

_________. *Pauline and Other Studies in Early Church History*. Reprint. Grand Rapids: Baker Book House, 1979. New York: A. C. Armstrong & Son, 1906.

_________. "Roads and Travel (in New Testament)." 5:375–402 in *Dictionary of the Bible*. 5 vols. Edited by James Hastings. Edinburgh: T. & T. Clark; New York: Charles Scribner's Sons, 1898–1923.

_________. *The Teaching of Paul in Terms of the Present Day*. Reprint. Grand Rapids: Baker Book House, 1979; London: Hodder & Stoughton, 1913.

Rawson, Beryl. "The Roman Family." Pp. 1–57 in *The Family in Ancient Rome: New Perspectives*. Edited by Beryl Rawson. Ithaca, N.Y.: Cornell University, 1986.

Reeder, E. D. "The Mother of the Gods and a Hellenistic Bronze Matrix." *American Journal of Archaeology* 91 (3, 1987): 423–40.

Reekmans, Tony. "Juvenal's Views on Social Change." *Ancient Society* 2 (1971): 117–61.

Reicke, Bo. *The Epistles of James, Peter, and Jude*. Anchor Bible 37. Garden City, N.Y.: Doubleday & Co., 1964.

_________. *The New Testament Era: The World of the Bible from 500 B.C. to A.D. 100*. Philadelphia: Fortress, 1974.

Reinhold, Meyer. *Diaspora: The Jews among the Greeks and Romans.* Sarasota and Toronto: Samuel Stevens & Co., 1983.

Reitzenstein, Richard. *Hellenistic Mystery-Religions: Their Basic Ideas and Significance.* Translated by John E. Steely. Pittsburgh Theological Monograph Series 15. Pittsburgh: Pickwick, 1978.

Richards, J. R. "Romans and I Corinthians: Their Chronological Relationship and Comparative Dates." *New Testament Studies* 13 (1, October 1966): 14–30.

Richardson, Don. *Peace Child.* Ventura, Calif.: Regal Books, GL Publications, 1976.

Richardson, Peter, and Peter Gooch. "Logia of Jesus in 1 Corinthians." Pp. 39–62 in *The Jesus Tradition Outside the Gospels.* Gospel Perspectives 5. Edited by David Wenham. Sheffield: JSOT, 1984.

Ridderbos, Herman. *Paul: An Outline of His Theology.* Translated by John Richard De Witt. Grand Rapids: Eerdmans, 1975.

"Ritual Against Impotence." Translated by A. Goetze. Pp. 349–50 in *Ancient Near Eastern Texts Relating to the Old Testament.* Edited by James B. Pritchard. 2d ed. Princeton: Princeton University, 1955.

Robertson, Archibald, and Alfred Plummer. *A Critical and Exegetical Commentary on the First Epistle of St. Paul to the Corinthians.* 2d ed. International Critical Commentary. Edinburgh: T. & T. Clark, 1914.

Robinson, J. Armitage. *St Paul's Epistle to the Ephesians.* 2d ed. London: James Clarke & Co., 1904.

Robinson, John A. T. *Jesus and His Coming.* 2d ed. Philadelphia: Westminster, 1979.

__________. *Twelve New Testament Studies.* Studies in Biblical Theology 1/34. London: SCM, 1962.

Rogers, Cleon L., Jr. "The Dionysian Background of Ephesians 5:18." *Bibliotheca Sacra* 136 (543, July 1979): 249–57.

Roon, A. Van. *The Authenticity of Ephesians.* Supplements to Novum Testamentum 39. Leiden: E. J. Brill, 1974.

Ross, James F. "Prophecy in Hamath, Israel, and Mari." *Harvard Theological Review* 63 (January 1970): 1–28.

Rost, Leonhard. *Judaism Outside the Hebrew Canon: An Introduction to the Documents.* Translated by David E. Green. Nashville: Abingdon, 1976.

Ruck, Carl A. P. "Solving the Eleusinian Mystery." Pp. 35–50 in *The Road to Eleusis: Unveiling the Secret of the Mysteries.* By Robert Gordon Wasson, Albert Hofmann, and Carl A. P. Ruck. New York: Harcourt Brace Jovanovich, 1978.

Rupprecht, Arthur W. "Attitudes on Slavery Among the Church Fathers." Pp. 261–77 in *New Dimensions in New Testament Study.* Edited by Richard N. Longenecker and Merrill C. Tenney. Grand Rapids: Zondervan, 1974.

Russell, D. S. *The Method and Message of Jewish Apocalyptic.* Old Testament Library. Philadelphia: Westminster, 1964.

Rutenber, Culbert Gerow. "The Doctrine of the Imitation of God in Plato." Ph.D. dissertation, University of Pennsylvania, 1946.

Ryan, Rosalie. "Lydia, A Dealer in Purple Goods." *Bible Today* 22 (5, 1984): 285–89.

Safrai, S. "Education and the Study of the Torah." Pp. 945–70 in *The Jewish People in the First Century: Historical Geography, Political History, Social, Cultural and Religious Life and Institutions.* 2 vols. Edited by S. Safrai and M. Stern with D. Flusser and W. C. van Unnik. Section 1 of Compendia Rerum Iudaicarum ad Novum Testamentum. Vol. 1: Assen: Van Gorcum & Co., B.V., 1974. Vol. 2: Philadelphia: Fortress, 1976.

_________. "Home and Family." Pp. 728–92 in *The Jewish People in the First Century: Historical Geography, Political History, Social, Cultural and Religious Life and Institutions.* 2 vols. Edited by S. Safrai and M. Stern with D. Flusser and W. C. van Unnik. Section 1 of Compendia Rerum Iudaicarum ad Novum Testamentum. Vol. 1: Assen: Van Gorcum & Co., B.V., 1974. Vol. 2: Philadelphia: Fortress, 1976.

_________. "Religion in Everyday Life." Pp. 793–833 in *The Jewish People in the First Century: Historical Geography, Political History, Social, Cultural and Religious Life and Institutions.* 2 vols. Edited by S. Safrai and M. Stern with D. Flusser and W. C. van Unnik. Section 1 of Compendia Rerum Iudaicarum ad Novum Testamentum. Vol. 1: Assen: Van Gorcum & Co., B.V., 1974. Vol. 2: Philadelphia: Fortress, 1976.

_________. "The Synagogue." Pp. 908–44 in *The Jewish People in the First Century: Historical Geography, Political History, Social, Cultural and Religious Life and Institutions.* 2 vols. Edited by S. Safrai and M. Stern with D. Flusser and W. C. van Unnik. Section 1 of Compendia Rerum Iudaicarum ad Novum Testamentum. Vol. 1: Assen: Van Gorcum & Co., B.V., 1974. Vol. 2: Philadelphia: Fortress, 1976.

_________. "The Temple." Pp. 865–907 in *The Jewish People in the First Century: Historical Geography, Political History, Social, Cultural and Religious Life and Institutions.* 2 vols. Edited by S. Safrai and M. Stern with D. Flusser and W. C. van Unnik. Section 1 of Compendia Rerum Iudaicarum ad Novum Testamentum. Vol. 1: Assen: Van Gorcum & Co., B.V., 1974. Vol. 2: Philadelphia: Fortress, 1976.

Salles, C. "Le monde gréco-romain du 1er siècle: une société interculturelle?" *Supplément* 156 (1986): 15–28. (NTA 31:85).

Sampley, J. Paul. *"And the Two Shall Become One Flesh": A Study of Traditions in Ephesians 5:21–33.* Society for New Testament Studies Monograph Series 16. Cambridge: Cambridge University, 1971.

Sanday, William, and Arthur Headlam. *A Critical and Exegetical Commentary on the Epistle to the Romans.* 5th ed. International Critical Commentary. Edinburgh: T. & T. Clark, 1902.

Sanders, E. P. *Jewish Law from Jesus to the Mishnah: Five Studies.* London: SCM; Philadelphia: Trinity Press International, 1990.

Sanders, E. P. et al., editors. *Jewish and Christian Self-Definition.* 3 vols. Philadelphia: Fortress, 1980–83.

Sanders, Jack T. *The New Testament Christological Hymns: Their Historical Religious Background.* Cambridge: Cambridge University, 1971.

Sarna, Nahum M. *Exploring Exodus: The Heritage of Biblical Israel.* New York: Schocken Books, 1986.

Scanzoni, Letha, and Nancy Hardesty. *All We're Meant to Be: A Biblical Approach to Women's Liberation.* Waco, Tex.: Word Books, 1974.

Schmithals, Walter. *The Office of Apostle in the Early Church.* Translated by John E. Steely. Nashville: Abingdon, 1969.

Scholem, Gershom G. *Jewish Gnosticism, Merkabah Mysticism, and Talmudic Tradition.* New York: Jewish Theological Seminary of America, 1965.

Scholer, David M. "1 Timothy 2:9–15 & the Place of Women in the Church's Ministry." Pp. 193–219 in *Women, Authority & the Bible.* Edited by Alvera Mickelsen. Downers Grove, Ill.: InterVarsity, 1986.

_________. "Paul's Women Co-Workers in the Ministry of the Church." *Daughters of Sarah* 6 (4, 1980): 3–6.

_________. "Women's Adornment: Some Historical and Hermeneutical Observations on the New Testament Passages." *Daughters of Sarah* 6 (1, 1980): 3–6.

Schreiner, Thomas R. "Head Coverings, Prophecies and the Trinity: 1 Corinthians 11:2–16." Pp. 124–39 in *Recovering Biblical Manhood and Womanhood: A Response to Evangelical Feminism.* Edited by John Piper and Wayne Grudem. Wheaton, Ill.: Crossway Books, 1991.

_________. "The Valuable Ministries of Women in the Context of Male Leadership: A Survey of Old and New Testament Examples and Teaching." Pp. 209–24 in *Recovering Biblical Manhood and Womanhood: A Response to Evangelical Feminism.* Edited by John Piper and Wayne Grudem. Wheaton, Ill.: Crossway Books, 1991.

Schulz, Ray R. "Romans 16:7: Junia or Junias?" *Expository Times* 98 (4, January 1987): 108–10.

Schwarz, Günther. "*Exousian echein epi tēs kephalēs* (1 Korinther 11:10)." *Zeitschrift für die Neutestamentliche Wissenschaft* 70 (3–4, 1979): 249.

Schweizer, Eduard. *The Letter to the Colossians: A Commentary.* Translated by Andrew Chester. Minneapolis: Augsburg, 1982.

Scott, E. F. *The Pastoral Epistles.* Moffatt New Testament Commentary. London: Hodder & Stoughton, 1936.

Scroggs, Robin. "Paul and the Eschatological Woman." *Journal of the American Academy of Religion* 40 (3, September 1972): 283–303.

Seager, Andrew R. "The Synagogue and the Jewish Community: The Building." Pp. 168–77 in *Sardis from Prehistoric to Roman Times:*

*Results of the Archaeological Exploration of Sardis 1958–1975.* By George M. A. Hanfmann. Edited by William E. Mierse. Cambridge: Harvard University, 1983.

"2 Baruch." Translated by A. F. J. Klijn. 1:615–52 in *The Old Testament Pseudepigrapha.* 2 vols. Edited by James H. Charlesworth. Garden City, N.Y.: Doubleday & Co., 1983–85.

"2 Enoch." Translated by F. I. Andersen. 1:91–221 in *The Old Testament Pseudepigrapha.* 2 vols. Edited by James H. Charlesworth. Garden City, N.Y.: Doubleday & Co., 1983–85.

Segal, Charles. "The Menace of Dionysus: Sex Roles and Reversals in Euripides' Bacchae." Pp. 195–212 in *Women in the Ancient World: The Arethusa Papers.* Edited by John Peradotto and J. P. Sullivan. SUNY Series in Classical Studies. Albany, N.Y.: State University of New York, 1984.

Selwyn, Edward Gordon. *The First Epistle of St. Peter: The Greek Text with Introduction, Notes, and Essays.* 2d ed. London: Macmillan, 1947.

Seneca. *Works.* 10 vols. Translated by John W. Basore et al. Loeb Classical Library. Cambridge: Harvard University, 1928–70.

*The Sentences of Sextus.* Edited and translated by Richard Edwards and Robert A. Wild. Society of Biblical Literature Texts and Translations 22. Society of Biblical Literature Early Christian Literature Series 5. Chico, Calif.: Scholars Press, 1981.

"Sentences of the Syriac Menander." Translated by T. Baarda. 2:583–606 in *The Old Testament Pseudepigrapha.* 2 vols. Edited by James H. Charlesworth. Garden City, N.Y.: Doubleday & Co., 1983–85.

Sernett, Milton C. *Afro-American Religious History: A Documentary Witness.* Durham: Duke University, 1985.

Sevenster, J. N. *Paul and Seneca.* Supplements to Novum Testamentum 4. Leiden: E. J. Brill, 1961.

_________. *The Roots of Pagan Anti-Semitism in the Ancient World.* Supplements to Novum Testamentum 41. Leiden: E. J. Brill, 1975.

Sextus Empiricus. *Works.* 4 vols. Translated by R. G. Bury. Loeb Classical Library. Cambridge: Harvard University; London: Wm. Heinemann, 1933–49.

Shapiro, Laura. "Guns and Dolls." *Newsweek* (May 28, 1990): 56–65.

Sheldon, Henry C. *The Mystery Religions and the New Testament.* New York: Abingdon, 1918.

Sherk, Robert K., editor and translator. *The Roman Empire: Augustus to Hadrian.* Translated Documents of Greece and Rome 6. New York: Cambridge University, 1988.

Shoemaker, Thomas P. "Unveiling of Equality: 1 Corinthians 11:2–16." *Biblical Theology Bulletin* 17 (2, April 1987): 60–63.

"Sibylline Oracles." Translated by J. J. Collins. 1:317–472 in *The Old Testament Pseudepigrapha.* 2 vols. Edited by James H. Charlesworth. Garden City, N.Y.: Doubleday & Co., 1983–85.

Sidebottom, E. M. *James, Jude, 2 Peter.* New Century Bible Commentary. Grand Rapids: Eerdmans, 1982; New York: Thomas Nelson Publishers, 1967.

*Sifra: An Analytical Translation.* 3 vols. Translated by Jacob Neusner. Brown Judaic Studies 138–40. Atlanta: Scholars, 1988.

*Sifre to Deuteronomy: An Analytical Translation.* 2 vols. Translated by Jacob Neusner. Brown Judaic Studies 98 and 101. Atlanta: Scholars, 1987.

*Sifré to Numbers: An American Translation and Explanation.* 2 vols. Translated by Jacob Neusner. Brown Judaic Studies 118–19. Atlanta: Scholars, 1986.

Smallwood, E. Mary. *The Jews Under Roman Rule: From Pompey to Diocletian.* Studies in Judaism in Late Antiquity 20. Leiden: E. J. Brill, 1976.

Smith, Morton. *Tannaitic Parallels to the Gospels.* Philadelphia: Society of Biblical Literature, 1951.

Sobol, Donald J. *The Amazons of Greek Mythology.* South Brunswick, N.J.: A. S. Barnes & Co., 1972.

Sokolowski, F. "A New Testimony on the Cult of Artemis of Ephesus." *Harvard Theological Review* 58 (4, October 1965): 427–31.

Spencer, Aída Besançon. *Beyond the Curse: Women Called to Ministry.* Reprint. Peabody: Hendrickson Publishers, 1989.

_________. "Eve at Ephesus (Should women be ordained as pastors according to the First Letter to Timothy 2:11–15)." *Journal of the Evangelical Theological Society* 17 (4, Fall 1974): 215–22.

Spittler, Russell P. *The Corinthian Correspondence.* Springfield, Mo.: Gospel Publishing House, 1976.

Stafford, Tim. "The Abortion Wars: What Most Christians Don't Know." *Christianity Today* (October 6, 1989): 16–20.

Stambaugh, John E., and David L. Balch, *The New Testament in Its Social Environment.* Library of Early Christianity 2. Philadelphia: Westminster, 1986.

Starr, R. J. "The Circulation of Literary Texts in the Roman World." *Classical Quarterly* 37 (1, 1987): 213–23.

Sterling, Dorothy, editor. *We Are Your Sisters: Black Women in the Nineteenth Century.* New York: W. W. Norton & Co., 1984.

Stern, M. *Greek and Latin Authors on Jews and Judaism: Edited with Introduction, Translations and Commentary.* 3 vols. Jerusalem: Israel Academy of Sciences and Humanities, 1974–84.

_________. "The Jews in Greek and Latin Literature." Pp. 1101–59 in *The Jewish People in the First Century: Historical Geography, Political History, Social, Cultural and Religious Life and Institutions.* 2 vols. Edited by S. Safrai and M. Stern with D. Flusser and W. C. van Unnik. Section 1 of Compendia Rerum Iudaicarum ad Novum Testamentum. Vol. 1: Assen: Van Gorcum & Co., B.V., 1974. Vol. 2: Philadelphia: Fortress, 1976.

Stowers, Stanley Kent. "The Diatribe." Pp. 71–83 in *Greco-Roman Literature and the New Testament: Selected Forms and Genres.* Edited by David E. Aune. Society of Biblical Literature Sources for Biblical Study 21. Atlanta: Scholars, 1988.

_________. *The Diatribe and Paul's Letter to the Romans.* Society of Biblical Literature Dissertation Series 57. Chico, Calif.: Scholars, 1981.

_________. *Letter Writing in Greco-Roman Antiquity.* Library of Early Christianity 5. Philadelphia: Westminster, 1986.

Streeter, B. H., and Edith Picton-Turbervill. *Woman and the Church.* London: F. Fisher Unwin, 1917.

Strabo. *Geography.* 8 vols. Translated by Horace Leonard Jones and John Robert Sitlington Sterrett. Loeb Classical Library. Cambridge: Harvard University, 1917–32.

Suetonius. *The Twelve Caesars.* Translated by Robert Graves. Baltimore: Penguin Books, 1957.

Sunderland, La Roy. *The Testimony of God Against Slavery, or A Collection of Passages from the Bible which Show the Sin of Holding Property in Man, with Notes.* Boston: Webster & Southard, 1835.

Sussman, Linda S. "Workers and Drones: Labor, Idleness and Gender Definition in Hesiod's Beehive." Pp. 79–93 in *Women in the Ancient World: The Arethusa Papers.* Edited by John Peradotto and J. P. Sullivan. SUNY Series in Classical Studies. Albany, N.Y.: State University of New York, 1984.

Swidler, Leonard. *Women in Judaism: The Status of Women in Formative Judaism.* Metuchen, N.J.: Scarecrow, 1976.

Tacitus. *The Complete Works of Tacitus.* Translated by Alfred John Church and William Jackson Brodribb. New York: Modern Library, 1942.

"The Tale of Aqhat." Translated by H. L. Ginsberg. Pp. 149–55 in *Ancient Near Eastern Texts Relating to the Old Testament.* Edited by James B. Pritchard. 2d ed. Princeton: Princeton University, 1955.

*Talmud of the Land of Israel: A Preliminary Translation and Explanation.* 34 vols. Translated by Jacob Neusner, et al. Chicago: University of Chicago, 1982–.

Tarn, W. W. *Hellenistic Civilisation.* Rev. by W. W. Tarn and G. T. Griffith. 3d rev. ed. New York: New American Library, 1974.

Taylor, Lily Ross. "Artemis of Ephesus." 5:251–56 in *The Beginnings of Christianity.* 5 vols. Edited by F. J. Foakes Jackson and Kirsopp Lake. Reprint. Grand Rapids: Baker Book House, 1979.

Taylor, Thomas. *The Eleusinian and Bacchic Mysteries: A Dissertation.* 4th ed. Edited by Alexander Wilder. New York: J. W. Bouton, 1891.

Tcherikover, Victor. "The Ideology of the Letter of Aristeas." *Harvard Theological Review* 51 (2, April 1958): 59–85.

Tertullian. *Apology; De Spectaculis.* Translated by T. R. Glover. Loeb Classical Library. Cambridge: Harvard University, 1931.

*The Testament of Abraham: The Greek Recensions.* Translated by Michael E. Stone. Society of Biblical Literature Texts and Translations 2. Pseudepigrapha Series 2. Missoula, Mont.: Society of Biblical Literature, 1972.

"Testament of Job." Translated by R. P. Spittler. 1:829–68 in *The Old Testament Pseudepigrapha.* 2 vols. Edited by James H. Charlesworth. Garden City, N.Y.: Doubleday & Co., 1983–85.

*The Testament of Job According to the SV Text.* Edited by Robert A. Kraft with Harold Attridge, Russell Spittler, and Janet Timbie. Society of Biblical Literature Texts and Translations 5. Pseudepigrapha

Series 4. Missoula, Mont.: Scholars, Society of Biblical Literature, 1974.

"Testament of Solomon." Translated by D. C. Duling. 1:935–59 in *The Old Testament Pseudepigrapha*. 2 vols. Edited by James H. Charlesworth. Garden City, N.Y.: Doubleday & Co., 1983–85.

*The Testament of Solomon* (Greek text). Edited by Chester Charlton McCown. Leipzig: J. C. Hinrichs'sche Buchhandlung, 1922.

"Testaments of the Twelve Patriarchs." Translated by Howard Clark Kee. 1:775–828 in *The Old Testament Pseudepigrapha*. 2 vols. Edited by James H. Charlesworth. Garden City, N.Y.: Doubleday & Co., 1983–85.

Theissen, Gerd. *The Social Setting of Pauline Christianity*. Edited and translated by John H. Schütz. Philadelphia: Fortress, 1982.

*Theognis, Ps.-Pythagoras, Ps.-Phocylides, Chares, Anonymi Avlodia, Fragmentvm Teliambicvm*. Edited by Douglas Young. Bibliotheca Scriptorvm Graecorvm et Romanorvm Tevbneriana. Leipzig: BSB B. G. Teubner Verlaggesellschaft, 1971.

Theon. *The Progymnasmata of Theon: a new text with translation and commentary*. By James R. Butts. Ann Arbor, Mich.: University Microfilms International, 1989.

"3 Baruch." Translated by H. E. Gaylord, Jr. 1:653–79 in *The Old Testament Pseudepigrapha*. 2 vols. Edited by James H. Charlesworth. Garden City, N.Y.: Doubleday & Co., 1983–85.

"3 (Hebrew Apocalypse of) Enoch." Translated by P. Alexander. 1:223–315 in *The Old Testament Pseudepigrapha*. 2 vols. Edited by James H. Charlesworth. Garden City, N.Y.: Doubleday & Co., 1983–85.

Thoma, Clemens. "Die Weltanschauung des Josephus Flavius. Dargestellt anhand seiner Schilderung des jüdischen Aufstandes gegen Rom (66–73 n. Chr.)." *Kairos* 11 (1, 1969): 39–52.

Thompson, Cynthia L. "Hairstyles, Head-coverings, and St. Paul: Portraits from Roman Corinth." *Biblical Archaeologist* 51 (2, June 1988): 101–15.

Thompson, Marianne Meye. "Response." Pp. 91–96 in *Women, Authority & the Bible*. Edited by Alvera Mickelsen. Downers Grove, Ill.: InterVarsity, 1986.

Tigerstedt, E. N. "Plato's Idea of Poetical Inspiration." *Commentationes Humanarum Litterarum* 44 (2, 1969): 5–76.

Tinh, Tran Tam. "Sarapis and Isis." 3:101–17 in *Jewish and Christian Self-Definition*. 3 vols. Vol. 3: *Self-Definition in the Greco-Roman World*. Edited by Ben F. Meyer and E. P. Sanders. Philadelphia: Fortress, 1982.

*The Tosefta*. 6 vols. Translated by Jacob Neusner, et al. New York: KTAV, 1977–86.

Townsend, John T. "Ancient Education in the Time of the Early Roman Empire." Pp. 139–63 in *The Catacombs and the Colosseum: The Roman Empire as the Setting of Primitive Christianity*. Edited by Stephen Benko and John J. O'Rourke. Valley Forge, Pa.: Judson, 1971.

Treggiari, Susan. "Jobs for Women." *American Journal of Ancient History* 1 (1976): 76–104.

———. "Jobs in the Household of Livia." *Papers of the British School at Rome* 43 (1975): 48–77.

Trompf, Garry W. "On Attitudes Toward Women in Paul and Paulinist Literature: 1 Corinthians 11:3–16 and Its Context." *Catholic Biblical Quarterly* 42 (2, April 1980): 196–215.

Tucker, Ruth A. *From Jerusalem to Irian Jaya: A Biographical History of Christian Missions.* Grand Rapids: Zondervan, 1983.

———. "Response." Pp. 111–17 in *Women, Authority & the Bible.* Edited by Alvera Mickelsen. Downers Grove, Ill.: InterVarsity, 1986.

Tucker, Ruth A., and Walter Liefeld. "Women in Foreign Missions." Pp. 56–76 in *World Christian Summer Reader 1990.* Pasadena, Calif.: World Christian, 1990.

Turner, Nigel. "Second Thoughts—VII. Papyrus Finds." *Expository Times* 76 (1964): 44–48.

Ulrichsen, J. H. "Noèn bemerkninger til 1. Tim. 2,15." *Norsk Teologisk Tidsskrift* 84 (1, 1983): 19–25. (NTA 29:42).

Urbach, Ephraim E. *The Sages: Their Concepts and Beliefs.* 2d ed. 2 vols. Translated by Israel Abrahams. Jerusalem: Magnes, 1979.

Van Der Horst, Pieter W. "Hellenistic Parallels to the Acts of the Apostles." *Journal for the Study of the New Testament* 25 (Oct. 1985): 49–60.

———. "Musonius Rufus and the New Testament." *Novum Testamentum* 16 (4, October 1974): 306–15.

———. "The Role of Women in the Testament of Job." *Nederlands Theologisch Tijdschrift* 40 (4, 1986): 273–89. (NTA 31:212).

Varro. *On the Latin Language.* 2 vols. Translated by Roland G. Kent. Loeb Classical Library. Cambridge: Harvard University, 1938.

Vermaseren, Maarten J. *Cybele and Attis: The Myth and the Cult.* Translated by A. M. H. Lemmers. London: Thames & Hudson, 1977.

Vermes, Geza, translator. *The Dead Sea Scrolls in English.* 2d ed. New York: Penguin Books, 1981.

Verner, David C. *The Household of God: The Social World of the Pastoral Epistles.* Society of Biblical Literature Dissertation Series 71. Chico, Calif.: Scholars, 1983.

"The Vision of Ezra." Translated by J. R. Mueller and G. A. Robbins. 1:581–90 in *The Old Testament Pseudepigrapha.* 2 vols. Edited by James H. Charlesworth. Garden City, N.Y.: Doubleday & Co., 1983–85.

Vistozky, Burton L. "Overturning the Lamp." *Journal of Jewish Studies* 38 (1, Spring 1987): 72–80.

Wagner, Günter. *Pauline Baptism and the Pagan Mysteries: The Problem of the Pauline Doctrine of Baptism in Romans VI.1–11 in Light of its Religio-Historical "Parallels."* Translated by J. P. Smith. Edinburgh: Oliver & Boyd, 1967.

Walker, William O., Jr. "1 Corinthians 11:2–16 and Paul's Views Regarding Women." *Journal of Biblical Literature* 94 (1, March 1975): 94–110.

Waltke, Bruce K. "1 Corinthians 11:2–16: An Interpretation." *Bibliotheca Sacra* 135 (537, January 1978): 46–57.

Ward, Roy Bowen. "Musonius and Paul on Marriage." *New Testament Studies* 36 (2, April 1990): 281–89.

Wasson, Robert Gordon, Albert Hofmann, and Carl A. P. Ruck. *The Road to Eleusis: Unveiling the Secret of the Mysteries.* New York: Harcourt Brace Jovanovich, 1978.

Watson, Alan. "Roman Slave Law and Romanist Ideology." *Phoenix* 37 (1, Spring 1983): 53–65.

Watson, Gerard. "The Natural Law and Stoicism." Pp. 216–38 in *Problems in Stoicism.* Edited by A. A. Long. London: Athlone, 1971.

Watts, William. "Seneca on Slavery." *Downside Review* 90 (300, July 1972): 183–95.

Wegner, Judith Romney. *Chattel or Person? The Status of Women in the Mishnah.* New York: Oxford University, 1988.

_________. "Tragelaphos Revisited: The Anomaly of Woman in the Mishnah." *Judaism* 37 (2, Spring 1988): 160–72.

Weinfeld, Moshe. "Deuteronomy—The Present State of the Inquiry." *Journal of Biblical Literature* 86 (3, September 1967): 249–62.

Whitely, D. E. H. *The Theology of St. Paul.* Oxford: Basil Blackwell, 1964.

Whittaker, Molly. *Jews and Christians: Graeco-Roman Views.* Cambridge Commentaries on Writings of the Jewish and Christian World 200 BC to AD 200, 6. Cambridge: Cambridge University, 1984.

Wiefel, Wolfgang. "The Jewish Community in Ancient Rome and the Origins of Roman Christianity." Pp. 85–101 in *The Romans Debate—Revised and Expanded Edition.* Edited by Karl Donfried. Peabody: Hendrickson Publishers, 1991.

Wiles, Gordon P. *Paul's Intercessory Prayers: The Significance of the Intercessory Prayer Passages in the Letters of St Paul.* Society for New Testament Studies Monograph Series 24. Cambridge: Cambridge University, 1974.

Wilken, Robert L. "The Christians as the Romans (and Greeks) Saw Them." Pp. 100–25 in *Jewish and Christian Self-Definition.* 3 vols. Vol. 1: *The Shaping of Christianity in the Second and Third Centuries.* Edited by E. P. Sanders. Philadelphia: Fortress, 1980.

Williams, Don. *The Apostle Paul & Women in the Church.* Glendale, Calif.: Regal Books Division, Gospel Light Publications, 1977.

Willis, Wendell Lee. *Idol Meat in Corinth: The Pauline Argument in 1 Corinthians 8 and 10.* Society of Biblical Literature Dissertation Series 68. Chico, Calif.: Scholars, 1985.

Willner, Dorothy. "The Oedipus Complex, Antigone, and Electra: The Woman as Hero and Victim." *American Anthropologist* 84 (1, March 1982): 58–78.

Willoughby, Harold R. *Pagan Initiation: A Study of Mystery Initiations in the Graeco-Roman World.* Chicago: University of Chicago, 1929.

Wilmore, Gayrand S. *Black Religion and Black Radicalism: An Interpretation of the Religious History of Afro-American People.* 2d rev. ed. Maryknoll, N.Y.: Orbis Books, 1983.

Wilshire, Leland Edward. "The TLG Computer and Further References to *AUTHENTEŌ* in 1 Timothy 2.12." *New Testament Studies* 34 (1, 1988): 120–34.

Witherington, Ben III. *Women in the Ministry of Jesus: A Study of Jesus' Attitudes to Women and their Roles as Reflected in His Earthly Life.* Society for New Testament Studies Monograph Series 51. Cambridge: Cambridge University, 1984.

Wolf, Eric. "The Virgin of Guadalupe: A Mexican National Symbol." *Journal of American Folklore* 71 (1958): 34–39. (Reprinted in Lessa, William A. and Evon Z. Vogt, editors. *Reader in Comparative Religion: An Anthropological Approach.* 4th ed. New York: Harper & Row, 1979.).

Wolfson, Harry Austryn. *Philo: Foundations of Religious Philosophy in Judaism, Christianity, and Islam.* 2 vols. 4th rev. ed. Cambridge: Harvard University, 1968.

Yamauchi, Edwin M. *The Archaeology of New Testament Cities in Western Asia Minor.* Grand Rapids: Baker Book House, 1980.

_________. "Magic or Miracle? Diseases, Demons & Exorcisms." Pp. 89–183 in *The Miracles of Jesus.* Gospel Perspectives 6. Edited by David Wenham and Craig Blomberg. Sheffield: JSOT, 1986.

_________. *The Stones and the Scriptures: An Introduction to Biblical Archaeology.* Grand Rapids: Baker Book House, 1972.

Zuntz, Günther. *Persephone: Three Essays on Religion and Thought in Magna Graecia.* Oxford: Clarendon, 1971.

# Index of Modern Authors

# Index of Ancient Sources

## Other Ancient Near Eastern Literature

## Apocrypha



## New Testament

## Qumran Texts

## Rabbinic Texts: Midrash Rabbah



## Other Rabbinic Collections

## Other Early Jewish and Christian Literature

## Other Greco-Roman and Ancient Mediterranean Literature